Die Not hat ein Ende

The Swiss Art of Rock

Edition Patrick Frey
No. 177

Dedicated to

Peter Blumer, H.R. Giger, Martin Byland, Peter Wittwer
and Luc Torregrossa

Die Trilogie hat ein Ende

Lurker Grand, Buchautor und Ausstellungsmacher, veröffentlichte 2006 mit *Hot Love* ein Buchprojekt, welches als detaillierte Chronik einer einzelnen Musikszene die Pionierzeit des Punk und New Wave von 1976–1980 in der Schweiz dokumentierte. 2012 folgte das Monumentalwerk *Heute und Danach* das den Untergrund der Achtzigerjahre, das musikalisch prägendste schweizerische Jahrzehnt, als Anthologie aufarbeitete. Und mit *Die Not hat ein Ende* folgt nun das letzte Werk der Trilogie, wo ein allumfassender Bogen über die szenen- und stilspezifische Bildsprache der letzten fünfzig Jahre in der Schweizer Rockmusik gespannt wird. Dieses Buch öffnet somit den Bühnenvorhang vollends, um szenen- und epochenübergreifend die gegenseitige Anziehungskraft von Grafik und Musik in Form von Rock-Art aufzuzeigen und gleichzeitig der Ästhetik dieser oft anarchischen künstlerischen Avantgarde von ihren Anfängen bis heute eine Anerkennung zu gebieten.

Hierfür wurden Experten der hiesigen Musikgeschichte und themenspezifisch auch aus der Kunstakademie herbeigezogen. Sam Mumenthaler, selber Autor von diversen Schweizer Musikbüchern, Co-Kurator bei *Hot Love* und *Heute und Danach*, Sammler, Ausstellungsmacher und Musiker steuert die chronologische und detaillierte historische Einführung in Schweizer Rock und dessen Erscheinungsbild bei.

Im umfangreichsten Teil des Buches wird die Schweizer Rock-Art anhand von fünfzehn ausgewählten Künstlerporträts präsentiert. Zu einzelnen Werken werden zudem anekdotische Kurzgeschichten von weiteren Autoren präsentiert. Die Selektion der kreativen Protagonisten, welche die visuelle Rockgeschichte der Schweiz exemplarisch illustrieren soll, wurde anhand der jeweiligen szenen- und epochenspezifischen, mitunter sogar stilprägenden Qualität ihrer grafischen Arbeiten vollzogen. Dabei kristallisiert sich die sehr «schweizerische» Qualität der Werke als gemeinsamer Nenner heraus, ohne dabei die zum Teil jeweils auch starken ausländischen Einflüsse verneinen zu wollen. Denn alle hier porträtierten Künstler haben in irgendeiner Art eine formale grafische Ausbildung durchlaufen. Dies bedeutet eine Schulung in Schweizer Grafik und Design, welche international einen hohen Stellenwert geniesst.

Den Abschluss bildet dann ein Diskurs zwischen Roland Fischbacher und Robert Lzicar über die Entwicklung der gestalterischen Erscheinungsformen der Rockkultur von ihren Anfängen bis zur heutigen Zeit. Roland, Studiengangsleiter für Visuelle Kommunikation an der Hochschule der Künste in Bern, hat die Rockmusikszene der Achtziger- und Neunzigerjahre als angeheuerter Grafiker im AJZ (Autonomes Jugendzentrum) und der Roten Fabrik in Zürich miterlebt. Robert, Designforscher, Gestalter und ehemals Partyveranstalter und DJ, fokussiert sich dank dem Post-Punk-Revival auf die alternative Rockkultur ab den Achtzigerjahren. Beide zusammen leisten Pionierarbeit mit ihrem Beitrag in diesem Buch, da ihr Text über Rock-Art in akademisch-analytischer Form für die Schweiz erstmalig ist!

The trilogy has an end

Lurker Grand, book author and exhibition organizer, published in 2006 a book project called *Hot Love* which, as a detailed chronicle of a single music scene, documented the pioneering days of punk and new wave in Switzerland from 1976–1980. In 2012, followed the epic anthology *Heute und Danach* that focused on the underground of the eighties, the most formative decade in Swiss music. And now, with *Die Not hat ein Ende*, follows the last work of the trilogy, spanning an all-encompassing arch over the scene- and style-specific visual language of the last fifty years of Swiss rock music. In order to reveal the mutual attraction of graphics and music in rock art, this book completely raises the curtain and stretches across scenes and eras; while, at the same time, bidding recognition to the aesthetics of a frequently anarchic artistic avant-garde from its beginnings to today.

For this purpose, experts were also drafted regarding local music history and related themes from the academic arts. Sam Mumenthaler, himself an author of miscellaneous Swiss music books, co-author of *Hot Love* and *Heute und Danach*, collector, exhibition organizer, and musician contributes the chronological and detailed historical introduction regarding Swiss rock and its appearance.

In the main bulk of the book, Swiss rock art is presented by means of fifteen select artist portraits. Furthermore, anecdotal short stories regarding specific works are presented by additional authors. The selection of these creative protagonists, which illustrates the visual rock history of Switzerland in an exemplarily fashion, was based on the respective scene-, era-, and on occasion even style-defining quality of their graphic art. Thereby, the very "Swiss" quality of the works became apparent as a common denominator, without negating the, in part, also strong respective foreign influences. Hence, all the portrayed artists have gone through some formal graphic artist education. This means a training in Swiss graphics and design, which enjoys a high international rating.

The conclusion of the book comes in form of a discourse between Roland Fischbacher and Robert Lzicar, analyzing the development of the creative manifestations and forms of rock culture from their beginnings to this day. Roland, head of the Bachelor study program "Visuelle Kommunikation" (Visual Communication) at the Hochschule der Künste Bern (Academy of Art Bern), witnessed the rock music scene of the eighties and nineties as a hired graphic artist at the AJZ (Autonomous Youth Centre) and the Rote Fabrik in Zurich. Due to the post punk revival, Robert, a design researcher, designer and former party organizer and DJ, focuses on alternative rock culture beginning with the eighties. With their academic-analytical text on rock art, the two of them achieve a pioneering feat, inasmuch as their contribution is a first for Switzerland in this form!

Synopsis der Rock-Gegenkultur in der Schweiz

Um es bereits vorwegzunehmen: Der Schritt vom musikalischen Randphänomen zum Massenerfolg gelang in der Schweiz nie wirklich. Der Rock musste entsprechend zweimal anklopfen, bevor er sich schlussendlich ab den Siebzigerjahren auch hierzulande in einer bemerkbar eigenständigen Form definieren konnte. Bezeichnend hierfür sind die Halbstarken der späten Fünfziger- und der Sechzigerjahre, welche, gemessen am Ruf der ihnen international anhaftete, in der lokalen Version dann eher bescheiden agierten. Meist waren es halbwüchsige Männer und Frauen, die ihr jugendliches Draufgängertum auslebten. Für die rigide bürgerliche Schweiz war es dennoch ein unerhörtes Gebaren, welchem man sogar mit dem Versuch, die Halbstarken zu kriminalisieren, Einhalt gebieten wollte. Dennoch, der oft realen und empfundenen «Freizeit-Langeweile» der Jugendlichen wurde damals aktiv, in Form einer gelebten Gegenkultur, entgegengewirkt.

Aber der zwingende weitere Schritt, Schweizer Rock'n'-Roll-Bands und später «YéYé»- und Beat-Gruppen, die mit selber komponierten Songs und eigenen Texten auftraten, erfolgte nicht. Denn Eigenständigkeit war für Schweizer Beat-Gruppen der Sechzigerjahre weder angesagt noch vonnöten: Am beliebtesten waren diejenigen Interpreten, welche schlicht am originalgetreuesten die aktuellsten Englischen Hits kopieren konnten. Generell fehlten die konsequenten Lebensideologien als Musiker oder Band. Denn, vom Rock'n'Roll der Fünfzigerjahre bis zum brachialen heutigen Metal stellt Rockmusik in seiner Grundfunktion immer den Anspruch, sich vom Konformismus und gesellschaftlich «Akzeptierten» abzugrenzen und einem selbstbestimmten alternativen Lebensentwurf gerecht zu werden. Rockmusik will/sollte/darf nicht Teil des Establishments sein, und allein das «Nichtpartizipieren» in allem, was massentaugliche Populärkultur darstellt, ist (mitunter auch identitätsstiftendende) Provokation; somit ein gewichtiger Stützpfeiler des Rocks.

Der Rock'n'Roll der Fünfzigerjahre fand somit hierzulande nie wirklich statt, die Beat-Periode der Sechziger verlief zumeist als Freizeitphänomen (mit ein paar zerbrochenen Stühlen im Zürcher Hallenstadion), gefolgt vom angeblichen Einfluss der 68er-Revolte auf die Schweizer Rockmusik. Die musikalischen Vertreter aus dieser politisch geladenen Zeit waren aber mehr auch die Repräsentanten einer Protesthaltung des «Spezialistentums» der progressiven Rockbands. Und, völlig konträr zum Geiste der 68er, begann auch die erste kommerzielle Verwertung der Gegenkultur. Dies jedoch meistens ohne die Partizipation lokaler Bands, denn hierfür bevorzugte man den internationalen Rock-Zirkus.

Viel instrumentaler für die hiesige Musik- und Kunstentwicklung, als Folge des 68er-Aufbruchs, waren die losen kleinen Szenen, mit Leuten aus verschiedensten kreativen Kreisen, die sich in den wenigen urbanen Zentren bildeten. Diese bestanden oft aus Musikern, Dichtern, Künstlern, Filmern, Fotografen, welche zusammen mit Halbstarken, Beatniks, Dealern, Vertretern des Rotlichtmilieus und Randständigen das ganze «Pack» oder «Gschlüder» (Gesindel), wie man es nannte, bildeten. Sie hoben sich ab vom gängigen Erscheinungsbild und lieferten während der Siebzigerjahre durch ihr eigen-

Synopsis of rock counterculture in Switzerland

To come straight to the point, the step from a marginal musical phenomenon to massive success never really panned out in Switzerland. Rock had to effectively knock twice before it, beginning with the seventies, ultimately could define itself in a noticeably distinct local form. Characteristic for this are the Halbstarken (rowdies) of the late fifties and early sixties, who when measured against the international reputation that preceded them, in the local version acted out rather modestly. In most cases they were adolescent men and women that lived their youthful bravado. For the rigid bourgeois Switzerland it was nevertheless an egregious behaviour and one that, by even attempting to criminalize the Halbstarken, they wanted to put to a halt. Yet, against the often real and perceived "recreational boredom" experienced by juveniles at that time, there was an active resistance in the form of a live counterculture.

However, the mandatory next step, Swiss rock'n'roll bands and "Yé-Yé" and beat groups that performed self-composed songs and own lyrics, did not happen. For unique local individuality was neither trendy nor required for Swiss beat bands of the sixties: the most popular acts were simply those that could most faithfully copy the latest hits from England. In general, the consequent ideologies for life as musicians or bands were missing. Because, from rock'n'roll of the fifties to today's brute metal, rock music in its basic function always lays claim to distance itself from conformity and the socially "acceptable" and seeks to meet the requirements of a self-determined alternative design for life. Rock music will/ought/must not be part of the establishment and simply the "non-participation" in anything that represents suitable popular mass culture is (on occasion even an identity-establishing) provocation; thus, a weighty buttress of rock.

Hence, the rock'n'roll of the fifties never actually took place around here, the beat period of the sixties passed as mostly a recreational phenomenon (with a few broken chairs at the Hallenstadion, a venue in Zurich), followed by the alleged influence of the 1968 revolt on Swiss rock music. However, the musical representatives from this politically-charged time were the exponents of a protest attitude by the "specialism" of progressive rock bands. And, completely contrary to the spirit of '68 began the first commercial exploitation of the counterculture. Though, mostly without the participation of local bands, because for this the international rock circus was clearly preferred.

Much more instrumental for the local music and art development was, as a consequence of the 1968 awakening, the loose small scenes of people from all sorts of creative circles, which formed in the few urban centres. These comprised of musicians, poets, artists, filmmakers, photographers, who together with rowdies, beatniks, drug dealers, representatives of the red light district and bums made up the entire "Pack" or "Gschlüder" (riffraff) as it was called back then. They contrasted from established appearances and delivered the necessary, in part also highly subversive, impulses by virtue of their wayward demeanour and the unconventional manner by which they lead their lives. As

williges Auftreten und die unkonventionelle Art, ihr Leben zu gestalten, notwendige und zum Teil auch stark subversive Impulse. Als direkte Konsequenz begegnete man während der Punkrevolte deshalb nicht nur den «Füdlibürgern» (Spiessbürgern) mit Abscheu, sondern rechnete gleichzeitig mit der langhaarigen, verkrusteten 68er-Generation ab. Zudem liess man sich (mit Ausnahmen und auch nur für eine kurze Zeit) weder politisch noch kommerziell vereinnahmen. Aber die Punkszene ab 1976–1980 (siehe das Buch *Hot Love*) legte einen Schwelbrand, der nicht mehr zu löschen sein sollte.

In den Achtzigerjahren fand dann mit den zahlreichen Post-Punk-Szenen der endgültige, breite Einzug der Rockmusik mit Schweizer Prädikat statt. Man vollzog zudem die ersten Schritte in Richtung der modernen Freizeitgesellschaft, welche sich heutzutage durch die unzähligen lokalen Jugendhäuser und traditionsreichen Musikclubs und Bars aufzeigen lässt sowie der Schweiz die weltweit grösste Dichte an Open-Air-Festivals beschert hat. Auch der Begriff «Jugendkultur» wurde als Teil der gesellschaftlichen Matrix anerkannt und verankert. Zum ersten Mal wurden auch Schweizer Rockbands international wahrgenommen oder etablierten sich sogar als stilprägende Vertreter von Musikgenres.

Der Unterschied zu den vorherigen Gegenkultur-Entwicklungen war jedoch, dass diese und weitere markante Veränderungen, welche von der hiesigen Jugend selbst initiiert wurden, nun tatsächlich auch in der Schweiz in vielen Lebensbereichen realpolitische Folgen hatten. Doch vielerorts galten weiterhin restriktive Gastgewerbegesetze mit Bedürfnisklauseln für Alkoholausschank, rigide nächtliche Sperrstunden, Lärmvorschriften oder sogar Tanzverbote. Die Antwort darauf waren unzählige illegal betriebene Bars und Clubs, welche in den Achtzigerjahren für die Explosion der eigenständigen Schweizer Musik (siehe das Buch *Heute und Danach*) die wohl gewichtigsten Auftritts- und musikalischen Entwicklungsplattformen boten.

Hier infrage zu stellen ist die «Eigenständigkeit» des bereits seit den Siebzigerjahren populären Mundart-Rock in der Schweiz. Weder ein «Rock»-Massenphänomen noch wirklich eigen, da es in anderen Ländern auch Musik mit lokalen Idiomen gibt, liegt ihm zudem keine wirklich innovativ gespielte Musik zugrunde: generell poppige Standard-Interpretation mit viel Referenzen zu vorangegangenem Rock'n'Roll, Blues-Rock, und Reggae. Das Label «Swiss Made» betrifft somit eigentlich nur Songtexte, die im Deutschschweizer Dialekt (bevorzugt aus der Region Bern) gesungen werden.

Ab den Achtziger- und Neunzigerjahren, hätten mit der endgültigen Etablierung von eigenständigen lokalen Rockszenen, die auch effektiv als Gegenkultur in der Schweiz agierten, somit auch die Zeiten des simplen Nachahmens vorbei sein können. Stattdessen wurden/werden nun auch immer wieder vorangegangene musikalische Meilensteine sowie obskurste Nischen ausgiebig referenziert und zelebriert. Als Konsequenz ist das ehemals stilbezogene «Retromania» jetzt der vollkommenste Über- und Inbegriff für den aktuellen gigantischen Rock- und Pop-Unterhaltungswahn; gesteuert von Grosskonzernen mit ihren digitalen und vernetzten Lifestyle-Zombie-Plattformen und kurzlebigen «Neualt-neu»-Hits von noch kurzlebigeren «Stars».

a direct consequence, one not only met "Füdlibürger" (bourgeois or squares) with disgust during the punk revolt, but settled the score with the long-haired crusted 1968 generation at the same time. Moreover, one did not let oneself become engrossed politically nor commercially (with exceptions and also only for a short time). However, the punk scene as of 1976–1980 (see the book *Hot Love*) set a smouldering fire that could no longer be extinguished.

During the eighties and due to the numerous post punk scenes, the final broad range of rock music with a Swiss predicate came to be. In addition, the first steps in the direction of the modern recreation society were taken, nowadays revealed by the countless youth centres and traditional music clubs and bars, as well as bestowing Switzerland with the worldwide greatest density of Open-Air festivals. Also, the term "Jugendkultur" (youth culture) was accepted and anchored as part of the societal matrix. And, for the first time, Swiss rock bands were also recognized or even established themselves as style-defining representatives of music genres.

However, the difference to previous counterculture developments was that all of the above and further striking changes, initiated by the local youth themselves, now actually had real ramifications in many areas of life even in Switzerland. Still, in many places, restrictive catering laws with necessity clauses governing the serving of alcohol, rigid nightly closing times, as well as noise regulations and dance bans, remained in place. The answer to that was the countless illegally operated bars and clubs that in the eighties offered the, probably, most important performance and musical development platforms for the explosion of distinct Swiss music (see the book *Heute und Danach*).

Here to challenge is the "distinctiveness" of "Mundart Rock" (vernacular rock), popular in Switzerland since the seventies. It is neither a "rock" mass phenomenon, nor truly distinct because in other countries there is also music with local idioms and, furthermore, there's not exactly an innovatively played music style that underlies it: generally poppy standard interpretations with many references to preceding rock'n'roll, blues rock, and reggae. Therefore, the label "Swiss Made" actually only concerns the song lyrics that are sung in Swiss German dialect (preferably from the region of Bern).

As of the eighties and nineties, with the definite establishment of distinct local rock scenes that effectively also acted as countercultures in Switzerland, the times of simple emulation could have therefore been over. Instead, musical milestones as well as the obscurest niches were/are now being referenced and celebrated time and again. Consequently, the former style-based "Retromania" is now the most quintessential umbrella term and pinnacle for the current gigantic rock and pop entertainment craze; driven by major corporations with their digital and interlinked lifestyle zombie platforms and transient "new-old-new" hits from even less long-lived "stars."

VORWORT

Rock-Art als verbindendes Element in der Schweizerischen Gegenkultur

Mit der klar ersichtlichen Abgrenzung einer Gegenkultur, welche über die Musik und Accessoires für alle rasch wahrnehmbar wird, geht generell auch eine neue Literatur (Untergrund-Postillen, Szenenmagazine, Fanzines etc.) und ein neues Repräsentationsverlangen (Konzertplakate, Flyer, Illustrationen für Plattenumschläge, Comics und Fotografien etc.) einher. Die grosse Vielfalt und Qualität der Publikationen, mit Bezug auf die letzten fünfzig Jahre Rockgeschichte in der Schweiz, wird noch überboten durch die oft herausragende und zuweilen auch künstlerische Eigenheit der hiesigen Rock-Art. Von den Anfängen in den Sechzigerjahren bis heute ist diese (meist gezielt öffentliche) Form visueller Kommunikation für die Eingeweihten, Fans und Neugierigen ein Medium, welches das Prädikat «Swissness» verdient.

Diesbezüglich beinhaltete die Rock-Art der Schweiz ab Anfang der Sechzigerjahre bis heute einen sehr eigenen, für die jeweiligen Gegenkulturen ent- und ansprechenden, für die Allgemeinheit aber auch oft absichtlich provokativen (Wieder-)Erkennungswert. Wie die Mücken vom Licht angezogen werden, kann man «seine» szenen- und stilspezifischen visuellen Produkte generell sofort erkennen. Deshalb wird den in diesem Buch zusammengebrachten Artefakten aus über fünf Jahrzehnten gemeinsamen musikalischen und künstlerischen Schaffens in der Schweiz eine stark verbindende Rolle zuteil. Denn Rock-Art ist wohl die einzige künstlerische Plattform, welche unabhängig von jeglicher Couleur und Stilrichtung der verschiedenen Epochen kontinuierlich Bestand hatte und sich als zentrales Element auch immer wieder neu zu definieren und manifestieren vermag!

André P. Tschan

FOREWORD

Rock art as a joining element in Swiss counterculture

With the clearly recognizable disassociation of a counterculture, quickly noticeable to anyone through the music and accessories, there's generally also an accompanying new literature (underground postils, scene magazines, fanzines etc.) and new representational iconography (concert posters, flyers, illustrations for record covers, comics and photographs etc.). The great variety and quality of the publications with regard to the last fifty years rock history in Switzerland is even surpassed by the often outstanding and at times also artistic distinctiveness of the local rock art. From the beginning in the sixties to today this (mostly public targeting) form of visual communication is a medium for the initiated, fans and the curious un-initiated, which also deserves the predicate "Swissness."

In this regard, the rock art of Switzerland has, for the respective countercultures from the beginnings of the sixties to today, a highly distinctive corresponding and appealing — for the general public, a frequently deliberately provocative — recognition value. Like moths are attracted to the light, "one's" scene- and style-specific visual products can generally be recognized immediately. For that reason, the artefacts from more than five decades of mutual musical and artistic crafting in Switzerland that have been brought together in this book are granted a highly joining role. For rock art is probably the only artistic platform that, independent of any shade and style of the different eras, has continually endured and as a central element always manages to define and manifest itself anew!

André P. Tschan

Rock over Switzerland

Eine Chronologie von Sam Mumenthaler

A chronology by Sam Mumenthaler

Welches sind die prägenden Meilensteine vom Rock'n'Roll der Fünfzigerjahre bis zum heutigen Rock in der Schweiz? Welche Rolle spielte die Rock Musik in der Schweiz mit Bezug auf gesellschaftliche Veränderungen – insbesondere, was die hiesige Freizeitkultur betrifft? Gingen starke individuelle Engagements an den «Schaltstellen» von Kulturinstitutionen und Musikhäusern gleichzeitig auch mit einer Evolution musikalischer Szenen einher? Sam Mumenthaler liefert zur Beantwortung dieser und weiterer Fragen im folgenden chronologischen und detaillierten Essay über die letzten fünfzig Jahre Rockgeschichte der Schweiz die Grundlage. Ausserdem beschreibt er den szenen-, epochen- und mitunter sogar stilprägenden musikalischen Kontext des Schweizer Rocks und zeigt spezifische Verflechtungen von «Sound and Vision» auf.

What are the milestones from fifties rock'n'roll to today's rock in Switzerland? What role did rock music play with regard to social changes — especially, concerning the local recreational culture? Were strong individual engagements at the "switch points" of cultural institutions and music houses accompanied simultaneously by an evolution of musical scenes? Sam Mumenthaler supplies the basis to answer these and additional questions with the following chronological and detailed essay highlighting the last fifty years of rock history in Switzerland. In addition, he describes the scene-, era-, and on occasion even style-defining musical context of Swiss rock and reveals the specific intertwining of "Sound and Vision."

UNKNOWN ARTIST, 1962, 420×580

UNKNOWN ARTIST, 1960, 610×810

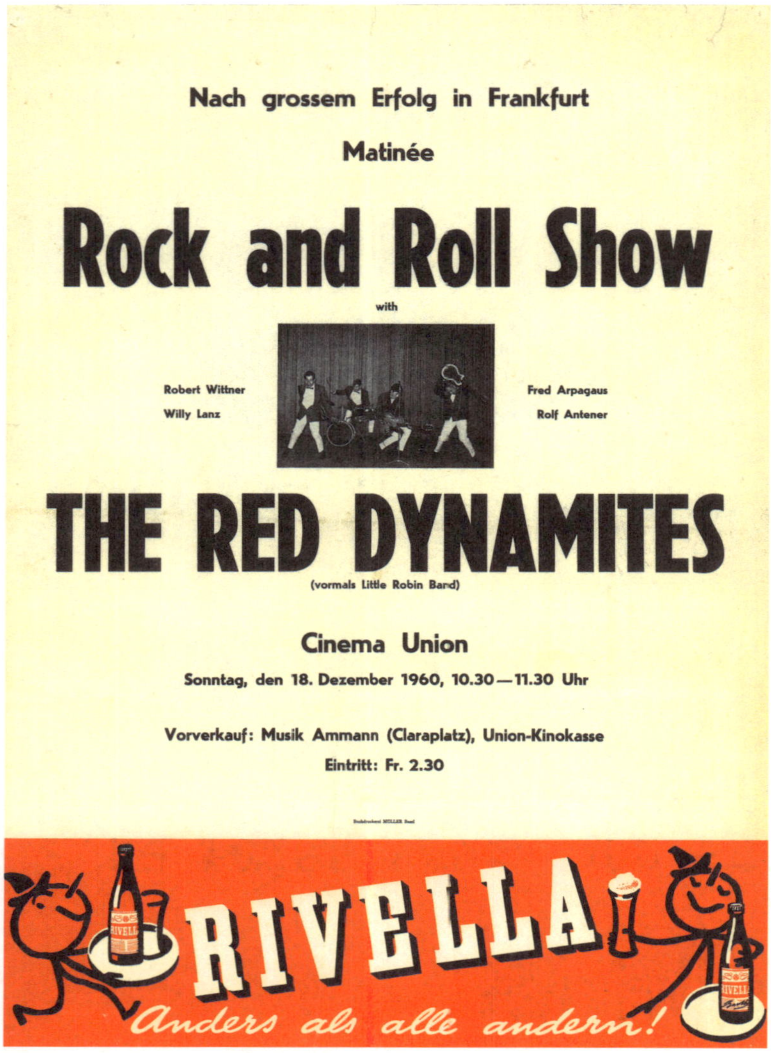

UNKNOWN ARTIST, 1965, 500×700

UNKNOWN ARTIST, 1965, 340×500

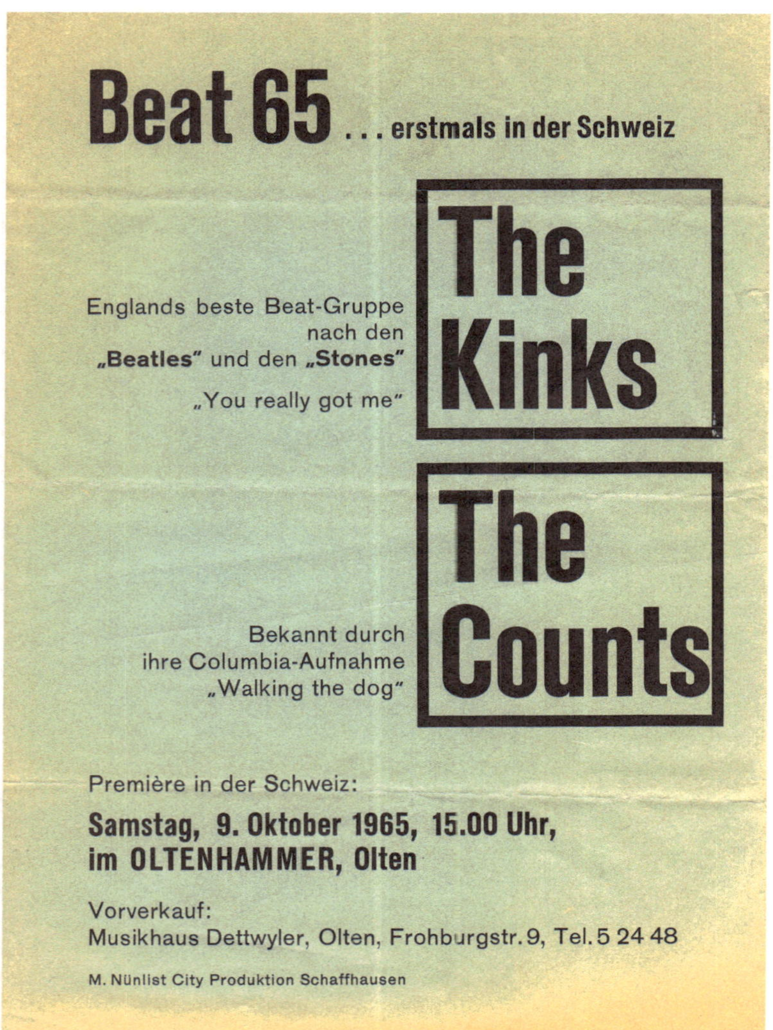

UNKNOWN ARTIST, 1964, 400×570

Beat Pop Protest

«Die Not hat ein Ende!», verkündete im April 1962 ein auf orangefarbenes Papier gedrucktes Plakat und doppelte nach: «Die Zeit der Dorfmusik ist vorbei.» Beworben wurde die Eröffnung des legendären Star-Club auf der Hamburger Reeperbahn, der als erstes wichtiges Lokal auf dem Kontinent dem Rock'n'Roll eine regelmässige Plattform bot. Doch das Poster, das diese kleine Sensation vermeldete und mit grossen Namen wie den Beatles protzte (die damals allerdings noch gar nicht so bekannt waren), blieb seltsam nüchtern. Illustrationen gab es keine, die Wahl der Schrift war unspektakulär – offensichtlich war das Plakat von einem der Club-Betreiber selbst gestaltet worden. Ein bisschen gewagt war einzig die Verwendung eines sechszackigen Sterns zur Illustration des «Star»-Status des Clubs. Hierfür hatten sich die Clubbesitzer beim Logo der deutschen Illustrierten *Stern* bedient – welche prompt intervenierte. Bald wurde der verwegene sechszackige Stern durch ein konventionelleres Fünf-Zacken-Modell ersetzt.

Das Star-Club-Plakat aus Deutschland wäre in der Schweiz der frühen Sechzigerjahre trotz seines nicht existenten Designs aufgefallen. Hier gab in dieser Zeit immer noch die «Dorfmusik» den Ton an, auch wenn sich – vor allem in den französischsprachigen Landesteilen und in grenznahen Städten wie Basel – erste Rock- und «YéYé»-Bands formierten. Eine der ältesten von ihnen waren The Dynamites aus Basel, die sich Ende der Fünfzigerjahre zunächst als Little Robin Band formiert hatten und später als Red Dynamites mit Rock'n'Roll-Shows auf sich aufmerksam machten. Von dieser Band stammt auch das älteste bekannte Rockplakat aus der Schweiz, das eine Rock'n'Roll-Matinee im Kino Union in Basel im Dezember 1960 bewarb – zu dieser Zeit hatten die Beatles gerade ihr erstes Gastspiel in Hamburg beendet. Dass die Red Dynamites auf diesem Plakat sogar auf einem Foto zu erkennen waren, sprengte die Norm und wurde in der noch sehr überschaubaren Basler Rock'n'Roll-Szene als kleine Sensation gewertet. Ansonsten war auch dieses Plakat aber nichts weiter als ein Vermittler von Information und nicht gross von den Aushängen der Verwaltung mit ihren offiziellen Verlautbarungen zu unterscheiden. Immerhin war unten auf dem Plakat das Logo des Sponsors Rivella zu sehen. Getränkehersteller und die Tabakindustrie stellten für Veranstaltungen gratis Plakatvorlagen zur Verfügung, unter der Bedingung, dass ihr Logo gut sichtbar platziert war. Derart gesponserte Plakate blieben bis weit in die Siebzigerjahre hinein die Norm – bis mit dem Punk auch dieser alte Zopf radikal abgeschnitten wurde.

"Die Not hat ein Ende!" declared a poster printed on orange paper announcing and emphasizing in April 1962 that "The era of oompah village music has come to an end". The poster advertised the opening of the legendary Star-Club in a side street of the Reeperbahn in Hamburg; the first important venue on the continent to offer a regular platform for rock'n'roll music. At the same time that it announced this small sensation, featuring big names such as the Beatles (who were actually not that big at the time), the poster used a strangely sober design. It showed no illustrations, the typeface was unspectacular—obviously one of the club managers had designed it himself. The only slightly daring element was the six-pointed star used to illustrate the "star" status of the club. The club manager had appropriated the logo from the German magazine *Stern*—which immediately intervened. Thus the daring six-pointed star was soon replaced by a more conventional five-jagged alternative.

During the early nineteen-sixties in Switzerland, the German Star-Club poster would have caught people's eye despite its lack of design. Back then, "oompah music" played by local village marching bands was still setting the tone, regardless of the fact that in the French-speaking parts of the country and border towns such as Basel, the first rock and "Yé-Yé" bands were cropping up. One of the earliest were The Dynamites from Basel, who began as the Little Robin Band at the end of the nineteen-fifties and later on attracted attention with their rock'n'roll shows as the Red Dynamites. This band was also responsible for the oldest known Swiss rock poster promoting a rock'n'roll matinee at the Union cinema in Basel, in December 1960—at the same time that the Beatles had just wrapped up their first guest appearance in Hamburg. The circumstance that the Red Dynamites could be seen by virtue of a picture on the poster, stretched the boundaries and was hailed as a minor sensation in the still small and managable rock'n'roll community of Basel. Beyond that, the poster was merely informative and didn't differ much from the way local authorities posted their official announcements. All the same, the logo of Rivella, who had sponsored the event, was featured at the bottom of it. Soft drink companies and the tobacco industry provided poster templates free of charge for events, on the condition that their logo was prominently displayed. These sponsored posters remained the standard until well into the nineteen-seventies —when punk radically broke with this hoary relic.

Der Jazz als «Grafiker-Sound»

Dass es in der Rockszene, die mit dem Aufkommen der Beatmusik ab 1964 auch in der Schweiz einen veritablen Boom erlebte, vorerst kaum künstlerisch gestal-

Jazz, the "Graphic Designer" Sound

The scarcity of artistically designed posters in the rock scene, which began to boom in Switzerland as of 1964 due to a growing interest in beat music, also had

tete Plakate gab, hatte auch soziale Gründe. Gespielt wurde die neue Musik meist an reinen Tanzanlässen, die Restaurants in den Städten, die Mitte der Sechziger regelmässig Beatbands zu engagieren begannen, befanden sich kaum an den besten Adressen und wurden regelmässig von Leuten aus dem Milieu frequentiert. Noch waren Rock'n'Roll und Beat etwas für sogenannte «Halbstarke»: Dem Mythos nach war Rock'n'Roll der rebellische Sound einer unterprivilegierten Klasse, und tatsächlich wurde diese Musik vorerst auch eher in den Arbeiterquartieren und im Rotlichtmilieu gespielt – in Zürich zum Beispiel im Kreis 4. Jugendliche mit höherem Bildungsniveau oder mit Jobs in den «kreativen» und «neuen» Berufen, die insbesondere die aufkeimende Werbewirtschaft anbot, lehnten Rock'n'Roll und Beat zunächst ab. Ihre Musik war der Jazz, nicht nur der moderne, wie man rückblickend annehmen möchte, sondern auch der wilde, urtümliche New-Orleans-Jazz, der gerade in Existenzialisten- und Grafikerkreisen der Soundtrack für wilde Feste mit exzessivem Alkoholkonsum war.

Dass Jazz bei den Kreativen beliebt war, zeigte sich auch in den Plakaten, die für Jazzanlässe warben. Seit den frühen Fünfzigerjahren gab es in der Schweiz aufwändig gestaltete Jazzplakate, wo es nicht nur um die Vermittlung von nüchterner Information, sondern auch um die Kultivierung einer eigentlichen Jazzästhetik ging. Der Schlagzeuger der Zürcher Jazzcombo Tremble Kids, Erwin Meierhofer, gestaltete attraktive Plakate für Schweizer Konzerte von Louis Armstrong oder Count Basie. Otto Dürst (der Bruder des späteren Sauterelles-Drummers Düde Dürst, der bei ihm Grafiker lernte) betrieb mit dem Basin' Street Club einen eigenen, berühmt-berüchtigten Zürcher Jazzkeller und prägte mit seinem Comicstil die Plakate der ersten Zürcher Amateurjazzfestivals. Er gestaltete auch Plattencover, Konzertwerbung und bemalte die Wände seiner Clubs gleich selber mit seinen Jazz-Figuren.

Von solchen visuellen Kreativitätsschüben war die aufkeimende Beat- und Rockszene noch weit entfernt. Doch es gab Ausnahmen. In Bern waren The Black Caps, eine ziemlich derbe Beattruppe, die man auch als Berner Rolling Stones apostrophierte, die Lieblingsband der damals auch international ausstrahlenden Berner Kunstszene. Man spielte an Vernissagen und Künstlerfêten und wurde vom Berner Sprengkünstler Willy «Widu» Weber gemanagt. Entsprechend haben von den Black Caps einige freche, vom Aufbruchgeist der Zeit geprägte Plakate überlebt, die von Künstlerfreunden wie Dieter Klein, dem späteren «Timmermahn», gestaltet worden waren. Doch solche «Kunstwerke» waren nach wie vor die Ausnahme in der von Coca-Cola, Peter Stuyvesant und Sinalco gesponserten Textwüsten-Plakatwelt der Schweizer Beat- und Rockszene.

Vom Beat zum Pop

Was als aufbegehrender Lärm von Jugendlichen begonnen hatte, entwickelte sich Mitte der Sechzigerjahre in den USA und England zur eigentlichen Popkultur – welche sich bald auch in der Schweiz verbreitete. Nun war die Musik nur noch ein Pfeiler eines neuen, jungen, frechen Kulturverständnisses, das sich auch in der

social reasons. This new music was usually played at pure dance events, while restaurants in the cities that started to book beat bands on a regular basis in the mid-sixties and were rarely located uptown, generally frequented by low-life. Rock'n'roll and beat music were still something for the so-called "Halbstarke" (young rowdies): for according to the myth, rock'n'roll was the rebellious sound for an underprivileged class and, initially, was mostly played in working-class and red light areas—in Zurich, for example, this was the Kreis 4 district. Young people with higher levels of education or jobs in the "creative" and "new" professions, particularly in the burgeoning advertising industry, at first rejected rock'n'roll and beat music. Jazz was their sound, not only the modern version as one would assume in retrospect, but also the untamed, primal New Orleans jazz; this was the soundtrack particularly favored by existentialists and graphic designers for their wild parties with excessive alcohol consumption.

The posters promoting jazz events, therefore, also reflected its popularity among the creative crowd. As of the early nineteen-fifties, elaborately designed jazz posters were produced in Switzerland that not only attempted to communicate dry facts but also sought the cultivation of an actual jazz aesthetic. Erwin Meierhofer, the drummer for Zurich-based jazz combo the Tremble Kids, designed eye-catching posters for the Swiss concerts of Louis Armstrong or Count Basie. Otto Dürst (the brother of Düde Dürst, who would learn graphic design from him and later become the drummer of Les Sauterelles), ran his own infamous jazz cellar, the Basin Street Club in Zurich and put his mark on the amateur jazz festivals in Zurich with his distinct comic book style. He also designed record covers, concert announcements and also painted the walls of his clubs with his own jazz figures.

The nascent beat and rock scene was, however, still miles away from such outbursts of visual creativity. However, there were exceptions. In Bern, The Black Caps, a rather rough beat combo also coined the "Rolling Stones of Bern," were the favorite band of the then internationally recognized Bernese art scene. Gigs were played at exhibition openings and artist parties, all the while being managed by the Bernese dynamite blasting artist Willy "Widu" Weber. Consequently, some bold Black Caps posters survived from this era, reflecting the spirit of this dawning era and designed by artist friends like Dieter Klein, the later "Timmermahn." Nonetheless, such "works of art" were the exception for the Swiss beat and rock scene, given the omnipresent text-based posters sponsored by Coca-Cola, Peter Stuyvesant, and Sinalco.

From Beat to Pop

What started out as the protest noise by young people, ultimately evolved as of the mid-sixties into the actual pop culture in the United States and England —that soon also spread across Switzerland. Now the music was merely an additional pillar for a new, young, and fresh vision of culture that also manifested itself

LES SAUTERELLES, 1962, © ARCHIV SM

LOUIS ARMSTRONG, THE TREMBLE KIDS, ZÜRICH AIRPORT, 1955, © ETH BIBLIOTHEK

MICHEL & KIESER, 1964, 840×600

MICHEL & KIESER, 1964, 840×600

UNKNOWN ARTIST, POP MAGAZINE NO.1, 1966, 210×285

UNKNOWN ARTIST, 1967, 496×694

DÜDE DÜRST, 1968, 500×700, SILKSCREEN

DÜDE DÜRST, 1966, 980×138

TRACE SHOP, BERN, 1969

POSTER SHOP, SAN FRANCISCO, 1967, ©H.H. KUNZ

Mode und der Kunst niederschlug. 1966 startete der 20-jährige Journalist Jürg Marquard seine Jugendzeitschrift *Pop*, die nach einer billigen handgemachten Schwarz-Weiss-Probenummer nun in Farbe und professionell gestaltet aufgelegt wurde. Das Plakat des von *Pop* gesponserten Zürcher Konzerts der Rolling Stones im April 1967 war zwar noch ein hässlicher Papierfetzen der konventionellen Sorte. Doch schon das nicht minder legendäre «Monsterkonzert» vom Mai 1968, wo Jimi Hendrix, Eric Burdon & The Animals und andere auftraten, wartete mit verschiedenen, poppig gestalteten Plakaten auf. Das auffälligste von ihnen hatte der junge Grafiker Peter Blumer gestaltet, der die Fachklasse F+F des experimentierfreudigen Künstler- und Lehrerpaars Doris und Serge Stauffer besuchte. Das Plakat war nicht für die Bewerbung des Anlasses an sich, sondern exklusiv als poppiges Accessoire für die jugendlichen Wohnstuben von 1968 konzipiert. Ob das Plakat von Peter Blumer wirklich je in Serie ging, ist bis heute unklar. Bislang ist kein gedrucktes Exemplar aufgetaucht – überlebt hingegen hat ein Probedruck.

Ein wahrer Posterboom

Im *Pop* fand sich damals eine ausführliche Würdigung einer neuen Posterkultur, die ein wichtiger Ableger der Hippies aus Haight-Ashbury, Kalifornien, war. Die aus den USA übernommene Posterkultur wurde Ende der Sechzigerjahre auch in der Schweiz zum Geschäftsmodell. Im *Pop* warben verschiedene Versandhäuser für «hippe» Poster als Wandschmuck – neben Musiksujets waren hier auch viel nackte Haut von jungen, attraktiven Menschen, allerlei Love-and-Peace-Symbolik und Sujets mit historischen Figuren wie Lord Kitchener zu sehen, die damals an der Carnaby Street in London und in der *Sgt. Pepper*-Ästhetik eine eigentümliche Renaissance erlebten. In den grossen Schweizer Städten gab es bald auf den Posterverkauf spezialisierte Läden und mit der Firma Wizard & Genius in Zürich einen eigentlichen Vertrieb poppiger Poster. Peter Blumer zeichnete für Wizard & Genius verschiedene Musikerporträts, etwa von den Beatles, Jimi Hendrix und den Rolling Stones – aber auch von Frank Zappa und seinen Mothers of Invention.

Die eigentlichen Veranstaltungsposter in der Schweiz blieben aber weiterhin meist nüchtern gehalten – Grossveranstaltungen gab es nach den Ausschreitungen bei den Konzerten der Rolling Stones und Jimi Hendrix ohnehin kaum mehr, und selbst die lokalen Bands kämpften mit einem Rückgang der Besucherzahlen –, das Aufkommen der Diskotheken machte sich für die Livemusiker erstmals schmerzlich bemerkbar. Der junge Schlagzeuger und Grafiker Düde Dürst war einer der wenigen, der für seine eigenen – erfolgreichen – Bands Les Sauterelles und Krokodil und für befreundete Musiker wie Hardy Hepp Konzertplakate und Plattenumschläge gestaltete, die mit den Einflüssen der Pop-Art aus den angloamerikanischen Ländern spielten. Das Logo seiner Band Les Sauterelles zum Beispiel war augenfällig dem *Rubber Soul*-Schriftzug der Beatles nachempfunden.

in fashion and art. At the same time, in 1966, the twenty-year-old journalist Jürg Marquard started his teen magazine *Pop,* that after an inexpensive, hand-made, black-and-white sample issue, became a professionally designed periodical published in color. *Pop* sponsored the poster for the Rolling Stones concert in Zurich in April 1967 but it was still one of those conventional, ugly scraps of paper. Yet, the no less legendary "Monster Concert" of May 1968, featuring Jimi Hendrix, Eric Burdon & The Animals and others, already boasted a series of posters with loud and trendy designs. The most striking one was created by the young graphic artist Peter Blumer, who attended the master class of experimental artists and teachers Doris and Serge Stauffer at the F+F (art school in Zurich). The poster had not been designed for promoting the event in itself, but conceived exclusively as a trendy accessory for sitting rooms of youngsters in 1968. Whether the poster by Peter Blumer actually had a production run remains unclear. No printed copy has emerged so far—though one trial proof has survived.

A veritable poster boom

An explicit appraisal was done by *Pop* at the time, regarding the new poster trend; which was an important offshoot of the hippie culture from the Haight-Ashbury area of San Francisco, California. The poster culture imported from the United States also became a business model in Switzerland towards the end of the nineteen-sixties. In the *Pop* magazine, various mail-order firms advertised hip posters for wall decoration. Aside from the music-related content there was plenty of naked skin of young, attractive people, all sorts of love and peace symbolism, as well as imagery depicting historical figures like Lord Kitchener, who experienced an odd revival on London's Carnaby Street and through the *Sgt. Pepper* aesthetics. Throughout the larger Swiss cities, shops specializing in posters appeared readily and, with Wizard & Genius in Zurich, also a dedicated distributor of trendy posters. Peter Blumer illustrated various portraits of musicians for Wizard & Genius, for instance, the Beatles, Jimi Hendrix and the Rolling Stones, as well as Frank Zappa and his Mothers of Invention.

Yet, the actual concert posters in Switzerland remained a mostly stale affair and major events were mostly nonexistent following the riots at the Rolling Stones and Jimi Hendrix shows. Local bands were also confronted with shrinking crowds and, for the first time, the arrival of discotheques dealt live music a painful blow. Young drummer and graphic artist Düde Dürst was one of the few people who designed concert posters and record covers for his own successful bands, Les Sauterelles and Krokodil, as well as for musician friends such as Hardy Hepp, all the while playing with the influences of Pop Art imported from the Anglo-American countries. For instance, the logo for his band Les Sauterelles, was strikingly similar to the lettering used by the Beatles for their *Rubber Soul* album.

The Art of Rock

Ende der Sechziger rühmte sich jeder einigermassen ambitionierte Pop- und Rockmusiker für seine Beziehungen zum sogenannten Underground: Kommerzielle Musik war out, nun sollte man – gegebenenfalls unter dem Einfluss von bewusstseinserweiternden Drogen – möglichst progressiv spielen, was sich insbesondere durch eine musikalische Annäherung der Rockmusik an den (modernen) Jazz, Blues und Soul, aber auch an die Klassik ausdrückte. Allerdings war «progressiv» oft nicht mehr als ein modisches Schlagwort für Leute, die den Anschluss an den Zeitgeist nicht verpassen wollten und musikalisch nicht selten weit über ihre Verhältnisse lebten. Dem «Spezialistentum» der progressiven Bands stand eine zunehmende Bagatellisierung beim breiten Publikumsgeschmack gegenüber: In der 1968 eingeführten Schweizer Radio-Hitparade tummelten sich nun «Bubblegum»-Schlager wie «Looky Looky», «Monja» und «Hanky Panky» auf den vordersten Plätzen.

Der eigentliche Vater eines echten, international vernetzten Underground war der Zürcher Poet und Performer Urban Gwerder, der seit Mitte der Sechzigerjahre seine von Dada und US-Untergrunddichtern wie Allen Ginsberg oder Ed Sanders (The Fugs) inspirierten Texte auch mit Musik kombinierte: Seine «Poëtenz»-Shows waren multimediale Spektakel mit Musikern der Band The Onion Gook, Filmvorführungen des späteren Oscar-Preisträgers Fredi M. Murer (der 1966 mit *Chicorée* ein auch heute noch sehenswertes avantgardistisches Porträt von Gwerder gedreht hatte) und Bildern des Künstlers H.R. Giger. Giger gestaltete auch Plakate für die Poëtenz-Auftritte und war später gelegentlicher Gast-Artist in Gwerders «Sippenzeitschrift» *Hotcha*, die dieser in eigenhändiger Fronarbeit und mit Hilfe von internationalen Mitarbeitern zwischen 1968 und 1971 herausgab. Diese Publikationen hatten ein eigenständiges visuelles Erscheinungsbild: Alles war hier handgemacht, Signet, Slogans und Textsatz. Eine Vielzahl von Künstlern lieferte Beiträge für *Hotcha* und zeichnete U-Comics. So sorgten Gwerder und sein Team dafür, dass der Underground in der Schweiz nicht einfach ein leeres Schlagwort einer auf Gewinnoptimierung ausgerichteten Schallplatten- und Unterhaltungsindustrie blieb.

Professionellere Strukturen

Inzwischen begann sich das Popgeschäft (auch) in der Schweiz zu internationalisieren und zu professionalisieren. Eine der treibenden Figuren hinter diesem Trend war Claude Nobs, der in dieser Zeit beim Tourismusbüro des vor sich hin dösenden Ferienkurorts Montreux am Genfersee arbeitete. Nobs war ein enthusiastischer Musikfan, der sich für Blues und Jazz begeisterte, aber weder intellektuellen Dünkel noch stilistische Berührungsängste kannte. Das von ihm 1967 ins Leben gerufene Montreux Jazz Festival öffnete sich bald auch dem

At the end of the sixties, every reasonably ambitious pop and rock musician took pride in his relations with the "underground": commercial music was passé, now one was to play progressive stuff—ideally under the influence of mind-altering drugs—which notably expressed itself through rock music approaching (modern) jazz, blues, soul, as well as classical music. However, "progressive" was rarely more than a hip catchword for people that didn't want to lose the connection to the prevailing Zeitgeist and, more often than not, by way overestimating their actual musical abilities. This technical "specialization" of progressive bands was confronted with the increasingly trite musical taste of the broader public audience. The "Schweizer Hitparade" (Swiss Top of the Pops on the radio) launched in 1968, saw bubblegum pop songs like "Looky Looky," "Monja," and "Hanky Panky" cavorting in the top places.

The actual father of an internationally-networked underground was the Zurich poet and performer Urban Gwerder, who as of the mid-sixties also combined his writing, inspired by Dadaism and US underground poets like Allen Ginsberg and Ed Sanders (The Fugs), with music: his "Poëtenz" shows were multimedia spectacles with musicians from the band The Onion Gook, film screenings by later Oscar winner Fredi M. Murer (who with *Chicorée* in 1966 created an avant-garde portrait of Gwerder that's still truly worth watching today) and paintings by H.R. Giger. Giger also designed posters for Poëtenz performances and later became an occasional guest artist in Gwerder's "tribal magazine" *Hotcha*, which he produced single-handily with the aid of international contributors and published from 1968 to 1971. These publications had their own visual identity. Everything was handmade: logo, slogans, and typesetting. Many artists contributed to *Hotcha* and drew underground comics. In this fashion, Gwerder and his team made sure that Swiss underground remained not just an empty catchword used by the profit-oriented record and entertainment industry.

Professionalized structures

Meanwhile, the Swiss pop business was (also) becoming increasingly international and professional. One of the driving forces behind this trend was Claude Nobs, who at the time was working for the tourism office of the happily dozing holiday resort of Montreux, on Lake Genf. Nobs was an avid music fan with a passion for blues and jazz, who neither knew intellectual conceit nor fear of other music styles. The Montreux Jazz Festival, which he founded in 1967, soon also opened up to rock—in 1969, Ten Years After became the first

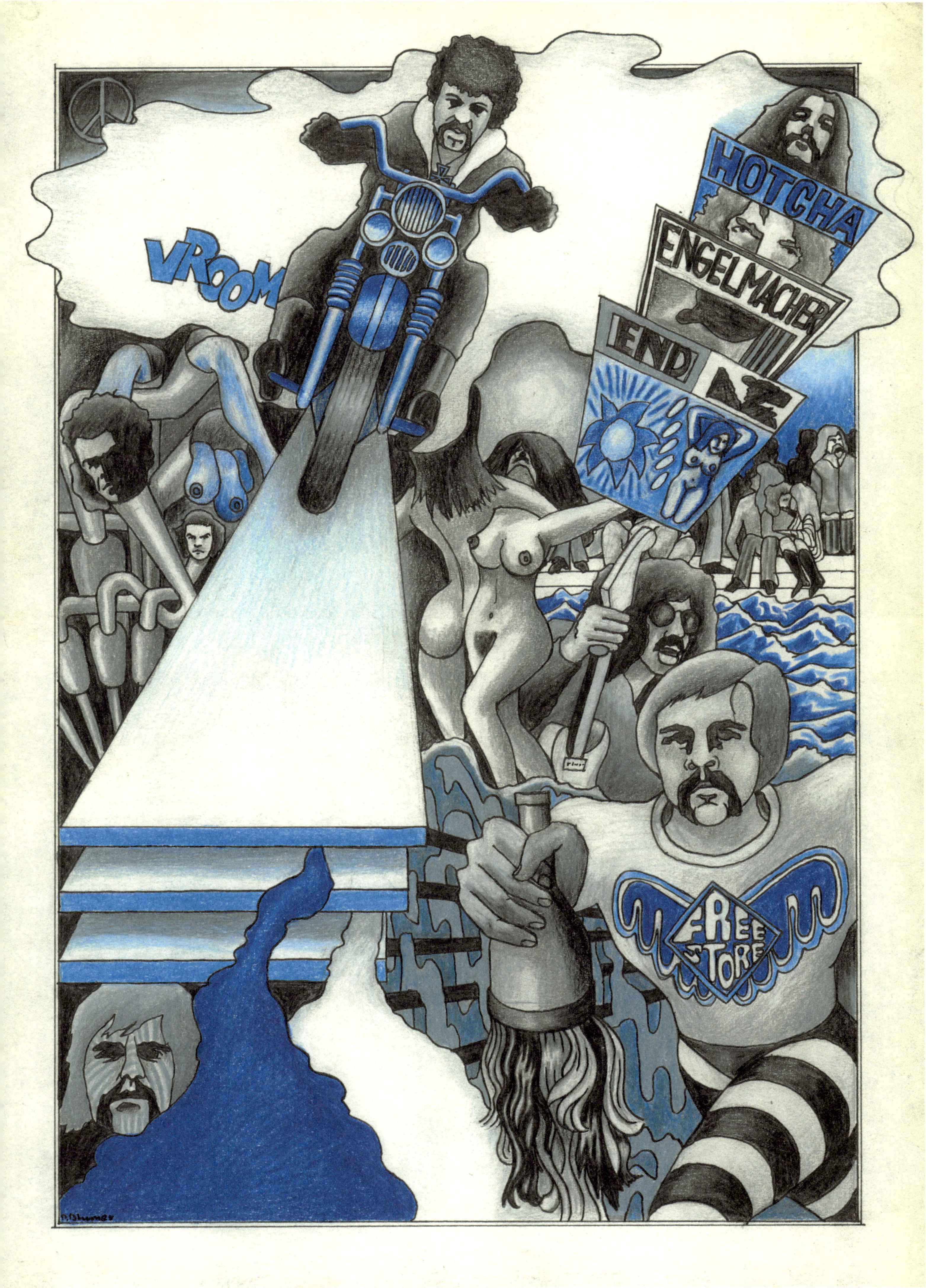

PETER BLUMER, 1969, 210×297, CRAYONS

CASINO MONTREUX, 1971, © ALAIN BETTEX

THE ROLLING STONES, HALLENSTADION ZÜRICH, 1967, © ERIC BACHMANN

Rock – Ten Years After waren 1969 die erste «richtige» Rockband in Montreux, die dort kurz vor ihrem bahnbrechenden Auftritt am Woodstock-Festival auftrat. So etablierte sich Montreux als Pilgerort für Hippies und Musikfans, die mit Schlafsäcken und allerlei illegalen Rauchwaren anreisten. Sie wurden ausserhalb des Jazzfestivals im Sommer auch mit rocklastigen Auftritten am Fernsehfestival «Rose d'Or» (wo 1964 die Rolling Stones ihren ersten Auslandsauftritt überhaupt hatten) oder im Rahmen von sogenannten Super-Pop-Konzerten versorgt. Unter diesem Label traten spätere Superstars wie Led Zeppelin, Pink Floyd oder Deep Purple am Lac Léman auf. Zur Legende wurde das Konzert von Frank Zappa im Dezember 1971, als die Petarde eines Fans das Casino von Montreux in ein Flammenmeer verwandelte. Deep Purple, die zur gleichen Zeit in Montreux an einem neuen Album arbeiteten, machten den Vorfall zum Song und zimmerten ihm mit ihrem kantigen «Smoke on the Water»-Riff ein Denkmal. Von Anfang an setzte das Montreux Jazz Festival auf eine starke visuelle Identität und engagierte Jahr für Jahr neue Grafikkünstler von Weltformat, die das Festivalplakat gestalteten. Zu den bekanntesten unter ihnen gehörten im Lauf der Zeit etwa Milton Glaser, Niki de Saint Phalle, Keith Haring oder Julian Opie. Claude Nobs zeigte sich aber auch hier tolerant und liess zum Beispiel selbst Rolf Knie (Mitglied einer Schweizer Zirkusdynastie) oder Genesis-Drummer Phil Collins ein Plakat zeichnen.

Electric Circus und Good News

1970 trat in Zürich die erste grosse, international ausgerichtete Konzertagentur Good News auf den Plan, die bis heute besteht. Gründungsmitglieder waren Peter Zumsteg und seine spätere Frau Regula sowie Johannes Heinrich Kunz (H.H. Kunz), ein alternativer Jungunternehmer, der Zürich und bald die ganze Schweiz mit seinem dem Zeitgeist entsprungenen Free Store (wo alle angebotenen Sachen gratis waren), dem progressiven Plattenladen Musicland (mit Henry Cookson) und dem Posterversand Wizard & Genius versorgte. Peter Zumsteg war der erfahrenste Fuchs dieses Trios. Er hatte bereits in seiner Zeit als Kantonsschüler Konzerte organisiert und 1967 als Redaktor bei Jürg Marquards Musikzeitschrift *Pop* angeheuert.

1968 zog es ihn nach London, wo damals die Popkultur in all ihren Facetten auf dem Zenit stand. Zumsteg knüpfte Kontakte zu Musikern, Managern und Plattenfirmen und war dabei, als die Rolling Stones 1968 ihren zum Scheitern verdammten *Rock and Roll Circus* inszenierten. 1969 kehrte er zurück in die Schweiz, um in Lausanne mit dem Electric Circus quasi einen Londoner Club nachzustellen. Dort stieg mit Black Sabbath, Free und Taste die Crème der damals angesagten «Progressive Rock»-Bands ab, deren Medium nicht mehr die 45-Touren-Single, sondern die Langspielplatte war, und die weniger auf Charts-Erfolge als auf hochstehendes Instrumentalhandwerk und Konzeptkunst setzten. Stilistische Engstirnigkeit war bei den Musikfreaks, die sich mit den Londoner Szenezeitschriften regelmässig up to date hielten, out: So spielten im Electric Circus regelmässig auch Jazzformationen – dass diese allerdings aus der Free-Jazz-Ecke kamen und wenig mit der tra-

"real" rock band to play Montreux, shortly before their breakthrough gig at the Woodstock Festival. In this fashion, Montreux established itself as a site of pilgrimage for hippies and music fans alike, arriving with sleeping bags and all kinds of illegal "tobaccos". Beyond the jazz festival, the same audience was also provided for through rock performances at the "Rose d'Or" television festival (where the Rolling Stones back in 1964 played their very first gig abroad) or the so-called "Super Pop" concerts. Under the latter heading, superstars like Led Zeppelin, Pink Floyd or Deep Purple would later also perform at Lake Genf. The Frank Zappa concert in December 1971 became legendary when the flare of a fan turned Montreux casino into a fiery inferno. Deep Purple, who were recording a new album in Montreux at the same time, turned this incident into a song, thus building a monument with the edgy "Smoke On The Water" riff. From the very beginning, the Montreux Jazz Festival placed an emphasis on a strong visual identity, hiring new and world-renowned graphic artists each year to design the festival poster. Among the most famous, in the course of time, were Milton Glaser, Niki de Saint Phalle, Keith Haring and Julian Opie. Claude Nobs also showed a broadmindedness in this regard and allowed, for example, Rolf Knie (member of a Swiss circus dynasty), or Genesis drummer Phil Collins to illustrate posters.

Electric Circus and Good News

In 1970, Good News, the first large and internationally-oriented concert agency which still exists today, appeared on the scene in Zurich. Peter Zumsteg and his future wife Regula, were the founding members, along with Johannes Heinrich Kunz (H.H. Kunz); the latter a young entrepreneur who, obviously inspired by the spirit of the time, would provide Zurich and soon thereafter the rest of Switzerland with his Free Store (where all things offered were for free), plus the progressive Musicland record store (together with Henry Cookson) and the poster distributor Wizard & Genius. Peter Zumsteg was the most wily fox of this trio. He had already organized concerts as a high school student and, in 1967, signed on as an editor for Jürg Marquard's music magazine *Pop*.

In 1968, he was drawn to London, where pop culture with all its facets had reached its peak. Zumsteg established contacts with musicians, managers and record labels and was on the scene when the Rolling Stones staged their destined to fail *Rock and Roll Circus* in 1968. He returned to Switzerland in 1969, essentially in order to reenact a London club called the Electric Circus, in Lausanne. There the cream of the crop of the then top progressive rock bands, Black Sabbath, Free and Taste, stopped over; whose medium was no longer the 45-rpm single, but rather Long-Play (LP) records and who also focused on high-level instrument skills and concept art rather than chart success. Brought up to date regularly by virtue of London music magazines, the music freaks shrugged off any stylistic parochialism: therefore, the Electric Circus often also presented jazz acts — however, that

ditionellen Spielweise aus New Orleans am Hut hatten, war selbstredend. «Wir wollen beweisen, dass die Popmusik Kultur unserer Zeit ist», liess sich Zumsteg damals in den Medien zitieren, «es gibt zu viele Veranstalter, die unsere Branche in Verruf gebracht haben.» Tatsächlich hatten sich unter dem Einfluss des Woodstock-Festivals windige Geldmacher und unerfahrene Hippies gleichermassen als Organisatoren von Schweizer Tourneen und Pop-Festivals versucht – wobei für die Beteiligten und das Publikum meist im besten Fall ausser Spesen nichts gewesen war.

Oft erschienen die angesagten Musiker gar nicht oder verweigerten wegen prekärer Verhältnisse vor Ort einen Auftritt. Ein Beispiel für solchen Dilettantismus war «The Greatest Show at Bodensee». Auf die Beine gestellt wurde das von Woodstock inspirierte Open-Air-Festival in Konstanz von einer «Non-Profit-Konzertagentur». Sie versprach, die grössten Namen des Underground-Rock in die Provinz zu holen. Auf dem Plakat prangten Namen wie Fleetwood Mac, Country Joe & The Fish, Humble Pie, Chicken Shack, Man und Marsha Hunt. Von diesen angekündigten Acts erschien am verregneten Festivalwochenende leider kein einziger – als Ersatz konnten immerhin die grossartigen MC5 engagiert werden, die aber kaum jemand kannte. «Schwindel am Pop-Festival in Konstanz: Top-Stars nicht da», titelte darauf der *Blick*. Auch wenn seitens der Veranstalter kaum böser Wille der Grund für die Leere auf der Bühne war, entpuppte sich die fehlende Erfahrung als fatal: Für die erwarteten 10'000 Zuschauer pro Tag stellten sie einen einzigen Toilettenwagen auf. Am Schluss war das «Woodstock am Bodensee» ein Fiasko. Ingesamt waren nur 3500 Zuschauer pro Tag erschienen – dafür blieb für die Veranstalter ein Schuldenberg.

Drei Affen und ihr Wiedererkennungswert

Zwar waren auch die Good-News-Konzerte vorerst kein grosses Geschäft – dazu waren die engagierten Gruppen eine Spur zu progressiv und die Gagen und Spesen zu hoch. Doch Good News entwickelte sich nicht nur rasch zur führenden Schweizer Konzertagentur, sondern setzte auch von Anfang an auf eine starke optische Identität. In Fortsetzung seiner strikt in Schwarz-Weiss gehaltenen Visuals beim Electric Circus vertrieb Peter Zumsteg auch bei Good News eine Gratis-Programmzeitschrift, die vorerst in Schwarz-Weiss gehalten war. Weil es Anfang der Siebzigerjahre noch kaum Plakatsäulen gab, der Platz in den potenziell interessierten Musikgeschäften beschränkt und wildes Plakatieren meist hoffnungslos war, entwickelte Good News eigene, in einem streifenförmigen Hochformat gehaltene Konzertposter. Für deren visuelle Gestaltung war von 1971 an bis zu seinem frühen Tod 1976 Peter Blumer zuständig, der mit seinen Pop-Art-Zeichnungen und ungewöhnlichen Farbvariationen einen grossen Wiedererkennungswert bei Popmusikfans erreichte. Dazu kam das nicht minder auffällige Good-News-Logo, das auf den drei japanischen Affen basierte, die nichts sehen, nichts hören und nichts sagen. In der Good-News-Variante wurden die Affen nun aber mit Megaphonen, Feldste-

these emphasized free jazz and had little regard for the traditional New Orleans style, is self-explanatory. "We wanted to prove that pop music is the culture of our time," Zumsteg was quoted in the media at the time, "there are too many organizers that have brought disrepute to our business." Sure enough, under the influence of the Woodstock Festival, hustlers and inexperienced hippies likewise attempted the organization of Swiss tours and pop festivals—while for the participants and audience, at best, it was a waste of time and effort.

Often, the announced musicians didn't appear or refused to perform, due to the precarious conditions they encountered once on site. A prominent example for this kind of dilettantism was the "The Greatest Show at Bodensee." The Woodstock-inspired open-air festival set in Constance (a German town right on the border to Switzerland) was organized by a "non-profit concert agency." They promised to bring the biggest names in underground rock to the province (*i.e.*, the boonies). On the poster shone names like Fleetwood Mac, Country Joe & The Fish, Humble Pie, Chicken Shack, Man and Marsha Hunt. Unfortunately, of the acts announced not a single one actually appeared during the rainy festival weekend—the organizers at least managed to recruit the brilliant, but hardly known, MC5 as a replacement. *Blick* (the largest Swiss tabloid), then wrote as a headline: "Constance Pop Festival Scam: Top Stars weren't there". Although no ill will could be placed on the organizers for the resulting emptiness on stage, their lack of experience turned out to be fatal: for the anticipated 10,000 spectators per day, only one lone toilet trailer was put up. In the end, the "Woodstock am Bodensee" (Woodstock at Lake Constance) was a fiasco. Altogether, a mere 3500 people turned up per day—consequently, the organizers faced a huge mountain of debt.

Three monkeys and their recognition value

As a matter of fact, the Good News concerts weren't big business either at first—inasmuch as the booked groups were a tad too progressive and the fees and expenses too high. Yet, Good News not only rapidly evolved and became the leading Swiss concert agency but, as of the onset, they also focused on a strong visual identity. Based on the strictly black and white visuals he had designed for the Electric Circus club, Peter Zumsteg also distributed a free Good News program guide that, for the time being, was kept in black and white. Inasmuch as there were hardly any outdoor advertising pillars in Switzerland at the beginning of the nineteen-seventies, space in potentially interested music stores was limited and to fly-poster generally hopeless, Good News developed their own strip-type, vertical format concert posters. Responsible for the visual design of these was, from 1971 to his early death in 1976, Peter Blumer, whose Pop Art drawings and unusual color variations achieved a high value of brand recognition among pop music fans. Add to this the no less conspicuous Good News logo, based on the three Japanese monkeys that see nothing, hear nothing, and say nothing. However, with the version used by Good News, the monkeys were, equipped with mega-

BOFINGER & REINHARDT, 1970, 420×585

NIKLAUS TROXLER, 1972, 410×600

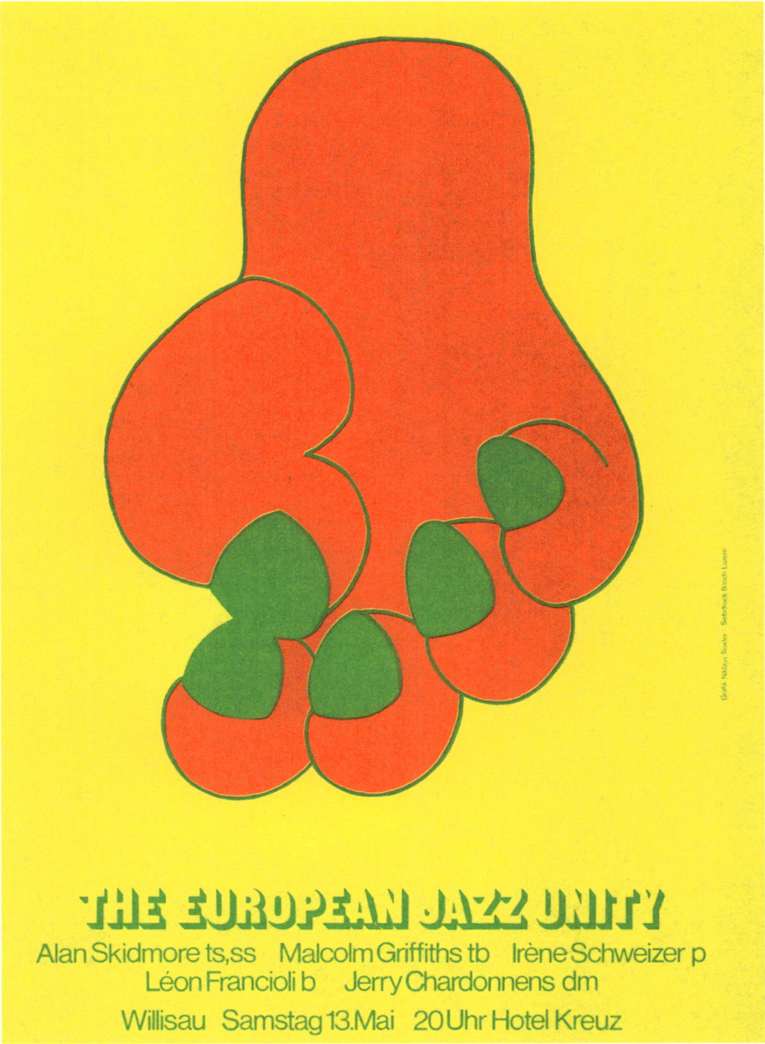

WERNER JEKER, ELECTRIC CIRCUS MAGAZINE, 1968, 180×240

PETER BLUMER, GOOD NEWS MAGAZINE NO.19, 1973, 210×297

KROKODIL, 1969, © EDI SEEBACH

H.R. GIGER WITH ELP, H.H. KUNZ & PETER ZUMSTEG, 1973, © BRUNO TORRICELLI

chern und Kopfhörern ausgestattet, um ein sinnliches Erlebnis zu symbolisieren. Die Kleber mit dem Affenlogo waren bald überall zu sehen – zum Beispiel bei Paul McCartney, der 1972 für Good News im Zürcher Kongresshaus und im Pavillon von Montreux zu einem Ticketpreis von 15 bis 25 Franken spielte und von dessen Basskoffer nun prominent die drei Good-News-Affen grüssten.

Nachdem die Good-News-Gründer ihre Aktien grösstenteils an André Béchir verkauft hatten, fanden die Konzerte ab 1972 zunehmend in grossen Hallen wie dem Zürcher Hallenstadion oder der Berner Festhalle statt. Solche Grossproduktionen waren nicht zuletzt wegen der Kooperation von Good News mit Claude Nobs möglich, der nach dem Brand des Casinos von Montreux vorübergehend ohne geeignetes eigenes Konzertlokal dastand und darum auch in die Deutschschweiz ausweichen musste.

Neben Good News hatten andere Agenturen zunehmend einen schweren Stand und suchten zum Teil eine Kooperation. In Bern machte Patrick Linder mit seinen Kohinoor Productions gutes Geld mit zwei Grosskonzerten von Jethro Tull und Ten Years After, brach sich dann aber an einer geplatzten Jeff-Beck-Tournee den Hals. Die Plakate zu diesen Happenings waren übrigens in Format und Gestaltung den Good-News-«Originalen» nachempfunden, wie auch die frühen Poster der Free & Virgin Agency, die auf dem Platz Zürich als einzige nennenswerte Konkurrenz zu Good News formierte und sich einige Jahre später mit den ersten Punkkonzerten in der Schweiz und dem Management der Solothurner Hardrocker Krokus einen Namen machte. Ansonsten sind aus den Siebzigerjahren kaum eigenständige Schweizer Konzertgrafiken im Rockbereich in Erinnerung. Dafür entwickelte der Grafiker Niklaus Troxler mit den Aushängen für das von ihm organisierte Jazz Festival Willisau eine neue Ästhetik für Konzertplakate. Seine Werke werden heute in Grafiksammlungen gehortet – ganz im Gegensatz zu den frühen Good-News-Postern, die nirgends systematisch gesammelt wurden, wohl auch deshalb, weil Rock- und Popkultur vorschnell als kurzlebige Auswüchse der kommerziellen Ausbeutung von jungen Leuten abgeschrieben wurden.

Progressive Cover-Art

Die Schweizer Rockbands der Siebzigerjahre waren mehr auf die musikalischen Anforderungen als auf eine eigenständige und konsequent durchgezogene visuelle Ästhetik fixiert. Nun waren lange Soli, Anleihen bei der Klassik und rhythmisch Verzwacktes aus der Jazzecke gefragt, und wer als enthusiastischer Autodidakt an den Start gegangen war, kam unter Druck – in einer Prog-Rock-Band zu spielen verlangte Können und Konsequenz, auch was den Lebensstil und Drogenexperimente betraf. Immerhin: Einige der LP-Cover der ersten Hälfte der Siebzigerjahre haben den Test der Zeit bestanden. Man denke an den wächsernen Totenschädel auf dem Cover der Basler Band McChurch Soundroom und das «reale» Exemplar auf dem Cover von Pacific Sound aus dem Val-de-Travers wie auch an die an naive afrikanische Kunst erinnernde Grafik auf dem Album der Lau-

phones, binoculars, and headphones, to symbolize a sensory experience. Soon stickers with the monkey logo were seen all over the place—for example, Paul McCartney's bass guitar case, from which the three monkeys greeted prominently when he played for Good News in 1972 at the Kongresshaus in Zurich and the Pavillon in Montreux; at a ticket price between fifteen and twenty-five Swiss francs.

After the founders of Good News had mostly sold their shares to André Béchir, concerts from 1972 onward increasingly took place in large halls like the Hallenstadion in Zurich or the Festhalle in Bern. These large-scale productions were not the least made possible because of the cooperation between Good News and Claude Nobs who, after the fire at the casino in Montreux, was temporarily without a suitable concert venue of his own and, therefore, had to sidestep his activities to the German-speaking part of Switzerland.

Aside from Good News, other agencies were also having an increasingly hard time and were, in part, looking for cooperation opportunities. In Bern, Patrick Linder with his Kohinoor Productions made good money from two large concerts by Jethro Tull and Ten Years After, but then went broke due to a cancelled Jeff Beck tour. Incidentally, the posters for these happenings were based on the original Good News format and design template, as were the early posters of the Free & Virgin Agency—the only competition to Good News that formed in the Zurich area that's worth mentioning; and who then also made a name for themselves a few years later with the first punk concerts in Switzerland and the management of Krokus, a hard rock band from Solothurn. Apart from the aforementioned, there's hardly any other distinct Swiss graphic art that was used for promoting rock concerts. On the other hand, graphic designer Niklaus Troxler, the organizer of the Wilisau jazz festival, developed a new aesthetic for concert posters through his placards. His works are nowadays hoarded treasures in graphic art collections—in sharp contrast to the early Good News posters, which were not collected systematically anywhere; maybe because rock and pop culture were prematurely written off as short-lived excesses in the commercial exploitation of young people.

Progressive cover art

The Swiss rock bands of the nineteen-seventies were more fixated on musical achievements than on a distinctive and consequently pursued visual aesthetics. Now, long solo parts, borrowing from classical music and rhythmically vexing elements from the jazz corner, were the flavor of the time. Whoever once had entered the starting block as an enthusiastic autodidact came under pressure—playing in a progressive rock band required skill and perseverance, also with regard to the lifestyle and the drug experiments. Oddly enough, some of the LP covers from the first half of the seventies have stood the test of time. One could think of the wax skull on the record cover by McChurch Soundroom from Basel and the "real" specimen on the cover of Pacific Sound from the Val-De-Travers, as well as the graphic design reminiscent of naïve African art on

sanner Band Cardeilhac: alles Platten, die auch wegen ihrer musikalischen Qualitäten auf dem Sammlermarkt gefragt sind.

Die St. Galler Band Shiver konnte für ihr Debütalbum (und für eine Singleauskoppelung) von 1969 H.R. Giger als Covergestalter gewinnen – hier ist es allerdings vor allem die Cover-Art, die in Erinnerung bleibt. Gigers morbider, am fantastischen Realismus geschulter und von okkulter Symbolik geprägter Stil schien wie vorbestimmt für die Gestaltung von Albumcovern: Mehr als zwanzig «offizielle» Cover gestaltete der Künstler – ausser für Shiver unter anderem auch für die Schweizer Bands Island, Celtic Frost und aktuell im Jahr 2014 für Triptykon –, doch waren oder sind es vor allem zahllose kleine Bands aus dem Heavy-Hardcore-Rockbereich, die sich ohne das Wissen Gigers bei ihm mit Sujets für ihre Albumhüllen bedienten.

Dank Vermittlung von Peter Zumsteg, der nach seinem Weggang von Good News die Leitung von Manticore Records, dem Plattenlabel von Emerson, Lake & Palmer (ELP), übernommen hatte, kam Gigers Kunst auch auf das Cover des ELP-Albums *Brain Salad Surgery* (1973) – und wurde so einem breiten Rockpublikum bekannt.

Selbst ist das Krokodil

Eine der wenigen progressiven Schweizer Bands der Siebzigerjahre, die ihr visuelles Erscheinungsbild in die eigenen Hände nahmen und diesem auch einen entsprechenden Stellenwert beimassen, war die Zürcher Formation Krokodil. Da der Schlagzeuger und inoffizielle Bandleader Düde Dürst eine (wegen der Musik allerdings abgebrochene) Grafikerausbildung absolviert hatte, prägte sein von den Einflüssen der Pop-Art geprägter Stil die Schriftzüge, Cover und Plakate der Band und war wesentlich daran beteiligt, dass Krokodil sich ihren «Underground»-Status bis zu ihrer Auflösung 1973 bewahren konnten.

Ab Mitte der Siebzigerjahre stiess der Rockgigantismus, der sich nach den bescheidenen Anfängen im Untergrund auch in der Schweiz breitzumachen begann, an Grenzen. Die Limousinen und die Gitarrensoli der international angesagten Rockstars wurden immer länger. Die Aufbruchstimmung, die der progressive Rock einst versprochen hatte, war einem diffusen Völlegefühl gewichen.

the album of Cardeilhac from Lausanne. All of these records are also sought after among the collectors market due to their musical qualities.

Shiver from St. Gallen won over over H.R. Giger as the cover designer for their debut album (as well as a single release) in 1969, although in this case, it is primarily the cover art that is actually memorable. Giger's morbid style, trained in fantastical realism and characterized by occult symbolism, seemed virtually predetermined for designing album covers: this artist created more than twenty official record covers aside from Shiver and, among many others, made covers for the Swiss bands Island, Celtic Frost and, most recently in 2014, for Triptykon. And, there were or still are the countless small heavy hardcore rock bands that have helped themselves to Giger's work for their album covers without his knowledge or consent.

Thanks to the connection made by Peter Zumsteg, who after leaving Good News took over the management of Manticore Records (the record label of Emerson, Lake & Palmer), Giger's art also came to be on the cover of the ELP album *Brain Salad Surgery* (1973)—thereby making Giger known to a broad rock audience.

Krokodil do it themselves

One of the few progressive Swiss bands of the nineteen-seventies that took their visual appearance into their own hands and ascribed a correspondingly high status to it, was Krokodil from Zurich. Because Düde Dürst, the drummer and unofficial band leader, was in a graphic artist training program (which he chucked in for the sake of music), his style, which was influenced by Pop Art, shaped the band's lettering, covers, and posters; it also was a major contributing factor so that Krokodil maintained its "underground" status up to the point of their split in 1973.

As of the mid-seventies, the rock gigantism that, after the modest beginnings in the underground had also began to spread in Switzerland, hit a brick wall. The hot rock stars' limousines and guitar solos grew ever longer. The spirit of optimism that progressive rock once had promised, gave way to a diffuse bloating feeling.

Hot Love

Der Journalist Bob Fischer erinnert sich an seine erste Begegnung mit Kleenex, nachdem er irgendwo über das «künstlerische Statement» der Zürcher Band geschrieben hatte: «Pfui Kunst! Widerlich Kunst! Überheblich, langweilig, tiefschürfend, überholt...», habe ihn Klaudia Schifferle, die Kleenex-Bassistin, wütend wissen lassen.

Trotz «No More Heroes», einem der Slogans der Punkbewegung: Eigentlich ein erstaunliches Statement einer Frau, die eben die F+F Schule für experimentelle Gestaltung abgeschlossen hatte, die schon früh begonnen hat, ihre Bilder auszustellen, und heute als eine der profilierten Schweizer Malerinnen gilt. Kleenex, die Zürcher Frauenband, die als einzige Schweizer Punkformation der ersten Stunde auch international ausstrahlte, 1979 auf einer Package-Tour mit anderen Rough-Trade-(Plattenlabel)-Bands durch England tingelte, vom grossen Popschreiber Greil Marcus als Fortsetzung der Dada-Bewegung gefeiert und von Kurt Cobain als eine seiner Lieblingsbands genannt wurde, waren von Anfang an ein Gesamtkunstwerk. Natürlich lässt sich das Wort «Kunst» durch andere ersetzen. Was zählte, waren die «Attitude», das (vermeintlich) Triviale, der Moment. Doch bei Kleenex spielte neben der Musik mehr noch als bei anderen Bands das Visuelle eine zentrale Rolle. Auf Fotos legten sie von Anfang an Wert auf einheitliche Erscheinung, man zeigte sich in weissen Jeansanzügen und später in Kostümen im Hugo-Ball-Stil. Das Cover der ersten Kleenex-EP von 1978 erschien in einem auffälligen Postercover, welches vom befreundeten Künstler Peter Fischli gestaltet worden war und von der Band von Hand gefaltet wurde. Man war weit weg von jener Fotokopie-Schnellbleiche, für die Punk heute eigentlich steht.

Treffpunkt der Aussenseiter

Es war nicht die Kunst an sich, die die Avantgarde der Punks ablehnte, es war das Künstliche. Der Dünkel, den die etablierten Kunstinstitutionen verbreiteten, war den Punks suspekt, ebenso wie es die zur Selbstüberschätzung neigenden «ernsthaften» Rockbands der Post-68er-Zeit waren, die sich zwar «progressiv» nannten, aber eigentlich längst nur noch um sich selbst kreisten und zunehmend den Draht zum Publikum verloren. Punk hingegen war frech und schnell, man besetzte ohne Federlesen die Nischen, die sich in der lustlosen Schweiz der Siebziger überall öffneten. Wenn die Anderen die besagten Nischen auch entdeckten, waren die Punks schon wieder weg. Denn Punk war das Gegenteil eines sicheren Werts. So tummelten sich in dieser Szene die verschiedensten Aussenseiter, viele unter ihnen kreative Geister.

Mit ihrem künstlerischen Statement, das sich von der heutigen Wahrnehmung von Punk als Schlägersound für Unterprivilegierte und Trinkfreudige abhob, war die

The journalist Bob Fischer recalls his first encounter with Kleenex after writing somewhere about the Zurich-based band's "artistic message": "Yuck, art! Art's Revolting! Pretentious, boring, profound, obsolete..." Kleenex' bassist Klaudia Schifferle let him know angrily.

Despite "no more heroes", one of the punk movement's slogans, it is essentially a surprising statement from a woman who had just graduated from the F+F School of Experimental Design, exhibited her paintings at an early stage and nowadays is considered to be one of the high-profile Swiss painters. Kleenex, the all-female band from Zurich, the only Swiss punk group from the pioneer phase to achieve international recognition, who hoofed it all over England in 1979 as part of a package tour with other "Rough Trade" (record label) bands, celebrated by the great pop author Greil Marcus as the continuance of the Dada movement and mentioned by Kurt Cobain as one of his favorite bands, were, as of the outset, an artistic synthesis. Of course it's possible to replace the word "art" by another. What mattered was the "attitude", the (supposedly) trivial, the moment. Yet, for Kleenex, aside from their music and to a much greater extent than for other bands, the visuals played a central role. From the beginning they placed importance on photographs with a uniform appearance, presenting themselves in white denim suits and later in Hugo-Ball-style costumes. The cover of the first Kleenex EP from 1978 was a striking foldout poster, designed by their artist friend Peter Fischli and hand-folded by the band. One was far removed from the quick and dirty photocopies representitive of punk nowadays.

Meeting point for outsiders

It was not art in itself, that the punk avant-garde rejected, but artificiality. The snobbery propagated by the established art institutions was suspect to the punks, likewise the "serious" rock bands of the post-'68 era, inclined to hubris, calling themselves "progressive"; for a long time had only been spinning around themselves, thereby, increasingly losing touch with their audience. In contrast, punk was brazen and fast and without further ado, occupied the niches that were opening up throughout a languid Switzerland of the nineteen-seventies. As soon as others also discovered said niches, the punks had already moved on. For punk was anything but a safe bet. Thus, a variety of outsiders were romping around in this scene, many of them creative spirits.

The Swiss punk movement wasn't alone with its artistic assertions, in contrast to the current perception of punk as goon squad music for the less privileged and drunks. Additionally, the Sex Pistols, who effectively

Schweizer Punkbewegung nicht allein. Auch die Sex Pistols, die in England quasi den Urknall der Punkbewegung ausgelöst hatten, waren ein Produkt, um nicht zu sagen ein Gesamtkunstwerk. Sie entstanden in der SEX-Boutique von Vivienne Westwood und Malcolm McLaren an der Londoner King's Road, einem Laden, der zunächst mit Rock'n'Roll-Mode und -Accessoires von sich reden machte und dann zunehmend radikalere und provokativere Kleidungsstücke lancierte, die den neuen Lifestyle verkündeten. Sex-Pistols-Manager McLaren persiflierte später den mithilfe der Boulevardpresse kreierten Mythos um seine Band als unterprivilegierte Teenager-Rüpel, die mit wuterfüllten Brachialriffs die Anarchie ausriefen und die verehrte Queen vom Sockel stiessen («she ain't no human being!»), im Film *The Great Rock'n'Roll Swindle*.

Doch Punk war mehr als nur ein Schwindel. Er war in der zweiten Hälfte der Siebzigerjahre ein Phänomen, das sich in den verschiedensten Ländern simultan entwickelte. Auch wenn es grosse soziale und wirtschaftliche Unterschiede gab: Punk war plötzlich überall. Das Bedürfnis nach einem Bruch mit dem Bestehenden war allgegenwärtig – auch wenn das, von dem man sich verabschieden wollte, nicht überall das Gleiche war. Peter Fischli spricht im Buch *Hot Love* von einem eigentlichen Flächenbrand, der die herkömmlichen kulturellen Muster auf den Kopf stellte. Punk «hatte keine Geschichte, sondern setzte viele verschiedene Geschichten neu zusammen, wie ein Schüttelbecher. Bei aller Konkurrenz kam damals keiner auf die Idee, den anderen zu kopieren. Das Copyright war kurzfristig abgeschafft, und Kopieren war Teil dieses Spiels, solange man mit den Versatzstücken eine eigene Geschichte erzählte. [...] Jeder sagte: ‹Wenn der das kann, dann kann ich das auch.› Du wolltest keine grossen Prozesse auf dich nehmen, alles musste schnell gehen.»

Der Collage-Charakter von Punk zeigte sich mehr noch als in der Musik in der visuellen Gestaltung: Fanzines für die eingeschworenen Szenegänger und auch Poster/Flyer für die vorerst noch in kleinem Rahmen stattfindenden Partys und Konzerte wurden oft fotokopiert oder möglichst billig gedruckt. Farbige Plakate und Plattenumschläge (vorerst fast ausschliesslich Singles mit extrem kurzer Spielzeit) gab es kaum, für die Farbe war wenn schon die Spraydose zuständig. Die «Erpresserbrief-Schrift» mit montierten Buchstabenschnipseln aus Zeitungen war quasi die Verbildlichung des Collage-Stils und tauchte auch in vielen Schweizer Fanzines und Flyern auf. Doch die Punkästhetik zitierte auch die Pop-Art von Andy Warhol und Roy Lichtenstein, die russische Avantgarde, die Fotomontagen von Heartfield, den Heimatkitsch der Nazis und selbst die rustikale Schweizer Volkskultur.

«Woodstock isch Scheisse gsy»

Musikalisch blieb der Spielraum vorerst begrenzt. Auch – aber nicht nur –, weil Punk der Sound der genialen Dilettanten war und keine instrumentalen Vorkenntnisse verlangte, beschränkten sich die Schweizer Bands vorerst auf Rock'n'Roll der kruden Sorte, der meist von schlecht gestimmten Gitarren dominiert war. Ein forsches Tempo war dagegen essenziell, einiger-

triggered the big bang for the punk movement in England, were a product; a complete work of art, so to speak. They were created by Vivienne Westwood and Malcolm McLaren in their boutique called SEX on King's Road in London; a shop that at first made a name for itself through rock'n'roll fashion and accessories and then launched evermore radical and provocative articles of clothing that announced the new lifestyle. Malcolm McLaren, the Sex Pistol's manager, later satirized the myth surrounding his band, also created with the support from the tabloids, that they were underprivileged teenage louts, using rage-filled brute riffs to shout out anarchy and push the "beloved" Queen off her pedestal (she ain't no human being!), in the movie *The Great Rock'n'Roll Swindle*.

But punk was more than just a swindle. It was a phenomenon that developed simultaneously in a number of countries during the second half of the nineteen-seventies. Even though there were great social and economic differences, punk was suddenly omnipresent. Yet, the focus for good riddance of the old was not always the same in all places. In the book *Hot Love*, Peter Fischli speaks of a veritable wildfire that turned conventional cultural patterns upside down. Punk "had no history, but rather, it pieced many different stories together to create something new, like a cocktail shaker. With all the competition around, no-one even considered the idea of copying others. Copyright was temporarily abandoned, and copying was part of the game, as long as you used the mismatched pieces to tell your own story. [...] Everyone said: 'If he can do that, so can I.' You didn't want to endure long, drawn-out processes, everything had to happen fast."

The collage characteristic so typical of punk, manifested itself even more prominently than in the music, through visual design: fanzines for the dedicated followers of the scene as well as posters and flyers for the, initial small parties and concerts, would often be photocopied or printed as cheaply as possible. There were hardly any color posters or record sleeves. The first singles featured short songs—if color was needed, a can of spray paint was all that was required. The "blackmail typeface" composed from cut out newspaper letters was, effectively, the visualization of the collage style and appeared in many Swiss fanzines and flyers. Yet, the punk aesthetic also pulled from the Pop Art style by Andy Warhol and Roy Lichtenstein, the Russian avant-garde, the photomontages of John Heartfield, Nazi fatherland kitsch and even rustic Swiss folk culture.

"Woodstock was a load of crap"

The musical leeway was quite confined in the beginning. Swiss bands restricted themselves initially to a crude variety of rock'n'roll, mostly dominated by badly tuned guitars, and not just because punk was the sound of ingenious dilettantes with no requirement to actually be able to play one's instrument. A brisk tempo was essential, as were some reasonably provocative lyrics.

MARCO REPETTO, 1978, 210×297, PHOTOCOPY

SERGIO GALLI, 1980, 440×615

NOËL SAUGY, 1980, 210×297, PHOTOCOPY

ANDREAS HOFER, 1982, 210×297, PHOTOCOPY

NASAL BOYS, ROTE FABRIK ZÜRICH, 1977, © SUSAN DE HAVILLAND

THE LIARS, GERSAG CHÄLLER LUZERN, 1979, © BRUNO STETTLER

massen provokative Lyrics ebenso. In der Welschschweiz wurden diese schon von Anfang an in der eigenen Sprache gesungen.

Bands wie Technycolor oder die Yodler Killers gaben Gas, mokierten sich über längst vergessene Nazis oder empfahlen Sexualpraktiken. Die ersten Punkplatten aus der Deutschschweiz – so etwa die 1977 erschienene Single *Hot Love* von den Nasal Boys als erste ihres Genres – waren noch mit englischen Texten versehen und wirkten bei aller Schroffheit reichlich «sophisticated». Doch auch diesseits des Röstigrabens machte sich bald ein Trend zu kernigen und für alle verständlichen Botschaften bemerkbar: «D'Zyt vom Flower Power isch verbi», höhnte Peter Sänger von Sperma zu den langhaarigen Kollegen von den «seriösen» Rockbands hinüber und doppelte nach mit «Woodstock isch Scheisse gsy!», während Crazy auf Selbstbestimmung pochten («Ech will frei si»). Richtig dringlich wurden TNT mit «Züri brännt». In der geschrienen Version von Sara verstand man allerdings ausser dem Songtitel kaum ein Wort. Egal. Die Stimmung, die sie transportierte, war allen verständlich. Genauso wie die aufs absolute Minimum reduzierten englischen Texte von Kleenex, die sich auf einige wenige Worte beschränkten und vor allem einen lautmalerischen Effekt hatten, der Assoziationen auslöste.

So wurde in der englischen Musikpresse aus dem Songtitel «Hedi's Head» schnell einmal «Heidi's Head», und als nächstes wurde erkannt: «These girls do yodel!» (Diese Mädchen jodeln!) Das stimmte zwar nicht. Doch irgendwie war die naiv anmutende Frische von Kleenex und vielen anderen Schweizer Punkbands der ersten Generation wohl nur möglich, weil man aus geordneten Verhältnissen stammte und noch weit entfernt von einer urbanen Gesellschaft war, wie sie zum Beispiel in London und New York längst Realität war. Swiss Punk nahm seinen Anfang zwar in den «Miniatur-Metropolen» Zürich und Genf, schwappte aber schon auf kleinere Städte, die Agglos und die ländliche Provinz über.

Undogmatisch und flexibel

Mit Ausnahme der Cover und Plakate von Peter Fischli (der neben Kleenex/Liliput etwa auch für Expo und Hertz arbeitete) und den Arbeiten von Martin Byland, der mit seinem Freund Peter Wittwer das Plattenlabel Off Course betrieb, das ein Heimathafen für manche Schweizer Punkband war, blieb auch der visuelle Teil des Punk in der Schweiz in der Hand der Dilettanten. 1980 wurde die neue Kultur an der von Bice Curiger kuratierten Ausstellung *Saus und Braus – Stadtkunst* im Strauhof Zürich erstmals in einem professionellen Umfeld und einem grösseren Kontext gezeigt.

Punk war undogmatisch und flexibel – so wurden viele der frühen Veranstaltungsplakate noch auf Vorlagen gedruckt, die diverse Getränkehersteller unter der Bedingung der Präsenz ihres Logos gratis abgaben. Das hörte spätestens dann auf, als die Punks ihre Veranstaltungen selber in die Hand nahmen, und war in den

As of the outset, in the French-speaking area of Switzerland these were sung in their mother tongue.

Bands like Technicolor or the Yodler Killers opened the throttle, sneered at long-forgotten Nazis or recommended sexual practices. The first punk records from the German-speaking part of Switzerland—the likes of the single *Hot Love* by the Nasal Boys and released in 1977 as the first of its genre—still featured English lyrics and, despite its ruggedness, came across as considerably "sophisticated." Yet, even on this side of the "Röstigraben" (a colloquial term used to set the French and German areas apart, according to the so-called "hash brown trench"), a trend was soon establishing itself for lyric messages that were gritty and intelligible for everyone. "D'Zyt vom Flower Power isch verbi" (The flower power era is over), jeered Peter Sänger of Sperma toward the long-haired members of "serious" rock bands and went one better with "Woodstock isch Scheisse gsy!" (Woodstock was a load of crap), while Crazy insisted on self-determination "Ech will frei si" (I want to be free). Really pressing were TNT with "Züri Brännt" (Zurich's Burning). However, in the version where Sara simply screams, hardly any word is intelligible, except for the song title. Whatever. Everyone understood the mood it conveyed. Exactly like the English lyrics by Kleenex that were reduced to a minimum and solely restricted to a few words which mostly imitated "natural sounds" and, thereby, triggered associations.

For example, in the English music press, the song title "Hedi's Head" quickly became "Heidi's Head" and the next thing published was: "These girls do yodel!" That wasn't true though. Yet, the seemingly naïve freshness of Kleenex and the many other Swiss punk bands of the first generation, may only have been possible because of the ordered circumstances that were still far removed from a truly urban society, as had long since been a reality, for example, in London and New York. Although Swiss punk had its inception in the "miniature metropolis" of Zurich and Genf, it was spilling over into smaller towns, the suburbs and the rural provinces.

Undogmatic and flexible

With the exception of the covers and posters by Peter Fischli (who, in addition to Kleenex/Liliput, also worked for Expo and Hertz) and the works of Martin Byland, operating the Off Course record label (a home port for many Swiss punk band) together with his friend Peter Wittwer, the visual side of punk in Switzerland remained in the hands of dilettantes. In 1980, the new culture was presented for the first time within a professional environment and larger context at the *Saus und Braus —Stadtkunst* exhibition at the Strauhof in Zurich and curated by Bice Curiger.

Punk was undogmatic and flexible—thus, many of the early event posters were still printed on the templates that were supplied free-of-charge by various soft drink companies; continuing the condition that their logo was featured. This practice ended, at the latest, when the punks took the organization of events into their own

politisierten Achtzigerjahren in «bewegten» Kreisen definitiv ein No-Go.

Ende der Siebzigerjahre stand der Punk auch in der Schweiz am Scheideweg. Einige der Musiker, die sich via Punk einen Namen gemacht hatten, versuchten die Nische zu verlassen, was angesichts der beschränkten Möglichkeiten dieses Stils als nachvollziehbar erscheint. Viele von ihnen veröffentlichten auch in der Post-Punk-Zeit der frühen Achtziger weiterhin Platten auf Independent-Labels, einige wenige weckten das Interesse von Major-Labels.

Aufgestaute Spannung

Auf der anderen Seite rüsteten die politisch aktiven und organisierten Kreise am Rand der Punkbewegung zum Kampf um Freiräume. Anders als die Punks, die ihre Freiräume ungefragt besetzt und bei der erstbesten Gelegenheit auch wieder verlassen hatten, rief die «Bewegung» nun nach dauerhaften Lösungen. Dass nun mit dem Staat ein monolithisches Feindbild installiert wurde, dem man gewisse Leistungen oder gar Subventionen abtrotzen wollte, entsprach nicht dem lustbetonten, aus dem Moment herausgeschrienen Protest, wie ihn die Punks für sich beanspruchten. Als sich die aufgestaute Spannung nach dem Konzert von Bob Marley im Zürcher Hallenstadion im Mai 1980 entzündete, wurde Punk zunehmend von politischen Parolen übertönt. Zwar spielte an den meisten Festen der bewegten Jugend eine Band auf, doch oftmals nur, um das festfreudige Publikum bei der Stange zu halten. Dass sich die Unruhen der Achtziger beim Krawall um das damals umstrittene Zürcher Opernhaus (und die hohen staatlichen Subventionen, welche diese Institution erhalten sollte) entzündeten, soll nicht unerwähnt bleiben. Auch die bewegten Kids der Jugendbewegung hatten für die etablierte Kunst nur das «Pfui»-Wort übrig. Die freche Kreativität, mit denen die Punks das Kulturestablishment erschüttert hatten, ging ihnen aber ebenso ab. Es kamen die Zeiten der Agitation, und die Musik spielte vorderhand nur noch im Hintergrund.

hands and it definitely became a "no-go" in the politically-charged "youth movement" circles of the eighties.

At the end of the seventies, punk was standing at a crossroad, also in Switzerland. Some of the musicians who had made a name for themselves with punk, attempted to leave the niche, which was understandable considering the limited possibilities of this music style. Many of them continued releasing records on independent labels during the "post-punk" era of the early eighties, a few attracted the interest of major labels.

Built-up tension

On the other side, the politically active and organized groups on the fringe of the punk movement were gearing up to fight for free (autonomous) zones. Unlike the punks, who had occupied their free spaces without asking and left them again at the first convenient opportunity, the "youth movement" now called for long-term solutions. The state — installed as a monolithic enemy stereotype from whom one should wrest particular services or even subsidies — did not match the pleasure-oriented, spur of the moment shouts of protest that the punks claimed for themselves. When the built-up tension ignited after Bob Marley's concert at the Hallenstadion in Zurich in May of 1980, punk was increasingly drowned out by political slogans. Yet, bands would still play at most of the parties thrown by the youth movement; it was usually only in order to keep the festive crowd in line. Worth mentioning is the fact that the "eighties unrest" was ignited by the violent Zurich Opera House demonstrations (protesting against the huge state subsidies intended for this institution). The kids participating in the rebellious "youth movement" had also only a "Pfui" (yuck) left over for established art. The brash creativity with which the punks had shaken up the cultural establishment, was also lost on them. The period of agitation had come and, for the time being, music was playing only in the background.

PETER FISCHLI & PIETRO MATTIOLI, 1978, 420×297

UNKNOWN ARTIST, 1979

AJZ ZÜRICH, 1980, © KLAUS RÓZSA

OPERA HOUSE DEMONSTRATIONS, ZÜRICH, 1980, © KLAUS RÓZSA

Heute und Danach

«We z'Bärn öpper Kultur macht, chunnt meischtens nume d'Polizei», singt Kuno Lauener im Song «Hans Dampf», in welchem er als Beobachter die Besetzung der Berner Dampfzentrale 1987 beschreibt. Seine Kritik richtete sich nicht an ein vermeintlich desinteressiertes Publikum, denn das strömte in Scharen zu den Strafbars und illegalen Partys, die Mitte der Achtzigerjahre in der Schweiz überall dort aufmachten beziehungsweise stattfanden, wo die Jugend den Behörden noch keine «autonomen» Jugendzentren abgetrotzt hatte. Besonders populär, wenn Laueners Band Züri West, die den Berner Mundart-Rock vom Räucherstäbchenduft der Hippies befreite, spielte. Nein, Lauener beklagte das fehlende Interesse bei den Politikern und dem Kulturestablishment. «Z'Bärn diskutiert me gärn u grad über Kultur u de chöme si drhär / Politiker u d'Vereine u mängisch gseht me sogar dr Kultursekretär / Aber wo sii die Lüt wes einisch Äkschn git / de sii si irgendwo daheim», heisst es in «Hans Dampf».

«We z'Bärn öpper Kultur macht, chunnt meischtens nume d'Polizei» (when one engages in culture in Bern, in most cases only the police show up) Kuno Lauener sings in the song "Hans Dampf," in which he describes the 1987 occupation of the Bernese Dampfzentrale as a witness. His criticism was not directed at a supposedly apathetic audience, for people flocked in hordes to the illegal bars and unauthorized parties that started up all over Switzerland during the mid-eighties; particularly also in those places where young people still hadn't succeeded in wresting autonomous youth centers from the authorities. Location were especially crowded when Lauener's band Züri West, who had freed Bernese dialect rock from the scents of hippie joss sticks, would also play. No, Lauener was bemoaning the lack of interest by politicians and the cultural establishment. "In Bern they readily like to discuss culture and then they arrive / The politicians and assemblies, sometimes you'll even see the Secretary of Culture / but where are these folks, when for once there's "action" / then they're sitting around at home somewhere," exclaim the lyrics of "Hans Dampf" further.

Kurz und heftig

So lange die alternativen Jugendszenen in den Schweizer Städten noch keine festen Zentren hatten, musste alles schnell gehen: Verstärkeranlagen wurden aufs Minimum reduziert, um bei etwaigen Polizeieinsätzen nicht unnötig ins Gewicht zu fallen. Die Songs waren kurz, heftig und für den Moment geschrieben, auch allerlei alternativ-bewegte Coverbands waren unterwegs. Die Anlässe in besetzten Häusern, auf Kiesgruben oder mitten in den Stadtzentren wurden kurzfristig angesagt, oft genügte Mund-zu-Mund-Propaganda, um innert weniger Tage oder gar Stunden Hunderte anzulocken. Plakate für solche Anlässe gab es aus naheliegenden Gründen keine, im besten Fall ein Flugblatt, auf dem selbst der Veranstaltungsort meist fehlte. Bandnamen standen nicht im Vordergrund, auch wenn an den Festen der bewegten Achtziger-Jugend die Livemusik das treibende Element war – anders als an Demonstrationen, wo die Wortführer und Ideologen den Ton angaben. Für viele junge Musiker war diese Zeit «uf der Gass» dennoch eine wichtige Aufbruchsphase. Geld liess sich bei den improvisierten Festen keines verdienen, aber einige Bands erspielten sich mit Engagement und Spielfreude einen Ruf. Einen Ruf, der nachhaltiger ist als viele der Promotionshypes der Unterhaltungsindustrie, die jede Saison neue, potenziell mehrheitsfähige Stars und Sternchen zu lancieren versucht.

Es scheint paradox: Mit der Etablierung von fixen alternativen Kulturzentren in den Schweizer Städten wurde es für viele Bands nicht einfacher, zu Auftritten zu kommen. Denn die Rote Fabrik in Zürich, das Fri-Son in Fribourg, die Coupole in Biel, die Usine in Genf oder die

Fast and furious

As long as the alternative youth scenes in the Swiss cities didn't have established centers, things had to happen fast: amplifier systems were reduced to a minimum, thus avoiding unnecessary weight in the case of police raids. The songs were fast and furious and written for the moment. Also all kinds of alternative youth movement cover bands were out and about. The events in squatted buildings, gravel quarries or even in the midst of city centers, were announced at short notice and, quite often, word of mouth was sufficient to attract hundreds within a few days or even hours. For obvious reasons there were no posters for such events, at best, a flyer with the location usually undisclosed. The names of the bands were not the priority even though music was the driving force at the parties of the eighties youth movement—unlike at the demonstrations, where the spokespersons and ideologists set the tone. Yet, for many young musicians these times "uf der Gass" (on the streets) were an important period of awakening. It was impossible to earn money at these improvised parties, but some bands made a name for themselves due to their commitment and enthusiastic playing. A reputation that was more sustainable than many of the entertainment industry's promotion hypes, seeking to launch new stars and starlets each season.

It seems paradoxical: for many bands it was no easier to get gigs despite the establishment of permanent alternative cultural centers in Swiss cities. This, because the Rote Fabrik in Zurich, the Fri-Son in Fribourg, the Coupole in Biel, the Usine in Genf, or the Reitschule in

Reitschule in Bern – um nur einige derjenigen zu nennen, die noch heute existieren – wurden zunehmend zu Stationen, an denen Bands aus den USA, England oder vom europäischen Festland auf ihren ausgedehnten Tourneen Halt machten. So bewarben auffallend viele der Schweizer Konzertplakate aus den Achtzigerjahren Auftritte internationaler Bands. Immerhin: Ihre lokale Verwurzelung äusserten die Veranstalter darin, dass sie regelmässig stilverwandte Schweizer Bands als Vorgruppen für die internationalen Acts verpflichteten. Trotz der angestrebten Internationalität gaben sie überdies eigene Konzertplakate bei lokalen Gestaltern in Auftrag oder nahmen, statt der Einfachheit halber auf die lieblose, oft von den Managern der Bands erhaltene Dutzendware abzustellen, deren Gestaltung gleich selber in die Hand.

Musik-Aficionados werden Gestalter

Die interessantesten Beispiele von Konzertplakaten dieser Phase wurden ohnehin von Aficionados gestaltet. Diese gingen als Veranstalter auch selber ein Risiko ein und organisierten in den neuen Konzerträumlichkeiten, die dank dem Druck der Strasse nun zur Verfügung standen, Konzerte auf eigene Rechnung. Der Berner Dirk Bonsma lebte seit Mitte der Achtzigerjahre mit der Veranstaltergruppe Project Blue seine Liebe für psychedelischen Rock der US-Westküste aus. Zunächst suchte er nach alten Beizensälen, in denen er besondere Happenings mit «seinen» Bands organisieren konnte und durch die die gleiche Wehmut von verlebter Grandezza wehte wie im legendären Avalon Ballroom in San Francisco. Später wich Bonsma auch auf konventionellere Orte aus und liess seine Bands etwa in der Berner Reithalle, dem Fri-Son oder der Kaserne in Basel auftreten. Die Plakate gestaltete der begeisterte Zeichner und gelernte Schriftsetzer selber. Sobald er mit den Betreibern der alternativen Zentren zusammenarbeitete, musste er erfahren, dass auch die Plakatgestaltung nicht frei von ideologischen Vorbehalten war: Als er im Winter 1989 für ein von ihm organisiertes Konzert mit der Henry Rollins Band in der Reithalle ein paar Gummientchen auf dem Plakat drapierte, musste er sich dafür ausführlich vor der «Vollversammlung» des AJZ rechtfertigen. Am Schluss setzte sich Bonsma durch – sein «Entenplakat» gilt heute als Klassiker des Genres.

Grafik, wie sie in den Achtzigerjahren im Zusammenhang mit Konzerten oder Tonträgern von alternativen Bands entstand, war für die Gestalter nicht lukrativ. Viele der Veranstalter griffen aus Kostengründen zur Selbsthilfe und gestalteten die Plakate für ihre Anlässe gleich selber. Da traf es sich gut, dass einige von ihnen über grafische Kenntnisse oder gar eine entsprechende Ausbildung verfügten – spätestens seit den Tagen des Existenzialisten-Jazz in den Fünfzigerjahren standen sich die kreativen, gestalterischen Berufe und die Musiker nahe. Martin Schori, der seit den frühen Achtzigerjahren selber Musik machte und bald begann, seine geliebten Indie-Pop-Bands aus England oder Neuseeland ins AJZ seiner Heimatstadt Biel zu holen, war ein Prototyp der Multitasking-Fähigkeiten der neuen «Kulturtäter»: Er war Musiker, Veranstalter und Gestalter in Personalunion und blieb dabei – vor allem – ein Fan.

Bern — to name but a few of the centers that still exist to-date — became more and more stations for a stopover by bands from the United States, England or mainland Europe, on their extensive tours. A striking number of Swiss concert posters from the eighties therefore promoted international bands. Still, event organizers revealed their local roots by regularly booking Swiss bands with related styles to play support for the international acts. And, despite aspiring to a level of "internationality", they commissioned local designers for their own concert posters or, for the simplicity of it, took the designing of posters into their own hands rather than relying on the uninspired, dime a dozen wares received from band managers.

Music aficionados become designers

The most interesting examples of concert posters during this period were designed by aficionados. As promoters, they also took a personal risk by organizing concerts at their own expense in the newly opened venues; now available, thanks to the pressure from the streets. Bernese native Dirk Bonsma, together with the event organizers Project Blue, was living his love for psychedelic West Coast rock since the mid-eighties. In order to stage special happenings with "his" (choice of) bands he initially looked for old tavern halls, through which the same melancholy of spent grandeur flowed as in the legendary Avalon Ballroom in San Francisco. Later, Bonsma also diverted to more conventional locations and, for example, let his bands perform in the Reithalle in Bern, the Fri-Son in Fribourg, or the Kaserne in Basel. Being a passionate illustrator and trained typesetter, he designed the posters himself. But, as soon as he started working with the operators of the alternative centers, he had to experience that even poster design isn't free from ideological caveats: after draping some yellow rubber ducks onto the poster for the Henry Rollins Band show he organized in the Reithalle in the winter of 1989, he was called to justify himself at length in front of the "general assembly" of the AJZ (autonomous youth center). Ultimately, Bonsma prevailed — nowadays his "duck poster" is considered a classic of the genre.

Graphic design that arose in the eighties in connection with concerts or music media of alternative bands, was lucrative for the designers. To save costs, many organizers reached for self-help and simply designed the posters for their events themselves. It was therefore convenient that some of them possessed some know-how or had training in graphic design — for ever since the days of existentialist-jazz in the fifties, the creative design professions and musicians stood close to each other. Martin Schori, who himself was a musician since the early eighties and soon began to bring his beloved indie pop bands from England and New Zealand to play the AJZ in his home town of Biel, was a prototype of the multitasking abilities concentrated within the new species of "culture perpetrators." He was a musician, event organizer and designer all in one person and — above all — remained a fan.

MARTIN SCHORI, 1988, 415×590

MARTIN SCHORI, 1990, 415×590

MARTIN SCHORI, 1988, 415×590

MARTIN SCHORI, 1989, 415×590

JACQUES SCHOUWEY, 1986, 210×297

UNKNOWN ARTIST, 1990, 400×580

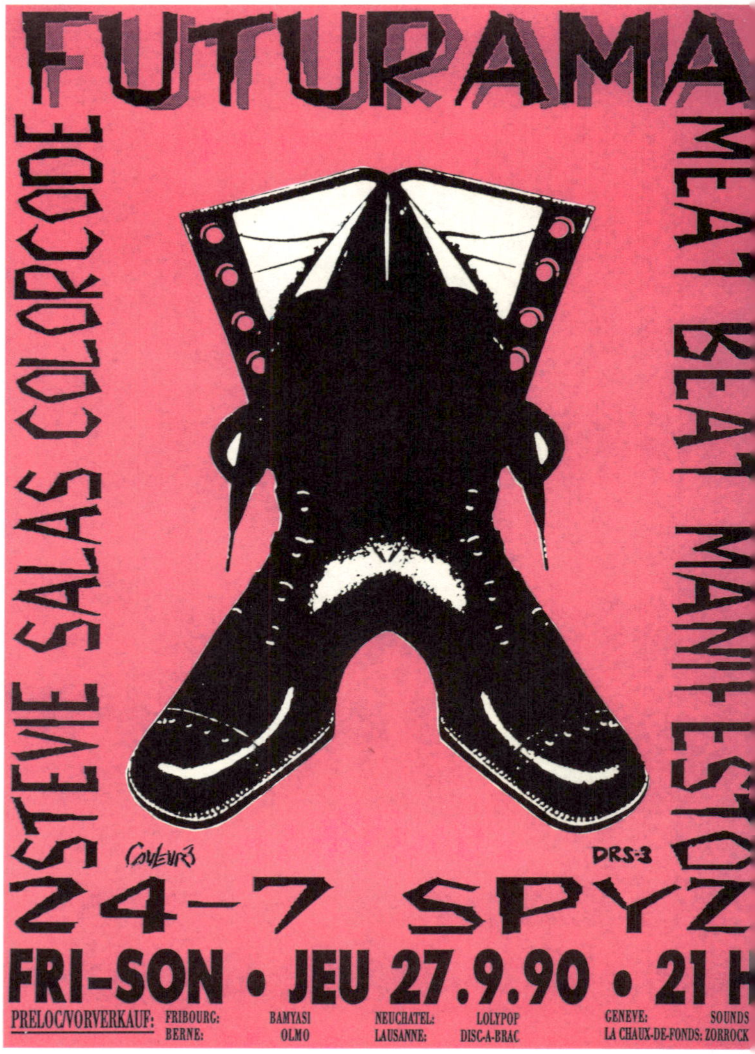

REMO KELLER, 1988, 210×297, PHOTOCOPY

REMO KELLER, 2005, 210×297, PHOTOCOPY

Teil eines Ganzen

Das verbindet ihn mit Leuten wie Jacques Schouwey oder Peter Bäder, die mit Leidenschaft Konzertplakate gestalteten und deren Handschrift leicht erkennbar ist. Schouwey holte ab 1983 zusammen mit seinem Freund Pascal Hunkeler viele der wichtigsten Namen der internationalen Indie-Szene ins erzkatholische Städtchen Fribourg, und er war nah dabei, als dort mit The Young Gods eine der wenigen Schweizer Bands entstand, die auch international einflussreich wurden. Schouwey hatte zuvor in einer Band namens Jof & The Ram getrommelt (Kurzform von Johnny Furgler & The Raclette Machine), bei der der spätere Young-Gods-Sänger Franz Treichler mitspielte – zusammen mit Treichler gehörte er zu den Mitgründern des alternativen Konzertlokals Fri-Son, das Fribourg auf die Karte der internationalen Konzertagenten brachte.

Peter Bäder wiederum bewegte sich in den Kreisen rund um das Zürcher RecRec-Label und -Musikvertrieb von Veit Stauffer und Daniel «Dewe» Walder. Er rückte mit seinen Plakaten und Schallplattencovern etwa die experimentelle No-Wave- und Avantgarde-Rock-Szene aus den USA ins Bild, die dank RecRec in der Schweiz über eine Art Exklave verfügte und zur gleichen Zeit von der temporär nach New York ausgewanderten Welschschweizer Fotografin Catherine Ceresole dokumentiert wurde. Bäder verstand sich – wie Bonsma, Schouwey, Cédric Magnin, Alain Straubhaar und Luc Torregrossa – als Teil eines Ganzen und setzte auf Teamarbeit. Dank dieser emotionalen Bindung der Gestalter an die Bands, Labels und Auftrittsorte, für die sie – nicht selten zum Nulltarif – die Plakate gestalteten, entstand ein visuelles «Branding» mit Wiedererkennungswert.

So verkörperten Bäders Plattencover und Konzertplakate den avantgardistisch-alternativen Geist hinter den RecRec-Produktionen, während Schoris aus alten Zeitschriften zusammengeschnipselte Retro-Ästhetik klarmacht, dass hier Popmusik für neugierige Connaisseure statt für die anonyme Masse angeboten wurde. Dirk Bonsma wiederum prägt seit mittlerweile einem Vierteljahrhundert die Ästhetik der Basler Garage-Rock-Band Lombego Surfers – eine solch enge und langfristige Verbindung zwischen einer Band und einem Gestalter dürfte nicht nur für die Schweiz einmalig sein. Gestalter, die untrennbar mit einem musikalischen Genre verbunden sind – Martin Schori mit dem Indie-Pop, Jacques Schouwey mit (Post) Industrial – waren früher so etwas wie die Regel, heute sind sie aber eher die Ausnahme. Eine solche stellt neben Dirk Bonsmas Engagement für die Lombego Surfers etwa Remo Keller vom Art-Label Milk + Wodka dar, in den Achtzigerjahren für seine Band Smelly Gambas, heute Denner Clan. Oder Martin Gössi, der mit Vehemenz und Konsequenz bis zum heutigen Tag für das punkige Erscheinungsbild des Luzerner Sedel (alternatives Musikzentrum) sorgt.

Part of a whole

This connected Martin Schori with people like Jacques Schouwey or Peter Bäder, who all designed concert posters with a passion and had easily recognizable distinctive styles. As of 1983, Schouwey, together with his friend Pascal Hunkeler, brought many of the most important names in the international indie scene to the small, staunchly Catholic town of Fribourg and he was closely present when The Young Gods were founded, one of the few Swiss bands that would become internationally influential. Schouwey had previously drummed in a band called Jof & The Ram (short form of Johnny Furgler & the Raclette Machine), where the later Young Gods singer Franz Treichler was playing, and, together with Treichler, he was a co-founder of the alternative concert venue Fri-Son, which putFribourg on the map of international concert booking agents.

Peter Bäder, in turn, belonged to the circle around the Zurich-based RecRec label and music distribution company run by Veit Stauffer and Daniel "Dewe" Walder. With his posters and record covers he, for instance, brought into focus the experimental no-wave and avant-garde rock scene from the United States who, thanks to RecRec, had an enclave of sorts in Switzerland and, at the same time, was being documented by the French-speaking Swiss photographer Catherine Ceresole; having temporarily emigrated to New York. Bäder—like Bonsma, Schouwey, Cédric Magnin, Alain Straubhaar, and Luc Torregrossa—perceived himself as a part of a whole and focused on teamwork. Due to this emotional bond between designers and bands, labels, and venues, for whom they designed the posters—more often than not free of charge—a visual "branding" developed with a recognition value.

Thus, Bäder's record covers and concert posters embodied the avant-garde, alternative spirit behind the RecRec productions, while Schori's retro aesthetics pieced together cutouts from old magazines and pointed out that this kind of pop music was being offered to curious connoisseurs rather than the anonymous masses. Dirk Bonsma, on the other hand, had been shaping the aesthetics of Basel-based garage rock band Lombego Surfers for a quarter of a century already—such a close and longstanding connection between a band and a graphic designer is quite likely unique, not just for Switzerland. Formerly, designers that were inseparably linked with a musical genre —Martin Schori with indie pop, Jacques Schouwey with (post) industrial sounds—were more often the rule, but nowadays they are rather the exception. One of these, besides Dirk Bonsma's commitment to the Lombego Surfers, is for example, Remo Keller from the art label Milk + Wodka, who already worked in the eighties for his band Smelly Gambas, presently, Denner Clan. Or then Martin Gössi, who, with a vehemence and consistency continues to care for the punk-referenced visual appearance of the Sedel (alternative music center) in Luzern.

Heterogene Szene

Musikalisch sind die Achtzigerjahre ohne die Punk-Explosion der Siebziger nicht denkbar. Die Unbeschwertheit und die freche Do-it-yourself-Mentalität der ersten Punkgeneration war schnell verglüht – auch weil die Musik nun Teil einer eigentlichen gesellschaftlichen Bewegung war, die auch zunehmend politische Anliegen formulierte und diese radikal einforderte. Die Szene der Bewegten war heterogen, die verschiedensten Strömungen von Alternativ- und Subkultur und politischen Gesinnungen flossen hier zusammen. Zeitweise wurde der Sound der Post-Punk-Bands, die zunächst noch auf New Wave, Power-Pop, Ska, aber auch auf die erste Industrial- und Noise-Musik setzten, von den Megaphonen der bewegten Jugend übertönt. Als dann in vielen Städten alternative Zentren mit Auftrittsmöglichkeiten entstanden, näherte sich auch die vom Post-Punk geprägte Musikszene einem regulären Kulturbetrieb an.

Musik setzte zunehmend einen logistischen Backbone voraus, zumal die Medien den Sounds abseits des Mainstreams mehr Platz einzuräumen begannen und mit der Entstehung der Schweizer Pop-Radios 1983 auch Bands aus der Post-Punk-Szene eine Möglichkeit erhielten, gespielt zu werden. Der Konkurrenzdruck wurde grösser, aber auch die stilistische Bandbreite. Während man sich in den Gründerjahren von 1977 bis 1980 noch weitgehend auf archaischen Gitarrenpunk und die ungestüme Kraft des primitiven Rock'n'Roll einigen konnte, wurden nun immer häufiger elektronische Instrumente eingesetzt, die den Achtziger-Sound im Rückblick geprägt haben. Schweizer Achtziger-Bands, die auch international ausstrahlen, sind etwa Yello oder The Young Gods: beides personell radikal abgespeckte Formationen, die auf Synthesizer, Sampler und später auf den Computer setzten. Stephan Eicher, der zusammen mit der Band Grauzone schon 1980 einen Wechsel der Tonalität in der Schweizer Post-Punk-Szene einläutete und mit dem Song «Eisbär» ein grosses Echo fand, trat zu Beginn seiner Solokarriere ganz alleine auf, umgeben von einem Park mit Drummaschinen und Keyboards.

Regionale Besonderheiten

Zunehmend begannen sich in der Post-Punk-Szene auch regionale Besonderheiten auszuprägen. Die Westschweiz pflegte seit jeher eine leidenschaftliche Liaison mit dem einfachen, traditionsbewussten Rock'n'Roll – was sich auch in der Ästhetik der Konzertplakate äusserte, die auf einem klassischen BD-Stil (*bandes dessinées* oder Comics) baute. Mitte der Achtziger kam es von Genf aus zu einem eigentlichen Revival des Gitarrenrock. The Maniacs und The Needles waren nur die Speerspitze einer ganzen Armada von Bands aus der selbst ernannten Guitar Town. In Bern setzte sich im Gefolge von Bands wie Ex-Trem-Normal und Züri West zunehmend eine neue, hektischere Art des Mundart-Rock durch. Daneben gab es aber einen noch radikaleren Untergrund, der von der dunklen No Wave einer Band wie Dnjepr bis zum kompromisslos handgemachten Noiseabilly der Szene rund um Beat «Beat-Man» Zeller reichte. Basel gab sich anglophil und frönte mit Bands wie The Wondergirls oder

A heterogeneous scene

Musically, the eighties are unimaginable without the punk explosion of the seventies. The lightheartedness and insolent do-it-yourself mentality of the first punk generation soon vaporized—also because music was now part of an actual social movement that increasingly formulated political requests and radically demanded the subsequent implementation of them. The scene of the youth movement was heterogeneous and, within it, the most diverse currents of alternative culture and subcultures as well as political persuasions coalesced. At times, the sound of the post-punk bands, that at first still relied on new wave, power pop and ska, but also the vanguards of industrial music and noise, was being drowned out by megaphones of the youth movement. Once alternative centers with gig opportunities came to be in many cities, the music scene, shaped by post-punk, also approached regular operations that govern such cultural institutions.

Music increasingly required a logistical backbone, especially since the media had started to give more space to the sounds beyond the mainstream and with the inception of the Swiss pop radios in 1983 also offered an opportunity for post-punk bands to be played. Over time, the spectrum of styles also grew due to competitive pressure. While during the founding years between 1977 and 1980 the scene mostly agreed on archaic guitar punk and the boisterous energy of primitive rock'n'roll, more and more electronic instruments were being applied that, in retrospect, shaped the sound of the eighties. Swiss bands of this time that also achieved international recognition were, for example, Yello or The Young Gods: both of them radically downscaled band formations relying on synthesizers, samplers and later computers. Stephan Eicher, who already in 1980, together with the band Grauzone, heralded a change of tonality in the Swiss post-punk scene and by virtue of the song "Eisbär" also received much attention, performed at the beginning of his solo career entirely by himself, surrounded by an arsenal of drum machines and keyboards.

Regional peculiarities

The increasing growth of regional peculiarities also started to develop in the post-punk period. The French-speaking part of Switzerland had always maintained a passionate liaison with the simple, traditional rock'n' roll—that also expressed itself in the aesthetics of the concert posters, building on a classic BD (*bandes dessinées* or comics) style. In the mid-eighties, a revival in the proper sense of the word, came out of Genf. The Maniacs and The Needles were merely the spearheads of an entire armada of bands from this self-proclaimed "Guitar Town". In the wake of bands such as Ex-Trem-Normal and Züri West a new, more hectic form of Swiss German dialect rock asserted itself In Bern. Next to this, there was a still greater radical underground, reaching from the dark no wave of a band like Dnjepr, all the way to the uncompromising, handmade "noiseabilly" encompassing the scene around "Beat-Man" Zeller. Basel acted anglophile and indulged in classic pop songs, with bands such as The Wondergirls or The Arhoolies.

HOT POINTS FESTIVAL, LAUSANNE, 1988, © YVON BAUMANN

MIX & REMIX, JEAN-PIERRE PABST, JACQUES SCHOUWEY, FRANZ TREICHLER, FRI-SON LAUSANNE, 1983

THE NEEDLES, BERNHARD TRONTIN, FLORENCE GROSJEAN, SERGE PULFER, DANIEL GAUTIER, 1994, © THE NEEDLES

GRAUZONE, MARCO REPETTO, G.T., MARTIN EICHER, BOLLWERK BERN, 1980

The Arhoolies dem klassischen Popsong. Daneben blühte eine vielfältige avantgardistische Musik-Kunst-Szene um die beiden Labels Winterschatten (Musik für andere Ohren) und Vision (The Sound of Vision), die heute noch immer durch Plattfon Records in Basel repräsentiert wird. Zürich blieb auch in den Achtzigerjahren die Stadt mit der grössten musikalischen Diversität. Hier koexistierten der rohe Power-Punk von The Bucks, die multimedial inszenierte Electronica von UnknownMix, die LoFi-Punk-Chansons von Baby Jail und die melancholisch-düsteren Klangwelten von Blue China.

Wie in jeder Grossstadt bildeten sich Szenen und Subszenen, die sich voneinander abgrenzten beziehungsweise zu ignorieren versuchten. An den Rändern und neben den urbanen Zentren der Schweiz bildeten sich eigene Zirkel, die teils zu eigenständigen Zentren für spezifische Stile wurden: In Schaffhausen und Romanshorn spielte die Szene rund um Der Böse Bub Eugen und Guz deutsch gesungenen Diskurspop Avant La Lettre (vor dem Buchstaben oder bevor es das überhaupt gab), in der Uhrenstadt La Chaux-de-Fonds im Kanton Jura trafen sich die Liebhaber von alternativem Gitarrenpop in verschiedenen Lokalitäten, bevor sich mit dem Bikini Test Ende der Achtzigerjahre ein fixer Club etablierte. Mit dem an Velvet Underground geschulten Jivaros Quartet hatte La Chaux-de-Fonds auch eine eigene Szeneband. Noch war der Alternative Rock mit seinen Post-Punk-Wurzeln die Musik der Stunde, noch trafen sich die Exponenten der verschiedenen Stile in denselben Lokalen. Zwar gab es schon in den Achtzigern einzelne Retroströmungen, wie das Revival des Garagenbeat der Sechziger, doch auf diese Musik bezogen sich Rockbands, die auf Gitarren setzen, ohnehin immer wieder. Gegen Ende der Achtzigerjahre geriet der Rock als prägende Musik der jugendlichen Subkultur langsam, aber sicher unter Druck. Mit Hip-Hop und insbesondere mit Techno kamen zwei neue Musikgenres ins Spiel, um die sich neue Jugendszenen gruppierten. Das wirkte sich auch auf die Selbstwahrnehmung und -darstellung der Rock- und Popkultur aus.

In addition, a multifaceted avant-garde music and art scene flourished around the two labels Winterschatten ("Musik für andere Ohren" or music for other ears) and Vision ("the sound of vision"), to this day still represented by Plattfon Records in Basel. Zurich still remained the city with the greatest musical diversity during the eighties. Here coexisted the raw power punk by The Bucks, the staged multi-media electronica by UnknownMix, the lo-fi punk chansons by Baby Jail and the melancholic, gloomy soundscapes of Blue China.

As in every big city, scenes and sub-scenes evolved that separated themselves from each other, or rather, attempted to ignore one another. On the edges and next to the urban centers of Switzerland, other circles developed that, in part, became distinct centers for particular styles: in Schaffhausen and Romanshorn, the scene played discourse pop avant la lettre (before the letter or before it actually existed) sung in German by Der Böse Bub Eugen and Guz. In the watchmaking town of La Chaux-de-Fonds in the canton of Jura, lovers of alternative guitar pop met in various localities, before a permanent club, the Bikini Test, entrenched itself at the end of the eighties. With the Jivaros Quartet "tutored" by Velvet Underground, La Chaux-de-Fonds also had its own scene band. Yet, alternative rock with its post-punk roots remained the flavor of the day and the representatives of the different styles still met at the same venues. There were also already the first occasional retro currents in the eighties, like the sixties garage beat revival, but it was still guitar-oriented rock bands that concerned themselves with this kind of music, incidentally, over and over again. Toward the end of the eighties, rock as the characteristic music of the youth subculture, slowly but surely came under pressure. With hip-hop and, especially techno, two new musical genres came into play, around which new youth scenes grouped themselves. This also affected the self-perception and image cultivation of the rock and pop culture.

The Art of Modern Rock

In den Neunzigerjahren beginnt sich die Musikszene in der Schweiz endgültig zu diversifizieren. Nach bisher ungeahnten Verkaufszahlen einiger Berner Mundart-Rockbands, die ihre Alben bei Independent-Vertrieben verlegen, springt die Zürcher Musikindustrie auf den fahrenden Zug auf und durchkämmt das Mittelland nach Züri-West- und Patent-Ochsner-Klonen. «Bruuchsch e Bärner i dr Bänd», singt Polo Hofer, der Chronist der laufenden Ereignisse. Doch es geht auch ohne. «Kauft keine Berner Tonträger!» heisst es auf einem Kleber, der Mitte der Neunziger in alternativen Plattenläden aufgelegt wird. Bands wie Baby Jail («Nei») und Eugen («Lied für Mani») singen gegen die latente Überdosis Bern und deren Resultate wie die umstrittene Hommage der Szene an den Chansonnier Mani Matter («MatterRock») an. Kommt dazu, dass das öffentliche und private Pop-Radio, das in seinen Anfängen in den Achtzigerjahren musikalisch noch erstaunlich offen war, sich nun die «Durchhörbarkeit» in die Handbücher schreibt und die Musikprogramme gnadenlos formatiert. Alles, was auffällt, ist unerwünscht, säuselnder amerikanischer RnB wird zum Mass aller Dinge. «Ist das besser als Janet Jackson?», müsse der Programmleiter seine Musik- und Nachrichtenredaktoren fragen, wenn diese mit einem neuen Song oder Thema vor seinem Chefpult stünden, meint ein deutscher Berater und Pop-Konfektionist an einer Tagung der Radiobranche in den späten Neunzigerjahren. Dass nach seiner Meinung Gitarrenmusik, erst recht, wenn sie von Schweizer Musikern gespielt wird, dieses Kriterium nicht erfüllt, liegt auf der Hand.

Drohende Banalisierung

Doch es ist nicht in erster Linie der schnöde Mainstream, der die alternative Rockmusik in Bedrängnis bringt: Hat sie sich mit Prog, Metal, Punk und Post-Punk bisher stets an den eigenen Haaren aus dem Sumpf der drohenden Banalisierung gezogen und darum weiter in Anspruch nehmen können, der prägende Sound einer Jugendkultur zu sein, erhält sie nun mit dem Boom von Techno und House erstmals ernsthafte Konkurrenz. Wer jung ist und etwas auf sich hält, geht nun nicht mehr zwingend ins alternative Kulturzentrum, um dort die neuesten Bands auszuchecken, von denen es seit der Wiederbefeuerung des harten Rock durch die Grungebands aus Seattle eine ganze Menge gibt. Als Alternative sind durchtanzte Nächte an spontan aufgezogenen Technopartys in improvisierten Lokalen durchaus valabel. Einige der Punks der ersten Stunde wie Arnold Meyer, Markus «Punky» Kenner oder Marco Repetto (Drummer bei Glueams und Grauzone) fühlen sich vom neuen Underground-Feeling und der maschinellen Präzision der elektronischen Musik mindestens ebenso angezogen, wie sie früher der brachiale Urschrei des Punk fasziniert hat.

In the nineties, the music scene in Switzerland ultimately began to diversify. Following the previously unimaginable sales figures by some Bernese dialect rock bands, whose albums are shifted by independent distributors, Zurich's music industry jumps on the moving train and combs through the Swiss Central Plateau area for Züri West and Patent Ochsner clones. "Bruuchsch e Bärner i dr Bänd" (You need a Bernese in the band), sings Polo Hofer, the chronicler of current events. Yet, it is possible without. "Kauft keine Berner Tonträger!" (don't buy any Bernese sound media!) declares a sticker placed in alternative record shops in the mid-nineties. Bands like Baby Jail (Nei) and Eugen (Lied für Mani) sing against the latent overdose of Bernese music and the results thereof; for example, the controversial tribute sampler (Matter Rock) of the scene to the Bernese chanson singer Mani Matter. Adding to this, public and private pop radio that at the start of the eighties remained surprisingly open in terms of music, now write "listen carefully first" into their handbooks and mercilessly format their music program. Anything that sticks out is now unwanted and sighing American R&B becomes the measure of all things. "Is this better than Janet Jackson?" the program director should ask his music and news editors when they stand in front of his executive chair with a new song or topic, reckons a German consultant and pop "confectionist" at a radio industry convention in the late nineties. That, in his opinion, guitar music, especially when played by Swiss musicians, doesn't satisfy this criteria, is apparent.

Impending banality

But it isn't the vile mainstream that first and foremost brings hardship on alternative rock music. By virtue of progressive rock, metal, punk, and post-punk, it had always been possible, by the scruff of one's own neck, to pull out from the swamp of impending banality and continue the claim that it is the defining sound of youth culture. But now, for the first time, serious competition comes from the boom of techno and house. Anybody that's young and self-respecting is no longer compelled to visit the alternative culture center in order to check out the newest bands, of which there were a good many since the resuscitation of hard-played rock by Seattle grunge bands. As a viable alternative, there were nights to dance through at spontaneously organized techno parties in improvised locales. Some punks from the early days like Arnold Meyer, Markus "Punky" Kenner or Marco Repetto (the drummer of Glueams and Grauzone) are more or less equally drawn to the new underground feeling and the machine-made precision of electronic music, much like they had been previously fascinated by the brute primal scream of punk.

UNKNOWN ARTIST, 1993, 105×148

UNKNOWN ARTIST, 1993, 105×148

CORNEL WINDLIN, 1994, 104×147

CORNEL WINDLIN, 1994, 102×148

UNKNOWN ARTIST, JUNKZ MAGAZINE NO.29, 1999, 210×297, PHOTOCOPY

Techno arbeitet mit ganz anderen Codes als die Rockkultur. Erstmals seit Punk – und noch radikaler – werden das Publikum beziehungsweise die Partygänger ins Zentrum gestellt, die das Geschehen an den Partys und Happenings vor Ort auch visuell mitgestalten können. Zur Promotion der Partys steht – ähnlich wie zuvor beim Punk – der kleinformatige Flyer im Vordergrund. Nur ist dieser, anders als das noch bei Punk der Fall gewesen ist, oft aufwändiger und grafisch sauberer gestaltet.

Ein Bindeglied zwischen dem aufblühenden Techno und dem bereits gut abgehangenen Rock ist der eben aus London zurückgekehrte Innerschweizer Cornel Windlin, der ab 1993 als Koorganisator der von Zürichs Party- und Kulturszene rege frequentierten «Reefer Madness»-Anlässe fungiert, für deren Flyer zuständig ist und für zwei Jahre auch die Veranstaltungsplakate der Roten Fabrik gestaltet. In seinem Stil finden sich Elemente aus beiden Genres, und er ist einer der wichtigen Neuerer der Schweizer Konzertgrafik, dessen Einfluss sich bis heute bei jungen Gestaltern wiederfindet.

Sport und Musik

Neben Techno, House und den verschiedenen damit assoziierten Stilen und Variationen wird Hip-Hop zur neuen Nische der Jugendkultur. Auch wenn in der reichen Schweiz die Adaptionen des urbanen Ghetto- und Gangsta-Raps vorerst weder besonders glaubwürdig noch eigenständig sind und erst mit der Verwendung der eigenen Sprache an Bedeutung gewinnen, die in der Romandie etwa von Crews wie Sens Unik und Silent Majority propagiert und vom Basler Rapper Black Tiger 1992 auch in einem Deutschschweizer Dialekt umgesetzt wird: Hip-Hop ist vor allem bei jungen Männern wegen seines kompetitiven Geistes und der sportlichen Herausforderungen von Breakdance und DJ-ing attraktiv. Dazu kommen nächtliche (Graffiti) Spray-Streifzüge durch die Städte und Agglos, wo sich die konkurrierenden Vertreter der Hip-Hop-Szenen buchstäblich im Untergrund bewegen, um dort ihre Tags zu hinterlassen. Visuell ist die Hip-Hop-Szene stark an ihren amerikanischen Vorbildern orientiert, sei es, was die Marken der getragenen Kleider anbetrifft, sei es bei Tonträgerhüllen und Flyern, sei es bei der Gestaltung von Tags und Logos. Einer, der Ende der Neunzigerjahre als Sprayer aktiv ist, ist Eric Andersen, heute einer der profilierten Gestalter von Konzertplakaten in der Schweiz. Andersen, der in dieser Zeit eine Lehre als Grafiker absolviert, trennt seine gestalterischen Kenntnisse und seine Aktivitäten als Sprayer. Erst als er Anfang der Nullerjahre damit beginnt, Konzertplakate im Rock-Umfeld zu gestalten, greift er aktiv und bewusst auf das zurück, was er während seiner Berufsausbildung gelernt hat.

Müffelnder Rock'n'Roll

Der neuen Konkurrenz der Jugendkulturen hat die klassische Rockkultur vorerst wenig entgegenzusetzen. Die Urkraft des Grunge inspiriert in der Schweiz nur we-

Techno works with completely different codes than rock culture. For the first time since punk—and even more radically—the audience, respectively the party-goers, are put centre stage and then help to fashion the local proceedings visually at parties and happenings. For the promotion of techno parties—similar to punk prior—stands the small-format flyers in the foreground. Only these, unlike as it was still the case with punk, are often more elaborate and designed graphically in a cleaner manner.

A link between the blossoming techno and the already well-established rock is Cornel Windlin from Central Switzerland, who has just returned from London and, as of 1993, functions as a co-organizer of the "Reefer Madness" events heavily frequented by Zurich's party and culture scene. Windlin is in charge of flyers for said event and for two years designs the event posters for the Rote Fabrik. In his design style, elements from both genres are found and he is one of the important innovators of Swiss concert graphic art, whose influence is still found among young graphic designers nowadays.

Sports and music

Next to techno, house, and the different associated styles and variations, hip-hop becomes a new niche for youth culture. Even though the adaptation of urban ghetto and gangsta rap in wealthy Switzerland are, at first, neither particularly credible nor distinct. Through the utilization of the mother tongue ultimately, this achieves a relevance that, for example, in the French-speaking part of Switzerland, is propagated by crews like Sens Unik and Silent Majority; and used a Swiss-German dialect with Basel rapper Black Tiger in 1992. Hip-hop is especially attractive to young men due to its competitive spirit and the sportive challenges of break dance and DJ-ing. Also included are nocturnal (graffiti) spraying sprees through the cities and suburbs, where the competing representatives of the hip-hop scene literally move around in the underground, leaving their tags behind. Visually, the hip-hop scene is strongly oriented on its American role models, be it with regard to the brands of clothes worn, the record covers and flyers or through the design of tags and logos. One active sprayer at the end of the nineties is Eric Andersen, now one of the high-profile graphic designers of concert posters in Switzerland. Andersen, who at the time is completing an apprenticeship as a graphic designer, keeps his design skills and his activities as a sprayer separate. Only at the beginning of the noughties, as he starts to design concert posters within the rock environment, does he consciously draw on what he had learned during his professional training.

Musty rock'n'roll

At that moment, the classic rock culture has little to hold against the new youth culture competition. The primal force of grunge inspires few Swiss bands

nige Bands zu ähnlichen Ausdrucksweisen – obschon Kurt Cobain seinerseits in seinen Tagebüchern *Alles von Kleenex* zu seinen fünfzig Lieblingsplatten gezählt hat. Sportsguitar aus Luzern veröffentlichen zwar eine Single auf dem US-Label SubPop, das quasi als Homebase des Grunge-Rock gilt. Doch ihre Musik ist eher schrammelnder Indie-Pop als mächtiger Swiss Grunge. Eine der wenigen Schweizer Bands, die die emotionale Rockkraft von Grunge wirklich glaubwürdig adaptiert – beziehungsweise sie Jahre vorher antizipiert hat –, sind The Young Gods. Dieses Trio hat seine Wurzeln zwar im Industrial und verzichtet konsequent auf Gitarren. Die Liveshows der Young Gods sind aber an Intensität kaum zu überbieten und stossen auch in den USA auf Interesse. Als sich 1994 Kurt Cobain das Leben nimmt, nur knapp zwei Monate nach einem fiebrigen Nirvana-Konzert in den Patinoires du Littoral in Neuchâtel, scheint Grunge und mit ihm die ganze alternative Rockkultur dem Tod geweiht. Rock ist zwar noch nicht ganz tot, doch er beginnt definitiv seltsam zu riechen.

Und doch hinterlassen Grunge und der neue, in den USA populäre Alternative Rock deutliche Spuren, auch in der Schweizer Musik- und Clublandschaft. Gerade im visuellen Bereich: In den USA hat sich rund um die neue Rockszene ein Zirkel von Gestaltern gebildet, die – erstmal seit den «Heydays» der psychedelischen Plakate der San-Francisco-Szene – wieder aufwändige, meist im Siebdruck hergestellte Plakate und Vinyl-single-Hüllen der angehenden Rockstars unter die Leute bringen. Der einflussreichste Protagonist dieser Szene – auch mit Bezug auf die Schweiz – ist der gebürtige Spanier Frank Kozik, der zuerst von Austin, Texas, und später von San Francisco aus mit seinem Label Man's Ruin agiert.

Sein erstes Siebdruckplakat gestaltet er 1991 für die Industrial-Rocker Pigface aus Chicago, und es sollten bis zum heutigen Tag über deren 1000 werden. Wie schon ein Vierteljahrhundert davor Hans Kunz, besucht Lurker Grand 1993 die Haight-Ashbury-Gegend in San Francisco und bringt nach einem Besuch in Koziks Atelier eine Mappe mit dessen neuesten Plakaten und weitere von Lindsey Kuhn und Chris Coop in die Schweiz. Im darauf folgenden Frühling kommt Kozik auf Einladung für seine erste Ausstellung in Europa nach Zürich. Dafür gestaltet er exklusiv ein Plakat, in dem er den Schweizer Comichelden Globi im Heroinrausch vom Zürcher «Needle Park» abheben lässt. Das «Posterhappening» ist ein voller Erfolg und beeinflusst zumindest den visuellen Auftritt der einheimischen Rockkultur nachhaltig. Unter dem direkten oder indirekten Einfluss von Kozik beginnen auch hiesige Zeichner und Gestalter mit der Herstellung von aufwändigen, im Siebdruck vervielfältigten Plakaten. Das Bewusstsein, dass hier mehr als nur Ankündigungen für Veranstaltungen entstehen, deren Verfallsdatum mit dem Konzertdatum identisch ist, steigt.

Die neue Schweizer Rock-Art

Nun beginnt sich so etwas wie eine Rock-Art zu etablieren. Auch, weil viele weitere Ausstellungen in diesem Kontext folgen und in den Städten neue Clubs, Plattenläden und Labels entstehen, die sich ganz auf die alter-

to similar modes of musical expression—even though Kurt Cobain, in his diaries, counted *everything by Kleenex* in his 50 favorite records list. Sportsguitar from Luzern releases a single on the American SubPop label, that was effectively deemed the home base of grunge. Yet, their music is closer to a strummed indie pop than mighty Swiss grunge. One of the few Swiss bands that adapted the emotional rock power of grunge in a truly credible manner—or rather had anticipated it years before—are The Young Gods. However, this trio has its roots in industrial music and steadfastly eschewes guitars. But the intensity of the Young Gods' live shows is hard to beat and also attracts attention in the United States. When Kurt Cobain commits suicide in 1994, barely two months after a feverish Nirvana concert at the Patinoires du Littoral in Neuchâtel, grunge and, with it the entire alternative rock scene, seems doomed. Although rock is not quite dead yet, it definitely begins to smell funny.

But grunge and the new type of alternative rock popular in the United States still leave clear marks, also on the Swiss music and club landscape. Particularly in the visual realm: a circle of graphic designers has formed around the new rock scene in the United States that —for the first time since the heyday of the psychedelic posters of the San Francisco scene—once again makes elaborate posters and vinyl single covers available to the general public; mostly produced as silkscreen prints. The most influential protagonist of this scene—also with regard to Switzerland—is the native Spaniard Frank Kozik, who at first operates from Austin, Texas and later on from San Francisco with his label Man's Ruin.

He designs his first silkscreen poster n 1991 for industrial rockers Pigface from Chicago and, to-date, there's over a thousand. As Hans Kunz had already did a quarter of a century earlier, Lurker Grand goes to the Haight-Ashbury district in San Francisco in 1993 and, after a visit at Kozik's studio, brings back to Switzerland a folder with his newest posters, as well as additional ones by Lindsey Kuhn and Chris Coop. The following spring, Kozik comes per invite to Zurich, for his first exhibition in Europe. For the occasion, he designs an exclusive poster where he let the Swiss comic hero called Globi lift off, high on heroin, from Zurich's "Needle Park." The "poster happening" is a great success and has a sustaining affect on, at least, the visual appearance of the domestic local rock culture. Under Kozik's direct or indirect influence, local illustrators and designers start with the production of elaborate posters, duplicated by means of silk-screening. The awareness rises that here there was something more emerging than just announcements for events, where the expiration date is also identical to the date of the concert.

The new Swiss rock art

Now something akin to "rock art" is entrenching itself. Also because many similar exhibitions follow within this context and new clubs, record shops, and labels emerge that totally focus on alternative rock, often

FRANK KOZIK, 1993, 570×890, SILKSCREEN

MICHEL CASARRAMONA, 2002, 500×700

MÄRT INFANGER, 2011, 500×700, SILKSCREEN

BEAT-MAN, 1996, 420×590

ROBERT BUTLER, 2010, 460×640, SILKSCREEN

ROBERT BUTLER, 2008, 420×595

ROBERT BUTLER, 2009, 370×500, SILKSCREEN

ROBERT BUTLER, 2009, 400×550, SILKSCREEN

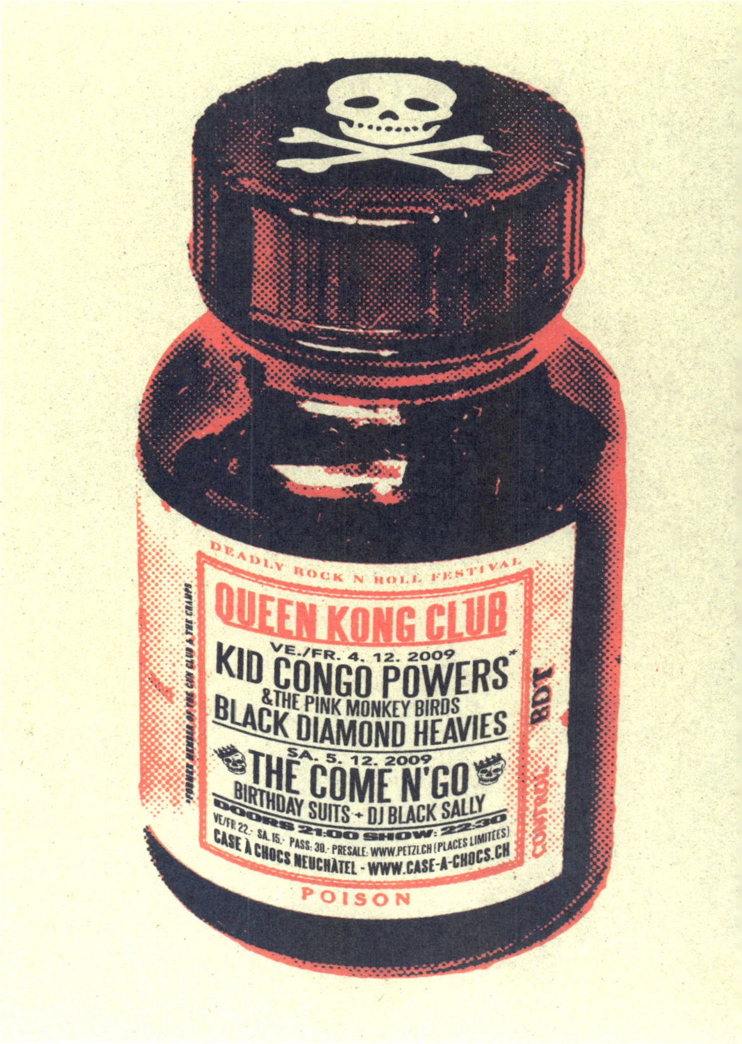

native Rockmusik konzentrieren und ihre Konzertplakate und Plattenhüllen oft bei lokalen Gestaltern in Auftrag geben. Der in Aarau aufgewachsene und seit Langem in Zürich ansässige Michel Casarramona ist einer der profiliertesten Vertreter der «Art of Modern Rock». Er ist von Raymond Pettitbon (dem Bruder von Greg Ginn, dem Gitarristen der US-Hardcore-Band Black Flag und Inhaber des SST-Label, für den er diverse Plattencover gestaltet) ebenso beeinflusst wie von der Comic-Art. Auch die Begegnung mit Frank Kozik ist für ihn wichtig – als Inspiration, aber auch als Hinweis darauf, was er *nicht* machen will und kann. Wie Kozik verwendet Casarramona häufig «vermenschlichte» Tiere für seine Zeichnungen, er meidet aber bekannte Trickfilm- und Comicfiguren, weil dieses Feld schon besetzt ist. Michel Casarramona ist ein leidenschaftlicher Musikfan, der in den besetzten Häusern, in denen er während seiner ersten Jahre in Zürich wohnt, regelmässig Konzerte mit Bands wie The Mekons, Killdozer oder den Goldenen Zitronen organisiert.

Die Flyer für diese Anlässe sind noch strikt schwarzweiss und werden billig vervielfältigt und unter die Leute gebracht. 1997 gestaltet Casarramona sein erstes Siebdruckplakat für ein Konzert der englischen Urpunker UK Subs im Zürcher Rockclub Luv. Seither sind Siebdrucke seine Spezialität. Anfangs noch an jeder Ecke in der Stadt gut sichtbar, werden diese heute kaum noch auf der Strasse aufgehängt, denn Aufwand und Nutzen würden hier in keinem rechten Verhältnis stehen: Meist werden solche Plakate innert Minuten von jemandem abgehängt und nach Hause genommen. Doch in den Szeneläden und -treffpunkten fallen seine aufwändig gestalteten Plakate auf. Sie erfüllen so ihren Zweck als Konzertankündigungen, wirken aber nachhaltig: Es finden sich immer wieder Interessenten, die Siebdruckplakate zu älteren Konzerten kaufen wollen und so für ihn und seine Gestalterkollegen ein weiteres finanzielles Standbein bilden. Ähnlich wie Casarramona hat auch der Innerschweizer Grafiker Märt Infanger noch eine Grafikausbildung ohne Computer absolviert. Während Casarramona aber der bedingungslose Zeichner ist, arbeitet Infanger oft mit Collagen, für die er Bildmaterial verwendet, das mittlerweile schon bis ins späte 19. Jahrhundert zurückreicht. Der Handorgelspieler von Jolly and the Flytrap (die Engelberger Folk-Punk-Band nennt sich bei der Gründung 1986 nach einer damaligen Lieblingslektüre des jungen Comicfans Infanger) ist um den visuellen Auftritt seiner Band besorgt, gestaltet Plakate für Konzerte in der Luzerner Boa-Halle oder im Sedel und macht sich zunehmend mit seinen LP/CD-Covers für Bands der Garagenrock-Szene einen Namen. Wann immer möglich, setzt auch er auf Siebdrucke.

Im Universum der Trash-Kultur

Wenn Rock als einer der musikalischen Motoren der Jugendkultur auf dem Plan bleiben will, muss er mehr sein als Musik. Das hat Beat «Beat-Man» Zeller schon früh realisiert. 1992 gründet der Frontmann und Gitarrist von The Monsters in Bern sein eigenes Label Voodoo Rhythm und lanciert eine Solokarriere als wrestlender und maskierter Anti-Rocker Lightning Beat-Man. Mit seinen ungestümen Liveshows zieht er ein Nischenpublikum weit über die Landesgrenzen hinaus in seinen

commissioning local designers for their concert posters and record covers. Michel Casarramona, who grew up in Aarau and domiciled in Zurich for some time, is one of the most high-profile representatives of the "Art of Modern Rock." He is likewise influenced by Raymond Pettibon (brother of Greg Ginn, the guitarist of U.S. hardcore band Black Flag and owner of the SST label, for whom he designs a number of record covers), as well as comic art. Furthermore, his encounter with Kozik is seminal to him—as inspiration but also as a clue as to what he *doesn't* want to do and what he can't do. Like Kozik, Casarramona often uses "humanised" animals for his drawings, but shirks from well-known animation and comic figures, as this field is already occupied. Michel Casarramona is a passionate music fan, who regularly organizes concerts in the squats where he lives during his first years in Zurich, featuring bands like The Mekons, Killdozer, or Die Goldenen Zitronen.

The flyers for these events are still strictly in black and white, cheaply produced and distributed among the public. In 1997, Casarramona designs his first silkscreen poster for a concert by the English proto-punks U.K. Subs at the Zurich rock club Luv. Since then, silkscreen prints are his specialty. At first, clearly visible on every corner of town, they are nowadays hardly ever hung in the streets anymore, because the costs and benefits would bear no proper relation: in most cases, such posters are removed within minutes by someone and simply taken home. However, in scene shops and gathering places his elaborately designed posters stand out. Thus, they fulfill their purpose as concert announcements, but also function in a sustainable way: time and again interested parties want to buy silkscreen posters of past concerts, thereby building another financial mainstay for himself and his fellow designers. Similar to Casarramona, the graphic designer Märt Infanger, a native of Central Switzerland, also completes training as a graphic designer without the use of computers. But, while Casarramona is the implicit illustrator, Infanger often works with collages, for which he uses picture materials that already reach as far back as the late nineteenth century. The accordion player for Jolly and the Flytrap (the folk punk band from Engelberg whose name, when forming in 1986, is based on one of young comic fan Infanger's favorite reads at the time) concerns himself with his band's visual appearance, designs posters for concerts at the Boa-Halle or Sedel in Luzern, and is increasingly making a name for himself with his LP/CD covers for bands from the garage rock scene. Whenever feasible, he also embraces silkscreen printing.

In the trash culture universe

If rock wants to stay on the map as one of the musical engines of youth culture, it has to be more than music. That's what "Beat-Man" Zeller already realized at an early stage. In 1992, the front man and guitarist of The Monsters founds his own label, Voodoo Rhythm, in Bern and launches a solo career as masked wrestling anti-rocker Lightning Beat-Man. With his boisterous live shows he casts a spell on a niche audience far beyond the Swiss borders. Thereunto, Beat-Man creates

Bann. Dazu kreiert Beat-Man eigene Albumcover und Plakate für seine Projekte (aus Lightning Beat-Man wird später der Trash-Prediger Reverend Beat-Man) und die Voodoo-Rhythm-Bands.

Dafür arbeitet er auch mit dem in Bern hängen gebliebenen Miracle-Workers-Bassisten Robert Butler aka Panti Christ zusammen, der ebenfalls stark an Visuals interessiert ist. Butler gestaltet seit geraumer Zeit Siebdruckplakate und betreibt sein eigenes Unterwäsche-Label, wenn er nicht mit seiner aktuellen Band The Shit unterwegs ist. Beat-Man und Panti Christ inszenieren ihre Acts in einem Universum der amerikanischen Trash-Kultur der Fünfziger- und Sechzigerjahre; des dreckigen Garagenrock und Blues, kombiniert mit mexikanischen Wrestling (Lucha Libre)- und Burlesque-Shows. Aufgestellt wie eine Freak-Sideshow, präsentieren sie sich als Barker (Marktschreier Panti Christ) und Wanderprediger (Reverend Beat-Man) und setzen dies visuell mit der Ästhetik der B-Movies um. Sie etablieren Voodoo Rhythm zum Kultlabel, das weltweit ausstrahlt und Beat-Man zum international berühmt-berüchtigten Prototypen des Rock-Preachers macht.

his own album covers and posters for both his projects (Lightning Beat-Man later becomes the trash preacher Reverend Beat-Man) and the Voodoo Rhythm bands.

To this end he also collaborates with Robert Butler aka Panti Christ, the Miracle Workers' bass player, who got stuck in Bern and also has a strong interest in visuals. For a considerable time now, Butler designs silkscreen posters and runs his own underwear label, when he isn't on the road with his current band The Shit. Beat-Man and Panti Christ stage their acts in a universe ruled by American trash culture of the fifties and sixties; dirty garage rock and blues combined with Mexican wrestling (Lucha Libre) and burlesque shows. Set up like a freak sideshow, they present themselves as a barker (Panti Christ) and a journeyman (Reverend Beat-Man), visually staging the performances using the aesthetics of B-movies. They entrench Voodoo Rhythm as a cult label that resonates world-wide and makes Beat-Man the internationally infamous prototype of the rock preacher.

BOGEN 13 ZÜRICH, 2004, © MICHI VOLLENWEIDER

GARAGE 29 ZÜRICH, 2014, © JAN HOFER

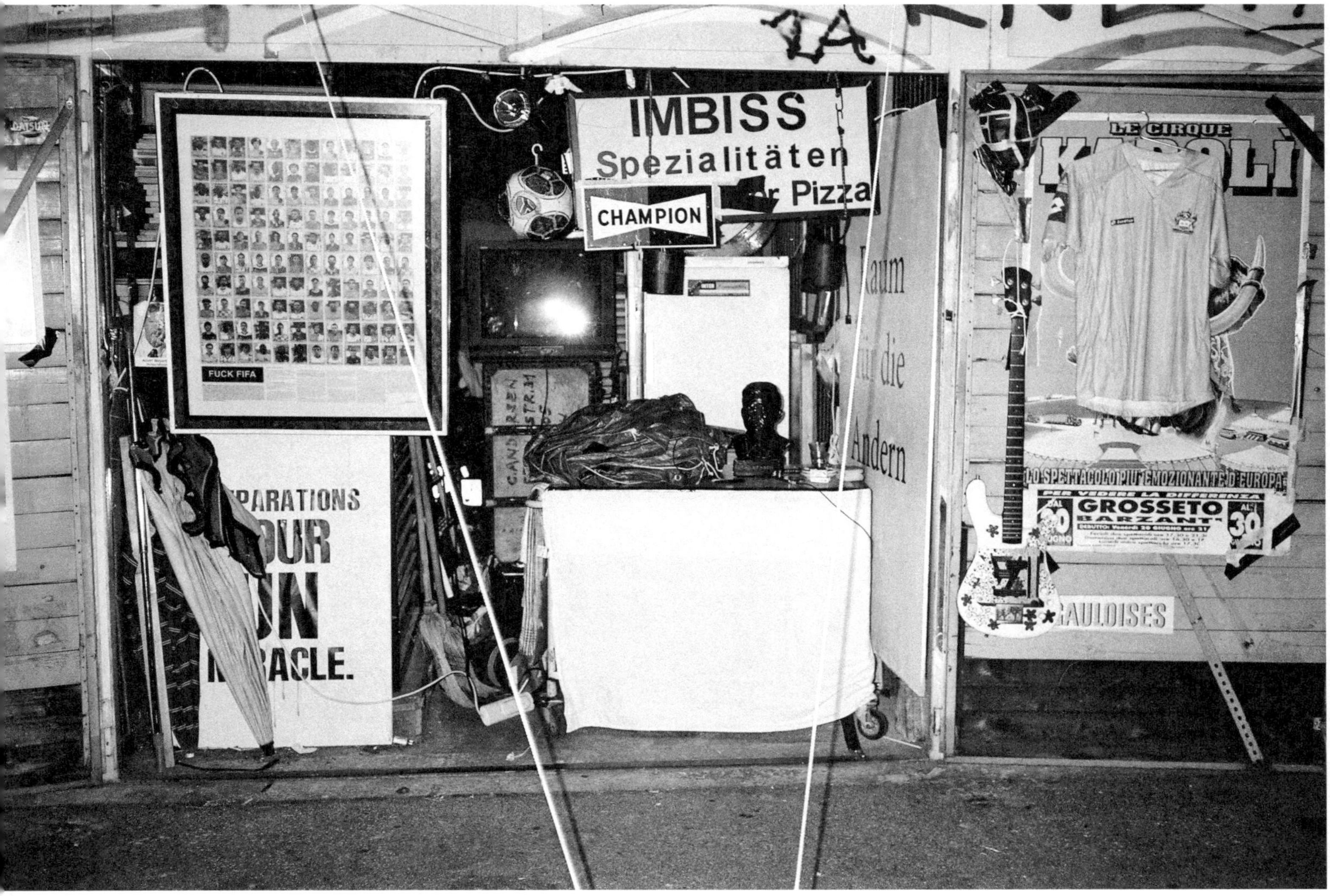

ERIC ANDERSEN, 2010, 500x720, WOODCUT

ERIC ANDERSEN, 2011, 700x1000, SILKSCREEN

ALAIN C. KUPPER, 2003, 460×640

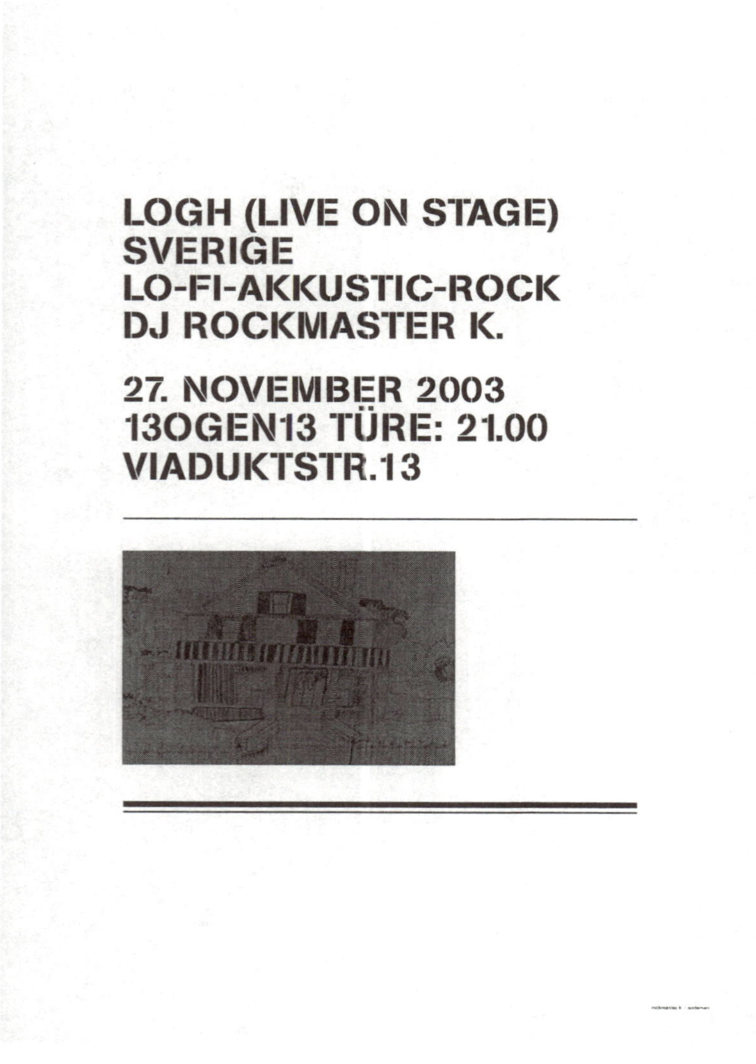

ALAIN C. KUPPER, 2004, 460×640

Die Not hat ein Ende

Simon Reynolds beschreibt in seinem Buch *Retromania* die zunehmende Fixierung der Popkultur der Nullerjahre auf ihre eigene Geschichte und konstatiert, dass die wachsende Zahl von Revivals die mangelnde Innovation in der Popkultur nicht zu kaschieren vermöge. Das mag bis zu einem gewissen Punkt auch für die Garagen- und Indie-Rock-Szene gelten, die heute den rockorientierten Teil des hiesigen Untergrunds beherrscht (wenn man einmal von der konstant operierenden Hardrock- und Metalszene absieht, die mit der Band Eluveitie einen neuen erfolgreichen Export hervorgebracht hat). Hier wird offen auf die Geschichte der (alternativen) Rock- und Undergroundkultur Bezug genommen. Der Zugang zur Geschichte ist allerdings oft spielerisch und alles andere als verkrampft. Viele aktuelle Akteure der alternativen Musikszene sind selber Sammler und Connaisseure, die ihre Bezüge und Querverbindungen nicht vernebeln. Und das ist gut so – wie selbst Simon Reynolds trotz aller Kritik einräumt.

Vom Computer zum Holzschnitt

Innovative Elemente lassen sich gerade im visuellen Auftritt der alternativen Rockkultur durchaus finden. Konzerte dienen nicht mehr einfach als nüchterne Promotion von Tonträgern, sondern werden oft in den grösseren Kontext eines Happenings gestellt. Auch bei der Gestaltung von Konzertplakaten begnügt sich die Szene nicht mit blossem Recycling und Zitaten aus der mittlerweile gut sechzigjährigen Rock- und Popgeschichte. Stillstand kann im digitalen Zeitalter, wo herkömmliche, physische Promotionsmittel zunehmend der mobilen Kommunikation und Newslettern aller Art weichen, nicht das Programm sein. So bemühen sich die jüngsten Vertreter der «Art of Modern Rock», die anders als die Klassiker des Genres zur Generation der Digital Natives gehören, um neue Zugänge zur Vermittlung.

Eric Andersen, der die Generation der jungen, wenn auch bereits nicht mehr ganz Wilden repräsentiert, knüpft zwar an die Tradition der handgemachten Plakatkunst an. Seine ersten Plakate in den frühen Nullerjahren sind Holzschnitte, die anschliessend im Siebdruckverfahren vervielfältigt werden: ein gigantischer Aufwand, den sich der junge Gestalter nur so lange leisten kann, wie er als Bewohner von besetzten Häusern die Lebenskosten auf einem Minimum halten und sich diese durch «Brotjobs» tagsüber verdienen kann. Heute arbeitet Andersen als selbstständiger Grafiker und muss seine Ressourcen einteilen. Doch immer noch legt er grossen Wert darauf, seine Plakate nicht nur selber zu gestalten, sondern auch in Handarbeit zu drucken. Diese Manufaktur passt gut zu einer Musik, die sich heute – zumindest im Rockbereich – auch wieder verstärkt auf Handgemachtes besinnt. Dass die Digital Natives dabei keine Berührungsängste zu allem Digitalen kennen, liegt auf der Hand. Andersen arbeitet heute im Auf-

In his book *Retromania*, Simon Reynolds describes the mounting fixation of pop culture during the 00s on its own history and establishes that the growing number of revivals cannot conceal the lack of innovation in pop culture. To a certain extent this may also apply to the garage and indie rock scene which nowadays, dominate the rock-oriented part of the local underground (when one clearly disregards the steadily operating hard rock and metal scene that with the band Eluveitie has spawned a new successful export). Here there's a frank reference to the history of (alternative) rock and underground culture. However, the approach to history is often playful and anything but uptight. Many contemporary players in the alternative music scene are themselves collectors and connoisseurs, who don't obfuscate their references or cross-connections. And that's good that way—even Simon Reynolds concedes, despite all criticism.

From computer to woodcut

It is definitely possible to find innovative elements, especially in the visual appearance of alternative rock culture. Concerts no longer simply serve as a sober promotion tool for sound media, but rather are often put in the context of a happening. Also, for the design of concert posters, the scene isn't content by mere recycling approaches and quotes from the, meanwhile, more than sixty-year-old history of rock and pop. Stagnation can't be the program in the digital age, where traditional physical means of promotion are being increasingly replaced by mobile communication tools and newsletters of all sorts. Thus, the youngest representatives of the "Art of Modern Rock" that, unlike the classics of the genre, belong to the generation of digital natives—strive for these new approaches in communication.

Eric Andersen, who represents the generation of the young digital natives, albeit no longer quite so wild, actually ties back to the tradition of hand-produced poster art. His first posters from the early noughties are woodcuts that later are duplicated using silkscreen printing: a huge effort that the young designer can only afford as long as he can keep his living costs at a minimum; as an occupant of squats and earning his keep through odd-jobs during the day. Currently, Andersen works as a freelance graphic designer and has to ration his resources. But he still attaches great importance on not only designing his own posters but also to print them by hand. This manufacture actually suits music well that nowadays—at least in the field of rock—also reinforces a greater reflection on manual crafting. The fact that digital natives have no fear of contact with everything digital is stating the obvious. At this point, Andersen works on commission—but also con-

trag – gibt sich aber nach wie vor auch selber Aufträge. Etwa, wenn er Plakate für die Konzerte zeichnet, die er nach wie vor im intimen Rahmen seiner Garage an der Zürcher Geroldstrasse organisiert. Die Ästhetik, die Andersen für seine Plakate verwendet, hat kaum etwas mit rocktypischen Accessoires zu tun, wie man sie noch eher in der ersten «Art of Modern Rock»-Generation bei Zeichnern wie Casarramona und Infanger findet.

Andersens Arbeiten sind stark grafisch orientiert und konzentrieren sich nicht selten auf die Typografie, die dank der sorgfältigen und aufwändigen Druckverfahren auch richtig zur Geltung kommt. Plakate für befreundete Bands wie Disco Doom, Demolition Blues oder Fai Baba, die abseits des Mainstreams musizieren, sind immer noch seine Leidenschaft. Doch daneben wendet er sein Augenmerk immer mehr auf das politische Plakat und gestaltet regelmässig für die 1.-Mai-Demos, einen palästinensischen Grill oder aktuelle, umstrittene Abstimmungsvorlagen. Das, was ihn stört, zu benennen, gestalterisch umzusetzen und dann unter die Leute zu bringen, ist hier sein dringliches Anliegen.

Selbstversorgung und Genügsamkeit

Die aktuelle Schweizer Rock-Art steht also in einem historischen Kontext und referenziert auf die Popkultur wie auf die lange Tradition der Schweizer Plakatgrafik. Diese Retroelemente passen zu einer kleinen, übersichtlichen, alternativen Musikszene, die sich mit Händen und Gitarren gegen die unerträgliche Leichtigkeit der mehrheitsfähigen Popmusik zwischen HitMill (eine Schweizer Musikproduktionsfirma) und Leutschenbach (Schweizer Fernsehen) wehrt. Eine Szene, in der kommerzielle Aspekte zwar durchaus mitgewichtet werden, aber nach wie vor das Prinzip der Selbstversorgung und einer gewissen Genügsamkeit gilt. Und die gerade darum Aussichten auf ein langes Leben hat.

Sam Mumenthaler

tinues to give commissions to himself. For example, when he illustrates for those concerts he still organizes in the intimate setting of his garage on Geroldstrasse in Zurich. The aesthetics Andersen applies in his posters have little to do with typical rock accessories and are more likely to be found in the first "Art of Modern Rock" generation and illustrators such as Casarramona and Infanger.

Andersen's works are strongly graphics-oriented and frequently concentrate on the typography, which truly comes into its own thanks to the meticulous and elaborate printing processes. Posters for friends' bands playing music beyond the mainstream such as Disco Doom, Demolition Blues or Fai Baba, continue to be his passion. Yet, aside from all this, he increasingly directs his attention to political posters and regularly designs them for the May 1st demonstrations, a Palestinian grill place, or current contentious bills put to popular vote. In this, his acute concern is to name what disturbs him, implement it graphically and then make it available to the public.

Self-sufficiency and contentment

Contemporary Swiss rock art, therefore, stands in a historical context and references pop and rock culture as well as the longstanding tradition of Swiss poster graphics. These retro elements fit a small, overseeable alternative music scene that makes a stand, by hands and guitars, against the unbearable lightness of the majority-appeal rock and pop music between HitMill (a Swiss music production company) and Leutschenbach (Swiss Television). Albeit a scene where commercial aspects are indeed evaluated accordingly, the principle of self-sufficiency and some degree of contentment still applies and, exactly because of these characteristics, has a chance for a long life.

Sam Mumenthaler

The Swiss Art of Rock

Fünfzehn Künstlerporträts mit Plakatgeschichten von verschiedenen Autoren

Fifteen artist portraits with poster stories by various authors

Ist eine direkte Beziehung der Rock-Art zu spezifischen Musikgenres zwingend? Findet mitunter sogar eine Verinnerlichung der Musik als Lebensideologie statt? In den nachfolgenden fünfzehn spezifisch ausgewählten Künstlerporträts wird ein breites Spektrum dieser Beziehungen sichtbar. Diverse Autoren setzen sich zudem in kurzen Anekdoten mit einzelnen Exponaten dieser Künstler auseinander. Zusammen vermögen die Texte und vielzähligen Abbildungen exemplarisch die visuelle Geschichte des Rocks in der Schweiz über die letzten fünfzig Jahre zu illustrieren.

Is a direct relationship of rock art imperative for specific music genres? Does, on occasion, an internalisation of the music in the form of an ideology for life take place? In the subsequent, specifically selected, fifteen artist portraits a wide spectrum of these relationships becomes apparent. In addition, several authors deal with individual works of these artists by recalling short “anecdotes.” Together, the texts and the numerous images allow an exemplary illustration of the visual history of rock in Switzerland over the last fifty years.

STEREO

Blick

PRÄSENTIERT:

(FROM THE FORTHCOMING LP «VIEW

DŪDE

Düde Dürst

Gelernter Grafiker und Profimusiker. War ab Ende 1965 Schlagzeuger bei der Zürcher Beatband Les Sauterelles und ab Anfang 1969 Gründungsmitglied bei der Progressiv-Rock-Band Krokodil. Diese wurde notabene als erste Schweizer «Super»-Gruppe bezeichnet. Er war bei beiden Bands für das visuelle Erscheinungsbild zuständig und entwickelte im Laufe der Zeit seinen ganz eigenständigen Stil – der von der Pop-Art der Sechziger und den psychedelischen Plakaten aus San Francisco stark beeinflusst war. Daneben zahlreiche grafische Arbeiten für Andreas Vollenweider, Dodo Hug, Hardy Hepp und weitere. Nach musikalischen Abstechern zu Hand in Hand, Ruby's Place und Jo Geilo & The Heartbreakers ist Jazz-Liebhaber Düde Dürst heute wieder regelmässig mit den «Swiss Beatles» von Les Sauterelles unterwegs.

Düde Dürst

Trained graphic artist and professional musician. As of the end of 1965, drummer for the Zurich beat band Les Sauterelles and from the beginning of 1969 founding member of the progressive rock band Krokodil. The latter were, nota bene, labelled the first Swiss "super group." For both bands, he was responsible for the visual appearance and, over time, developed his own style entirely — albeit, heavily influenced by the Pop Art of the sixties and the psychedelic posters from San Francisco. In addition, numerous graphical works forAndreas Vollenweider, Dodo Hug, Hardy Hepp and others. After musical excursions with Hand in Hand, Ruby's Place and Jo Geilo & The Heartbreakers, Düde Dürst is nowadays regularly on the road with the "Swiss Beatles" of Les Sauterelles.

DÜDE DÜRST, LES SAUTERELLES, REUNION CONCERT FLYER, 1971, 150×210

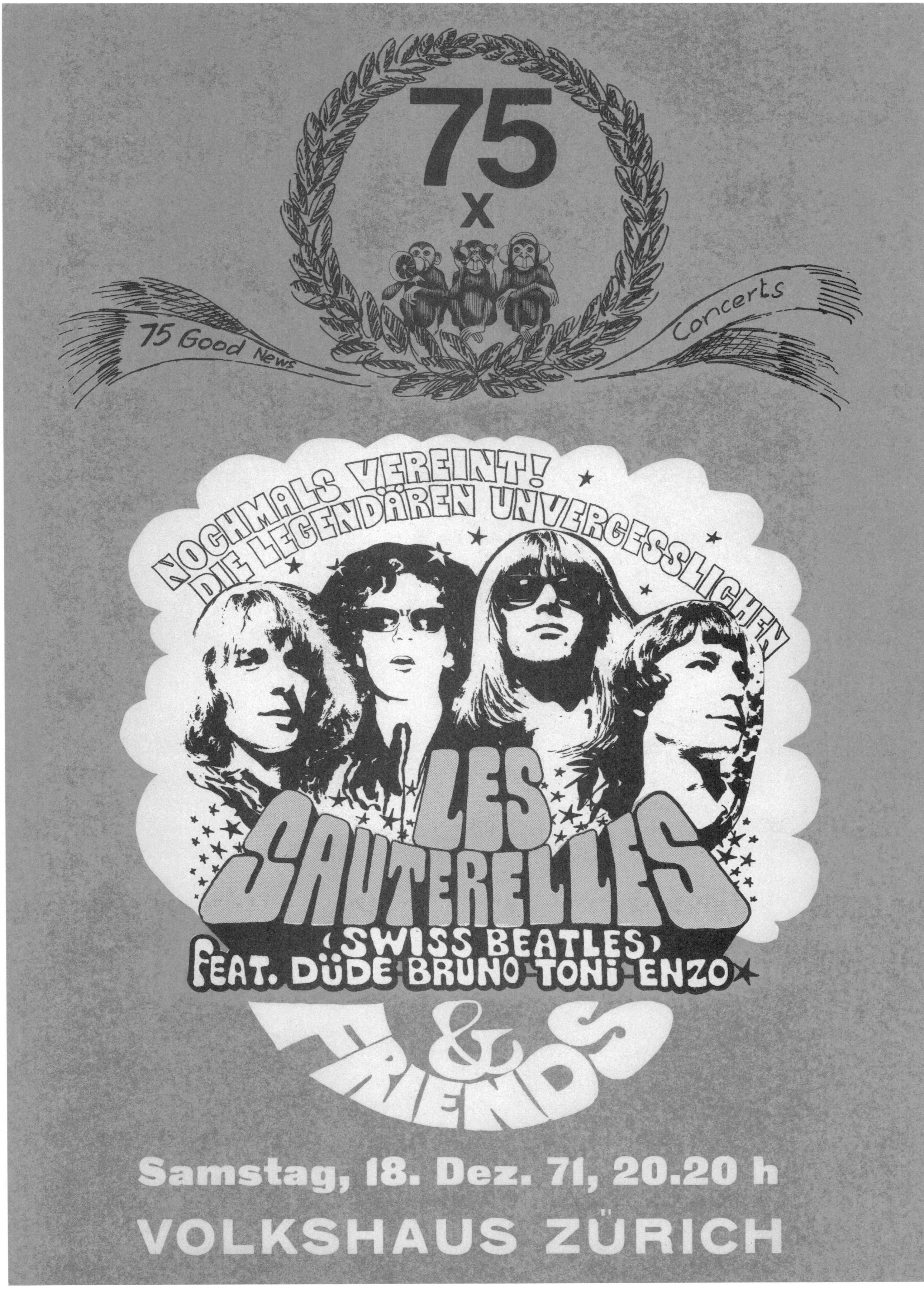

DÜDE DÜRST, LES SAUTERELLES, BASS DRUM LOGO, 1966

Les Sauterelles – Die «Swiss Beatles»

Die Bandmitglieder der schon im September 1962 von Toni Vescoli gegründeten Beatband Les Sauterelles konnten trotz vieler Engagements und der Veröffentlichung ihrer ersten Single am 15. September 1965 vorerst nicht von der Musik alleine leben. Die Platte enthielt zwei Eigenkompositionen: die Instrumentalnummer «Hongkong» auf der A-Seite und das von den Beatles inspirierte «Forget It All» auf der B-Seite. Sie verkaufte sich sehr gut und war notabene der erste in der Schweiz produzierte Hit seit dem «Träumli» der Kapelle Bossbuebe, der Ende der Fünfzigerjahre erschienen war. Auf der Plattenhülle starren die Musiker mit todernster Miene und leicht hochmütig aus dem Halbschatten in die Kamera. Sie hatten sich auf Anweisung ihres Managers Hansruedi Jaggi von dem stilbildenden Cover der ersten Rolling-Stones-LP (*The Rolling Stones*) inspirieren lassen, sprich dieses kopiert, obschon sie den Beatles musikalisch näher standen. Die Beatles sind nie in der Schweiz aufgetreten, und so wurden die Sauterelles, wo immer sie aufspielten, als die «Swiss Beatles» gehandelt, auch wenn sie anfänglich nur zwei Beatles-Songs im Repertoire hatten. Dies führte dazu, dass sich ihr Bekanntheitsgrad in der Schweiz und im nahen Ausland deutlich steigern sollte und sich ihr ohnehin schon gut gefüllter Terminkalender noch mehr zu füllen begann.

Anfang 1966 stiess der Schlagzeuger der befreundeten Beatband The Counts, Düde Dürst, zu den Sauterelles. Düde hatte zunächst die Kunstgewerbeschule in Zürich besucht und danach eine Grafikerlehre begonnen, die er aber abbrechen sollte, da er voll auf seine Profikarriere als Musiker setzte. Mit ihm kam nicht nur ein weiteres musikalisch versiertes Mitglied zu den Sauterelles, sondern auch eines, das die Zeichen der Zeit früh erkannte. Düde war nicht entgangen, dass sich die meisten erfolgreichen angelsächsischen Bands klar durch einen eigenständigen Bandschriftzug, ein «Bandlogo», definierten. Dies war gut sichtbar auf der Pauke eines jeden Schlagzeugers angebracht. Das wohl berühmteste Logo, obwohl nie für ein Albumcover verwendet, befand sich zu jener Zeit auf dem Paukenfell des Beatles-Drummers Ringo Starr, genannt «Drop-T».

Im Dezember 1965 erschien das Album *Rubber Soul* von den Beatles. Auf diesem Album brachte die Band neben amerikanischen Souleinflüssen auch neue Instrumente in ihre Musik ein, wie beispielsweise die von George Harrison im Song «Norwegian Wood» (der übrigens während John Lennons Ferienaufenthalt in St. Moritz Anfang 1965 entstanden war) gespielte Sitar. Düde orientierte sich am *Rubber Soul*-Schriftzug für sein rundes, geschwungenes Les-Sauterelles-Design. Dies übertrug er auf sein Paukenfell, und es wurde von da an für die meisten Tonträger, Konzert- und Promoplakate verwendet. Der «Psychedelic Trip» der Beatles läutete auch in der Schweiz den Abschied der klassischen Beat-Ära ein, und schon bald zogen Schwaden eines verheissungsvollen Rauchs namens Psychedelic Rock von San Francisco via England herüber. Dies führte nicht zuletzt dazu, dass Düde im Januar 1969 eine Band Namens Krokodil mitbegründen sollte …

Lurker Grand

Les Sauterelles—The “Swiss Beatles”

The members of the beat band Les Sauterelles, already established by Toni Vescoli in September 1962, could not make a living solely from their music at first, despite all their engagements and the release of their first single on September 15, 1965. The compositions on the record were their own: the instrumental “Hongkong” on the A-side, and “Forget It All,” inspired by the Beatles, on the B-side. It sold really well and was, notably, the first hit produced in Switzerland since “Träumli” by Kapelle Bossbuebe, released at the end of the nineteen-fifties. On the record sleeve the band members are staring into the camera dead serious from the half shade with somewhat arrogant expressions. As instructed by their manager Hans-Ruedi Jaggi, they received their inspiration from the influential cover of the first Rolling Stones LP (*The Rolling Stones*), thus copying it even though they were musically closer to the Beatles. The Beatles never performed in Switzerland, and wherever Les Sauterelles played in those days, they were welcomed as the “Swiss Beatles” (in spite of the fact that their repertoire initially only contained two Beatles songs). This hugely boosted their level of recognition in Switzerland and neighboring countries, and their already tight schedule was filled to the brim.

At the beginning of 1966, Düde Dürst, the drummer of The Counts, a beat band that they had befriended, joined Les Sauterelles. Düde had first attended the College of Applied Arts in Zurich and then started an apprenticeship as a graphic artist, although he later abandoned it in order to concentrate fully on his professional career as a musician. With him, Les Sauterelles had not only gained a further member and well versed fellow musician, but also a pundit who could read the signs of the times at an early stage. Düde registered that most successful Anglo-Saxon bands clearly defined themselves by means of a specific band lettering, a “band logo.” This logo was first of all applied clearly visible on the bass drum in all known bands. Although never used for an album cover, the likely most famous logo of that period, the “drop-T,” was to be found on the head of the bass drum played by Ringo Starr of the Beatles.

The Beatles’ *Rubber Soul* album was released in December 1965 and integrated both American soul influences and new instruments into their music, a sitar played by George Harrison in the song “Norwegian Wood,” among others (which, incidentally, was written during John Lennon’s vacation in St. Moritz at the beginning of 1965). It was the *Rubber Soul* logo from which Düde modelled his rounded, curvy design for Les Sauterelles on. From then on, the logo found its place on the head of his bass drum and was used on most of their records as well as concert and promotional posters. In Switzerland, the Beatles’ “psychedelic trip” also ushered in the end of the classic beat era and billows of a promising smoke called psychedelic rock arrived, coming from San Francisco and stopping over in England, in the wake of which Düde Dürst was to become one of the founding members of a band named Krokodil in January 1969 …

Lurker Grand

Hippies
FÜR TeenaGeR
im Dancing TABARIS
SONNTAG 8. und 15.10.67
15 30 – 18 00
MIT
Les SauTeRelles
JOSÉ MARCELLO
THE SPECTRES
Kein Tenue-Zwang
EINTRITT NUR 1.10
KONSUMATION 1.50
ALKOHOLFREI
KEIN TANZ

DÜDE DÜRST, LES SAUTERELLES, FAN CLUB CARD, 1966, 100×140

DÜDE DÜRST, LES SAUTERELLES, 1968, 297×420

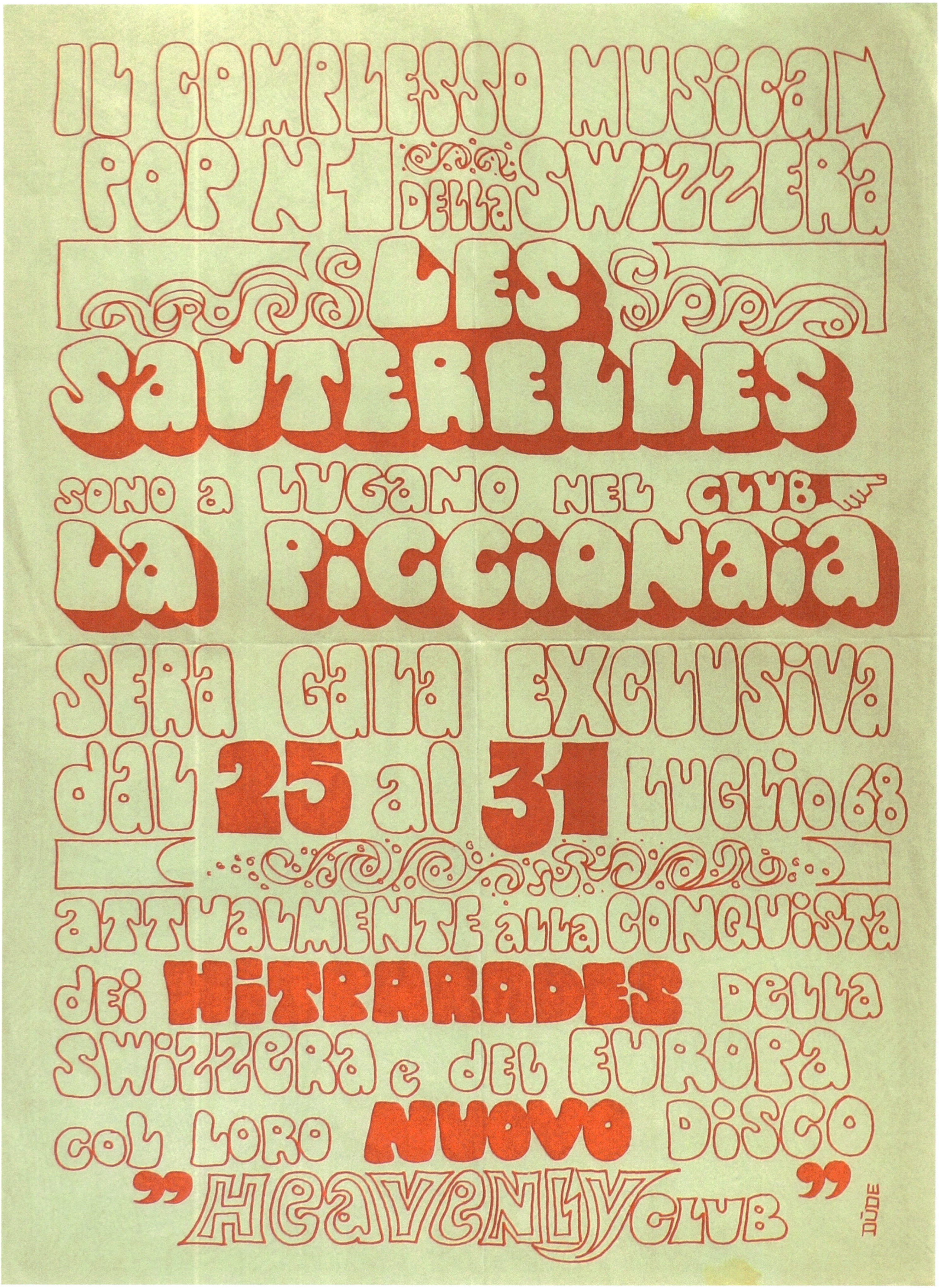

DÜDE DÜRST, LES SAUTERELLES – HEAVENLY CLUB, LP PROMO, 1968, 270×390

DÜDE DÜRST, LES SAUTERELLES – HEY GIRL, 7", 1966

LES SAUTERELLES – I LOVE HOW YOU LOVE ME, 7", 1968

LES SAUTERELLES – VIEW TO HEAVEN, LP, 1968

LES SAUTERELLES – YESTERDAY, CD, 2012

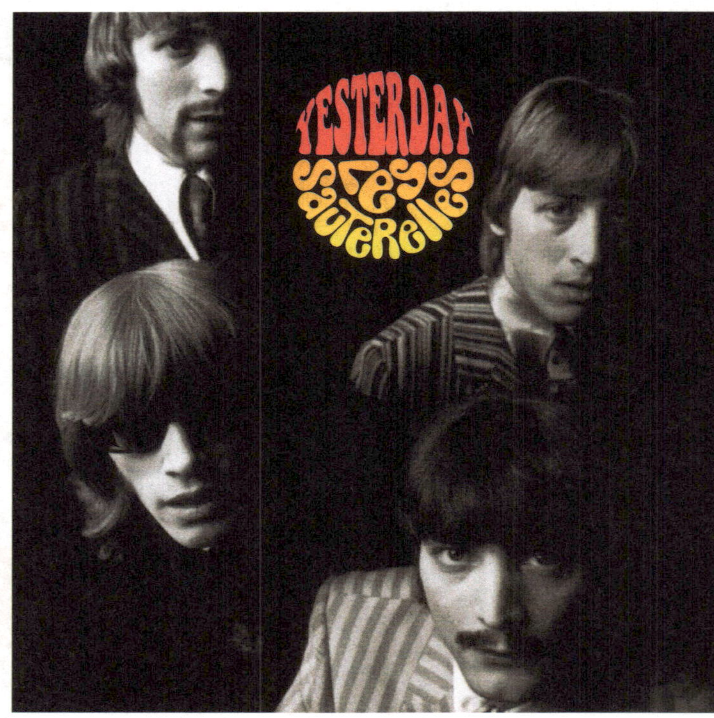

DÜDE DÜRST, KROKODIL - SWAMP, LP, 1970

KROKODIL - TELL ME WHAT YOU WANT, 7″, 1970

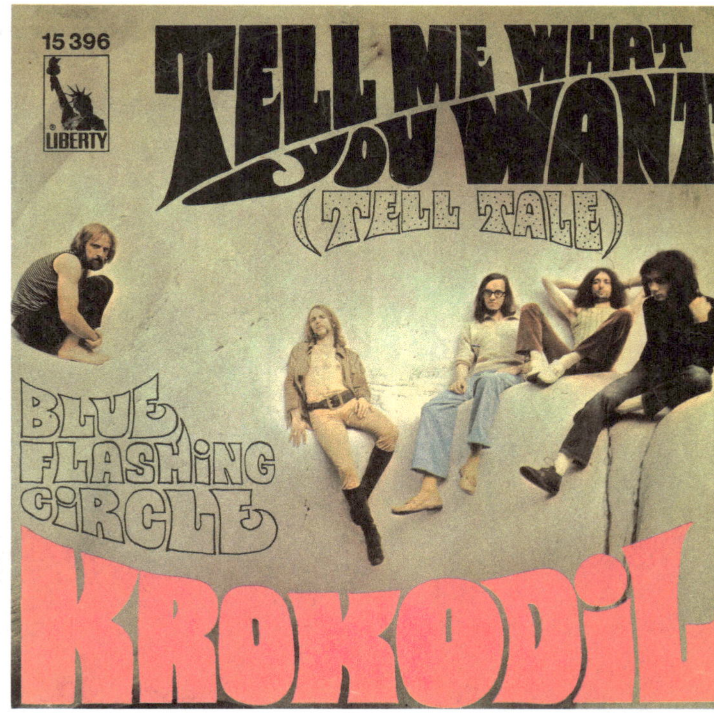

KROKODIL - YOU'RE STILL A PART OF ME, 7″, 1973

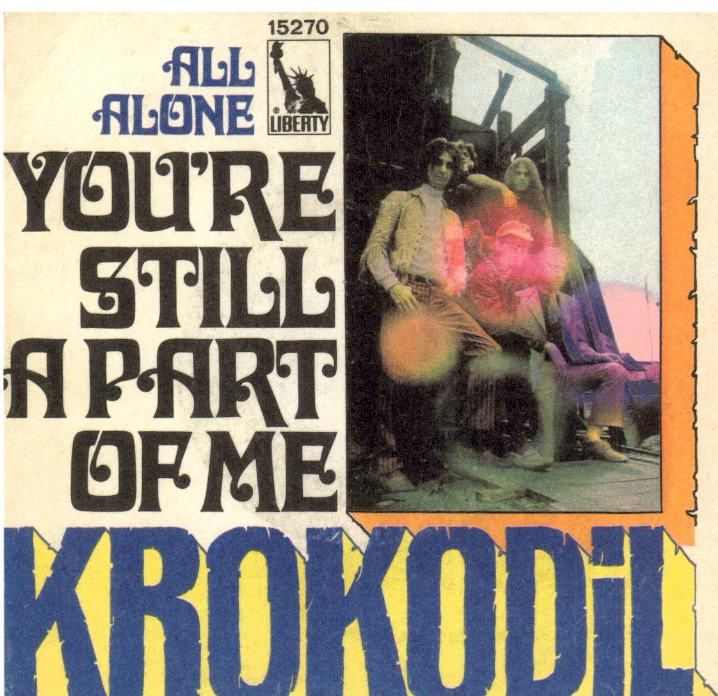

KROKODIL - DON'T MAKE PROMISES, 7″, 1969

DÜDE DÜRST, KROKODIL - SAME, LP FRONT COVER, 1969

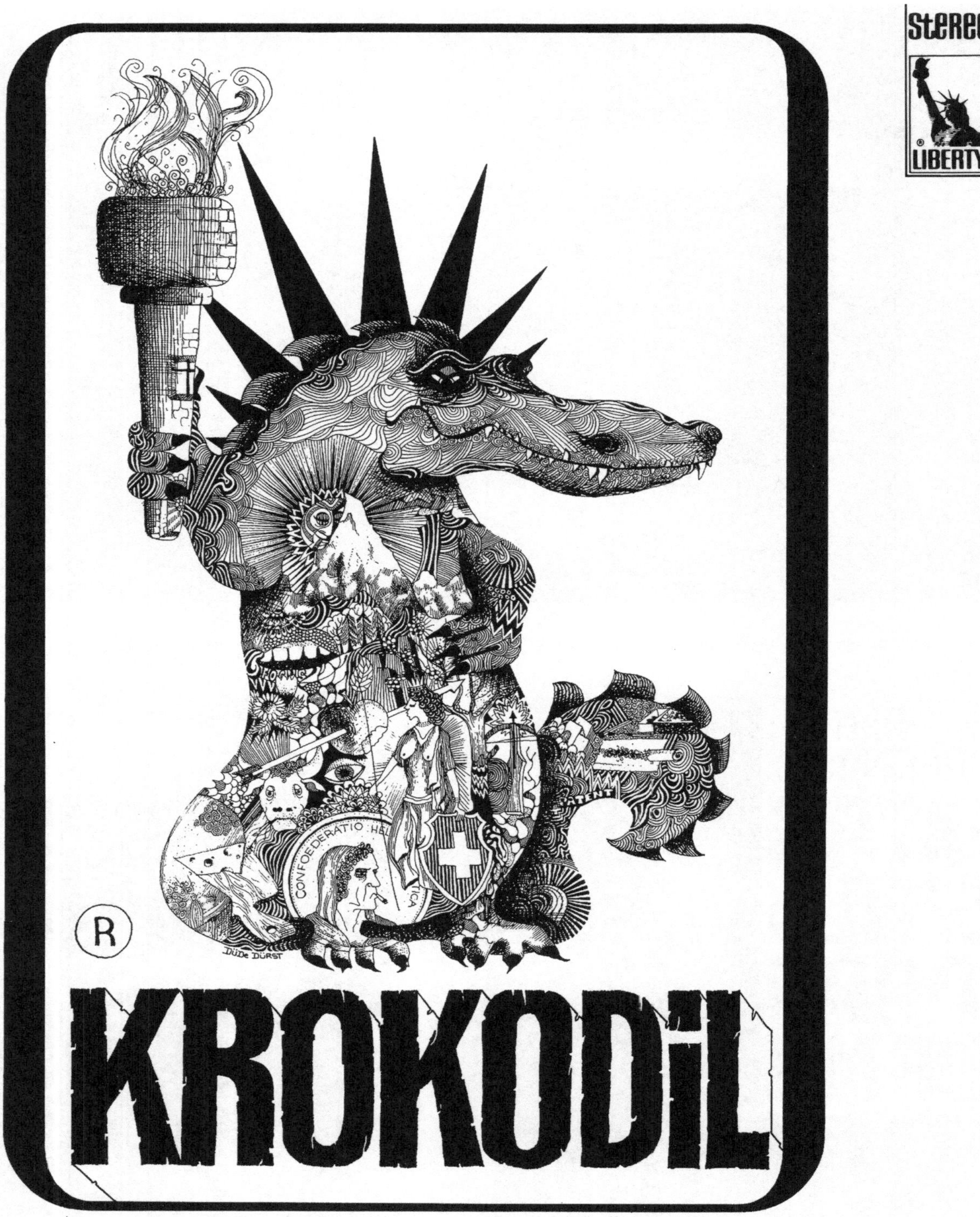

Krokodil – Ein Symbol der Freiheit

Januar 1969, dies war die Geburtsstunde von Krokodil, eines rockigen Untiers aus dem progressiven Underground von Zürich. Ihre Musik wollte schnell in Umlauf gebracht werden. Während der vielen Verhandlungen mit unterschiedlichen Plattenlabels zeigte sich direkt, dass Hardy Hepp, der Sänger und Violinist der Band, aufgrund seiner Schlager-Vergangenheit wohl den meisten Eindruck auf die Plattenbosse machte. Hepps persönliche Verbindungen zu Liberty-Direktor Siggi Loch (das Label hatte zuvor schon drei Solosingles von ihm veröffentlicht) führten dazu, dass die Band bei Liberty ihr professionell eingespieltes Demoband mit acht Songs vorspielen durfte. Daraus ergab sich ein Vertrag, der Krokodil mindestens zwei Singles und eine LP-Veröffentlichung garantierten sollte. Ebenso blieb der Band die Auswahl der Songs und auch die Gestaltung der Plattenhüllen vertraglich zugesichert. Kurz darauf, im Mai 1969, war es so weit: Für zwei Tage ging es ins Münchner Trixi-Studio, wo Krokodil ihre Songs zunächst als Demo aufnehmen sollten. Als Siggi Loch noch am gleichen Abend die Bänder präsentiert bekam, entschied er allerdings, das eingespielte Material unverändert für die Platte zu übernehmen. So kam es, dass das komplette Debütalbum bereits nach einem Durchgang fertig im Kasten lag – ein sensationelles Ergebnis, das den Live-Qualitäten der Band zu verdanken war.

Für die Gestaltung des Plattencovers kam natürlich niemand anderes als der Schlagzeuger und Bandgrafiker Düde Dürst infrage, der schon davor bei Les Sauterelles für die grafischen Belange zuständig gewesen war. Düde sagt dazu: «Dieser Plattendeal mit einem US-Major machte uns total ‹giggerig› – somit war es für mich naheliegend, irgendetwas mit dem Liberty-Logo zu machen. Zuerst ersetzte ich die Freiheitsstatue im Logo durch ein Krokodil. Da wir zu dieser Zeit enorm viel kifften, streckte sie nun statt einer Fackel ein rauchendes Chillum in den Himmel. Die Struktur des Körpers des Krokodils stellt eine Art Ganzkörper-Tattoo dar, darin finden sich Schweizer Klischees wie Armbrust, Helvetia, Matterhorn und Käse. Ein kiffender Tell auf der Fünf-Franken-Münze, eine ebenfalls kiffende Kuh und im Schwanz des Tieres ein Joint, der noch fertig zu drehen ist, rundeten das Ganze ab. Die Trademark hiess jetzt natürlich Krokodil.»

Für ein nicht-kommerzielles erstes Album verkaufte sich das unbetitelte Krokodil-Debüt in Europa erstaunlich gut. Das Mutterhaus in Amerika wollte die Platte nun ebenfalls herausbringen, dies aber mit einer «gewichtigen» Einschränkung: Das Krokodil auf dem Umschlag, das sich für die Freiheit des Kiffens starkmacht, ging aus Sicht der Plattenbosse im Land der unbegrenzten Freiheit gar nicht. Doch die Band beharrte wiederum auf dem ihr vertraglich zugesicherten Recht, zu bestimmen, wie die Plattenhülle auszusehen habe. Konsequenz war, dass ihre Alben in den USA nie offiziell veröffentlicht wurden. Im darauf folgenden Jahr erschien abermals bei Liberty Deutschland das Nachfolgealbum *Swamp*. Beide Alben fanden trotz aller Widerstände später den Weg von Europa in die USA. Krokodil sind bis heute bei Liebhabern progressiver Musik weltweit ein Begriff.

Düde Dürst im Gespräch mit Lurker Grand

Krokodil — A symbol of freedom

January 1969 saw the birth of Krokodil, a rock monster from Zurich's progressive underground. The band wanted their music to get into circulation quickly. At the same time, negotiations with various record labels soon revealed that Hardy Hepp, the band's singer and violinist, made the strongest impression on record label bosses due to his history in pop music. Hepp's personal connection to Siggi Loch, director of Liberty Records (the label that had already released three of Hepp's solo singles), gave the band the chance to record a professional quality demo tape containing eight songs for Liberty. The result was a contract that would guarantee Krokodil the release of at least two singles and one LP. It also gave the band full control over the selection of songs as well as the design of the record sleeves. A short time later, in May 1969, their dream came true: two days at the Trixi Studio in Munich, where Krokodil were to record their songs, initially only as a demo. But when Siggi Loch listened to the tapes that same evening, he decided to use the recorded material for an LP with no changes made. Thus the complete debut album was all in the box after only one session — a sensational outcome, thanks to the live qualities of the band.

Naturally the design for the album cover fell to Düde Dürst, the drummer and graphic artist of the band, who had already previously been in charge of the graphic design for Swiss band Les Sauterelles. To quote Düde: "The record deal with a major U.S. label really made us totally 'horny' and, in my opinion, to work with the Liberty Logo seemed the obvious choice. I started by replacing the Statue of Liberty in the logo with a crocodile. Since we were smoking huge amounts of pot at the time, the statue now held a smoking joint up to the sky instead of a torch. The structure of the crocodile's body was covered with a special whole body tattoo depicting Swiss clichés, such as a crossbow, the Swiss patroness Helvetia, the Matterhorn, and cheese. A pot-smoking William Tell on the five-franc coin, a pot-smoking cow, and a ready to roll joint in the animal's tail completed the setting. Now the trademark was, of course, called Krokodil."

For a non-commercial first album, the untitled Krokodil debut sold amazingly well. As a result, the American parent company wanted to release the record in the States, albeit with one severe restriction. In the opinion of the record company executives, the crocodile campaigning for the freedom to smoke pot depicted on the record cover just wouldn't work in the land of the free. But the band insisted on their contractually guaranteed freedom to determine the design of their record sleeves. Therefore their album was never officially released in the United States. The band's second album, *Swamp*, was released on Liberty Records Germany the following year. Despite all resistance, both albums later made their way from Europe to the United States, and to this day, Krokodil is still highly popular with lovers of progressive music the world around.

Düde Dürst in a conversation with Lurker Grand

DÜDE DÜRST, KROKODIL - SAME, LP BACK COVER , 1969

DÜDE DÜRST, KROKODIL, PRESS DOSSIER, 1969, 210×297

1.
KROKODIL
August
CHÜEBODE
ÄLPLI
HALDEN
UNTER-
WASSER
ALT
ST.
JOHANN
WILD-
HAUS
CA. AB 15[00] ODER WIE DU WILLST
DÜDE

DÜDE DÜRST, ELECTRIC MUSIC SCENE, 1969, 210×297

PARTY
KREUZFAHRT
70
FÜR
JUNGE LEUTE

KROKODILE IM MITTELMEER ?

Nein — so was gibt es doch nicht! Krokodile hausen doch nur in den feucht-heissen Regionen unseres Erdballes!

Weit gefehlt !! Unsere «Krokodile» im Mittelmeer existieren tatsächlich — die bekannten und extravaganten «Krokodil» begleiten unser Party-Schiff im April/Mai 1970.

Was ist die Party-Kreuzfahrt?

Etwas, das es noch nie gab! Ein Happening auf hoher See - Acht Tage unbeschwerten Tuns - Eine Fahrt für die Jugend - mit Pop - Beat - Jazz und Tanz - ohne Polizeistunde und Garderobe-Vorschriften - Ein Kreuzen durch das Mittelmeer exklusiv für die Jugend von 20 bis 35 - Mit Gags an die Sonne nach Dubrovnik - Malta - Tunis - St. Tropez - Eine Maxi-Fahrt zu Mini-Preisen . . . .

. . . . und mit den «Krokodil» !

Ohne Übertreibung: So was gab es tatsächlich noch nie !

Also - nichts wie los auf die Party-Kreuzfahrt 1970 - Die Plauschfahrt des Jahres.

Treffpunkt der Jugend 1970:

DIE PARTY - KREUZFAHRT !

DÜDE DÜRST, PARTY KREUZFAHRT, BACK SIDE, 1970, 210×297

DÜDE DÜRST, KROKODIL, INVITATION FOR THEIR FIRST CONCERT, 1969, 100×210

ELEC
CIRC

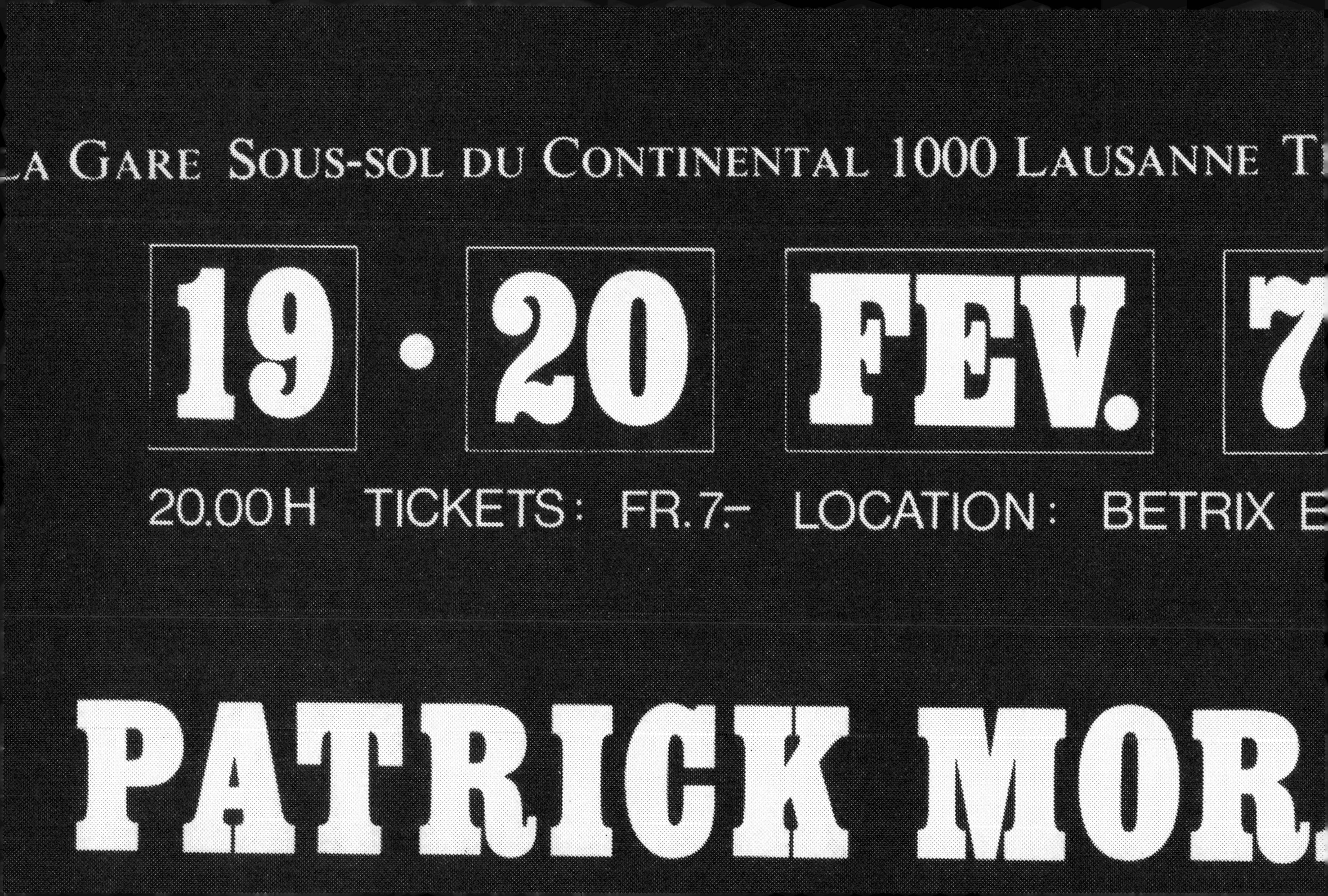
LA GARE SOUS-SOL DU CONTINENTAL 1000 LAUSANNE T
19 · 20 FEV. 7
20.00 H TICKETS: FR. 7.– LOCATION: BETRIX B
PATRICK MOR

Werner Jeker

Der ausgebildete Grafiker aus dem Kanton Solothurn war von 1969 an zwei Jahre lang zuständig für die Gestaltung der Konzertplakate im Electric Circus, einem progressiven Musikclub in Lausanne, dessen Bands vom späteren Good-News-Gründer Peter Zumsteg programmiert wurden. Jeker wurde später durch seine von ihm gestalteten Plakate und Bücher weltbekannt und erhielt zahlreiche Auszeichnungen. Jekers konsequent in Schwarz-Weiss gehaltene Konzertplakate aus dem Electric Circus werden hier zum ersten Mal in einer Publikation veröffentlicht. Er ist bis heute in der Grafik tätig und wirkt noch immer in Lausanne.

Werner Jeker

As of 1969, the trained graphic artist from the canton of Solothurn was responsible for two years regarding the design of the concert posters at the Electric Circus, a progressive music club in Lausanne; for whom the later Good News founder Peter Zumsteg did the band bookings. Jeker later became world-renowned for his designs of posters and books and received numerous awards. Jeker's consistently black/white concert posters from the Electric Circus are presented here for the first time in a publication. To-date, he works in graphic art and still operates in Lausanne.

WERNER JEKER, WRITING ON THE WALL, 1970, 326×465

WERNER JEKER, ASHTON GARDNER & DYKE, 1970, 322×487

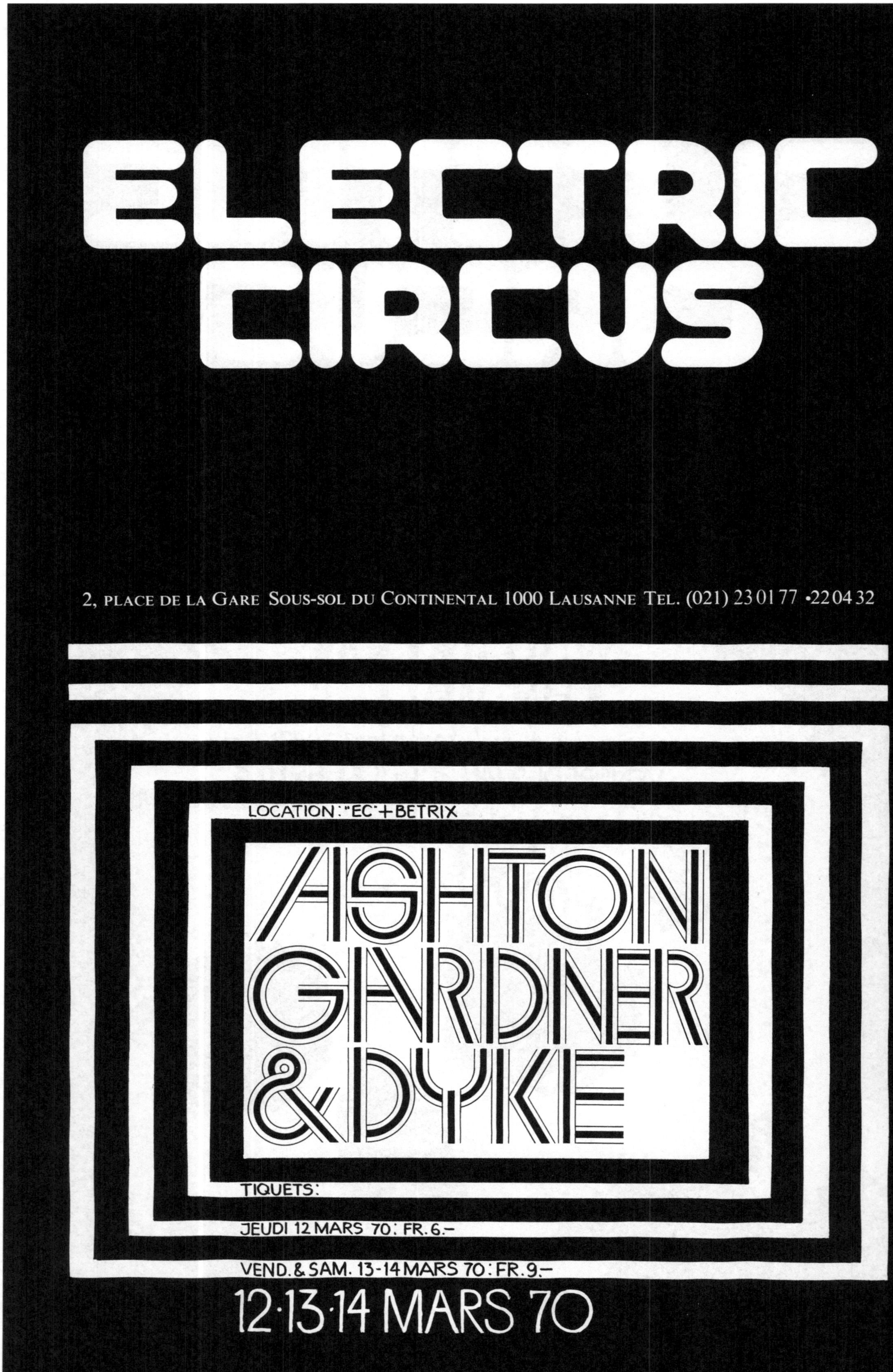

WERNER JEKER, PATRICK MORAZ, INTEGRAL, 1970, 322×487

WERNER JEKER, BLACK SABBATH, 1970, 322×487

Black Sabbath – Erde an Black Sabbath

Black Sabbath spielten zu Beginn ihrer Karriere einige Europa-Tourneen. Die erste brachte sie nach Hamburg in den Star-Club, nach Dänemark und Schweden. Die darauf folgende Tour im Winter 1969 führte sie in die Schweiz, nach St. Gallen, in den Club Africana, wo sie drei Tage nacheinander auftreten sollten. Das Africana war ein Veranstaltungsort, wo verschiedene, später berühmt gewordene Gruppen auftraten, und ein Anziehungspunkt für die alternative Szene der Schweiz der späten Sechziger- und frühen Siebzigerjahre.

Black Sabbath, die damals noch nicht ihr erstes Album veröffentlicht hatten, das ihnen den Durchbruch brachte, spielten vor wenig Publikum zwei Shows am Tag, der Eintritt kostete 2.50 Franken und beinhaltete eine Cola. Für die Nachbarn des Clubs war die dargebotene Musik viel zu laut, und der Besitzer des Africana, René Theiler, bat die Band deshalb, am folgenden Tag leiser zu spielen. Sie spielten natürlich am nächsten Tag ihre zwei Sets in der gleichen Art und Weise, sodass ihre verbleibenden Auftritte abgesagt wurden.

Tony Iommi, der Gitarrist der Band, erinnert sich in seiner Autobiografie *Iron Man*: «Die Gage bestand aus einem Glas Milch und einem Würstchen. In finanzieller Hinsicht ging es uns mehr als dreckig. Da wir absolut kein Geld hatten, musste sogar Geezer (der Bassist), der Vegeterier war, die Würstchen runterwürgen. Und das Hotel? Die gesamte Band schlief in einem winzig kleinen Raum über einem Café (Goliath), das gegenüber vom Club lag. Wenn man da nicht rechtzeitig ankam, schlossen die Besitzer einen aus. An einem Abend schliefen Ozzy und ich bei zwei Mädchen. Als Geezer auftauchte, stand er vor verriegelter Tür. Bill (der Schlagzeuger) schnappte sich die Bettlaken, knüpfte sie aneinander und versuchte, unseren Basser hochzuziehen. Und exakt in dem Moment fuhr eine Polizeistreife vorbei. Es dauerte einige Zeit, ihnen das ganze Dilemma, in dem Geezer sich befand, im Kauderwelsch zweier Sprachen zu erklären.»[1] Allerdings sollte man diese Aussagen, wie Gespräche mit anderen Zeugen der Ereignisse und dem damaligem Stammpublikum des Africana beweisen, sicher nicht ganz wörtlich nehmen.

Danach zogen Black Sabbath weiter nach Zürich, ins Hotel Hirschen, eines der ältesten Hotels der Stadt und Heimat des sogenannten Beat Clubs, einem Ort für Live-Konzerte seit den frühen Sechzigerjahren. Als sie dort ankamen, war der Club dicht gefüllt. Eine Band spielte, und die Musiker sahen glücklich aus und tranken sogar Champagner. «Das ist doch wunderbar, dachten wir uns», schrieb Iommi. «Uns steht eine tolle Zeit bevor. Keiner konnte wissen, dass die Musiker ihren letzten Abend von einem insgesamt sechswöchigen Engagement feierten. ... Als wir mit unseren Gigs begannen, war der Laden so gut wie ausgestorben. Moment mal! Was ist passiert? Wo sind die ganzen Leute hin? Täglich kam so ein Spinner vorbei, der einen Kopfstand machte, wobei ihm das ganze Geld aus den Taschen fiel. Er suchte es wieder zusammen und verzog sich dann. Und dann sass da noch eine uralte Nutte in der Ecke an der Bar. Das war's.»[2]

Da der Club ziemlich leer war und das Repertoire der Band relativ klein, fingen sie an, herumzuexperimentie-

Black Sabbath — Earth to Black Sabbath

At the beginning of their career, Black Sabbath played a couple of European tours. The first one took them to the Star Club in Hamburg, to Denmark and to Sweden. On their next tour, in the winter of 1969, they also visited Switzerland, where they were booked to play three days in a row at the Africana club in St. Gallen. This was a music venue that presented various bands that later became famous and a magnet for the alternative scene in Switzerland in the late sixties and early seventies.

Black Sabbath, who had not yet released their breakthrough first album at the time, played two shows a day to a tiny audience for an entry fee of 2.50 francs, a coke included. The music they played was, however, much too loud for the club's neighbors, and René Theiler, the owner of the Africana, had to ask them to tone it down a bit for the following performances. The next day, the band, of course, played their two sets at an unchanged volume, so the rest of their shows were cancelled.

As Tony Iommi, the band's guitarist, recalls in his autobiography, *Iron Man*, the general conditions at the club — and St. Gallen in general — were terrible: "All we'd get would be a glass of milk and a sausage. No money, we were poverty-stricken. Geezer (the bass player) was a vegetarian, but he had to eat the sausages because we didn't have any money to buy him any other food. We all stayed in this room above this café (the Goliath) across the road from where we played. If you weren't in on time, they'd lock you out. One night me and Ozzy went off with these two girls and stayed with them. Geezer came back from somewhere and couldn't get in. So Bill (the drummer) tied sheets together, trying to pull Geezer up. As they were doing this, the police came by. It took quite some explaining in two different languages to sort that one out."[1] Based on accounts by other witnesses to the events as well as former regulars of the Africana, these statements should definitely be taken with a grain of salt.

Black Sabbath then traveled on to the Hotel Hirschen in Zurich, one of the oldest hotels in the city and home to the so-called Beat Club, a venue for live concerts starting in the early sixties. When the band arrived at the club, it was filled to capacity and a band was playing happily, drinking champagne. Iommi writes, "We thought, this is marvelous. We'll have some! Little did we know that this band had been playing there for six weeks and it was now their last night ... As soon as we started, the place was dead. We went, wait a minute, what happened? Where's all the people? They had this one nutter coming in every day. He'd stand on his head, all his money would fall out of his pocket, he'd pick it up again and leave. And there was this old hooker sitting at the corner by the bar and that was it."[2]

Because the club was pretty much deserted and the band's repertoire was relatively small at the time, they started experimenting, having individual members of the band do set-long solos. This experiment supposedly led to the creation of "War Pigs," the song that later would open on their second album *Paranoid* — the first real heavy metal album per se. This is also supported

ren, jedes Bandmitglied spielte ein langes Solo. Das führte schliesslich zum Song «War Pigs», der später das zweite Album *Paranoid* eröffnen sollte – das erste echte Heavy-Metal-Album schlechthin. Gedeckt wird das von einer Frage, die Ozzy Osbourne 2011 dem Moderator von SRF 3 in einem Interview stellte: «Gibt es den Hirschen-Club noch?», und hinzugefügt hat: «Wir haben früher dort geprobt!»[3]

Wie Iommi erzählt, war das Experimentieren mit den langen Solos für einige Tage grossartig, bis «Doktor» Schwarzwald, der Besitzer des Ladens, dann natürlich gemerkt hat, was sie taten, und seine Tochter Trudy schickte, um zu sagen: «Hört auf mit dem Lärm! Wir zahlen euch, um zu spielen, und nicht für das!» Die Bedingungen im Beat Club allgemein liessen zu wünschen übrig. «Es war ein trostloser und düsterer Schuppen. Wir mussten erneut alle in einem Zimmer schlafen – zusammen mit einigen Ratten. Der Clubbesitzer hatte unsere Pässe einkassiert, damit wir nicht so leicht abhauen konnten. Die ganze Situation ähnelte einem Sklavenjob, denn die Band musste täglich fünf Mal jeweils 45 Minuten lang auftreten, an Wochenenden sogar sieben Mal, und wir spielten fast für lau.»[4] Aber ganz so schlimm kann es nicht gewesen sein, denn im April 1970 kamen Black Sabbath für vier weitere Konzerte in die Schweiz. Das erste war im Casino in Montreux, gefolgt von zwei weiteren im Electric Circus in Lausanne und einem im Atlantis in Basel. Doch diese Geschichten müssen erst noch erzählt werden.

Lurker Grand

Anmerkungen:
1 Tony Iommi, *Iron Man. Von Black Sabbath bis Heaven & Hell*, übersetzt von Alan Tepper (Höfen, 2012, S. 68).
2 Ebd.
3 Zitiert in Englisch auf: http://negativewhite.ch/rockgeschichte-im-hallenstadion/ (Zugriff am 17. Juni 2014).
4 Iommi, 2012 (wie Anm. 1), S. 68/69.

by a question Ozzy Osbourne asked the presenter in a radio interview on DRS 3 in 2011: "Does the Hirschen club still exist?" adding "We used it to rehearse!"[3]

According to Iommi, this experimentation with set-long solos was great for a few days until "Doc" Schwarzwald, the owner of the club, figured out what they were doing, and sent his daughter to tell them to stop the noise and play some real music. Once again, the general conditions at the Beat Club left much to be desired according to Iommi: "It was a really grim place. We all slept in one room, together with a bunch of rats. The owner of the club had taken our passports, so we couldn't get out. It was like slavery, with us playing five forty-five-minute sets and seven on weekends, and all that for hardly any pay."[4] Yet, the time in Switzerland couldn't have been that bad, since Black Sabbath came back to Switzerland to play four more shows in April 1970. The first one at the Casino in Montreux, followed by two at the Electric Circus in Lausanne, and one at the Atlantis in Basel. But those are stories yet to be told.

Lurker Grand

Notes:
1 Tony Iommi, *Iron Man: My Journey Through Heaven & Hell with Black Sabbath* (Boston, 2011, p. 58).
2 Ibid., p. 58.
3 Quoted at: http://negativewhite.ch/rockgeschichte-im-hallenstadion/ (accessed June 17, 2014).
4 Iommi, 2011, pp. 58–59.

WERNER JEKER, SWEET WATER CANAL, 1970, 322×487

WERNER JEKER, THE CLIMAX CHICAGO BLUES BAND, 1970, 322×470

WERNER JEKER, GURU GURU, 1970, 322×470

WERNER JEKER, SMALL FACES, YES, 1969, 322×470

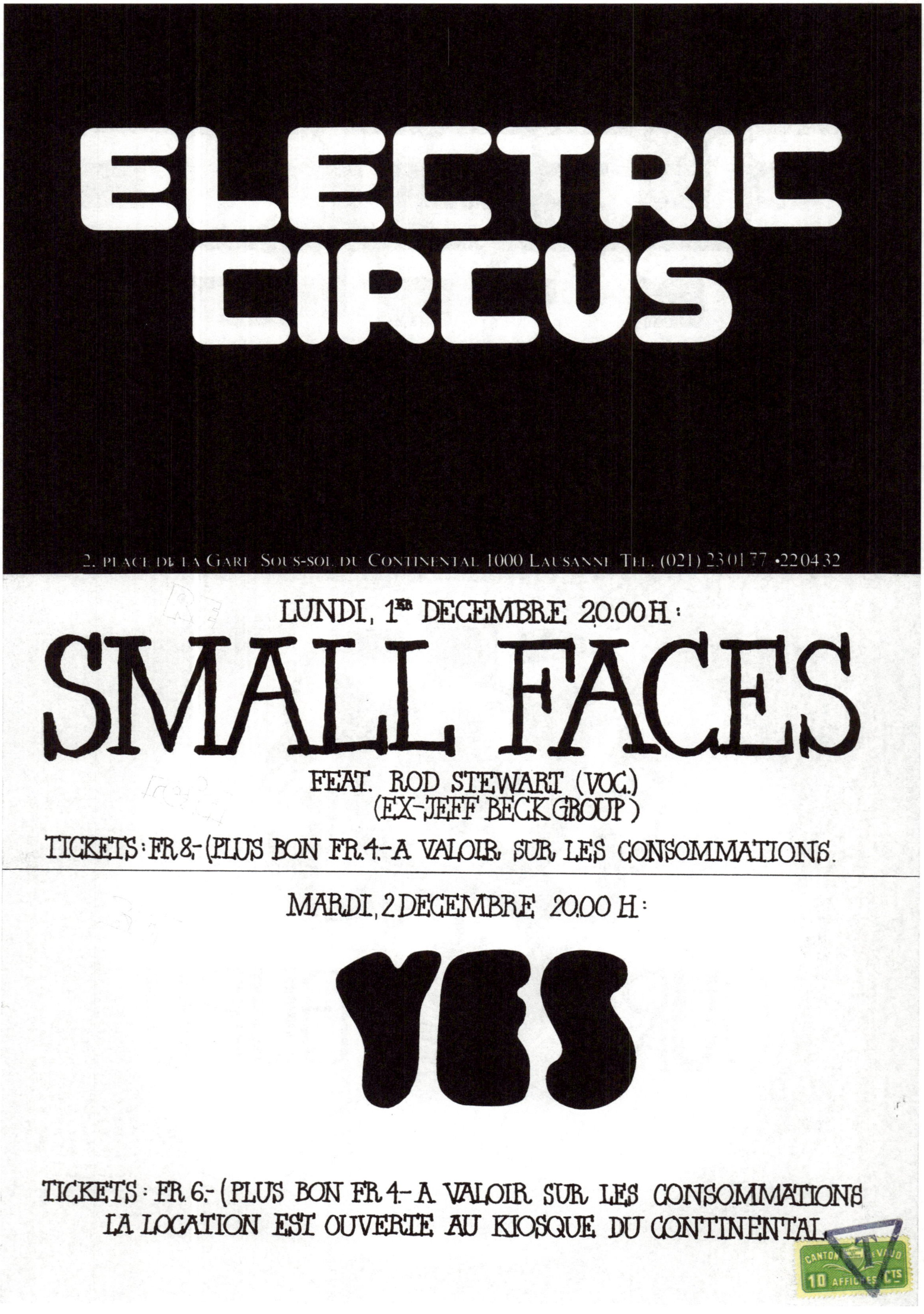

WERNER JEKER, GUN, 1970, 322×487

WERNER JEKER, RAHSAAN ROLAND KIRK, 1970, 322×487

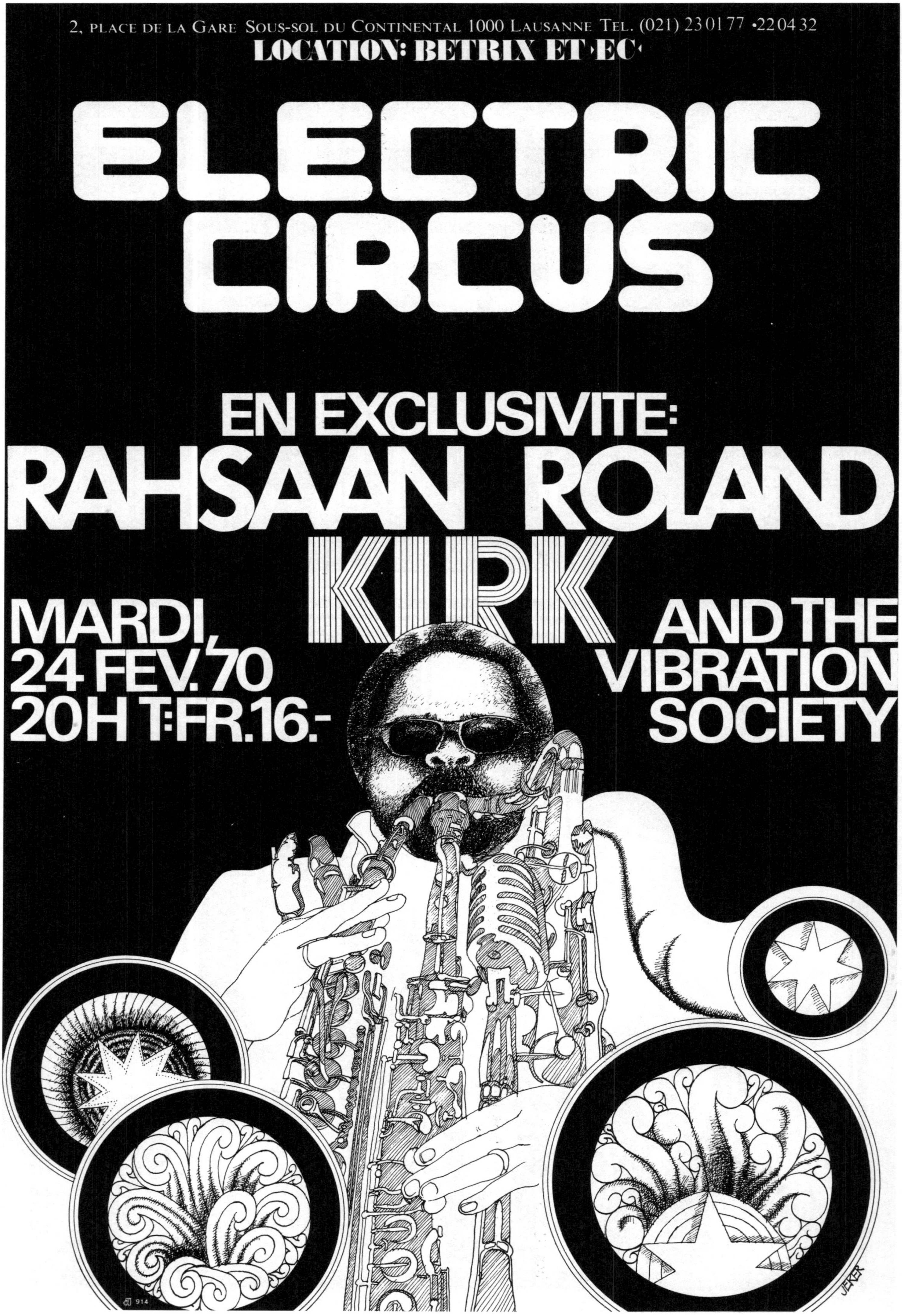

Rahsaan Roland Kirk im Electric Circus

Das Konzert mit Rahsaan Roland Kirk im Electric Circus war eines von vielen Highlights für mich. Ich hatte Kirk in London kennengelernt, wo ich 1968/69 als Journalist arbeitete und ganz nah dran war an der Szene – und dies in der vielleicht spannendsten Phase der Rockgeschichte. Meine allnächtliche Clubtour führte mich vom Marquee über Ronnie Scott's zum Speakeasy. Während dieser Streifzüge traf ich auch auf Leute wie Jimi Hendrix oder John Lennon – und stillte meinen Hunger nach Entdeckungen in der progressiven Rockszene. Ich war als junger Schweizer gern gesehen in den Londoner Musikerkreisen – eben weil ich ein Angefressener war, der fast alles wusste über die aktuellen Sounds und ihre Exponenten, aber auch darum, weil ich nie das Vertrauen der Musiker missbrauchte. Kirk, der damals einer der angesagtesten Jazzer war, traf ich *backstage* im Ronnie Scott's. Ich bot an, bei der Vermittlung in die Schweiz mitzuhelfen. Doch obwohl ich alle wichtigen Veranstalter kannte und eine wirklich vernünftige Gage ausgehandelt hatte, kam vorerst kein Schweizer Auftritt zustande.

Darum war es naheliegend, dass ich Kirk im Februar 1970 in «meinen» Club, den Electric Circus in Lausanne, holte. Dieses Lokal, das sich im Sous-Sol auf der ehemaligen Kegelbahn des Erst-Klasse-Hotels Continental befand, war das Schweizer Pendant zu den hippen Londoner Clubs und auf dem Kontinent einer der ersten seines Genres. Der Hotelier Caspar Manz suchte nach neuen Ideen, um seine Diskothek aufzuwerten, und ich schlug ihm einen Musikclub mit Livebands von internationalem Format vor, der täglich geöffnet war. Mein Ziel war es, ein Lokal zu betreiben, das auch ich selber frequentieren würde – schliesslich war ich wegen des Electric Circus aus London in die Schweiz zurückgekehrt. Das Lokal war optisch konsequent in Schwarz-Weiss gehalten (was sich auch im Grafikkonzept von Werner Jeker weiterzog), für die psychedelische Lightshow hatte ich den Zürcher Lichtkünstler Louis Stalder engagiert. Es gab einen Pop-Drug-Store, wo man sich die neuesten Ausgaben der aktuellen Musik- und Undergroundpresse kaufen konnte, vom *Melody Maker* bis zu den *International Times*. Musikfreaks, die wir ja explizit ansprechen wollten, konnten sich in den Nischen des Lokals die neuesten von uns programmierten Mixtapes ab Spulentonband anhören, natürlich war uns nur Revox-Qualität gut genug. Der Electric Circus war definitiv Rock'n'Roll, auch wenn die Sandwiches aus der gehobenen Vier-Sterne-Hotelküche stammten – dafür trugen sie Namen wie «Bonzo Dog» oder «Toast Woodstock».

Wir wollten besser sein als die Konkurrenz und boten stets hohe musikalische Qualität: Die Bands, die bei uns spielten, hatten sich in der englischen Musikszene bereits einen Namen gemacht. So spielten bei uns aufstrebende und bereits erfolgreiche Acts wie Mott the Hoople, Keith Relf's Renaissance, Free und Black Sabbath – meistens blieben sie gleich zwei Tage. Von den etablierten Medien wurden wir dennoch kaum wahrgenommen, schon gar nicht von deren Kultur-Redaktionen. Das war beim Konzert von Roland Kirk anders – wenn es um Jazz ging, bemühten sich auch die Feuilleton-Schreiber zu uns in den Underground. Ich hielt für Kirk eine besondere Überraschung bereit:

Rahsaan Roland Kirk at Electric Circus

The Rahsaan Roland Kirk concert at the Electric Circus was one of many highlights for me. I had got to know Kirk in London while working there as a journalist in 1968–69. I was quite close to the scene — during the perhaps most exciting phase in the history of rock. Every night my club crawl took me from the Marquee to Ronnie Scott's to the Speakeasy. During these rambles, I not only ran into people like Jimi Hendrix or John Lennon, but above all, also satisfied my hunger for discoveries in the progressive rock scene. As a young Swiss journalist, I was very welcome in London's music circles — not only because I was passionate and knew practically everything about current sounds and their exponents, but also because I never betrayed the musicians' confidence. I met Kirk, one of the hottest jazz musicians at the time, backstage at Ronnie Scott's. I tried to find a way to bring this fantastic musician to Switzerland. But although my connections made it possible to negotiate a truly reasonable fee no appearance in Switzerland materialized at first.

It therefore made sense for me to bring Kirk to "my" club, the Electric Circus in Lausanne, in February 1970. The club, located in the former basement of bowling alley of the first-class Continental Hotel, was the Swiss counterpart of the London clubs, and one of the first of its kind on the continent. Hotel owner Caspar Manz was seeking ideas for bringing young people to his discotheque, and I proposed a club that would be open every day, presenting live bands of international reputation. My goal was to run a club that I would want to visit myself — in the end, I returned from London to Switzerland because of the Electric Circus. The club was designed consistently in black and white (something that found its dramatically in Werner Jeker's graphic design concept), and I hired a lighting artist named Louis Stalder for the psychedelic light show. There was a "pop drug store" where people could buy the newest current music releases and underground press publications, from the *Melody Maker* to the *International Times*. Music freaks, whom I and my young team indeed explicitly sought to address, could sit in niches inside the club listening to the newest mixes, which we compiled on reel-to-reel audio tape, since of course only the best Revox quality audio equipment was good enough. The Electric Circus was definitely rock'n'roll, although the sandwiches were delivered from the upscale 4-star-hotel kitchen — at least they sported suitable names such as "Bonzo Dog" and "Toast Woodstock."

We wanted to be better than our competitors, and we always offered top notch musical quality: the bands playing our club had all already made a name for themselves in the British music scene. Thus, emerging and already successful acts such as Mott the Hoople, Keith Relf's Renaissance, Free, and Black Sabbath played the venue — often staying on for two nights. Nevertheless, we received little attention from the media and none at all from their culture journalists. The Roland Kirk concert was an exception — where jazz was concerned, the feuilleton journalists also found their way to our spot in the Lausanne underground. I had a special surprise in store for Kirk: he adored U.S. saxophonist Lucky Thompson, who was living in Lausanne at the time. So I invited him to the Electric Circus as a surprise guest.

Er verehrte den US-Saxophonisten Lucky Thompson, der in dieser Zeit in Lausanne lebte. So lud ich diesen als Überraschungsgast in den Electric Circus ein. Kirk war zu Tränen gerührt, stellte sein Programm völlig um, führte eine Polonaise an und spielte sich in dieser Nacht durch alle Jazzstile. Es war eines jener Konzerte, das man so nur einmal erleben kann.

Dennoch hielt es mich nicht allzu lange in Lausanne. Zum einen, weil man mich dort als jungen Deutschschweizer Rockpromoter stets kritisch beäugte und mir wegen einiger eigentlich belangloser Vorfälle, die meist mit allerlei illegaler Raucherware zu tun hatten, das Leben schwer machte. Doch es gab vor allem auch eine wirtschaftliche Sichtweise. Mit seinem offiziellen Fassungsvermögen von 300 Plätzen war dieses oft überfüllte Lokal einfach zu klein, um mit der steigenden Popularität «meiner» Bands mithalten zu können. Ich sah meine Zukunft ohnehin nicht als Clubmanager, und so verabschiedete ich mich im Sommer 1970 nach Zürich und gründete zusammen mit meiner späteren Frau Regula und Johannes Heinrich Kunz (H.H. Kunz) die Firma Good News, die sich auf Konzerte progressiver Bands spezialisierte. Das erste Good-News-Konzert spielten im September 1970 Rory Gallagher und seine Band Taste, die auch schon verschiedentlich im Electric Circus aufgetreten waren. Ich kann mich noch sehr gut erinnern, wie mir Rory und sein Bruder damals in Lausanne mit ihrem Band-Van halfen, von meinem Hotelzimmer in ein Appartement zu zügeln.

Peter Zumsteg im Gespräch mit Sam Mumenthaler

Kirk was moved to tears, completely restructured his program, led a polonaise, and played his way through all styles of jazz that night. It was one of those once-in-a-lifetime performances.

Nevertheless, I didn't remain in Lausanne for too long. On the one hand because, being a German-speaking Swiss concert promoter, I was always looked upon critically there, and had considerable trouble with the authorities, usually due to some insignificant incidents involving illegal smoking substances. On the other hand, being a young entrepreneur, I was also guided by economic considerations: with an official capacity of 300 visitors the often overcrowded Electric Circus was simply too small to accommodate the needs of "my" bands, who were constantly gaining popularity. Moreover, I didn't perceive myself as a club manager, so in 1970 I packed my suitcase and left for Zurich. Together with my later wife Regula and Johannes Heinrich Kunz (H.H. Kunz) I started the Good News music agency, specializing in concerts with progressive bands. The first Good News gig was played by Rory Gallagher and his band Taste — who had also earlier appeared several times at the Electric Circus — in September 1970. With this concert I also returned a favour Rory Gallagher and his brother had done for me back in the Lausanne days where they had helped out as "removal men" with their band van, when I had moved from my hotel room to an apartment.

Peter Zumsteg in a conversation with Sam Mumenthaler

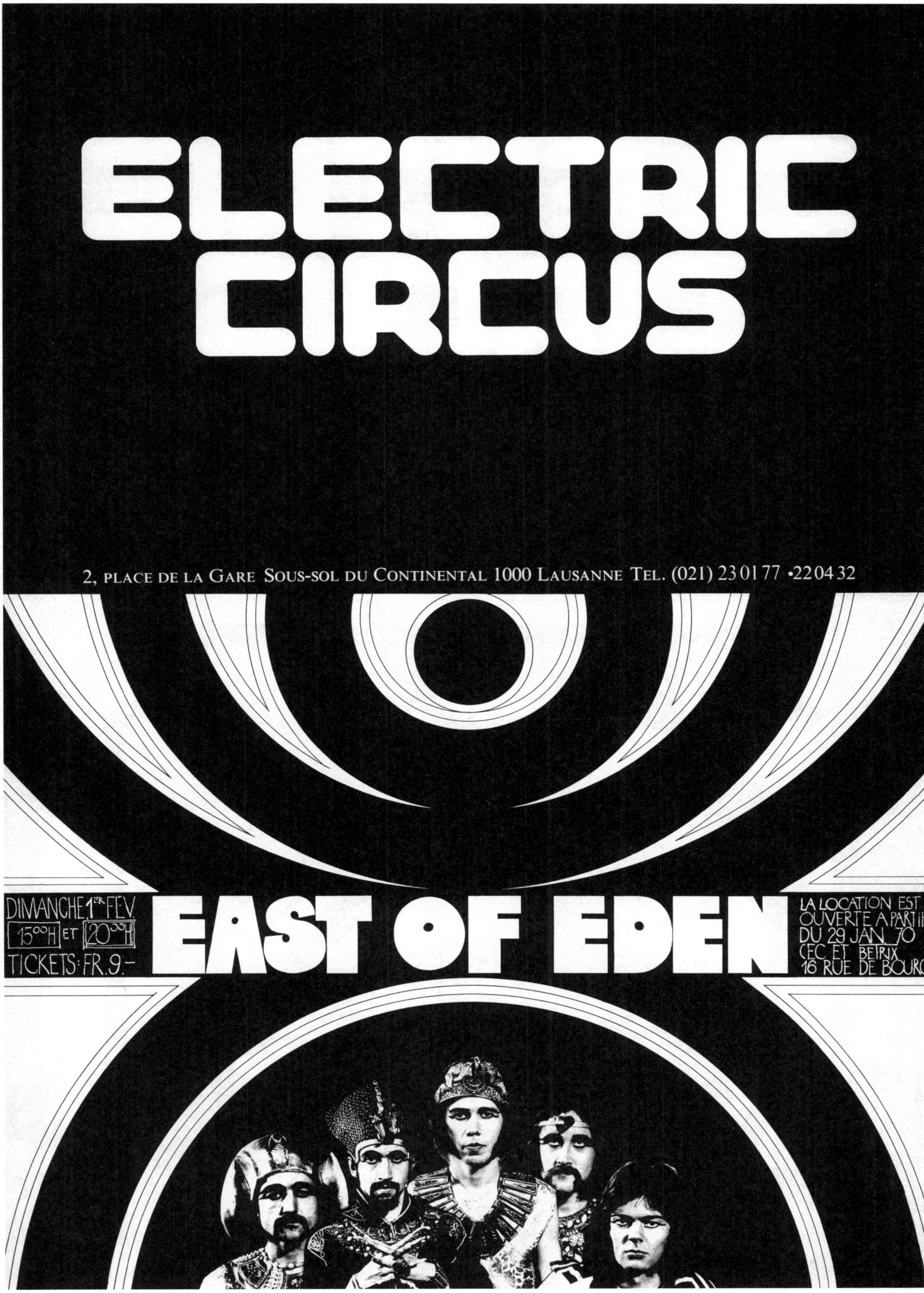

WERNER JEKER, EAST OF EDEN, 1970, 326×465

ELECTRIC
CIRCUS
2. PLACE DE LA GARE SOUS-SOL DU CONTINENTAL 1000 LAUSANNE TEL. (021) 23 01 77 •22 04 32
STEAMHAMMER
20.00 H
MARDI 14 AVRIL 70
MERC. 15 AVRIL 70
TICKETS: FR. 9.–

WERNER JEKER, RENAISSANCE, KEITH RELF, 1970, 322×470

WERNER JEKER, MAN, 1970, 326×465

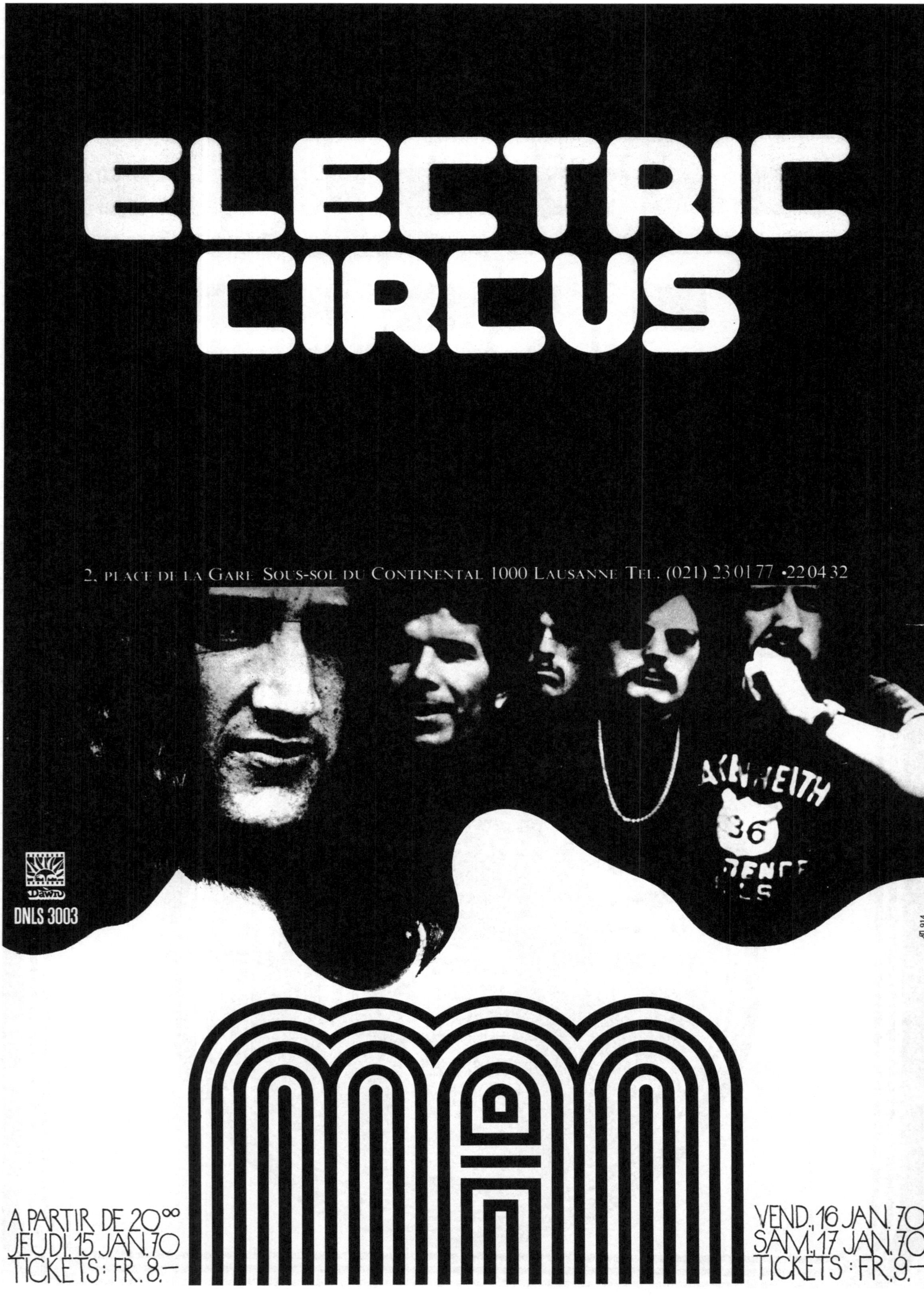

ENDRIX EXPERI

HE CREAM
SELMO TREND
30. MAI 31. MAI
P. Blumer
R POP-GENERATION

Peter Blumer

Aufgewachsen in Kloten. Gelernter Grafiker, der 1967/68 die F+F Schule für Gestaltung in Zürich besuchte. Ende der Sechzigerjahre organisierte der leidenschaftliche Musikfan Partys in Zürich. Ebenfalls während der späten Sechzigerjahre prägte Peter Blumer in der Schweiz zuerst als Mitarbeiter von Wizard & Genius und dann als «Hofgestalter» der Agentur Good News die visuelle Wahrnehmung der Popmusik einer ganzen Generation. Sein grafischer Stil orientierte sich an der Pop-Art und dem Comic-Stil seiner Zeit, als Person erinnerte Blumer an einen sensiblen Hippie. Bis zu seinem frühen Tod arbeitete der selbstständige Grafiker auch für Zeitschriften wie *annabelle*, *Playboy* und Jürg Marquards *Pop* (u.a. gestaltete er 1968 für *Pop* ein nie veröffentlichtes Plakat zum «Monsterkonzert» in Zürich) – daneben erhielt er gelegentlich Aufträge der Musikindustrie.

Peter Blumer

Raised in Kloten. Trained graphic artist, who in 1967/68 attended the F+F Schule für Gestaltung in Zurich. At the end of the sixties, the passionate music fan organized parties in Zurich. During the late sixties, Peter Blumer, who at first worked for Wizard & Genius and then as the "courts" designer for the Good News agency, shaped the perception of pop music for an entire generation. His graphical style was oriented on Pop Art and the comic book styles of the time, while Blumer as a person reminded one of a sensitive hippie. Until his early death, the freelancing graphic artist worked for magazines such as *annabelle*, *Playboy* and Jürg Marquards *Pop* (among others, he designed for *Pop* in 1968 a never published poster for the "Monster Concert" in Zurich) — in addition to receiving occasional commissions from the music industry.

PETER BLUMER, YES, 1974, 245×635

PETER BLUMER, FRANK ZAPPA, 1974, 245×635

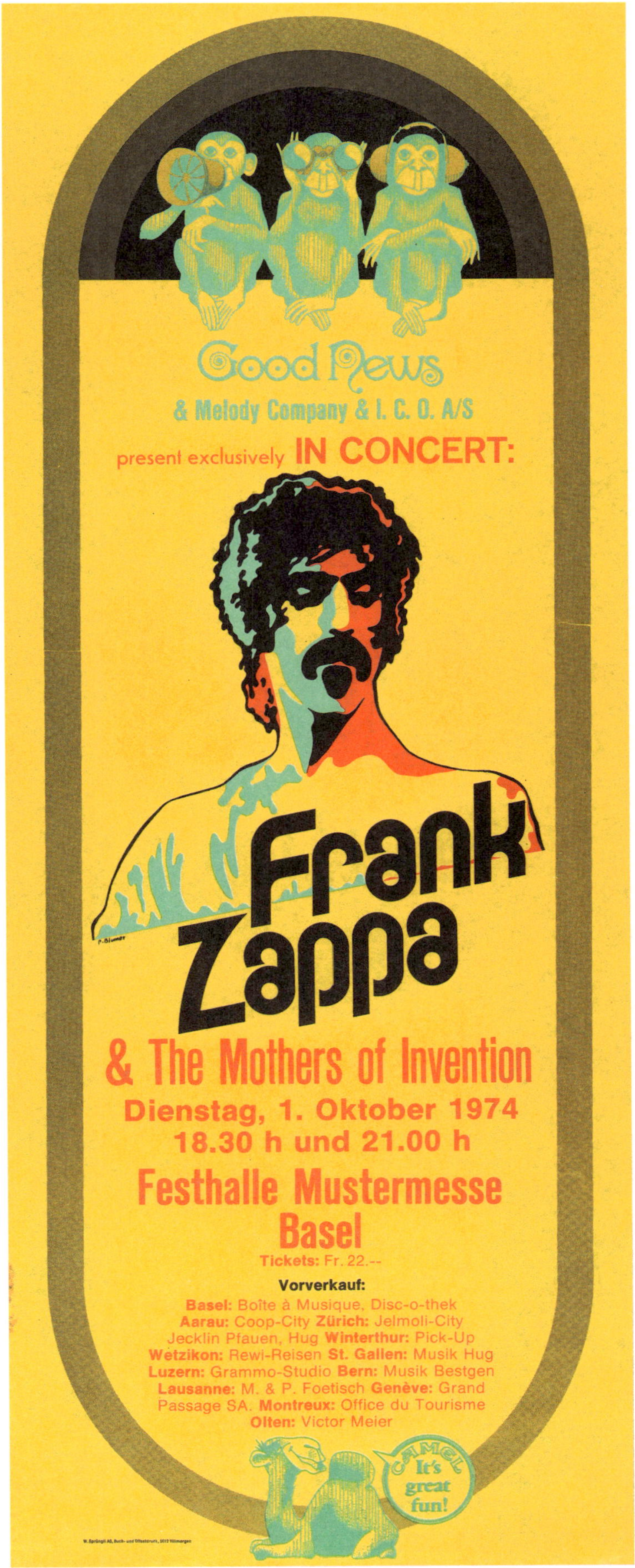

PETER BLUMER, HERBIE HANCOCK, 1972, 250×635

PETER BLUMER, ASHTON GARDNER DYKE & CO, 1972, 245×635

PETER BLUMER, BLACK SABBATH, 1973, 245×635

PETER BLUMER, DEEP PURPLE, 1973, 245×635

PETER BLUMER, MONSTER CONCERT, 1968, 445×630

Jimi Hendrix – Monsterkonzert

Einer aus London kommenden Chartermaschine entstieg am Nachmittag des 30. Mai 1968 auf dem Flughafen Zürich-Kloten eine Schar ungewöhnlicher Passagiere. Rund vierzig junge Musiker, auffallend bunt, mit Schlapphüten, wunderlichen Haartrachten, Klunkern und Tüchern, trollten sich die fahrbare Treppe hinunter. Der eigentliche Star der beiden anstehenden Konzerte, Jimi Hendrix, war unbemerkt schon am Morgen aus New York eingeflogen. Vor dem Konzert wollte Wachtmeister Guido Buchli von der Stadtpolizei Zürich der Presse die vielsagende Auskunft geben, man wisse noch nicht genau, wie viele Polizisten man aufbieten werde, «im Krieg sagt man ja auch nicht, wie gross das Heer ist, das ausrückt».

Statt der erwarteten 10'000 Besucher kam am ersten Abend nur die Hälfte. Für elf Franken erhielten sie einen Besuch mit bleibenden Eindrücken aus einer neuen Welt. Nach einer kurzen Modenschau mit farbenfrohen Kleidern von Bernie's, eröffnete Walty Anselmo, gehandelt als «der Schweizer Jimi Hendrix», mit seinen Musikern den Reigen. Anschliessend spielten nacheinander: The Koobas, John Mayall's Bluesbreakers, Traffic mit Steve Winwood, Eric Burdon & The New Animals, The Move und zum Schluss die Jimi Hendrix Experience.

Hendrix' Gitarre konnte sprechen, Geschichten erzählen, Bilder malen, knattern wie ein Maschinengewehr, zittern wie eine Frau, leuchten wie Phosphorbomben und weinen wie ein Kind. Das Konzert ging erst nach Mitternacht zu Ende. Die Musiker kehrten ins Hotel Stoller zurück, wo sie untergebracht waren. Hendrix nahm sich eine Begleiterin mit aufs Zimmer. Dem Portier entging dies nicht. Er informierte die Polizei, welche den Star aus dem Bett holte und seine Besucherin abführte. Stollers «Frauentraum» war strikt für die Glacekarte reserviert. Jetzt erst konnte Zürich ruhig schlafen gehen. Es war sauber geblieben.

Am zweiten Abend kamen nun tatsächlich die erwarteten 10'000 Besucher. Die Stimmung war glänzend. Die Bands leisteten saubere Arbeit. Einziger Unterschied zum Vorabend: The Move und Eric Burdon tauschten die Plätze. Burdon war beim Publikum besser angekommen. Weniger glänzend war die Stimmung hinter der Bühne. Uniformierte machten abfällige Bemerkungen über die Jugendlichen, titulierten die auf- und abtretenden Musiker «Söihünd» und «schwuli Söi».

Danach vergnügten sich die Musiker in der Diskothek Crazy Girl an der Zwinglistrasse in Zürich 4, wo später Hansruedi Jaggi, der Veranstalter der beiden Abende, seinen Club Revolution eröffnen sollte. Es war eine Abschiedsparty, man hatte verlängerte Polizeistunde eingegeben. Punkt 2.30 Uhr erschien, einem Überfallkommando gleich, ein mit Uniformierten vollgepackter Einsatzwagen vor der Diskothek, einige postierten sich am Haupteingang, andere sicherten die Hinterausgänge. Die Feiernden stürzten ins Freie, in der Meinung, es handle sich um eine Razzia. Die Ordnungshüter wollten aber lediglich der Polizeistunde etwas Nachdruck verschaffen. Dies war die Art, wie man mit Halbstarken umging, und so hielt man es damals auch bei internationalen Popstars für angemessen. Hendrix selbst war nicht unter den Gästen. Die Securitas-Wächter hatten ihn

Jimi Hendrix — Monster Concert

On the afternoon of May 30, 1968, a peculiar-looking assortment of passengers disembarked from a chartered plane arriving from London at Zurich's Kloten airport. Some forty young musicians in magnificent colorful garb, sporting floppy hats, odd hairdos, jewelry and scarves descended down the steps. The headlining star of the concerts, Jimi Hendrix, had already arrived that morning from New York City and retired to his hotel. Before the event, police constable Guido Buchli of the Stadtpolizei Zurich told the press that they did not yet know the exact number of officers to be put on duty, but he did tell them: "in war, you don't give away the strength of the forces you are about to deploy."

Only about half the expected 10,000 people showed up at the first concert. For eleven francs, they received the performance as well as some lasting impressions of a new world. Following a fashion show presenting colorful products from Bernie's, Walty Anselmo, who was announced as "the Swiss Jimi Hendrix," opened the evening with his band. After that, playing in this order: The Koobas, John Mayall's Bluesbreakers, Traffic with Steve Winwood, Eric Burdon & the New Animals, The Move, and finally the Jimi Hendrix Experience.

Hendrix' guitar could actually talk, tell stories, paint pictures, fire like a machine gun, tremble like a woman, glow like phosphorus bombs, and weep like a child. The concert ended just after midnight. Hendrix took a female companion up to his hotel room. This did not escape the watchful eye of the night porter. The police were informed and arrived to wake up the star and remove his visitor. The Hotel Stoller's offered *Frauentraum* (ladies' delight) was strictly reserved for the "ice-cream menu." Only now could Zurich find some sleep. It had been kept clean.

On the second night the expected 10,000 people showed up. The atmosphere was fantastic and the bands did a great job. The only difference between this night and the previous one was that The Move and Eric Burdon were to change places, since the night before Burdon's set had gone down better with the audience. Backstage the atmosphere was not half as good. Some uniformed officials made derisory remarks about the audience and called the artists cunts and faggots.

Afterwards, the musicians were having a good time at the Crazy Girl discotheque in Zurich's Kreis 4 district, where Rolf Jaggi the promoter of both nights would later open his club, Revolution. It was a farewell party and a late licence had been granted. At 2:30 AM sharp, a police car packed with officers stopped commando-like in front of the discotheque. Some officers took up positions at the front door while others secured the back entrance. The partygoers, taking the action for a raid, rushed outside. However, the police only wanted to make sure closing time was respected. This was the treatment beatniks usually received, so it was also deemed appropriate for pop stars. Hendrix was not among the guests. Club security had denied him entry earlier that evening. No chance to get in since Jimi's skin was way too dark. Being hungry, Hendrix took

an der Tür abgewiesen. Keine Chance, hereingelassen zu werden, zu dunkel war Jimis Haut. Hendrix bestieg ein Taxi, er wollte noch etwas essen. Der Fahrer brachte ihn nach Zürich-Altstetten, dort stand ein Automat, der panierte Schweinsschnitzel ausspuckte. Anständige Leute schliefen nachts, Hunger nach Mitternacht war noch nicht vorgesehen. In Gesellschaft einiger Prostituierter, Strichjungen und Taxifahrer kaute der höfliche Star sein kaltes Menü und liess sich anschliessend ins Hotel zurückfahren, wo er sich beim Chauffeur mit einer 100-Dollar-Note bedankte.

Zwei Wochen später forderte die mittlerweile organisierte Protestjugend das leerstehende Gebäude des Warenhauses Globus an der Bahnhofsbrücke in Zürich als autonomes Jugendzentrum. Tausende kamen zur Demonstration, auch aus dem Thurgau, sogar aus dem Wallis. Veranstalter Jaggi hatte unterdessen die Adressen der Teilnehmer am *Blick*-Wettbewerb des Hendrix-Konzerts erhalten, zwei Körbe voll Postkarten, 6000 Namen insgesamt. Diese gab er an Roland Gretler weiter, der im 16-köpfigen Globus-Komitee der Autonomen vertreten war. Als Globus-Krawall ging die lange Nacht vom 29. auf den 30. Juni 1968 in die Geschichte der Schweiz ein, man hatte zu Europa aufgeschlossen, das «Monsterkonzert» war der Auftakt gewesen.

Eugen Sorg (gekürzte Version)

a taxi. The driver took him to the outskirts of Zurich, where a snack vending machine spit out a schnitzel. Respectable people should sleep at night, munchies after midnight were not part of the plan. So the polite star chewed on his cold menu in the company of prostitutes, hustlers and taxi drivers before taking the taxi back to the hotel, where he expressed his gratitude to the driver with a 100-dollar bill.

Two weeks later, the now well organized '68 protest movement demanded the empty building of the Globus emporium at the Bahnhofsbrücke in Zurich as an autonomous youth center. Thousands came to the rally, even from far away regions as the Cantons of Thurgau and Valais. Incidentally, Jaggi, the organizer, had gotten hold of the addresses of the people who had participated in the *Blick* newspaper contest for the Hendrix concert: two clothes baskets full of postcards, containing some 6,000 names in all. He passed these on to Roland Gretler, now one of sixteen members of the autonomous Globus Committee. The long night of June 29–30, 1968 went down as the Globus Riots; the city of Zurich had caught up with the rest of Europe, and the "Monster Concert" had been the overture.

Eugen Sorg (abridged version)

PETER BLUMER, ALICE COOPER, 1972, 245×635

PETER BLUMER, STEPPENWOLF, 1972, 250×635

PETER BLUMER, LEONARD COHEN, 1974, 245×635

PETER BLUMER, DAVID BOWIE, 1976, 245×635

PETER BLUMER, ROXY MUSIC, 1974, 245×635

PETER BLUMER, SPARKS, 1974, 245×635

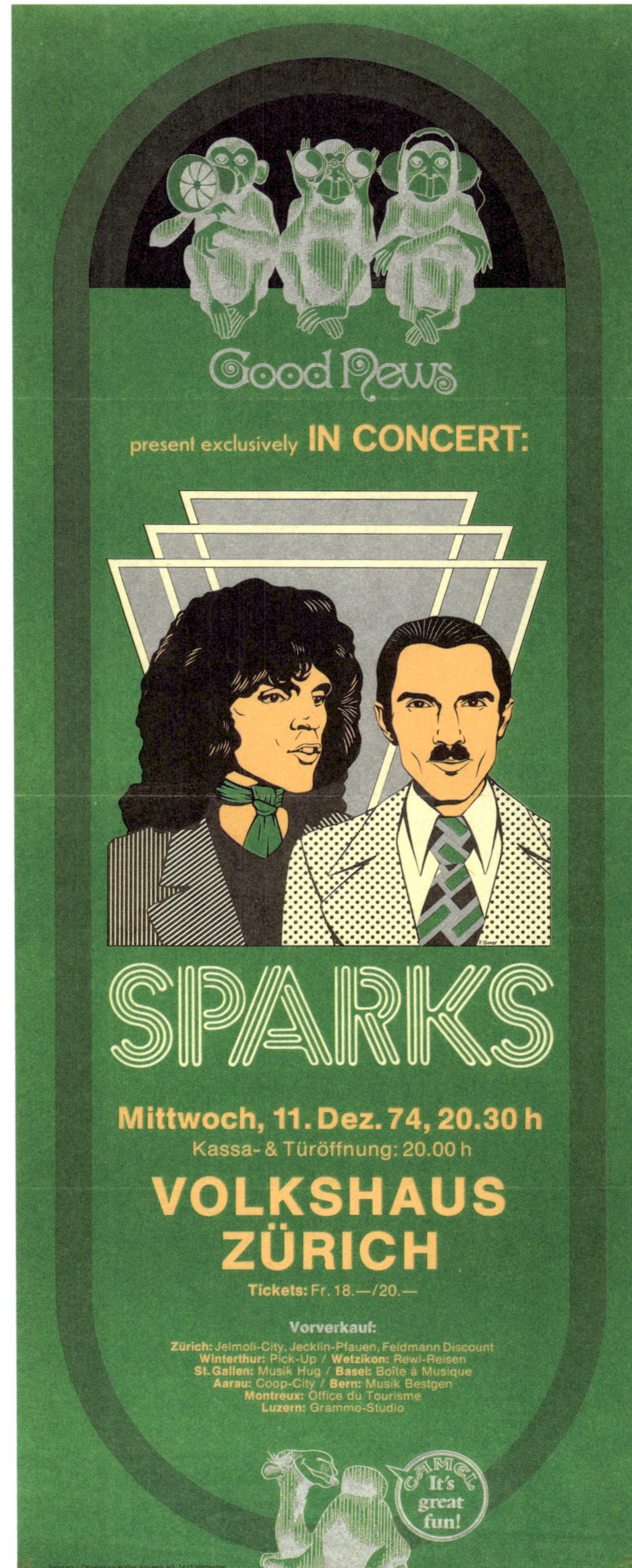

PETER BLUMER, JOHNNY CASH, 1975, 245×635

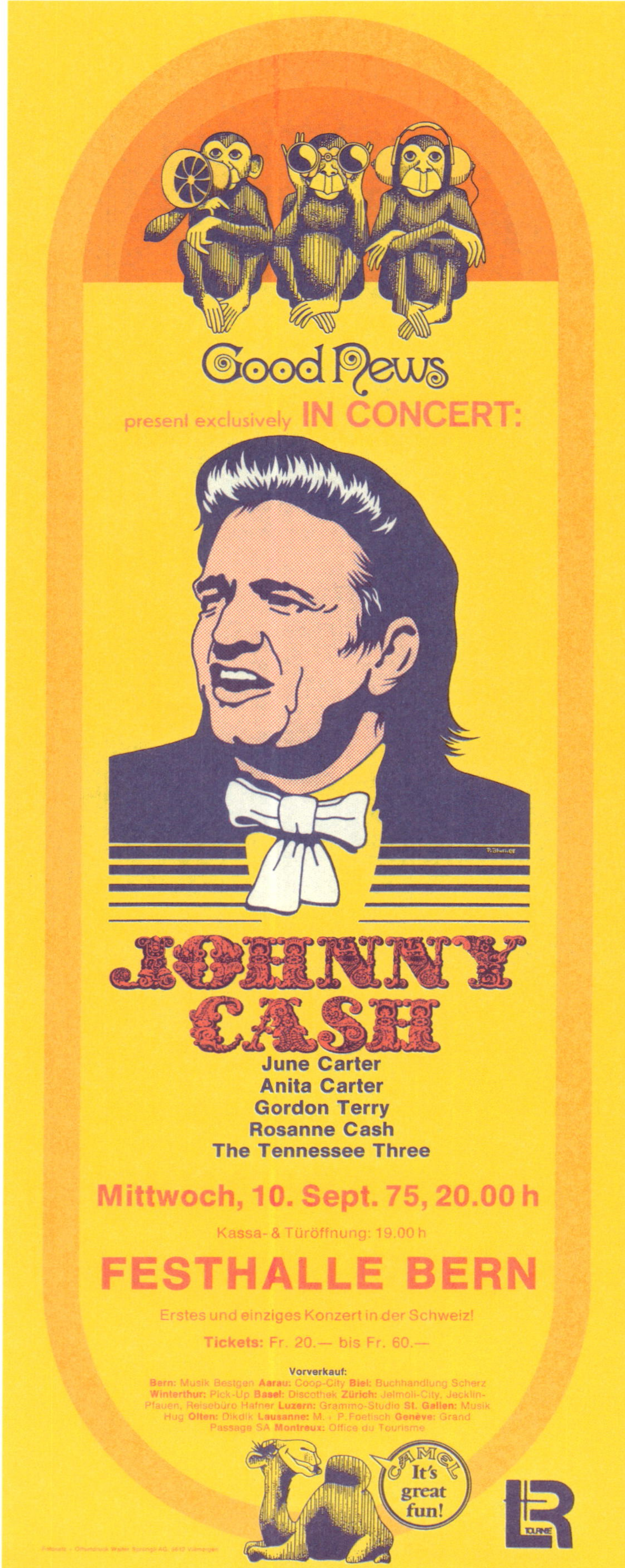

PETER BLUMER, LOU REED, 1975, 245×635

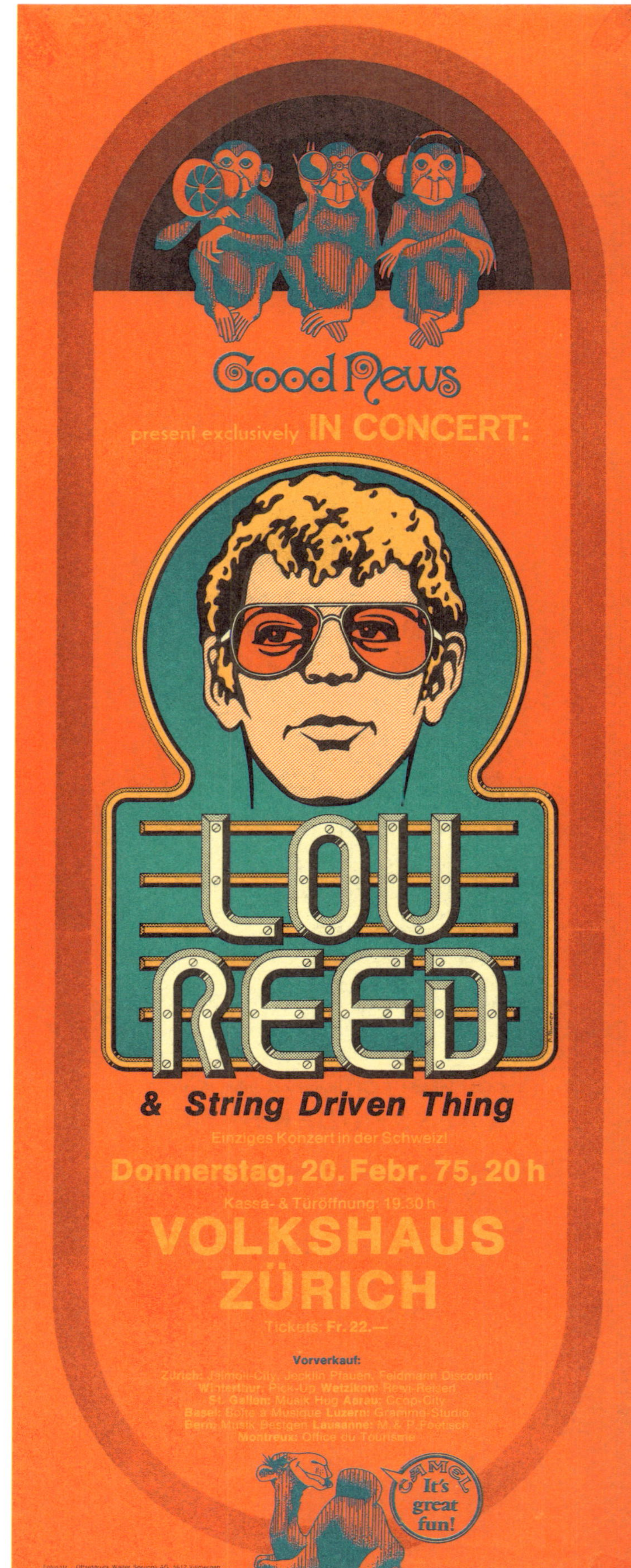

PETER BLUMER, DOLDLINGER JUBILEE ’75, 1975, 245×635

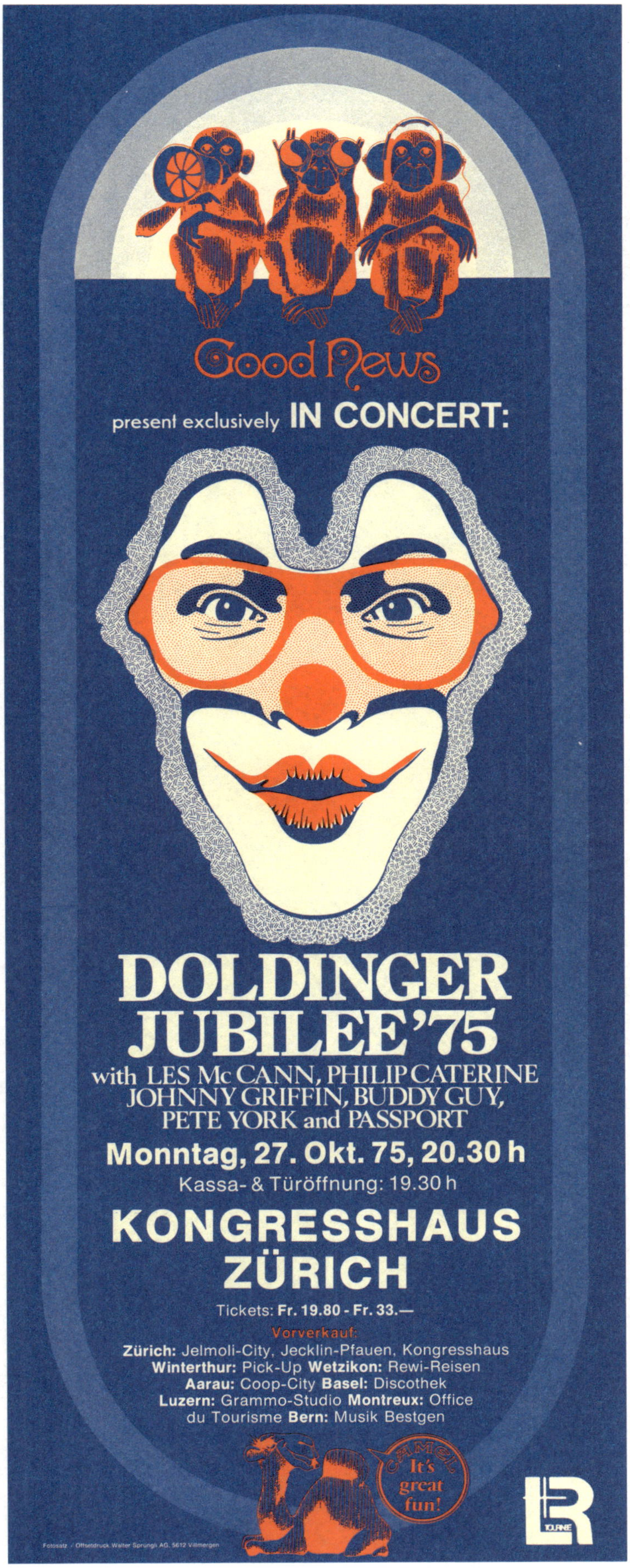

PETER BLUMER, FATS DOMINO, 1974, 250×635

PETER BLUMER, PINK FLOYD - ORIGINAL DRAWING, 1972, 297×420, PENCIL

PETER BLUMER, SUZI QUATRO – ORIGINAL DRAWING, 1974, 297×420, PENCIL

PETER BLUMER, KISS, 1976, 245×635

PETER BLUMER, P.F.M., 1973, 245×635

PETER BLUMER, RICK WAKEMAN, 1976, 245×635

PETER BLUMER, CAT STEVENS, 1973, 250×635

PETER BLUMER, SUZI QUATRO, 1974, 245×635

PETER BLUMER, IKE & TINA TURNER, 1974, 245×635

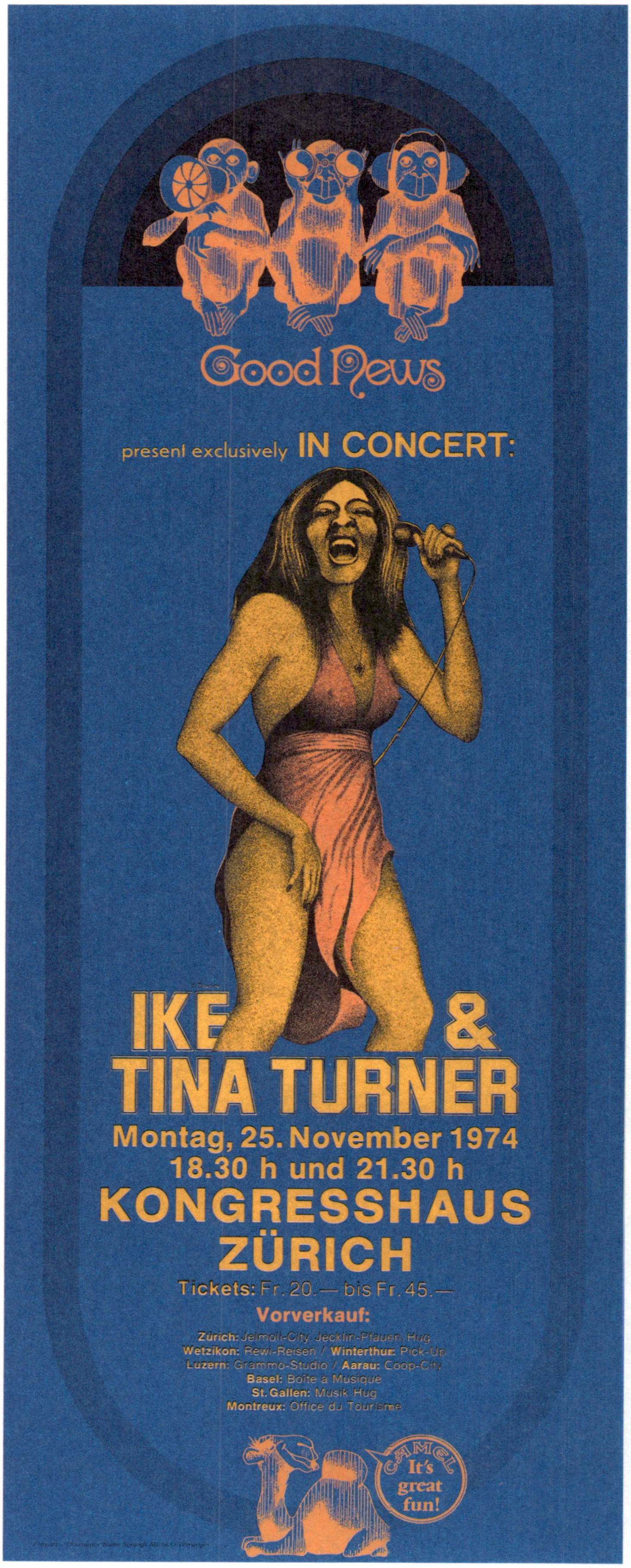

PETER BLUMER, CHUCK BERRY, 1973, 245×635

PETER BLUMER, RORY GALLAGHER, 1974, 245×635

PETER BLUMER, BACHMAN TURNER OVERDRIVE, 1975, 245×635

PETER BLUMER, PROCOL HARUM, 1974, 245×635

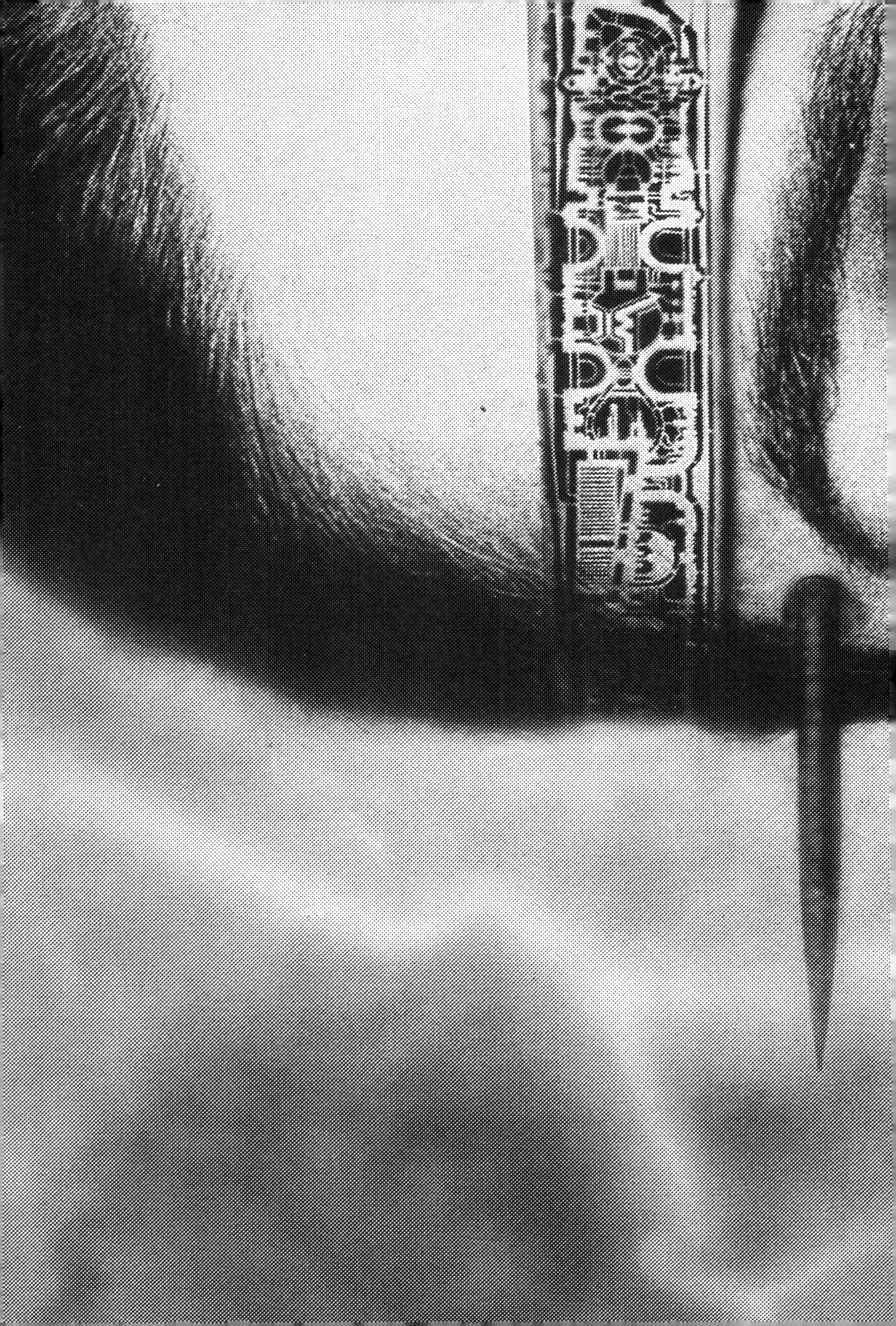

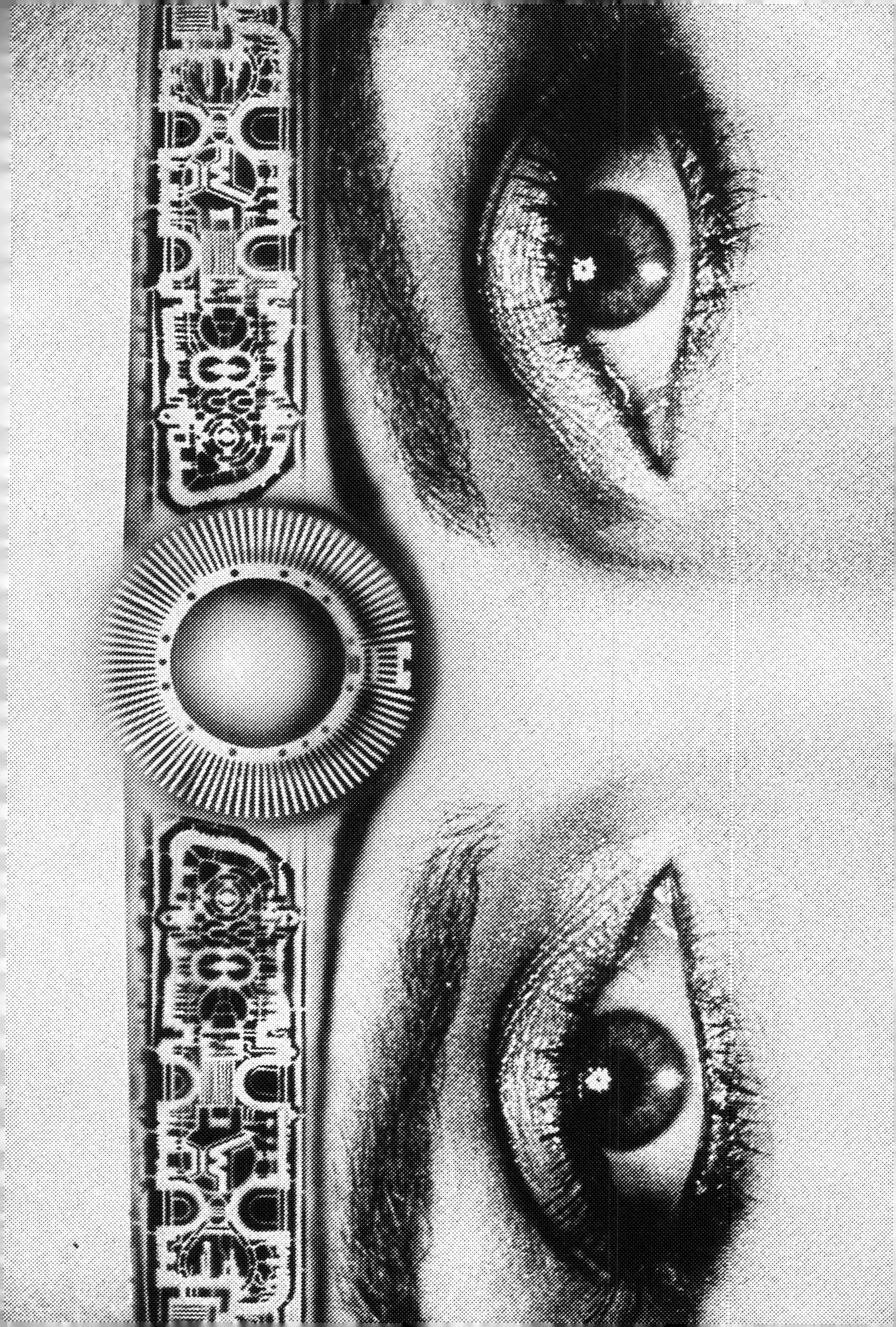

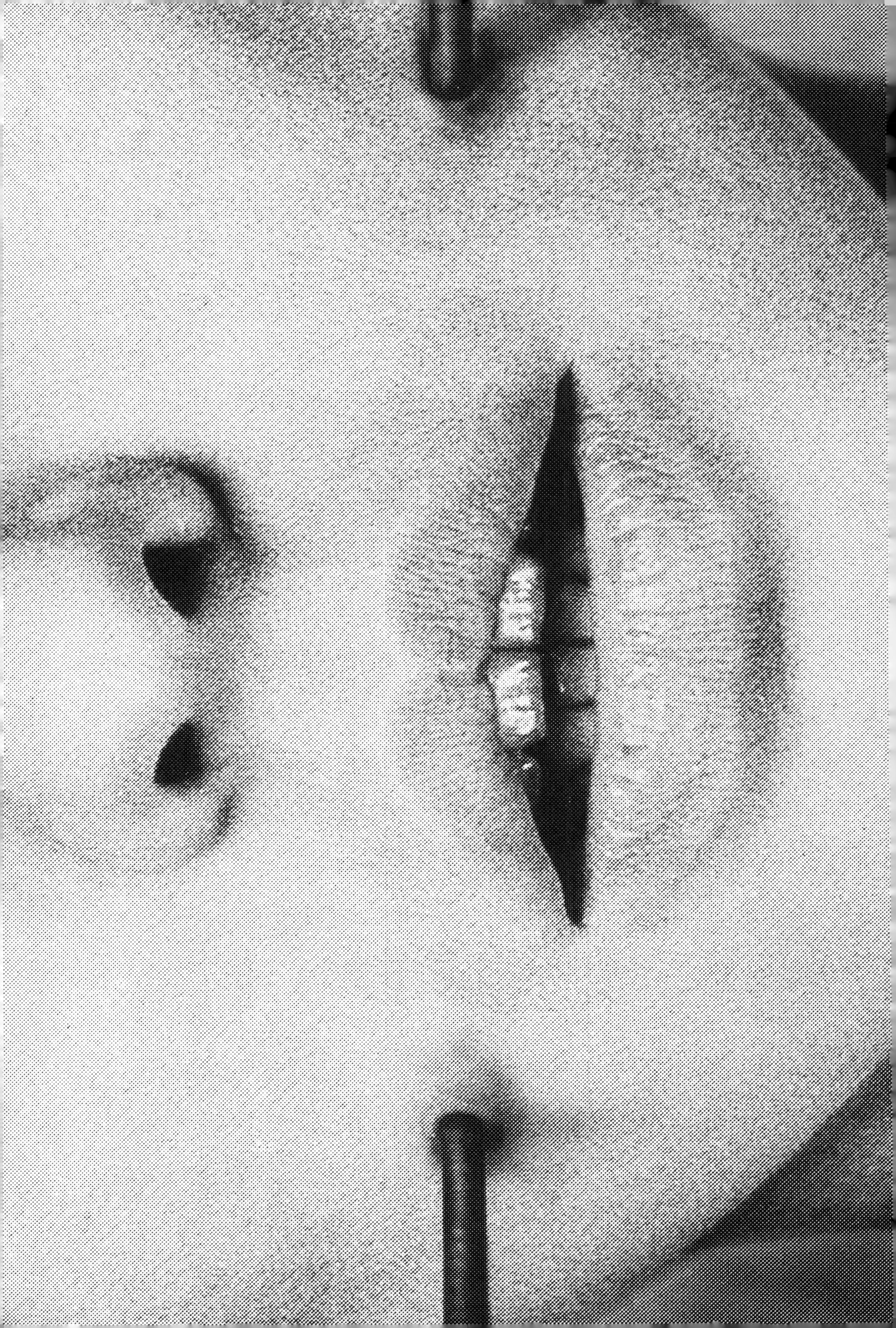

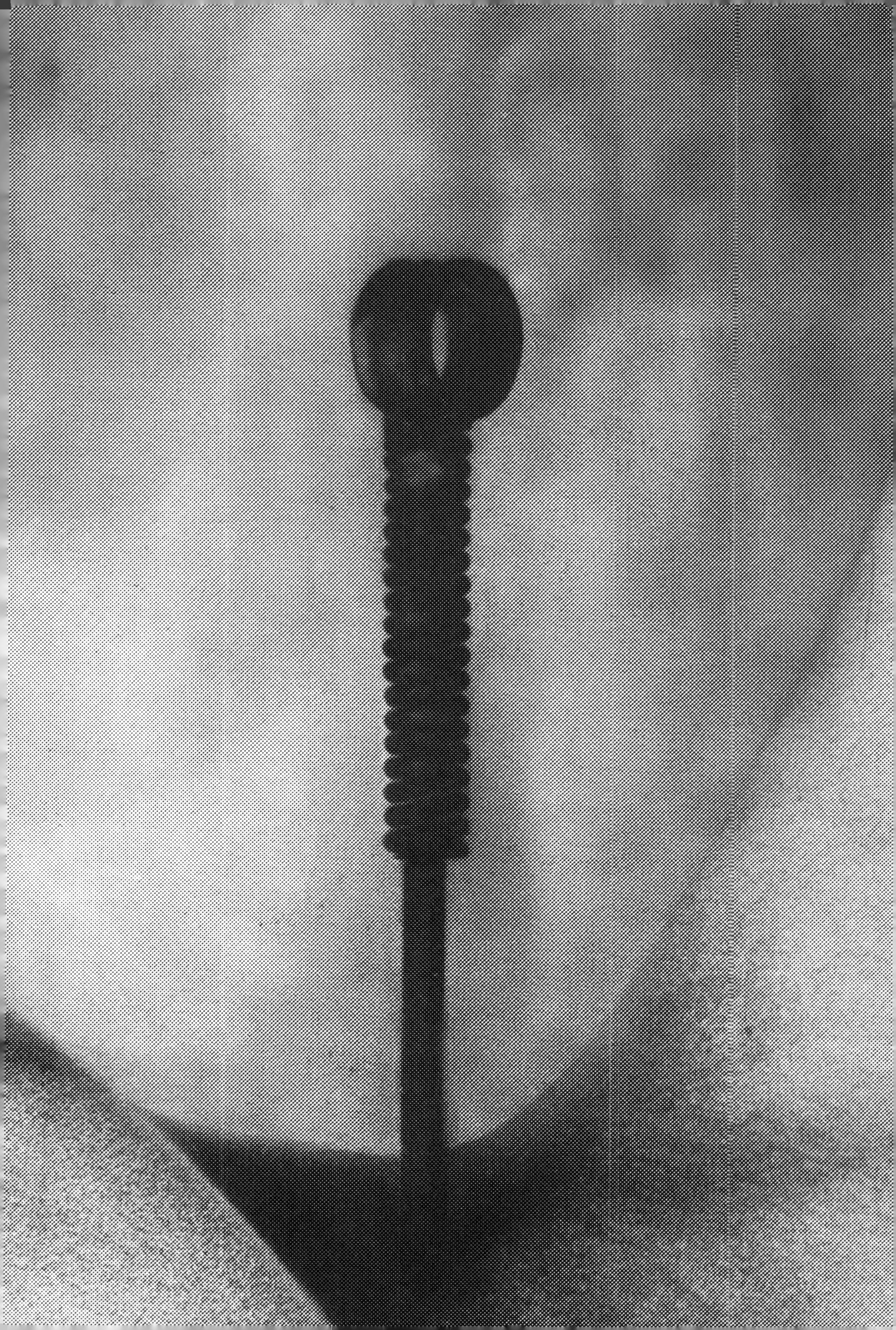

H.R. Giger

Geboren in Chur. Studierte in Zürich Architektur und Industriedesign. Während seines Studiums entstanden erste Tuschfederzeichnungen («Atomkinder»), worauf er seine Werke in der Untergrundzeitung *Hotcha* publizierte. Ab Ende der Sechzigerjahre wurden seine Bilder von der internationalen Rockszene wahrgenommen. Wie kein anderer transportiert sein Stil düstere Emotionen des Rock – etwa im ikonenhaften Umschlag für das ELP-Album *Brain Salad Surgery* (1972). Gigers zahlreiche weitere Umschläge für Schweizer und internationale Bands sind zu Klassikern der Rockgrafik geworden. Daneben war Giger auch für seine Mitwirkung als Szenen- und Kostümbildner in Hollywood-Filmen wie *Alien* bekannt. Für *Alien* erhielt er 1980 auch den Oscar in der Kategorie «Beste visuelle Effekte».

H.R. Giger

Born in Chur. Studied architecture and industrial design. During his studies, the first ink drawings (Atomkinder) developed, whereupon he published his works in the underground newspaper *Hotcha*. As of the end of the sixties, his pictures were noticed by the international rock scene. Like nobody else, his style transports the gloomy emotions of rock — for example, the iconic cover design for the ELP album *Brain Salad Surgery* (1972). Giger's numerous additional covers for Swiss and international bands have become classics of rock graphic art. In addition, Giger was known for his contribution as a set and costume designer for Hollywood films such as *Alien*. For *Alien* he also received the Oscar in 1980, in the category of «best visual effects».

H.R. GIGER, EMERSON LAKE & PALMER - THEN AND NOW, DOUBLE CD, 1998

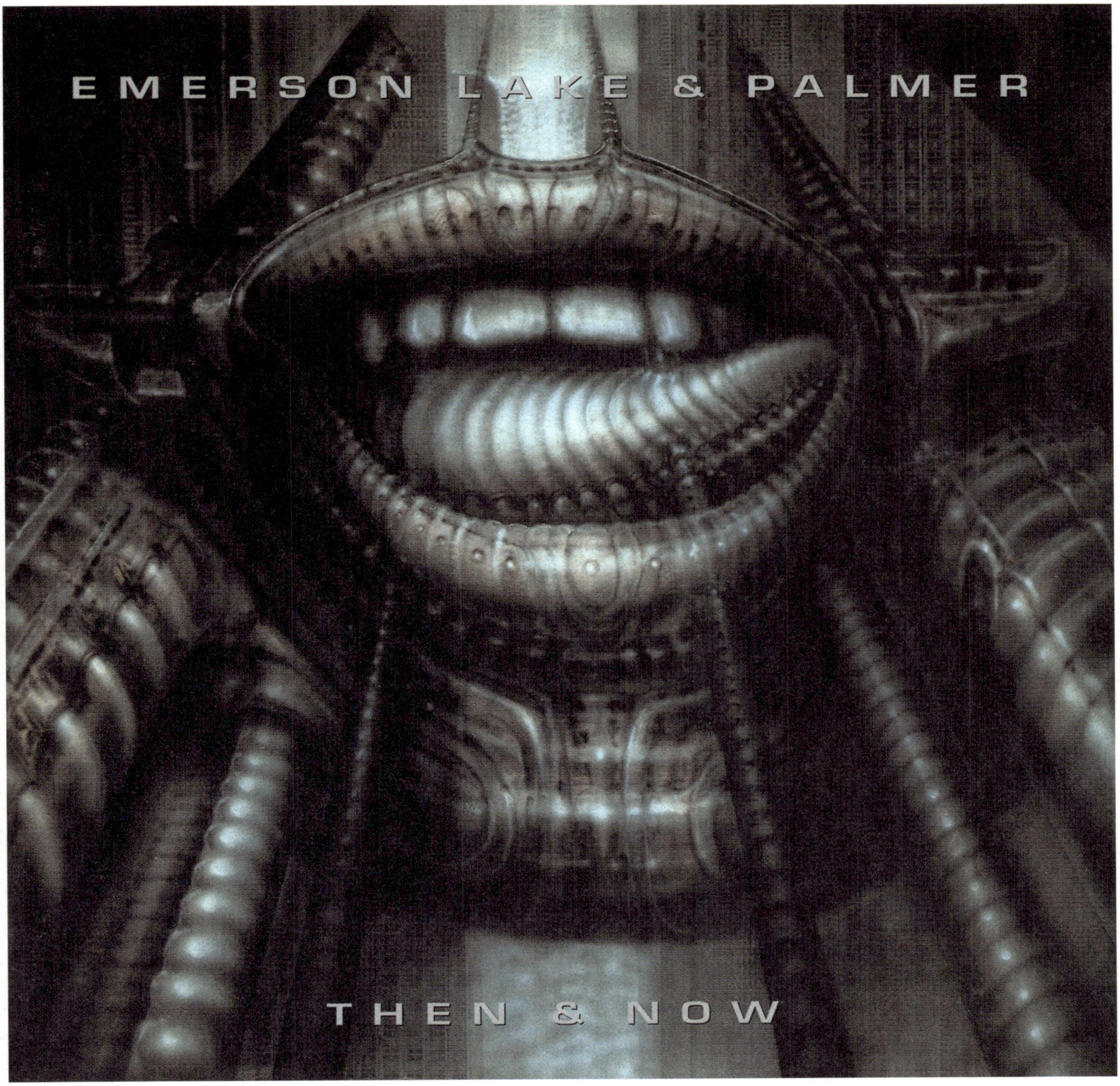

ELP – Brain Salad Surgery (Teil 1)

1973, Li Tobler und ich lebten seit drei Jahren zusammen in einer alten Wohnung/Studio in Zürich-Oerlikon. Ich hatte gerade das Bild *The Passage* fertig gemalt und arbeitete mit meiner neuen Spritzpistole am Gemälde *Temple*. Ich berauschte mich zu der Zeit vor allem mit der Musik von ELP, Miles Davis und Bowie und schuf das Triptychon *Penis Landschaften*. Darauf sind Abbildungen von Babys, Schädeln und Phalli zu sehen. Letzteres zog 1986 einen eineinhalbjährigen Porno-Rechtsstreit nach sich, weil es dem Album *Frankenchrist* der amerikanischen Punk-Rock-Gruppe Dead Kennedys beigelegt wurde. Zu diesem Zeitpunkt hatte ich meine produktivste und kreativste Phase als Maler. Ich erhielt dann die Nachricht von meinem Freund H.H. Kunz und von Peter Zumsteg, der damals ELP in der Schweiz vertrat, dass ELP Interesse an einem von mir für sie gestalteten Plattencover hätten. Die Band würde in zwei Tagen im Hallenstadion spielen, und bei dieser Gelegenheit könnte man das Design dafür begutachten. Dies war schon mein zweiter Vertrag für ein Albumcover, und ich begann umgehend mit der Arbeit.

Der Titel des Albums sollte *Whip Some Skull On Ya* heissen. Übersetzt bedeutet es Fellatio, und es war für mich offensichtlich, Lippen, Penisse und Totenköpfe zu kombinieren. Der Hausgrafiker von ELP hatte die Idee, dass der Umschlag wie ein Tor geöffnet werden könne; keine gute Idee, wie sich später herausstellte, als sie gestapelt wurden. Derselbe Grafiker wollte sich auch mit falschen Federn schmücken, als er meinen Namen mit seinem als Schöpfer für das Albumdesign versah. Ich war zu der Zeit sehr beleidigt, verzieh ihm jedoch, da er kurz darauf bei einem Autounfall sein Leben verlor.

Aber zurück zum Auftrag. Da ich mich zu dieser Zeit mit dem oben genannten Triptychon auseinandersetzte, flossen diese Elemente in das Bild ein. Ich erschuf das gewünschte Doppelbild wie nichts über Nacht. Nach dem Konzert kam Keith Emerson mit Peter Zumsteg und H.H. Kunz zu mir. Ich war schrecklich aufgeregt, da ich noch nie einem Popstar gegenübergestanden hatte, und mein Haus war, wie es der Zufall wollte, voll mit Leuten. Lake, Palmer und der Fotojournalist Bruno Torricelli kamen erst später. Ich wurde mit Komplimenten für meine Arbeit überschüttet. Nichtsdestotrotz teilte mir Keith plötzlich mit, dass der Titel des Albums nun *Brain Salad Surgery* heissen sollte. Ich war bestürzt, bis er mir erklärte, dass dieser Ausdruck ebenfalls Fellatio konnotiere. Nachdem die Band sich mit verständnisvollen und aufmunternden Bemerkungen für ein Foto aufstellte, verstummte die Aufregung.

Ein Teil der Auflage wurde wie von mir gewünscht mit metallischen Farben gedruckt, dies im Gegensatz zu denen, die in der Schweiz erhältlich waren. Diese wurden möglicherweise in einer Druckerei, die sich auf Pornografie spezialisierte, gedruckt. Dort haben sie nämlich die Tendenz, zur Verschönerung der Sache zu viel Rot zu geben. Der Druck war Kuh-Scheisse-Haufen-braun.

H.R. Giger

ELP — Brain Salad Surgery (Part 1)

In 1973, Li Tobler and I had been living together for three years in an old apartment/studio in Zurich-Oerlikon. I had just finished with the painting *Passage* and was working with my new spray gun on the painting *Temple*. At the time, I was getting high on the music of mainly ELP, Miles Davis and Bowie, and created the *Penis Landscapes* triptych, with its babies, skulls, and phalluses. The last of which led to a year-and-a-half-long porno lawsuit (1986), because it was sold to an American punk rock group called Dead Kennedys as a poster insert for their album *Frankenchrist*. This period was my most productive and creative phase as a painter. It was then that I received the news from my friend H.H. Kunz and from Peter Zumsteg, who was then the Swiss representative of ELP, that ELP was interested in having me do a record cover for them. The group would be playing at the Hallenstadion in two days, and on this occasion it would be possible to get an expert opinion on the design. This was already my second contract for an album cover, and I began working on it with enthusiasm.

The title of the album was supposed to be *Whip Some Skull On Ya*. Translated, it means fellatio, and the obvious thing was therefore to combine lips, penises, and skulls. The graphic artist for ELP had the idea that it should be possible to open up the cover like a gate; not a good idea, as would later become apparent when they were stacked. The same graphic artist wanted to take all the credit himself by substituting his name for mine as the creator of the album design. At the time, I was deeply offended. But I forgave him, since he lost his life in an auto accident shortly thereafter.

But back to the contract. Because I was working at this time on the aforementioned triptych, those elements flowed into the picture. I created the dual image desired, as it were, overnight. After the concert, Keith Emerson came over with Peter Zumsteg and H.H. Kunz. I was terribly excited, since I had never stood directly opposite a pop star before, and my house, as it happened, was also full of people. Lake, Palmer, and the photo journalist Bruno Torricelli arrived later. I was ceremoniously showered with compliments on my work. Nevertheless, Keith suddenly informed me that the title of the album was now going to be *Brain Salad Surgery*. I was dismayed until he explained to me that this expression also connoted fellatio. After the group posed for a photo with understanding and encouraging comments, the hubbub died down.

One part of the printing was done, as I had wished, with metallic color — in contrast to what was available in Switzerland. This was likely printed in a printing shop specializing in pornography. There, they have a tendency to beautify things by the application of too much red. The print came out "cow-pie-shit-brown."

H.R. Giger

ELP – Brain Salad Surgery (Teil 2)

Soweit ich mich erinnern kann, wurde mein erstes Treffen mit H.R. Giger durch unseren Promoter in Zürich, Peter Zumsteg, eingefädelt. Zu dieser Zeit, im Jahr 1973, waren ELP mitten auf einer Europatour. H.H. Kunz, der Freund meines Promoters, bestand darauf, mich zu Gigers Haus zu fahren. So wie ich mich erinnern kann, war es von aussen ein ziemlich bescheidenes «Häuschen», bis du hineingingst. Auf Anhieb fiel mir Giger als «HEAVY» auf, um es gelinde auszudrücken. Die Inneneinrichtung war überwältigend, Gothik auf die Spitze getrieben. Vom Boden bis zur Decke hatte er mit seiner einzigartigen Airbrush-Technik ein einfaches Zimmer in eine Kathedrale verwandelt, in der man sich nun quasi bewegte. Als wenn das noch nicht genug gewesen wäre, arbeitete Giger auch dreidimensional. Aus seiner Toilette kamen Arme hervor, die dich fast verschlingen wollten. Ich bemerkte, dass Bluttransfusionsschläuche in diese Arme gesteckt waren. Ein weiteres Einrichtungselement bestand aus Gasmasken. Giger zeigte mir seine V.D.-Landschaft, die sehr nach Science-Fiction aussah. Doch dann erzählte er mir, dass das Sujet von medizinischen Fotos her stammte.

Ich war gleichzeitig geschockt und fasziniert. Dieses Haus war dunkel und verheissungsvoll, und für mich repräsentierte es die Musik von ELP. Ich schlug vor, dass Greg und Carl das alles sehen sollten, und überredete sie, zu Gigers Haus zu kommen. Ich erinnere mich, dass sie skeptisch waren, doch wir brauchten ein Albumcover. Der Arbeitstitel für unser nächstes Album war *Whip Some Skull On Ya,* was gelinde gesagt zweideutig war. Schlussendlich einigten wir uns auf *Brain Salad Surgery*. Es war genauso suggestiv wie der ehemalige Titel, wenn du auf diese Art von Anspielungen standest. ELP waren sehr angetan von Gigers Arbeit, und einstimmig entschieden wir uns für zwei seiner bestehenden Arbeiten. Später wurde die Innenhülle für uns zu einem Problem. Die Druckerei der Plattenfirma hatte ein Problem mit dem phallischen Objekt vor dem Kopf der Dame mit dem explodierenden Metall-Kopfschmuck. Nach einigem Hin und Her mit unserer Plattenfirma mussten wir H.R. Giger widerwillig bitten, das phallische Objekt vor dem Munde der Dame «abzuschwächen», bis es so aussah wie eine «Welle des Lichts». Ich hoffe doch, dass sich Giger so stolz wie ich fühlt, da dieses Albumdesign einen Meilenstein darstellt, auch wenn Giger unfreiwillig ein paar Dinge daran ändern musste. Bis zu diesem Tag bleibt die Arbeit von H.R. Giger in jeder Hinsicht unverwechselbar. Er ist erschreckend einzigartig.

Keith Emerson

ELP — Brain Salad Surgery (Part 2)

As far as I can recall, my first meeting with H.R. Giger was engineered by Peter Zumsteg, our Zurich promoter at that time. ELP was in the middle of a European tour in 1973. My promoter's friend H.H. Kunz insisted on driving me to Giger's house. As I remember, from the outside, it was a fairly modest "bungalow," until you went in. Giger struck me straight away as "HEAVY," to put it mildly. The interior décor was overpowering, gothic to the extreme. From floor to ceiling, his unique airbrush technique had transformed a simple room into a cathedral, and it was virtually all around you. And as if this were not enough, Giger had gone three-dimensional. His toilet had arms coming out of it, almost engulfing the sitter. I noted that the arms had "drip feeds" going into them. Other décor consisted of gas masks. He showed me his V.D. landscape, which looked very science-fiction until he told me that he had taken the subject from medical photographs.

I was both shocked and fascinated at the same time. It was dark and very foreboding, and, for me, it represented ELP's music. I suggested that Greg and Carl view it all and finally persuaded them to come out to Giger's house. I remember them being reluctant, but we were at a loss for an album cover. Our working title for our next album was *Whip Some Skull On Ya*, which was suggestive, to say the least. We finally settled on *Brain Salad Surgery*. It was just as suggestive as the former title, if you were into that sort of thing. ELP viewed Giger's work and unanimously agreed on two of Giger's existing works. The inside sleeve would later bring us problems with the record company's printers because of the phallic object in front of the head of the lady with the exploding metal headdress. After some back and forth with our record company, we reluctantly had to ask H.R. Giger to "tone down" the phallic object in front of the subject's mouth until it looked like a "shaft of light." I hope that Giger feels as proud as I do about that landmark album cover, even though he was reluctant to alter a few things. To this day, H.R. Giger's work remains distinctive in every sense. He's frighteningly unique.

Keith Emerson

H.R. GIGER, EMERSON LAKE & PALMER - BRAIN SALAD SURGERY, LP GATEFOLD COVER - OUTSIDE, 1973

H.R. GIGER, THE SHIVER - WALPURGIS, LP FRONT COVER, 1969

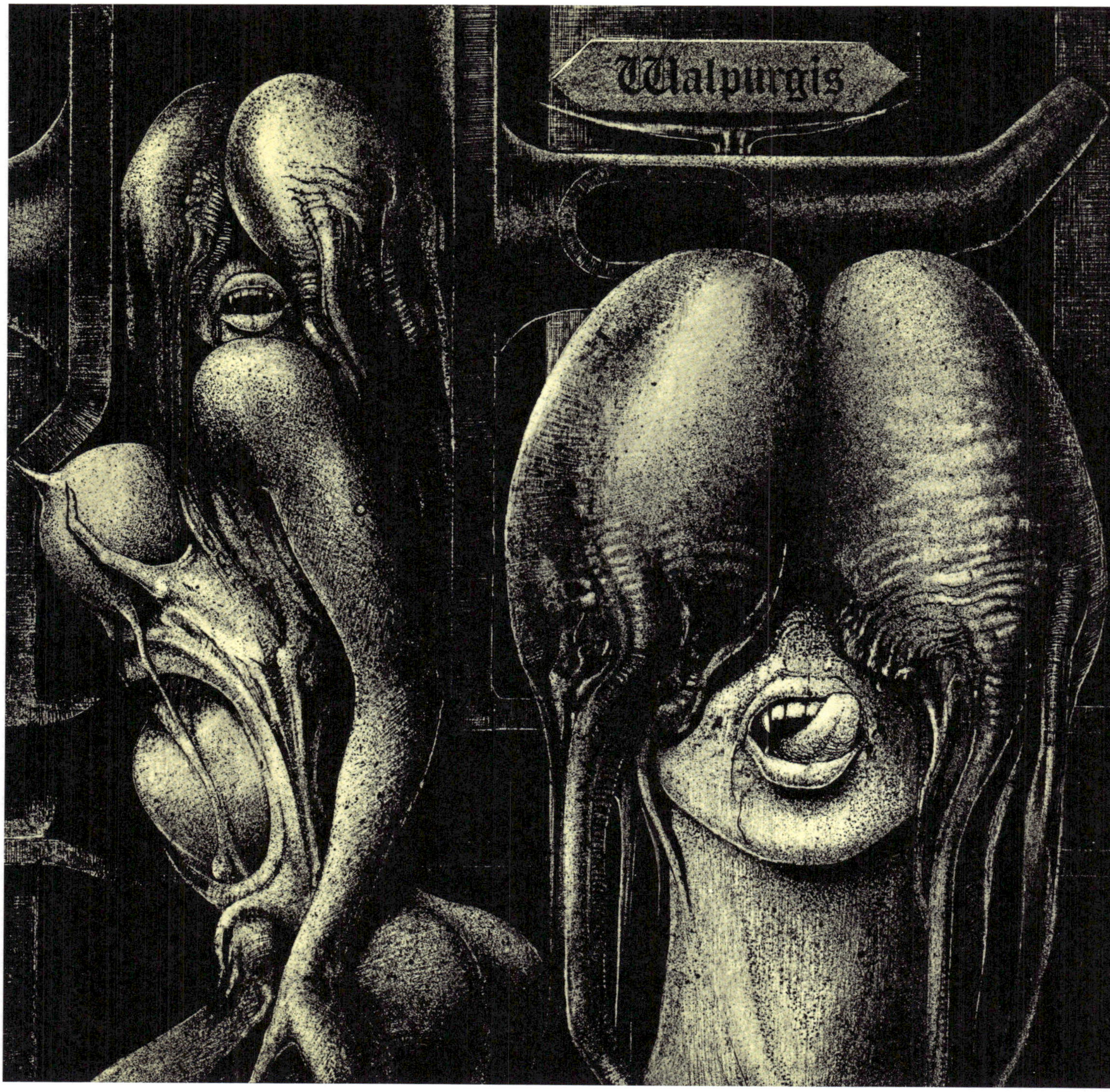

H.R. GIGER, THE SHIVER – WALPURGIS, LP BACK COVER, 1969

DEBBIE HARRY
KooKoo

H.R. GIGER, STEVE STEVENS - ATOMIC PLAYBOYS, LP, 1989

H.R. GIGER, ISLAND - PICTURES, LP, 1977

H.R. GIGER, DANZIG – MEISTER UND MARGERITHA, LP, 1992

H.R. GIGER, FLOH DE COLOGNE - MUMIEN, LP, 1975

H.R. GIGER, MAGMA - ATTAHK, LP, 1978

H.R. GIGER, TROCKI - PERMANENT REVOLUTION, UNLICENSED ARTWORK, CD, 2003

ELP – Brain Salad Surgery (Teil 3)

Kurz nach einer Ausstellung in Prag im Jahr 2005 verschwand das ikonoklastische Originalkunstwerk, das für das Cover von *Brain Salad Surgery* verwendet worden war. Dies ist nicht der einzige Schicksalsschlag, der H.R. Giger widerfahren ist, als es um seine ikonischen Gemälde mit der Rockwelt ging. Dasselbe Kunstwerk war schon 1997 Thema gewesen, als ELP mit dessen Sujet ein T-Shirt produzieren wollte. Im Jahr darauf hatten ELP infolge eines anderen Deals eine weitere Auswahl von Gigers Gemälden für ihr Album *Then And Now* verwendet. Während der Künstler für die Verwendung dieser Arbeiten bezahlt wurde, behauptet Gigers Berater Les Barany bis heute, dass der *Brain Salad Surgery*-T-Shirt-Deal zwischen dem Künstler und dem Management der Band nie honoriert worden sei. Er sagt: «Seit 17 Jahren gibt es keine Honorarabrechnung in der Angelegenheit, und angesichts der gut dokumentierten Geschichte und der gegenseitigen Vorteile, die für Giger und ELP bestanden, hatten wir auch nicht gedacht, dass die üblichen Vorauszahlungen notwendig gewesen wären. Die Rockwelt hat aufgehört, uns zu überraschen.»

Emerson Lake & Palmer sind nicht die Einzigen, wenn es darum geht, Rechte für die Verwendung der Bilder des Schweizer Künstlers einzufordern. Glenn Danzig musste sich vor Gericht verantworten, da er mit einem Sujet von Giger illegal T-Shirts produzierte, dieses aber nur für sein Album *Danzig III: How The Gods Kill* lizenziert worden war und nicht für weitere Merchandising-Produkte. Es heisst, Danzig seien die Gerichtsakten über einen Crowd-Surfing-Prozess-Server bei einem Konzert der Band im Roseland Ballroom in New York zugestellt worden. Die auffälligste unbefugte Nutzung eines Giger-Kunstwerks für eigene Zwecke gelang allerdings der polnischen Politik-Death-Punkband Trocki. Für ihr Album *Permanent Revolution* aus dem Jahr 2004 verwendeten sie einfach den Umschlag von *Brain Salad Surgery* und schrieben ihren eigenen Namen darauf, aber so, dass das von Giger gestaltet ELP-Logo trotzdem noch deutlich zu sehen war!

Leslie Barany

Für sachdienliche Hinweise, die zur Auffindung dieser beiden Gemälde führen, ist eine Belohnung von 10'000 US-Dollar ausgesetzt.

www.hrgiger.com

ELP — Brain Salad Surgery (Part 3)

The iconoclastic original artwork that was used for the cover of *Brain Salad Surgery* disappeared shortly after an exhibition in Prague in 2005. This is not the only blow of fate that befell H.R. Giger when it comes to both this iconic painting and the rock world. The same artwork was also the motif for a 1997 T-Shirt produced by the band in the wake of a deal struck with ELP to use a selection of Giger's paintings for their upcoming album *Then And Now*. While Giger was paid for the use of these works, his agent Les Barany maintains that the simultaneous merchandising deal for the *Brain Salad Surgery* T-Shirt that was agreed on by the artist and band management has never been honored. "It's been seventeen years without as much as a royalty payment," he says, "and given the anticipated well documented and mutual benefits for both Giger and ELP, we didn't think at the time that the usual payment advances were necessary. The rock world has ceased to surprise us."

Emerson, Lake & Palmer are not the only ones when it comes to failing to secure the necessary rights for the use of the Swiss artist's images. Glenn Danzig ended up settling out of court with Giger following the production of illegal T-Shirts with one of the artist's motifs that was only authorized for use on the cover of *Danzig III: How The Gods Kill* and not for other merchandising products. As the story goes, court papers were delivered to Danzig via a crowd-surfing process server at a concert by the band at the Roseland Ballroom in New York City. However, the most blatant unauthorized use of Giger's artwork was by the Polish political death punks Trocki, who simply used the cover of *Brain Salad Surgery* for their 2004 album, *Permanent Revolution*, and stuck their name on it, but in such a way that it was nevertheless possible to clearly see the logo that Giger designed for ELP!

Leslie Barany

A reward of 10'000 US-Dollars is being offered for information leading to the recovery of these two paintings.

www.hrgiger.com

Necromancer

MOURNFUL MELODIES
FOR DARKNESS

Chaotic Aeon

Military Wife
ENGINEERED FOR WAR

Dramafall
Foreshadow Seasons

ГАЛЕРЕЯ СНОВ

PROMO '98

CENOTAPH

f/windowpane
walking in the rain

MORBIUS

Ominous Eyes
DEUS MORTIS
OMINOUS EYES
LADO "A"
1- JUDGMENT DAY SUNRISE (INTRO)
2- ASSASSIN INSTINCTS
3- OMINOUS
5- ERRANT LEGION
LADO "B"
1- PRESENT FROM GOD
2- THE DAY EARTH VOMITED HER HORRORS
3- THE GREAT WHORE
4- SAME DESTINATION: DEATH

BEN SEBANELL
SLITHER

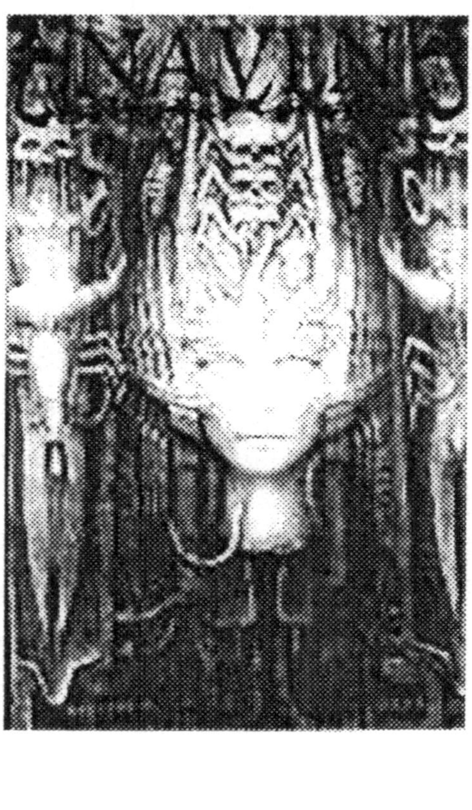

Whores of Babylon
ETERNAL

Ars Notoria

MOROK

THE DEATH METAL

T I T A N I U M

FALSE LIGHT GARDEN

ANSIA DE VOMITO

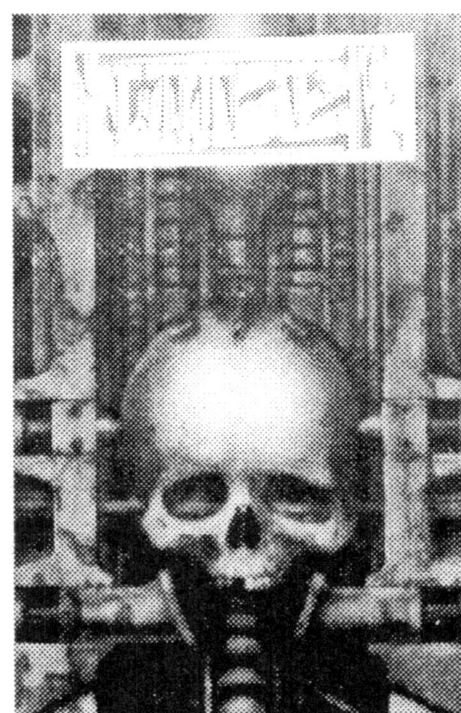

LED ZEPPELIN

SLAYER

DAWN OF IMMORTALITY

Soulless
Spirit of Damnation

BLACK SABBATH
DIES IRAE

Visions
Of

OUR
ALMIGHTY
LORDS

Dark Millennium

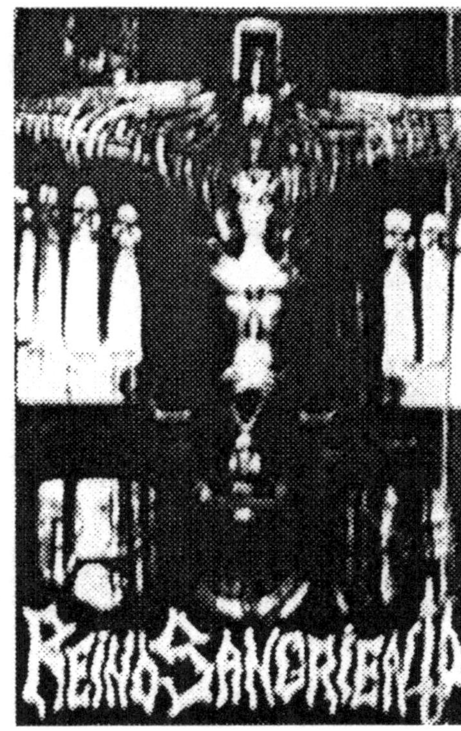
REINO SANGRIENTO

ORTHODOX

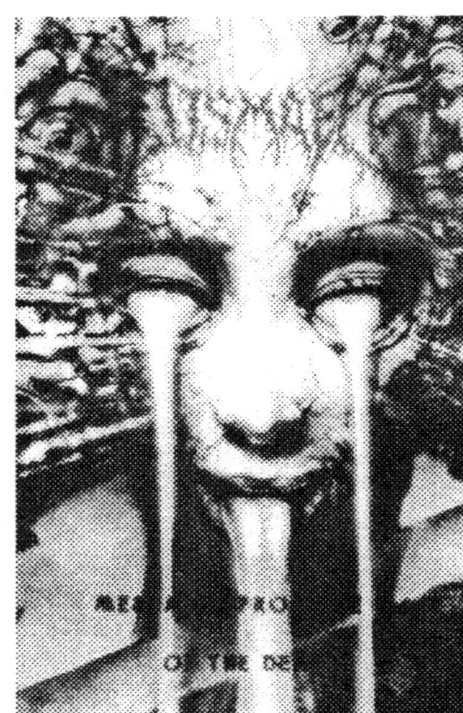

TECHNOPOLIS
VOL. I

TECHNOPOLIS
VOL. II

TECHNOPOLIS
VOL. III

TECHNOPOLIS
VOL. IV

TECHNOPOLIS
VOL. V

TECHNOPOLIS
VOL. VI

TECHNOPOLIS
VOL. VII

TECHNOPOLIS
VOL. VIII

TECHNOPOLIS
VOL. IX

TECHNOPOLIS
VOL. XII

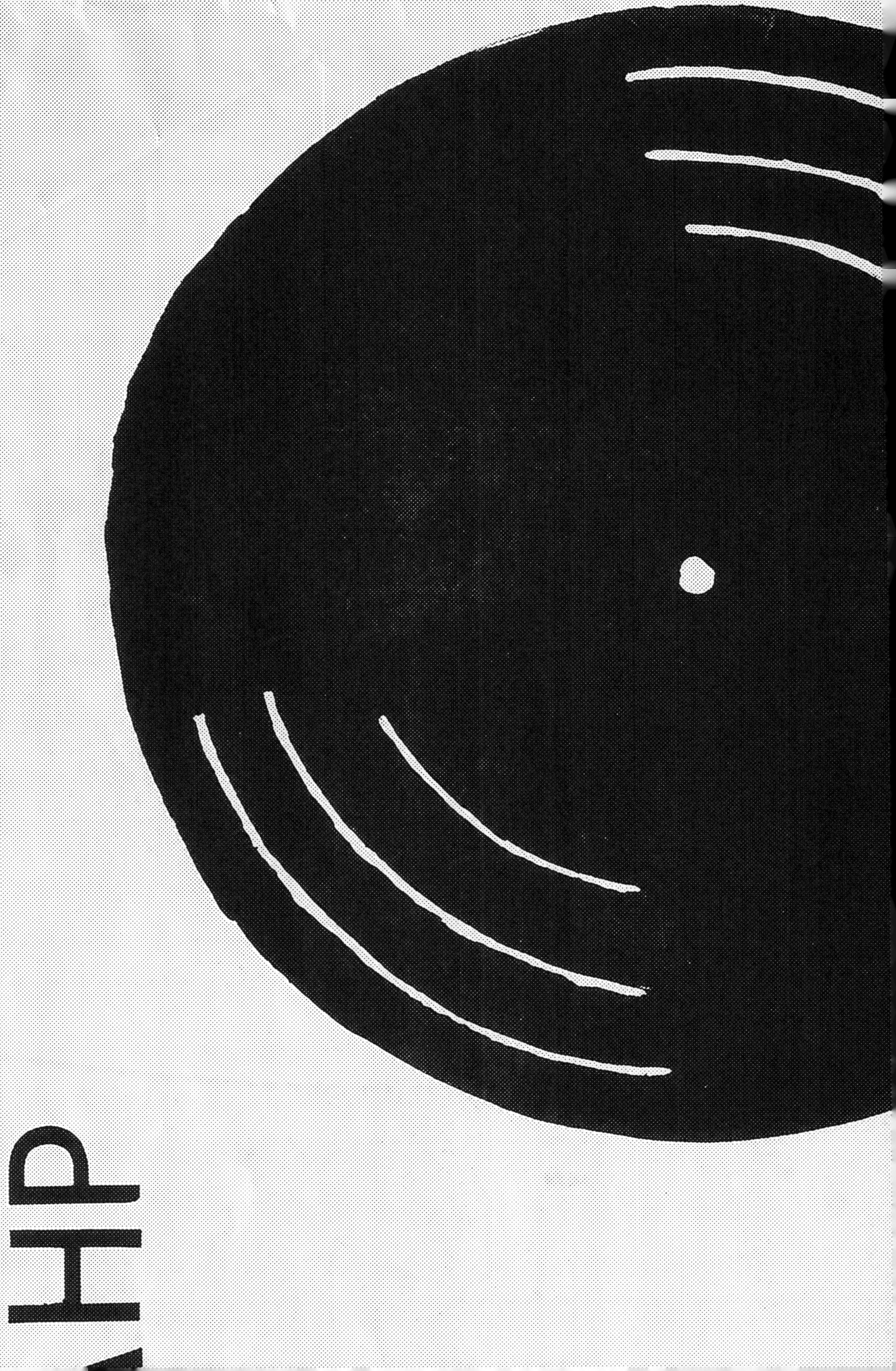

SCHALLPLATTEN

LADEN

BEI DER SCHIPFE
SIEHE SKIZZE

IM LADEN FUER SIE:
REGGAE JAMAICA DIREKTIMPORT

PUNK ROK GB UND USA
NEUE WELLE TECHNO

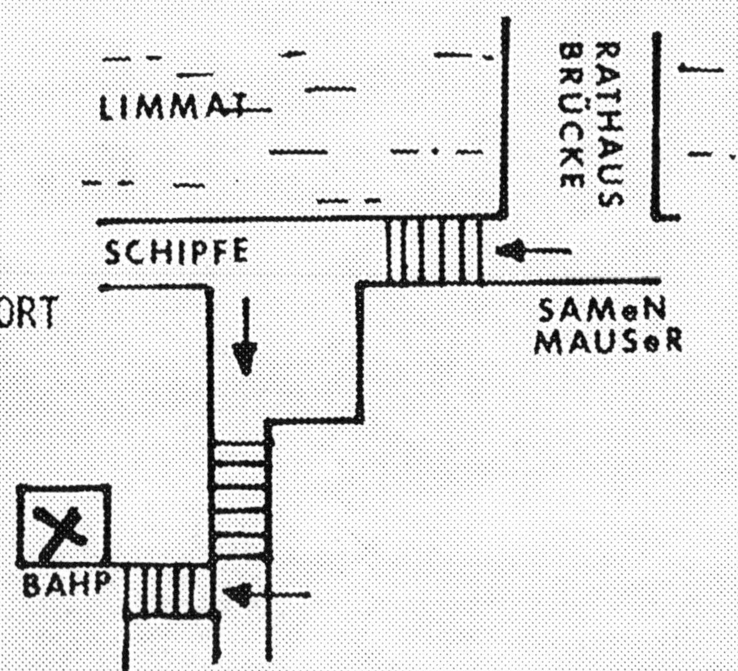

VERTRIEB

BAHP RECORDS DISTRIBUTION
POSTFACH
8021 ZUERICH
SWITZERLAND

VERTRIEB AUF BAHP LABEL:
KLEENEX HERTZ NOVAK
BEANS SURVIVORS RED CRAYOLA

Peter Fischli, Stephan Eicher

Peter Fischli studierte von 1975–1977 an der Academia di Belle Arti in Urbino und in Bologna. Er kam nach Zürich zurück, als aus New York und London erste Ausläufer einer neuen Musik- und Kunstbewegung mit dem Namen «Punk» die Schweiz erreichten. Im Sog dieses Umfelds gestaltete er Plakate und Schallplattencover für befreundete Bands und Musiker wie Kleenex/ Liliput, Hertz, Expo und Rudolph Dietrich.

Stephan Eicher absolvierte ab 1979 an der F+F Kunstschule in Zürich die Videoklasse. In dieser Zeit spielte er bei der Band Noise Boys und lernte, auf den ersten Musikcomputern zu komponieren. Im Jahr darauf wurde er Mitglied bei Grauzone. Zur selben Zeit erschienen seine ersten Musikkassetten und Schallplatten, deren Umschläge er selber gestaltete. Für seine weiteren Tonträger kooperierte er bis Ende der Achtzigerjahre gestalterisch mit Peter Fischli, David Weiss, Klaudia Schifferle, Urs Steiger, Martin Byland und Luciano Castelli.

Peter Fischli, Stephan Eicher

Peter Fischli studied from 1975 to 1977 at the Academia di Belle Arti in Urbino and in Bologna. He returned to Zurich, when the first offshoots of a new music and art movement from New York and London called "punk" reached Switzerland. In the undertow of this environment he designed posters and record covers for bands or musician friends such as Kleenex/Liliput, Hertz, Expo and Rudolph Dietrich.

Stephan Eicher was enrolled in the video class at the F+F Kunstschule in Zurich as of 1979. During this time, he played in the band Noise Boys and learned to compose on the first music computers. The following year he became a member of Grauzone. At the same time, his first music cassettes and records were released, for which he did the graphic designs himself. For his subsequent releases until the end of the eighties he cooperated artistically with the likes of Peter Fischli, David Weiss, Klaudia Schifferle, Urs Steiger, Martin Byland and Luciano Castelli.

PETER FISCHLI, KLEENEX, HERTZ, 1979, 293×420

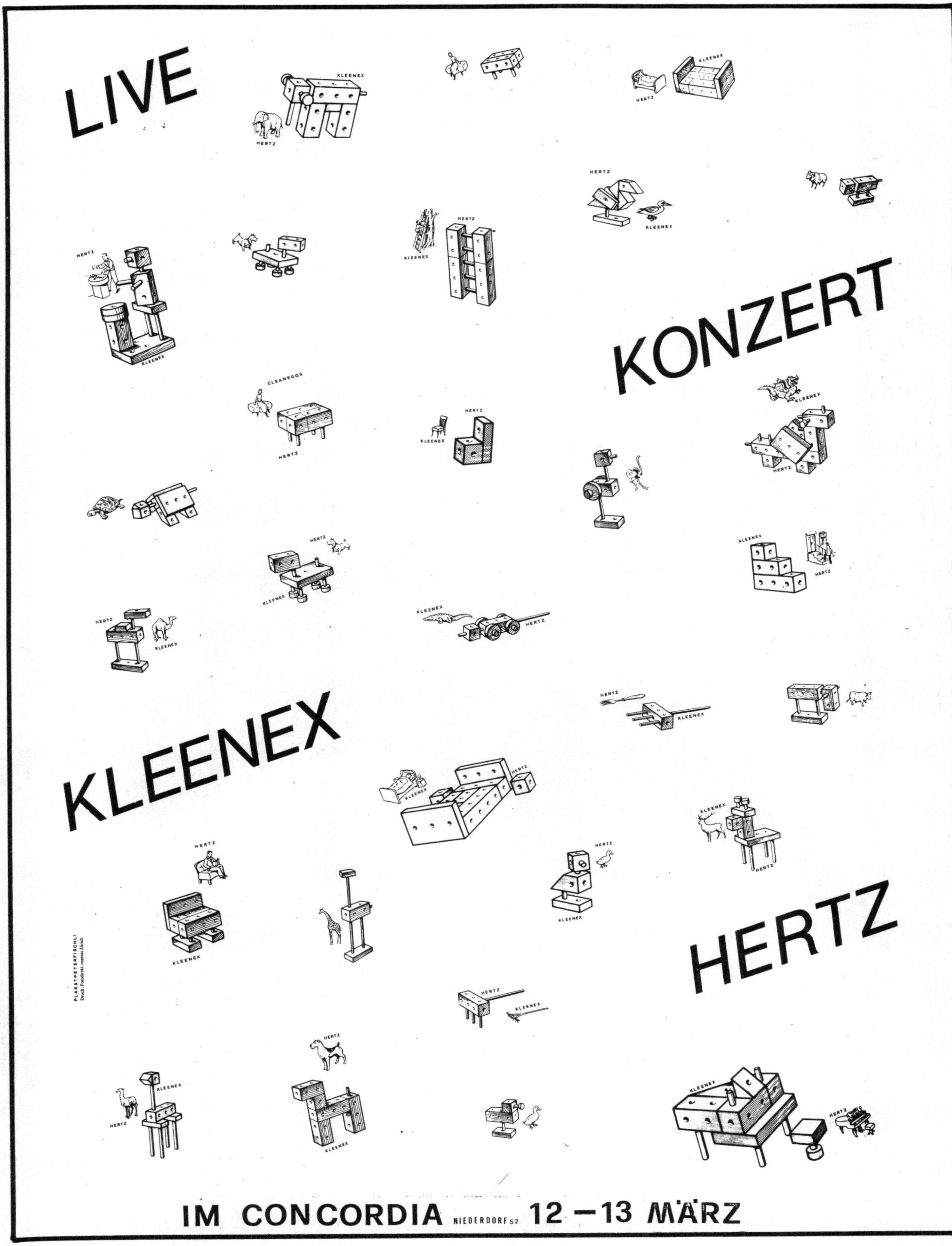

PETER FISCHLI & PIETRO MATTIOLI, KLEENEX - BERI-BERI, 7″ PROMO, 1978, 420×297

their impact is due to the personalities of the musicians
rent from each other.. There is an ironically lascivious drummer.
a (●) who when on stage just about manages to suppress her
lamourous) laugh, there is the singer, Regula Sing (●) with
itive and expressive matter-of-factness, Marlene Marder (●),
, who contributes a mixture of gentleness and opposition to
up and baseist Klaudia Schiff (●), who shows what sophisti-
in plastic age means.

It is nice to hear that Alan Lewis of SOUNDS writes: "really, this is one of the best records I've heard this year," and when he goes on: "if Kleenex can do it on stage they'll go down a bomb", we can answer without hesitation: "they will!"....

CURIGER & CASTELBERG

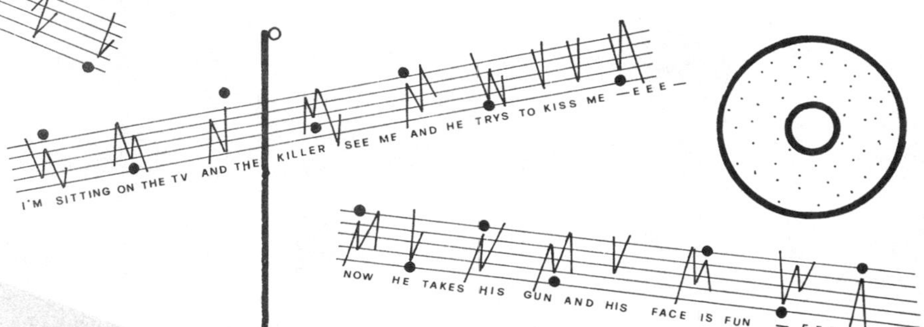

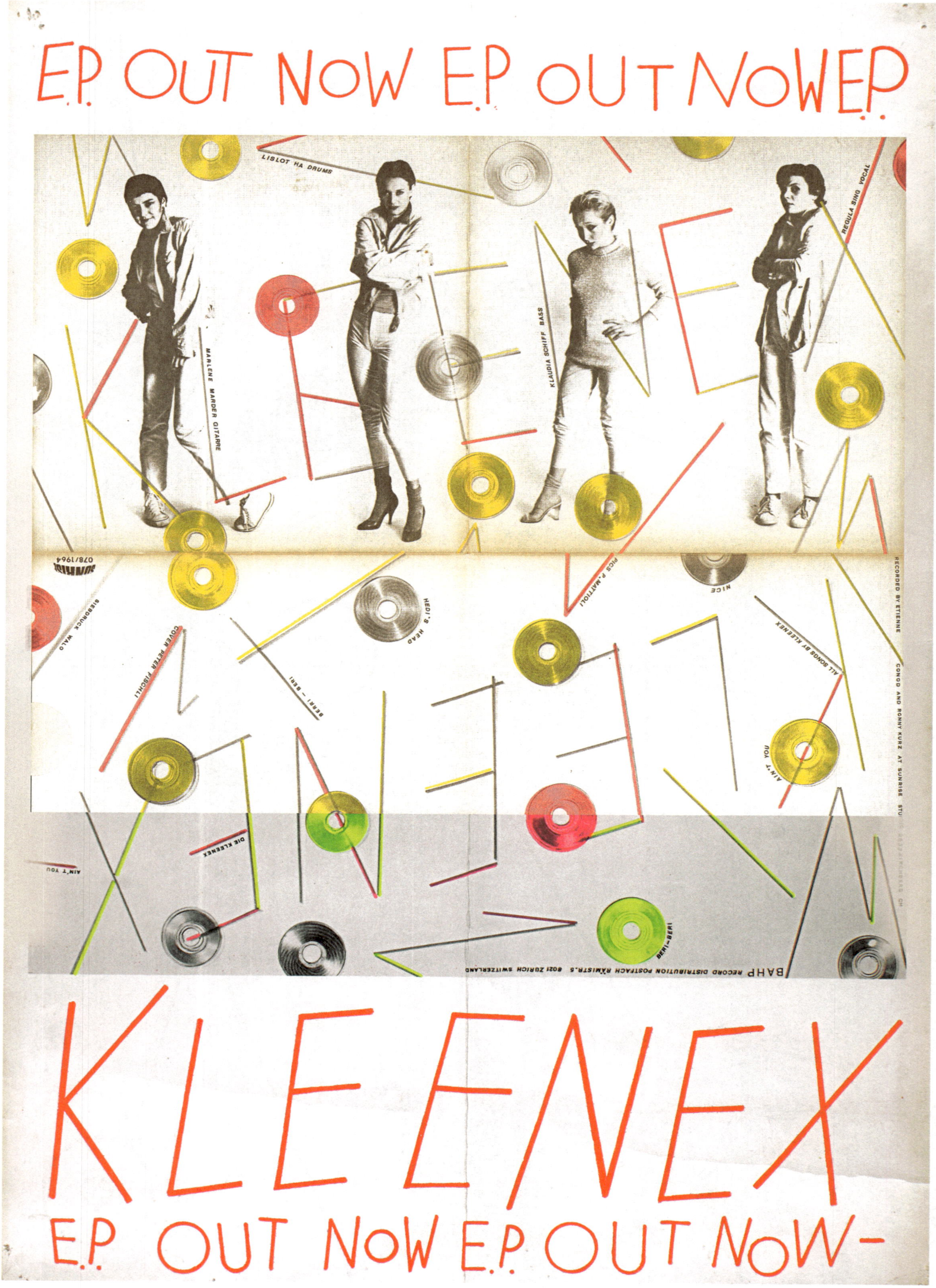
E.P. OUT NOW E.P. OUT NOW E.P.
LISLOT HA DRUMS
MARLENE MARDER GITARRE
KLAUDIA SCHIFF BASS
REGULA SING VOCAL
KLEENEX
E.P. OUT NOW E.P. OUT NOW -

Kleenex – «Art-Punks»

Pin-up Nr. 6/7 / Februar 1979:
Neulich hatte ich ein langes Gespräch mit Kleenex-Mastermind und Grafikberater Peter Fischli – der ein langjähriger Freund von der Bassistin Klaudia Schifferle ist ... Fischli hat das Kleenex-Logo entworfen, dies war zu der Zeit das Erste, was ich von der Band wahrgenommen hatte. Eine irgendwie seltsam kindliche aussehende Schrift, wie aus einer Clearasil-Werbung der frühen Sechzigerjahre, die dort im Hintergrund wie moderne Hieroglyphen aussieht (wie die bei den Vorhängen im Esszimmer, als wir noch SEHR kleine Jungs waren ...). Die Grafik zu einem Plakat zu einem der ersten Auftritte der Kleenex vereinnahmte mich stark, wobei auch eine gewisse Ähnlichkeit mit dem grafischen Auftritt von Devo zu sehen ist. Peter erklärte umgehend, dass man diese Art der Beschriftung erhält, wenn man «normale» Schriftzeichen durch ein Videogerät zieht. Unser Gespräch geriet somit zunehmend zu einem technischen Informationsaustausch – solche Themen interessieren mich ja auch sehr! Wie auch immer. Peter bezeichnete den modern-naiven Schriftzug als ein «unfertiges Produkt», als «work in progress». Dieser evoziert «Instabilität», so wie wenn du die Stäbe eines Mikado-Spiels auseinanderfallen lässt und dann versuchst, die «Message» zu entziffern. Was dabei herauskommt, ist eine Art primitives Alphabet ... und das alles, sagte Peter, ist charakteristisch für Kleenex.

Pin-up Nr. 8/9 / April 1979:
Okay, ich habe einen Fehler gemacht. Ich beschrieb in meinem ersten Teil die Band Kleenex als «Art-Punks», dies, nachdem ich ein langes Gespräch mit dem Kleenex-Grafiker Peter Fischli geführt hatte, der ein langjähriger Freund der Bassistin Klaudia ist. Und das ist genau das, was die vier Frauen NICHT sein wollen! Sie wollen, dass die Band für Spass und Unterhaltung steht, für Freude und Zufriedenheit, und vor allem für den Körper und NICHT für den Geist. Und während ich dies schreibe, habe ich die Worte von Klaudia noch in meinem Ohr, wie sie sagt, dass sie «von der Kunst angewidert» sei. Kleenex soll im Leben der vier Musikerinnen und im Leben von ihren Fans eine echte Alternative zu den altmodischen Kunstkonzepten sein. Und auch wenn es Künstler gibt, die einfach das machen, was sie wollen, die etablierte «Kunst»-Szene scheint derzeit nur Dreck für Kleenex zu sein. Und überhaupt, es wird einfach sooo viel geredet – was fehlt, ist die Aktion. Alle die kreativen Menschen sitzen allein in ihrer kleinen Ecke, dort produzieren sie etwas, und es gibt keine soziale Interaktion mit ihrer Kreativität. Dies wird erst später geschehen, wenn das Produkt fertig ist und der Künstler selbst herumrennen muss, um seine Werke zu verkaufen und eine Ausstellung zu organisieren.

Nachdem ich mit einigen Mitgliedern von Kleenex gesprochen hatte, war es offenkundig, dass sie untereinander intensive Gedanken und Gespräche über das Thema «Kunst» ausgetauscht hatten.

Bob Fischer (gekürzte Version)

Kleenex — "Art punks"

Pin-up No. 6/7 / February 1979:
The other day I had a long conversation with Kleenex mastermind and graphic counselor, Peter Fischli, who is a long-standing friend of bass player and backing vocalist, Klaudia Schifferle ... Fischli designed the Kleenex logo, which, at the time, had been the first thing to make me take notice of the band. A somehow strange lettering consisting of childish-looking characters, like a Clearasil advert in the early sixties, printed against a backdrop of modern-looking hieroglyphs (much like the curtains of our dining room when we were VERY little boys ...). The artwork on a poster advertising one of the first Kleenex gigs interested me intensely as it also bore some resemblance to the graphical imagery of Devo. Peter immediately explained that this sort of lettering was obtained by feeding "regular" characters through a video machine — at once we were involved in a technical discourse — as this sort of stuff usually catches my fervent interest! Anyhow, the "modern-naive" lettering outlines what Peter calls an "unfinished product," or, something "in progress." It evokes "instability," comparable to throwing the little sticks in a game of Mikado and attempting to decipher the "message." The result is a type of primitive alphabet ... and all this, Peter said, is characteristic of Kleenex.

Pin-up No. 8/9 / April 1979:
Ok, I made a mistake. In the first section, I described the band Kleenex as "art punks" — after a long conversation with Peter Fischli, the graphic designer of Kleenex, who is also a long-standing friend of the band's bass player, Klaudia. But that is exactly what the girls do NOT want to be! They want the group to stand for fun and entertainment, for pleasure and satisfaction, and above all for the body, and NOT the mind. As I am writing this, Klaudia's words still sound in my ears, when she says that she is "disgusted by art." In the life of the four musicians and in the lives of their fans, Kleenex should be a real alternative to the old-fashioned concepts of art. Even though there are artists who simply do the things they like to do, in Kleenex' world the whole established "art" scene appears as nothing but rubbish. Anyway, "there's just way too much talk — what's missing is the action. The creative individuals all work for themselves in their own little corner, creating products void of social interaction with their creativity. This only takes place later on, when the product is finished and the artist is hustling around trying to sell his stuff and organizing exhibitions."

So, having talked to some of the Kleenex girls, it became very clear that they had exchanged deep thoughts amongst each other and had profound conversations on the subject of "art."

Bob Fischer (abridged version)

KLEENEX SPIELEN AM 29.3 IM HEY-CL

BEIM BELLEVUE UM 21oo BIS 2oo OFFEN
© BY P.RASCHLI

HERTZ
PLAKATPETERFISCHLI
HIER IHRE SINGLE: DER MOND, DAS SCHICKSAL
DAHP RECORD DISTRIBUTION' POSTFACH 8021 ZUERICH

PETER FISCHLI, BAHP RECORDS, 1979, 440×620

PETER FISCHLI, KLEENEX, 1979, 213×295, PHOTOCOPY & PENCIL

PETER FISCHLI, LILIPUT & SPERMA, 1980, 293×420

PETER FISCHLI & PETER WITTWER & KATJA BECKER, LILIPUT, 7″, 1980

PETER FISCHLI, KLEENEX, 7″, 1979

PETER FISCHLI, EXPO, LP, 1978

PETER FISCHLI & PETER WITTWER, LILIPUT, 7", 1980

FISCHLI & WITTWER & SCHIFFERLE, LILIPUT, 7", 1982

PETER FISCHLI & DAVID WEISS, LILIPUT, LP, 1983

KLAUDIA SCHIFFERLE, LILIPUT, LP, 1983

STEPHAN EICHER, STEFAN EICHER – SPIELT NOISE BOYS, EP PROMO, 1980, 210×297, PHOTOCOPY

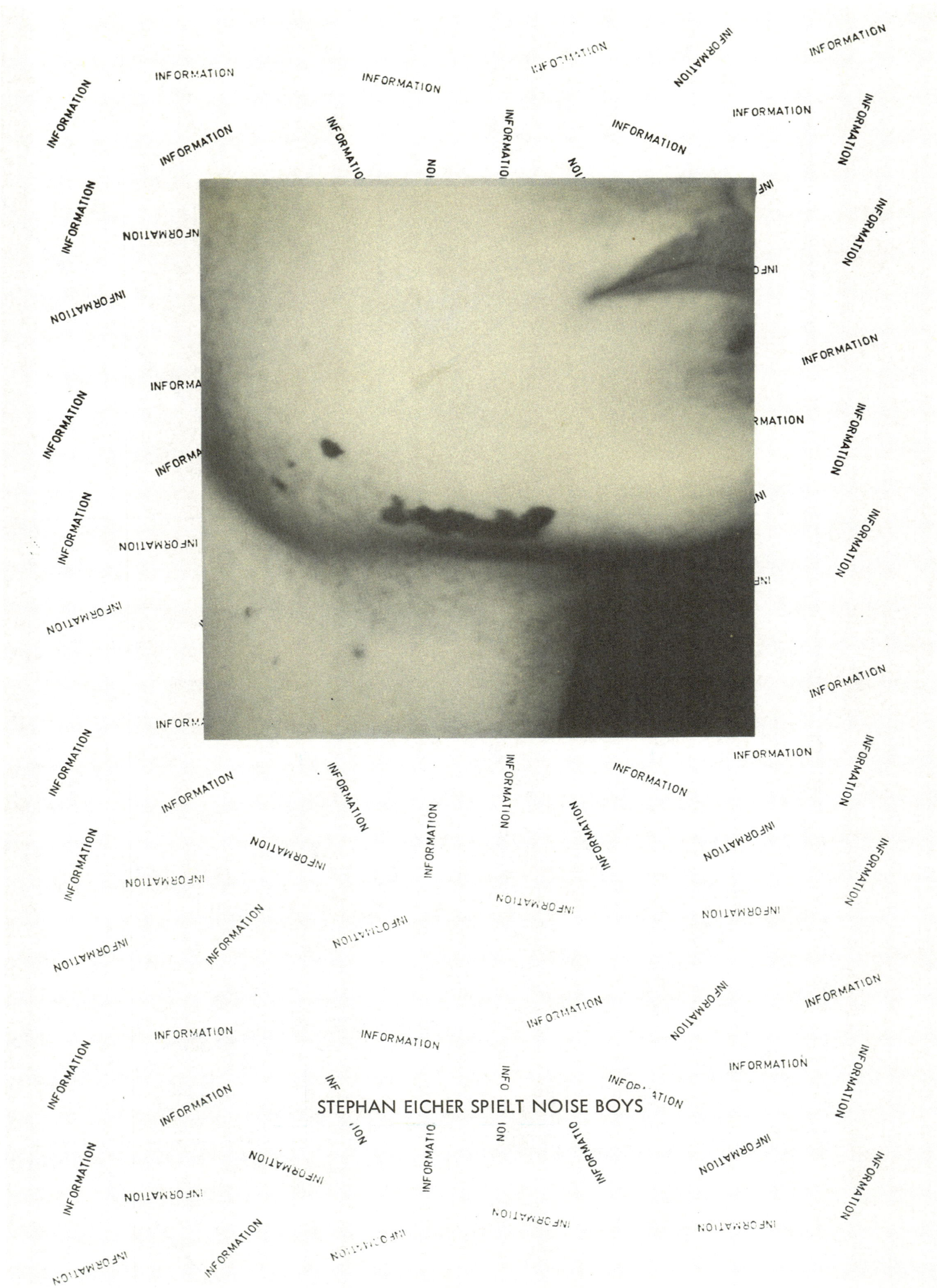
INFORMATION
STEPHAN EICHER SPIELT NOISE BOYS

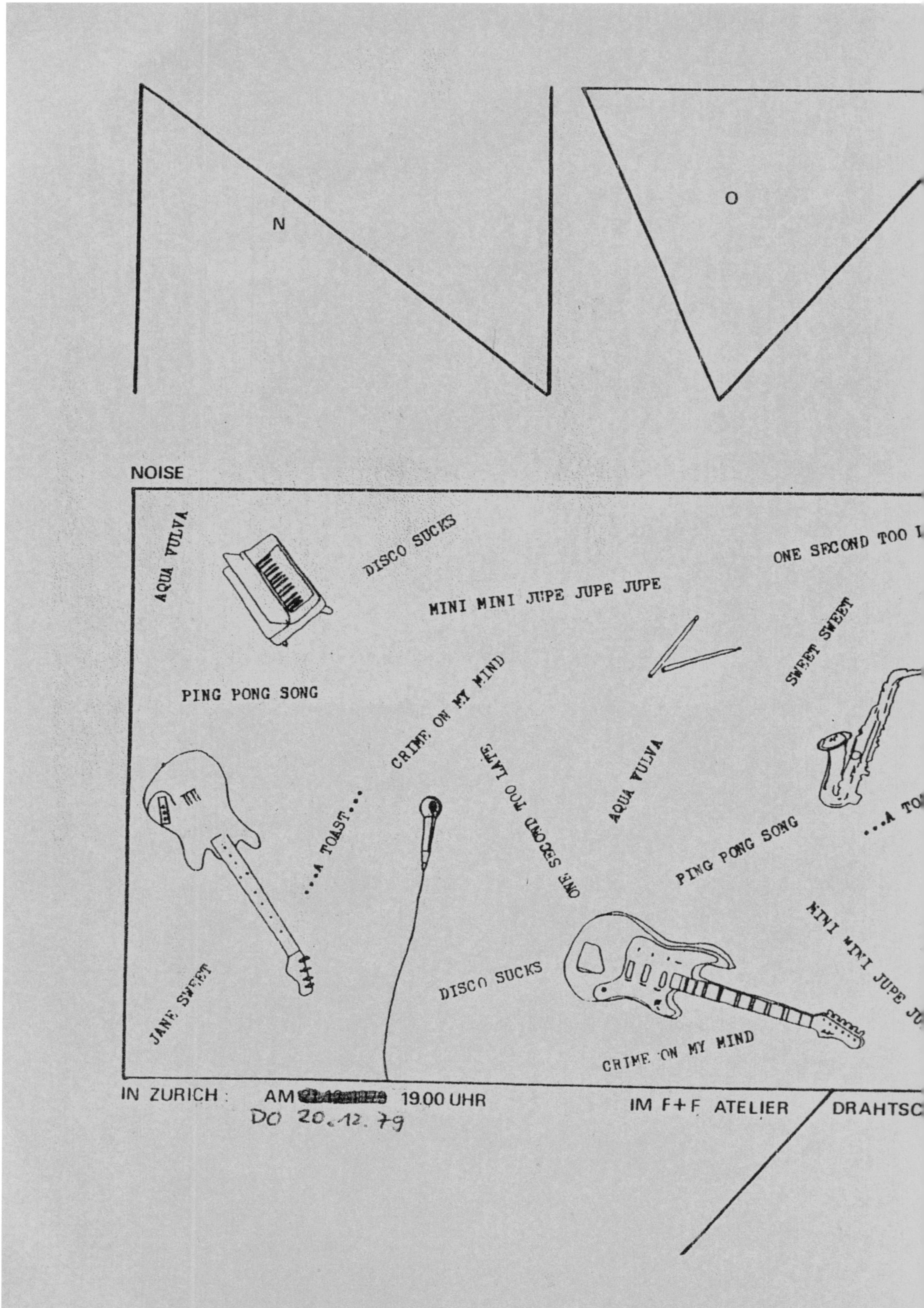
N
O
NOISE
AQUA VULVA
DISCO SUCKS
ONE SECOND TOO L
MINI MINI JUPE JUPE JUPE
SWEET SWEET
PING PONG SONG
CRIME ON MY MIND
ONE SECOND TOO LATE
AQUA VULVA
...A TOAST...
PING PONG SONG
...A TO
MINI MINI JUPE JU
JANE SWEET
DISCO SUCKS
CRIME ON MY MIND
IN ZURICH : AM 19.00 UHR
DO 20.12.79
IM F+F ATELIER
DRAHTSC

IN BERN : AM 29.12.1979 21.00 UHR (F+F AUSSTELLUNG)AK GALERIE OLMO LAUPENS

STEPHAN EICHER, GRAUZONE – EISBÄR/ICH LIEBE SIE, 12″, 1981

MAI
ZÜRI PUNX
Sperma

Lurch

VOLCAN

Urs Steiger, Martin Byland, Peter Wittwer

Martin Byland, Grafiker bei Graphis Annual, gründete Ende 1978 zusammen mit dem Fotografen Peter Wittwer das unabhängige Schallplattenlabel Off Course Records. Byland war mehrheitlich für das Erscheinungsbild des Labels und dessen Tonträger zuständig, Wittwer steuerte die dazu benötigten Fotos bei. Im Herbst 1980 erschien in Kooperation mit Urs Steigers Another Swiss Label, der auch für das erste Schweizer Punkfanzine *No Fun* zuständig war, der Sampler *Swiss Wave – The Album*. Darauf befand sich nicht nur Grauzones epochaler Song «Eisbär», der stellvertretend für das Lebensgefühl der damaligen Jugend stand – das Album prägte auch den Ausdruck «Swiss Wave», der einen eigenständigen Schweizer Musikstil definierte. Auf Off Course, dass dann auch mit Urs Steigers Another Swiss Label fusionierte, erschienen in der Folge einige der wichtigsten Plattenproduktionen der Schweizer Punk-, Wave- und Postpunkszene.

Urs Steiger, Martin Byland, Peter Wittwer

Martin Byland, graphic artist working for Graphis Annual, founded at the end of 1978 the independent label Off Course Records, together with the photographer Peter Wittwer. Byland was mostly in charge of the label's appearance and that of the recorded media. Wittwer contributed the required photographs. In the Autumn of 1980 and in cooperation with Urs Steiger's Another Swiss Label — who was also responsible for *No Fun*, the first Swiss punk fanzine — the compilation *Swiss Wave — The Album* came out. Not only was the epochal song "Eisbär" (by Grauzone on this record) representative of the youths' attitude towards life in those days, this album also established the term "Swiss Wave" as a distinct music style. Subsequently, some of the most important record productions of the Swiss punk, wave and post punk scene were released through Off Course, having also merged with Urs Steiger's Another Swiss Label.

URS STEIGER & PETER PREISSLE, HINTERBERGER'S WUT, 1980, 300×425

NO FUN
...Chaos...Volcan...Szene Genève...Wire...Red Crayola...
U.K. Subs...Cuddly Toys...Rudolph Dietrich...TNT...Mother's Ruin....
NR.16
...REGGAE-SPECIAL...REGGAE-SPECIAL...REGGAE-SPECIAL...REGGAE-SPECIAL...
FR. 2.-
DM 3.-
Nr. 16 April 1979
NO FUN erscheint monatlich
PC 80-36485 Peter Preissle, Hügelstr. 11, 8002 Zürich

URS STEIGER, NO FUN FANZINE NO.4, 5, 13, 17, 1978-1980, 210×297

PUNK
NASAL BOYS & DOG
& PUNK RECORDS FREIT
20 UHR I
EINTRIT
VORVER

ODYS
23. 12. 77
RAHTSCHMIDLI
FR. 7.70
AUF:
MUSIK MARKET
Bäckerstr.58
BOOSTER
Stüssihofstatt
RGANISATI ON
NO FUN
N NO FU
FREE & VIRGIN AGENCY

URS STEIGER, SPERMA, SOZZ, VOLCAN, 1979, 310×443

URS STEIGER, TNT, CHAOS, MOTHER'S RUIN, 1979, 310×443

YOUNG PEOPLES
HEY
TREND CLUB
DIENSTAG MITTWOCH
FREITAG SONNTAG
CLUB HEY FREIECKGASSE AM BELLVUE
FOTO PIETRO MATTIOLI
ART & DESIGN MARTIN BYLAND

HEY – Young Peoples Trend Club

Im Dezember 1976 eröffnete die Schweizerische Organisation der Homosexuellen den Club HEY unterhalb des Nobelclubs Mascotte an der Freieckgasse beim Bellevue in Zürich. Anfangs fehlten besonders unter der Woche die Besucher. Rudolph Dietrich, der Gitarrist der ersten Schweizer Punkband Nasal Boys, wurde deswegen bei den Betreibern vorstellig. Kurz danach wurde der Mittwochabend im HEY die erste Spielwiese für Punks hierzulande. Am 18. Mai 1977 dann der erste Auftritt der Nasal Boys vor Ort. Kurz darauf stiessen die Macher des Fanzines *No Fun*, Urs Steiger & Peter Preissle, sowie die zukünftigen Off-Course-Labelbetreiber Martin Byland und Peter Wittwer dazu. Bis in den Sommer '78 war das HEY *der* Ort für die lokale Punkszene schlechthin.

Im Frühling 1978 fing ich meine Lehre als Dekorateur an. Ein Feierabend-Treffpunkt bei den Dekorateuren war die Kon-Tiki Bar im Niederdorf. Dort trafen sich auch Teile der Punk/Wave- und neuen Kunstszene Zürichs. Der Weg von dort zum HEY war nicht weit, und eines Abends stand ich vor dessen Eingang. Im Programmkasten hing das hier abgebildete Plakat, das eigentlich nur die Besucher des HEY darstellte und dazu den Slogan «HEY Young Peoples Trend Club». Das Plakat hinterliess bei mir bis zum heutigenTag einen nachhaltigen Eindruck, und ich erhielt von Martin Byland, der für die Gestaltung zuständig war, ein Exemplar.

Am 13. Juni 1979 war Schluss mit Punk im HEY. Von nun an ersetzten Reggae und Black Music den Punkabend (dies notabene bis zur Schliessung des HEY im Jahr 2011). Reggae Music sprach breitere Kreise von Jugendlichen an, und ihre Sprengkraft war nicht zu unterschätzen. Bei weiten Teilen der Jugend war die Unzufriedenheit über lange Zeit gewachsen und die Geduld am Ende. Die Erwachsenengesellschaft wollte partout nicht verstehen, dass sie bei der Gestaltung ihres Lebens selbst Einfluss nehmen wollten und dafür ihre eigenen Freiräume benötigten.

Im Sommer desselben Jahres stürmte ich mit ein paar hundert weiteren Personen das Konzert von Peter Tosh im Zürcher Volkshaus. Dies unter anderem wegen des hohen Eintrittspreises, ebenso war es aber so was wie ein Probelauf für das, was noch kommen sollte ... «Get Up, Stand Up» war einer seiner bekanntesten Songs, den Peter Tosh zusammen mit Bob Marley geschrieben hatte. Als er selbst mitten im Tumult beim Eingang erschien und meinte, «alle können reinkommen», war dies für uns eine kleine Bestätigung, dass die Musik mit ihrer Sprengkraft etwas bewegen konnte. Im Jahr darauf, in der Nacht vom 30. Mai, als der grosse Bob Marley sein Konzert im Hallenstadion mit den Worten «Get up, stand up, stand up for your rights» beendete und Teile der Besucher im Tram via Durchsage der VBZ von den ersten Demonstrationen (Auslöser der Achtziger-Jugendunruhen) am Limmatquai hörten, stürzten sich nicht wenige am Central oder Bellevue in die Schlacht.

2005 erschien das Fotobuch mit dem Titel *1977* des Künstlers Pietro Mattioli. Er war damals selbst Teil der Szene gewesen und hatte fotografisch über ein Jahr hinweg die Besucher des HEY porträtiert. Diese Porträts

HEY — Young Peoples Trend Club

In December 1976, the Swiss Organization of Homosexuals opened the HEY club beneath the ritzy Mascotte club on Freieckgasse near Bellevue in Zurich. In the beginning there weren't many visitors, especially on weekdays. Rudolph Dietrich, guitarist of the first Swiss punk band, Nasal Boys, afterwards presented himself to the club managers. A short time later, Wednesday evenings at the HEY club became the initial playground for punks in Switzerland. On May 18, 1977, the Nasal Boys finally performed there for the first time. Shortly afterward, Urs Steiger and Peter Preissle, the producers of the *No Fun* fanzine, as well as Martin Byland and Peter Wittwer, the future managers of the Off Course label, also joined in. Until the summer of 1978, the HEY club was the absolute hot spot of the local punk scene.

In the spring of 1978, I began my apprenticeship as a display artist in Zurich. One place where we met after work was the Kon-Tiki Bar at the Niederdorf. Parts of Zurich's punk/wave and new art scene also used to meet there. It didn't take long to walk from there to the HEY and on one evening I found myself standing at the entrance. The poster you can see here, showing actual visitors to the Hey club accompanied by the slogan "HEY Young Peoples Trend Club," hung in the program showcase of the club. I received a copy from Martin Byland, who created the design, and the impression the poster made on me has remained strong to this day.

The end of punk at the HEY came on June 13, 1979. From then on, reggae and black music replaced the punk evenings (and did so until the HEY closed in 2011). Reggae music addressed broad circles of young people, and its explosive power should not be underestimated. Among many young people, dissatisfaction had been growing for a long time, and their patience had reached an end. Adult society simply ignored that we, the youth of the era, wanted to decide on how we wanted to shape our lives ourselves, and that we needed a free space to do so.

In the summer of the same year, I forced my way into the Peter Tosh concert at the Volkshaus in Zurich along with some hundred other people because of the high ticket prices, among other things. At the same time, this was something like a trial run for what was still to come ... "Get Up, Stand Up" was one of Peter Tosh's most popular songs, which he had written in collaboration with Bob Marley. When he himself then appeared in the midst of the turmoil saying "everyone can come in," it was a confirmation to us that music with its explosive power could make a difference. The following year, on the night of May 30, the great Bob Marley ended his concert at the Hallenstadion singing the words, "Get up, stand up, stand up for your rights." Some of the people who had attended the concert later heard about the first demonstrations on the Limmatquai — the catalyst for the youth unrest in Zurich at the beginning of the eighties — by way of an announcement made by the VBZ public transport operator. Many got off the trams at the Central and Bellevue stops, and threw themselves into the fray.

In 2005, artist Pietro Mattioli's photo book with the title *1977* was published. He was also part of the scene at

wurden immer frontal, als Brustbild, hart geblitzt, vor monochromen Wänden im und um den Club herum (vom WC bis zum Hofbereich) aufgenommen. Im Buch befinden sich teilweise dieselben Fotos wie auf unserem Plakat. Vermutlich erfuhren die Betreiber des HEY aus der Presse von der bevorstehenden Buchvernissage in der Galerie Art Magazin im Kreis 4, denn sie deponierten knapp dreissig Jahre später vor dem Eingang der Galerie eine Rolle der Plakate, die sich noch im Putzkasten befunden hatten.

Zur selben Zeit, als Pietros Buch erschien, arbeitete ich am Buch *Hot Love* über den Schweizer Punk & Wave, das im Herbst 2006 erscheinen würde. An einem Mittwochabend kam ich zufällig mit einigen Bekannten am Club HEY vorbei und konnte diese überreden, dort kurz reinzuschauen. Im Programmschaukasten befand sich noch immer eines dieser Originalplakate; *HEY Young Peoples Trend Club!* Ich konnte es fast nicht glauben!

Am Mittwoch – wann den sonst? –, dem 13. Oktober 2010, feierte André Gulewicz, der ehemalige Bassist der Punkband Mother's Ruin, mit zahlreichen Punks aus den Anfangszeiten, Freunden und mit der jungen Punkband Swamp Things im HEY seinen fünfzigsten Geburtstag. Zum letzten Mal vor der Schliessung des Clubs im März 2011 traf man sich im HEY. Die Betreiber des HEY sind in die Nähe des Bahnhofs Oerlikon umgezogen und ihr Club heisst heute HEY CITY.

Lurker Grand

the time and took photographic portraits of visitors at the HEY for more than a year. His portraits were always shot front on as half-length images, using a hard flash in front of monochrome walls in and around the club (from the toilets to the courtyard area). In part, the book contains the same photos as the poster does. Presumably, the people running the HEY club heard about the upcoming book presentation at the gallery Art Magazin in the Kreis 4 district via the press and, nearly thirty years later, they deposited a roll of these posters in front of the gallery.

At the same time as Pietro's book was published, I was working on *Hot Love*, a book about Swiss punk and wave that was published in the fall of 2006. One Wednesday evening I went past the HEY club by chance together with a friend, and I was able to persuade him to take a quick look inside. The original poster, "HEY young peoples trend club!" was still in the program showcase. I could hardly believe my eyes!

On Wednesday (when else?) October 13, 2010, André Gulewicz, former bass player of Swiss punk band Mother's Ruin, celebrated his fiftieth birthday at the HEY along with friends, lots of punks from the early days, and the young punk band Swamp Things. People met up at the HEY for the last time before the club closed in March 2011. The people who ran the HEY have moved to a space near the Oerlikon train station and their club is now called HEY CITY.

Lurker Grand

URS STEIGER & PETER WITTWER, SPERMA – SCHMIER, 12″ INSIDE & PROMO, 1979, 310×452

URS STEIGER & PETER WITTWER, SPERMA, 12", 1979

URS STEIGER & RETO RESSEGATTI, SPERMA, 7", 1980

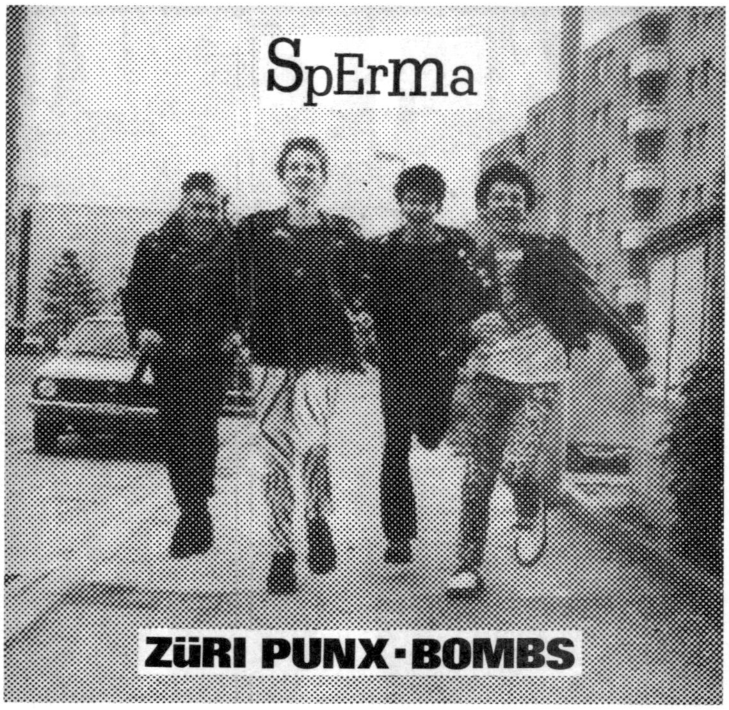

URS STEIGER & PETER WITTWER, SPERMA, 7", 1980

STEIGER & BYLAND & WITTWER, TECHNYCOLOR, 7", 1979

BYLAND & WITTWER & BECKER, MOTHER'S RUIN, LP, 1981

URS STEIGER, JACK & THE RIPPERS, 7", 1979

MARTIN BYLAND & PETER WITTWER, MOTHER'S RUIN, 7", 1979

MARTIN BYLAND & PETER WITTWER, MOTHER'S RUIN, 12", 1979

OFF COURSE
RECORDS
WAN
GET
MOTHER'S RU
SONGBOOK

MOTHER'S RUIN
IORE?
E ALBUM!
IT MORE (ASL-3303) LP AND
W.

SWISS WAVE
presents:
LIVE
KRAFT DURCH FREUDE
INTERNAT. STUDENTS CLUB
7.70 franken
augustinerhof ZÜRICH
20³⁰
OFF COURSE
DO. 28. 2. 80
ANOTHER SWISS LABEL

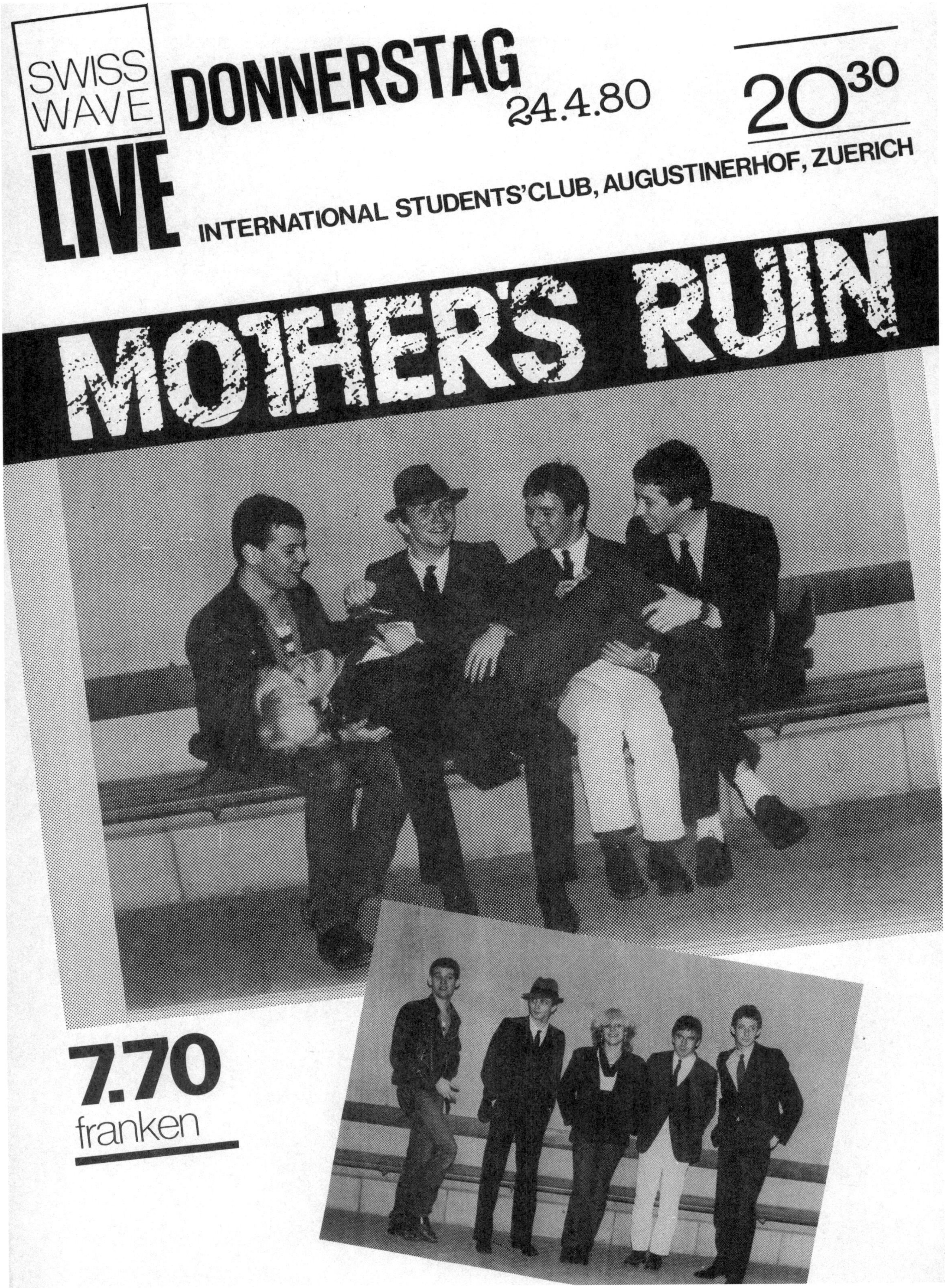

MARTIN BYLAND & PETER WITTWER, MOTHER'S RUIN, 1980, 300×425

IVES PENET & URS STEIGER, TECHNYCOLOR, 1979, 110×150

zürich
shift+++
+videoladen++
+tnt+

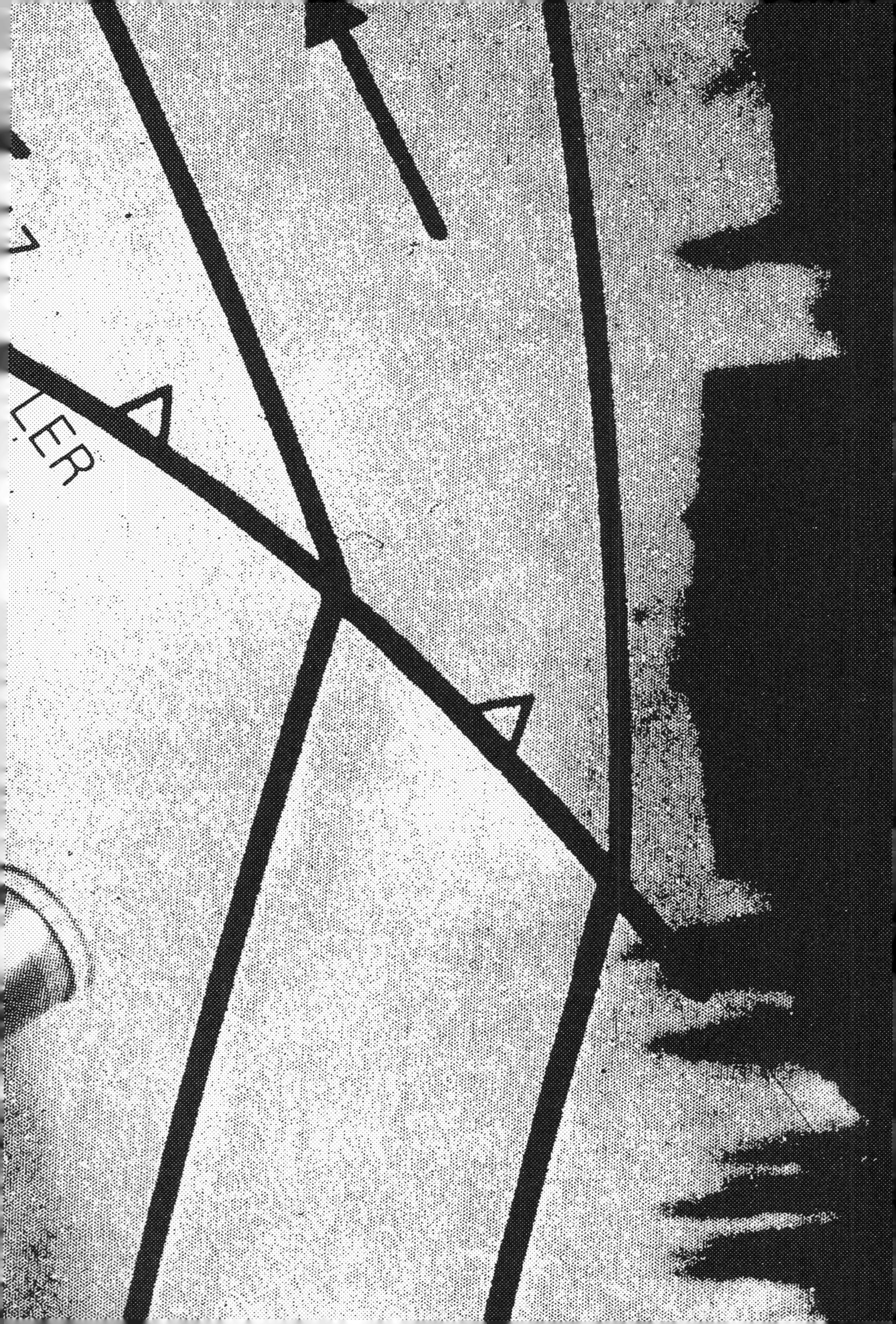
LER

Peter Bäder

Gelernter Hochbauzeichner und Grafiker. Seit den frühen Achtzigerjahren war er zuständig für den visuellen Auftritt von RecRec (Label, Vertrieb und Plattenladen) wie auch für verschiedenste Musikanlässe in der Roten Fabrik in Zürich. Ebenso gehörte er zu den ersten Zeichnern, die ihre Arbeiten im Comicmagazin *Strapazin* veröffentlichten. Bäder identifizierte sich in jener Zeit komplett mit der «Neuen Musik» und gestaltete über ein Jahrzehnt lang Konzertplakate, Platten- und CD-Cover, die bekannten Inseratekleber im *Strapazin* – und vieles mehr. Mitte der Neunzigerjahre lebte er für einige Jahre in Berlin. Als Gestalter setzte Bäder nun «nichtmusikalische» Schwerpunkte – auch, weil sein Umfeld sich veränderte und er sich vorgängig bei seinen Arbeiten im Musikumfeld immer als Player in einem Team verstanden hatte.

Peter Bäder

Trained construction draughtsman and graphic artist. As of the early eighties he was responsible for the visual appearance of RecRec (label, distributor and record shop) as well as various music events at the Rote Fabrik in Zurich. Furthermore, he belonged to the first illustrators that had their works published in the comic magazine *Strapazin*. At the time, Bäder completely identified himself with the "new music" and for over a decade designed concert posters, record and CD covers, the famous advertisement stickers for *Strapazin* and much more. During the mid-nineties he lived in Berlin for a few years. As a graphic designer he then set "non-music" priorities — also, because his surroundings had changed. For his previous work within the music environment he always considered himself as a player within a team.

SONIC
YOUTH NY
and ABT 409
GENEVE
SA
SUN
Sa 20.6. 21.00
Rote FaBRIK
AKTIONSHALLE

PETER BÄDER, GLENN BRANCA GROUP & ART ZOYD, 1983, 440×620

Sonic Youth – Protokoll einer Geburtshilfe

Der pockennarbige, leicht schielende Gitarrist Lee Ranaldo und sein schlacksiges, fast zwei Köpfe grösseres Pendant Thurston Moore spielten im Frühling 1983 erstmals in der Roten Fabrik in Zürich. Sie waren Teil eines zwölfköpfigen Ensembles des New Yorker Noise-Komponisten Glenn Branca. Mit offensichtlich selbst gezimmerten, flügelähnlichen Saitenkästen, deren Klang an frisierte Cembalos erinnerte, veranstaltete das Orchester zusammen mit den beiden jungen Sonic-Youth-Gitarristen und einem Drummer ein unerhörtes Klanggewitter.

Nach dem Soundcheck kamen die beiden Gitarristen auf mich zu. Damals arbeitete ich als Promoter bei Recommended Records und unterstützte das Glenn-Branca-Orchester auf seiner Europa-Tournee. Lee Ranaldo fragte mich, ob ich die erste Sonic-Youth-LP kenne. Selbstverständlich. Die Platte war nichts Besonderes, so und ähnlich klangen damals Hunderte von europäischen und amerikanischen Gitarrenbands (*Sonic Youth*, Neutral Records, 1982). Thurston Moore drückte mir eine Rohpressung in die Hand und meinte nur: «So klingen wir heute» – als hätte er meine Gedanken gelesen (*Confusion Is Sex*, Neutral Records, 1983). Das Album offenbarte ein fantastisches Gewühl aus Gitarrenloops und Feedbackschleifen, frei von jeder gängigen Songstruktur, getrieben von Bob Berts Schlagzeug, übermalt mit Kim Gordons Schreigesang. Brachial-lärmige, stilbildende Musik, wie sich im Lauf der kommenden Jahre weisen sollte. Unschwer erkennbar dabei: der mächtige Einfluss von Glenn Branca.

Ihren Platz in der Geschichte haben sich Sonic Youth aus New York hart erarbeitet. 31 Alben, produziert zwischen 1982 und 2011, zeugen davon. Ihr Einfluss auf die Entwicklung der Rockmusik in den Achtziger- und Neunzigerjahren war immens: So war es Gitarrist Thurston Moore gewesen, der 1990 den Leuten von Geffen Records die damals noch relativ unbekannte Band Nirvana empfahl. Sonic Youth waren es auch, die Anfang der Neunzigerjahre Kurt Cobains Kultband erstmals als Vorgruppe mit auf eine Europa-Tournee nahmen. Überhaupt: Noch zur Jahrtausendwende gab es kaum eine amerikanische Rockband, die sich nicht auf Sonic Youth berief. Es gehörte schon fast zum guten Ton in der Szene. Und konnte auch nerven.

Zurück nach Zürich: Lee und Thurston hatten den Wunsch, mit Sonic Youth erstmals den Sprung nach Europa zu wagen. Ob ich Lust hätte, eine Club-Tournee für sie zu organisieren? Ich war sofort dabei. Warum die Band damals Zürich als «Brückenkopf für die Erstürmung Europas» wählte, bleibt ein Rätsel. Ohne London ging damals nämlich gar nichts: Hatte man die britische Metropole einmal erobert, stand ganz Europa für Konzerte offen. Nur, Sonic Youth gingen ihren eigenen Weg. London nahmen sie wenig später praktisch im Vorbeimarsch ein: mit Pauken, Trompeten und Feedbackgitarren.

Da wartete ich also am Zürcher Hauptbahnhof auf Sonic Youth. Es war Anfang November 1983 und bitterkalt. Zu fünft waren sie direkt aus New York gekommen, mit eigenem Toningenieur und sechs Gitarren im Gepäck (Jahre später hatten sie ihren Sound konzeptionell derart

Sonic Youth — Log of obsterics

The pockmarked, slightly cross-eyed guitarist, Lee Ranaldo, and his slender, nearly two heads taller counterpart, Thurston Moore, played at the Rote Fabrik in Zurich for the first time in the spring of 1983. They were part of New York noise composer Glenn Branca's twelve-piece ensemble. With apparently self-carpentered, grand piano-like cases of strings making tones that brought tinkered harpsichords to mind, the orchestra accompanied by the two young guitarists of Sonic Youth as well as a drummer unleashed an as yet unheard storm of sound.

The two guitarists came up to me after the sound check. At the time I was working as a promoter for Recommended Records, supporting the Glenn Branca orchestra on its European tour. Lee Ranaldo asked me whether I knew the first Sonic Youth LP. Of course I did. The record (*Sonic Youth*, Neutral Records, 1982) was nothing special — hundreds of European and American guitar bands at the time sounded similar. Thurston Moore thrust a raw pressing (*Confusion Is Sex*, Neutral Records, 1983) into my hands and just said: "This is how we sound today" — as if he had read my mind. The album consisted of a fantastic melee of guitar and feedback loops without any conventional song structure, driven by Bob Bert's drum kit, with Kim Gordon's scream-singing on top. Brutally noisy, seminal music, as would become clear in the years to come when the powerful influence of Glenn Branca became clearly recognizable.

With New York as their base, Sonic Youth worked hard to earn their place in history. Thirty-one albums produced between 1982 and 2011 bear witness to this. Their influence on the development of rock music in the eighties and nineties was immense: it was guitarist Thurston Moore who recommended the as yet relatively unknown band Nirvana to the people at Geffen Records in 1990. It was also Sonic Youth that hired Kurt Cobain's cult band as support for a European tour at the beginning of the nineties. To sum it up, at the turn of the millennium, there was hardly an American rock band that didn't refer to Sonic Youth as a major influence. It was almost compulsory in the scene; and it could get on your nerves.

Back to Zurich, Lee and Thurston wanted Sonic Youth to venture to Europe for a first time. Did I feel like organizing a club tour for them? I said yes on the spot. Why the band had chosen Zurich as the "beachhead for conquering Europe" remains a mystery. At that time, nothing went without London: if you conquered the British capital, all of Europe stood entirely open for you to play. But Sonic Youth chose their own path. They took London a short time later by marching in as with a parade, complete with drums, trumpets, and guitar feedback.

So, there I was at the main train station in Zurich waiting for Sonic Youth. It was the beginning of November 1983 and bitterly cold. Five of them were coming directly from New York with their own sound engineer and six guitars in their luggage. (Years later they had fine-tuned their sound concept to such an extent that each individual song used one guitar specifically prepared for it. Once they allegedly dragged thirty guitar

durchgetrimmt, dass sie für jedes Stück eine eigens dafür präparierte Gitarre verwendeten. Da soll es schon mal vorgekommen sein, dass sie an die dreissig Gitarrenkoffer mitschleppten!) Die Band übernachtete bei uns in der WG. Die Kanonenöfen glühten vollrohr. Wir räumten ein Zimmer leer und kleideten es mit versifften Matratzen aus. Es sollte das Basislager für die Tournee werden.

Thurston Moore entpuppte sich als wandelndes Musiklexikon, wusste über alles Bescheid. Das passte wunderbar zu seinem Äusseren: ein College-Student, der unkontrolliert in die Höhe geschossen war. Als die Band 1986 unter dem Namen Ciccone Youth eine EP herausbrachte (mit Mike Watt von Firehose), wunderte ich mich sehr. Ciccone? Musste man das kennen, oder war das eine von Moores obskuren Bands aus dem mittleren amerikanischen Westen? Es stellte sich heraus, dass Ciccone der Mädchenname einer gewissen Madonna war, die just in jenen Jahren zur Popikone heranreifte. Ciccone Youths Version von Madonnas «Into the Groove» hatte nichts mehr mir dem Original gemein. Cuts und Schnipsel der Originalaufnahme wurden defragmentiert und neu zusammengesetzt. Warum aber ausgerechnet Madonna? Lee Ranaldos Antwort ist so nirgends verbrieft: 1981 hätten sich Sonic Youth und Madonna in Manhattans Lower East Side einen Übungsraum geteilt. Sie sei kaum auszuhalten gewesen und habe jede Gelegenheit wahrgenommen, irgendwie bekannt zu werden. Man habe sich dann aber rasch aus den Augen verloren ... Wen wundert's?

Eines von Sonic Youths ersten Konzerten in Europa fand also im November 1983 in Zürichs Roter Fabrik statt. Ein paar Dutzend Neugierige verloren sich im Theatersaal dieses alternativen Kulturzentrums. Das Konzert war laut, lärmig und genial. Einige Tage später spielte die Band in einem Keller der besetzten Häuser am Stauffacher ein *concert sauvage* – und begründete damit auch in Polit-Kreisen ihre Glaubwürdigkeit. Ihre späteren Zürcher Konzerte fanden übrigens alle in ausverkauften Hallen statt. Peter Bäders Konzertplakate zu jenen Gigs gehören zu seinen absolut besten. Er liebte die Band.

In jener Konzertnacht war noch mehr passiert: Es erwies sich, dass nicht nur wir, die Leute von Recommended Records, Sonic Youth als Geburtshelfer in Europa Pate standen – fast retournierten sie uns den Gefallen. Babsi war damals hochschwanger. Dennoch wollte sie sich das Konzert keinesfalls entgehen lassen. Obschon ich während der ersten paar lärmigen Riffs und Loops schützend vor ihr stand, hielt sie es nicht lange aus und eilte heim. Dann, spätnachts, die Band hatte sich bereits ins Matratzenzimmer verzogen, ein gellender Schrei. Ich schreckte auf und sah Babsi im Dämmerlicht mit aschfahlem Gesicht schluchzend inmitten einer sich ausweitenden Blutlache auf dem Bett kauern. Wir fuhren ins Spital, wo sie einige Wochen bleiben musste. Milos kam schliesslich im Januar 1984 gesund zur Welt und ist heute ein fescher junger Mann. Ein echter «Sonic Youth» eben.

Marcus May

cases around with them!) The band stayed overnight with us in our shared apartment. The potbelly stove was glowing red-hot. We cleared out a room and furnished it with some filthy mattresses. This was to be the base camp of the tour.

Thurston Moore turned out to be a walking encyclopedia of music, he knew about simply everything. This matched his appearance to a T, a college student who had shot to the sky without control. When the band brought out an EP in 1986 under the name Ciccone Youth (together with Mike Watt of Firehose), I was quite surprised. Ciccone? Was one supposed to know that name, or was this one of Moore's obscure bands from the American Midwest? It turned out that Ciccone was the surname of a certain Madonna, who was maturing into a pop icon in exactly those years. Ciccone Youth's version of Madonna's "Into the Groove" had nothing in common with the original. Cuts and snippets of the original recording were fragmented and rearranged. But why Madonna of all things? Lee Ranaldo's answer is not actually officially recorded, but ... In 1981, Sonic Youth and Madonna shared a rehearsal space on Manhattan's Lower East Side. She had been difficult to get along with and had taken every opportunity to somehow get known. They then quickly lost touch with her ... hardly surprising!

Hence, one of Sonic Youth's first concerts in Europe was played at the Rote Fabrik in Zurich in November 1983. A mere couple of dozen curious individuals meandered in to the auditorium of this alternative cultural center. The concert was loud, noisy, and inspired. A few days later, the band played in the cellar of one of the squatted houses on Stauffacher — a concert off the record — and, consequently, established their credibility in political circles by doing so. Their later concerts in Zurich incidentally were all played in sold-out venues. Peter Bäder's concert posters for those gigs are among his absolutely best. He just loved the band.

Something else happened on that concert evening. It turned out that not only we, the people of Recommended Records, had been the driving force behind Sonic Youth in Europe as their midwives — they nearly returned us the favor. Babsi, my partner, was in an advanced stage of pregnancy at the time. Nevertheless she didn't want to miss the concert. Although I stood protectively in front of her during the first couple of noisy riffs and loops, she couldn't endure them for too long and hurried home. Then, late that night, when the band had already disappeared into the mattress room, there was a piercing scream. I woke up startled, and in the halflight I saw Babsi with a face pale as ashes, sobbing, huddled on the bed in the middle of a spreading pool of blood. We drove to the hospital, where she then had to stay for some weeks. In January 1984, Milos finally made a healthy entrance to the world and today he is a handsome young man. A true "Sonic Youth" so to say.

Marcus May

PETER BÄDER, SONIC YOUTH & PALERMO, 1989, 425×610

PETER BÄDER, ZÜRI BRÄNNT, 1981, 297×420

PETER BÄDER, DÉBILE MENTHOL – EMILE AU JARDIN PATROLOGIQUE, PROMO LP, 1983, 440×600

KONZERT THE W
THE CASSANDRA C

ATHERMEN AND
OMPLEX
ROTE FABRIK
SA. 24. OKT. 21.00

IMPULS TRAVEL
TEL. 01-271 33 77

BLOOM!
COMIX SHOP
Comics, Cartoons, Bandes-Dessinées
4051 Basel, Theaterpassage, 061/22 66 86

SALINGER AG
WEINBERGSTR. 114 8006 ZURICH TEL. 01-362 16 06 FAX 363 45 70

OFFSETDRUCK- TASCHENBÜCHER- BROSCHÜREN
ADAG
LANDENBERGSTR. 10
8037 ZÜRICH
TEL.01-271 99 22

TALK SHOP
LEHRT SPRACHEN

hors série
>3, rue dizerens >1205 genève >022-29 63 70
librairie B.D.

PETER BÄDER, STRAPAZIN NO.29, 1992, 340×465

PETER BÄDER, REC REC, 1984, 385×440, PLASTIC BAG

PETER BÄDER, SOUNDS!, 1985, 390×480, PLASTIC BAG

PETER BÄDER, PIG BAG & SOPHISTICATED BOOM BOOM, 1982, 440×620

PETER BÄDER, APPENZELLER SPACE SCHÖTTL, 1988, 310×440

PETER BÄDER, M.A.K. FESTIVAL – MUSIK AUSSER KONTROLLE, 1982, 625×445

Druck: Printoset Zürich 202 93 41

PETER BÄDER, CASSIBER, 1981, 440×620

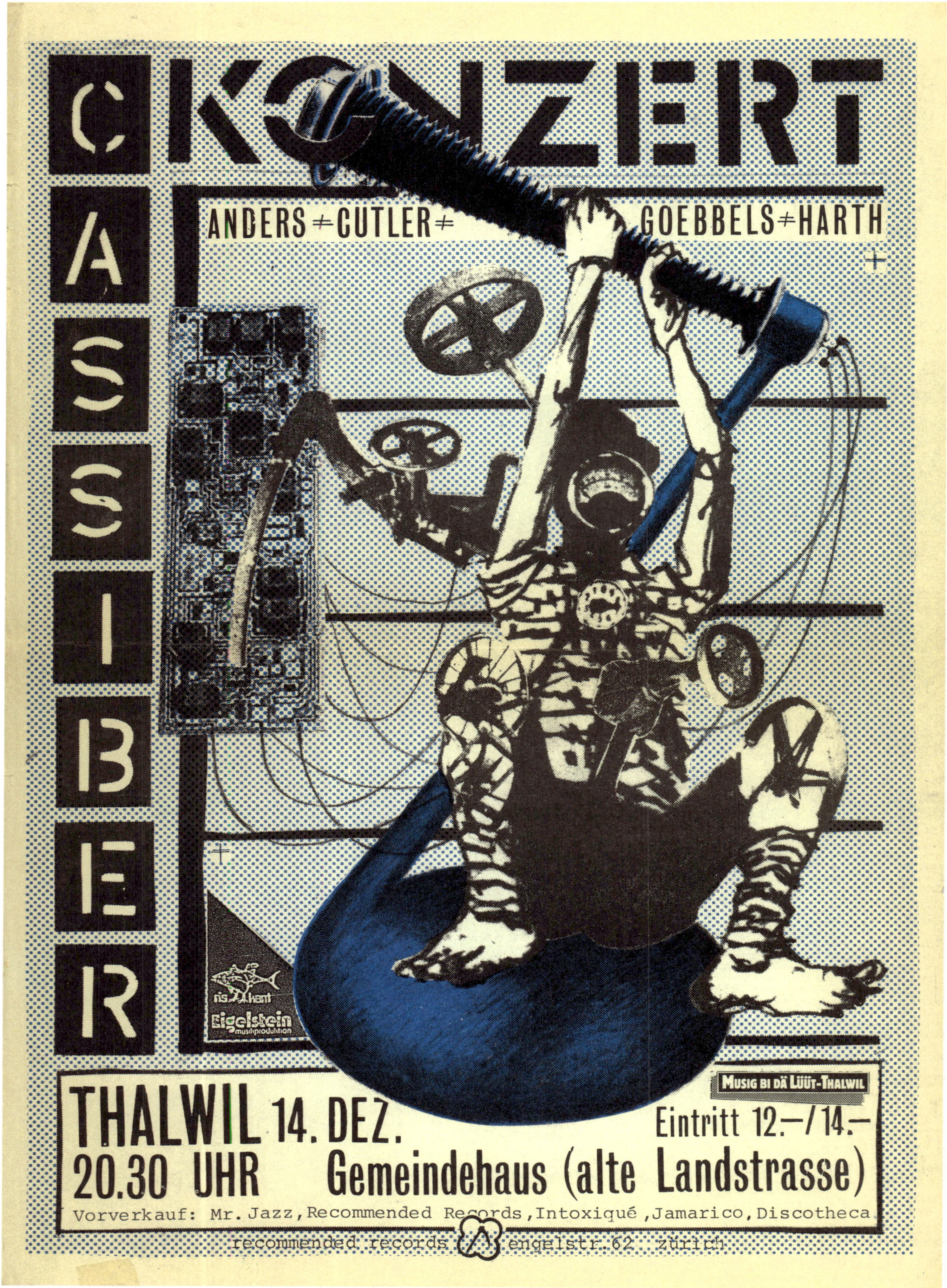

Dirk Bonsma

Der Berner Grafiker Dirk Bonsma lancierte nach einem USA-Aufenthalt Anfang der Achtzigerjahre den Club Boot in der Berner Altstadt. Von diesem Zeitpunkt an war er nicht nur Konzertveranstalter, sondern auch Hausgrafiker im Boot und bald auch beim Veranstalterkollektiv Project Blue, das diverse psychedelische Bands aus den USA und Europa in die Schweiz holte. Sein Stil orientierte sich klar an Vorbildern aus dem amerikanischen Musikuntergrund der Fünfziger- und Sechzigerjahre, doch Bonsma fand bald seinen eigenen, unverkennbaren Stil. Bonsmas Arbeiten fanden sich noch bis in die Neunzigerjahre im Raum Bern (Reithalle), Luzern (Sedel), Fribourg (Fri-Son) und Bikini Test (La Chaux-de-Fonds). 2012 erschien eine Monografie in Buchform unter dem Titel *Ding Dong* – ein Jahr später erhielt Bonsma eine Ausstellung in der Berner Kunsthalle. Bei der Basler Rockband Lombego Surfers ist Bonsma seit Ende der Achtzigerjahre für das visuelle Erscheinungsbild zuständig.

Dirk Bonsma

After a stay in the USA at the beginning of the eighties, the Bernese graphic artist Dirk Bonsma launched the Club Boot in the old quarter of Bern. As of this point, he wasn't just a concert promoter, but also the domestic graphic artist and soon thereafter part of the concert organizing collective called Project Blue, that brought various psychedelic bands from the USA and Europe to Switzerland. His graphical style oriented itself clearly on the paragons of the American music underground of the fifties and sixties, yet Bonsma soon found his own distinctive style. Bonsma's work could be found all the way into the nineties in the vicinity of Bern (Reithalle), Luzern (Sedel), Fribourg (Fri-Son) and La Chaux-de-Fonds (Bikini Test). In 2012, a monograph in the form of a book was published with the title *Ding-Dong* — a year later Bonsma had an exhibition in the Kunsthalle in Bern. For the rock band Lombego Surfers from Basel, Bonsma has been responsible for their visual appearance since the end of the eighties.

DIRK BONSMA, LOMBEGO SURFERS – ALL STRUNG OUT, 2006, 430×635

GOOD NIGHT CHILDREN
SCALPERS
NEW ALBUM «GOOD NIGHT CHILDREN» OUT NOW ON BIG BANG-RECORDS

DIRK BONSMA, MIRACLE WORKERS, CROPMÖNSTERS, 1989, 490×660

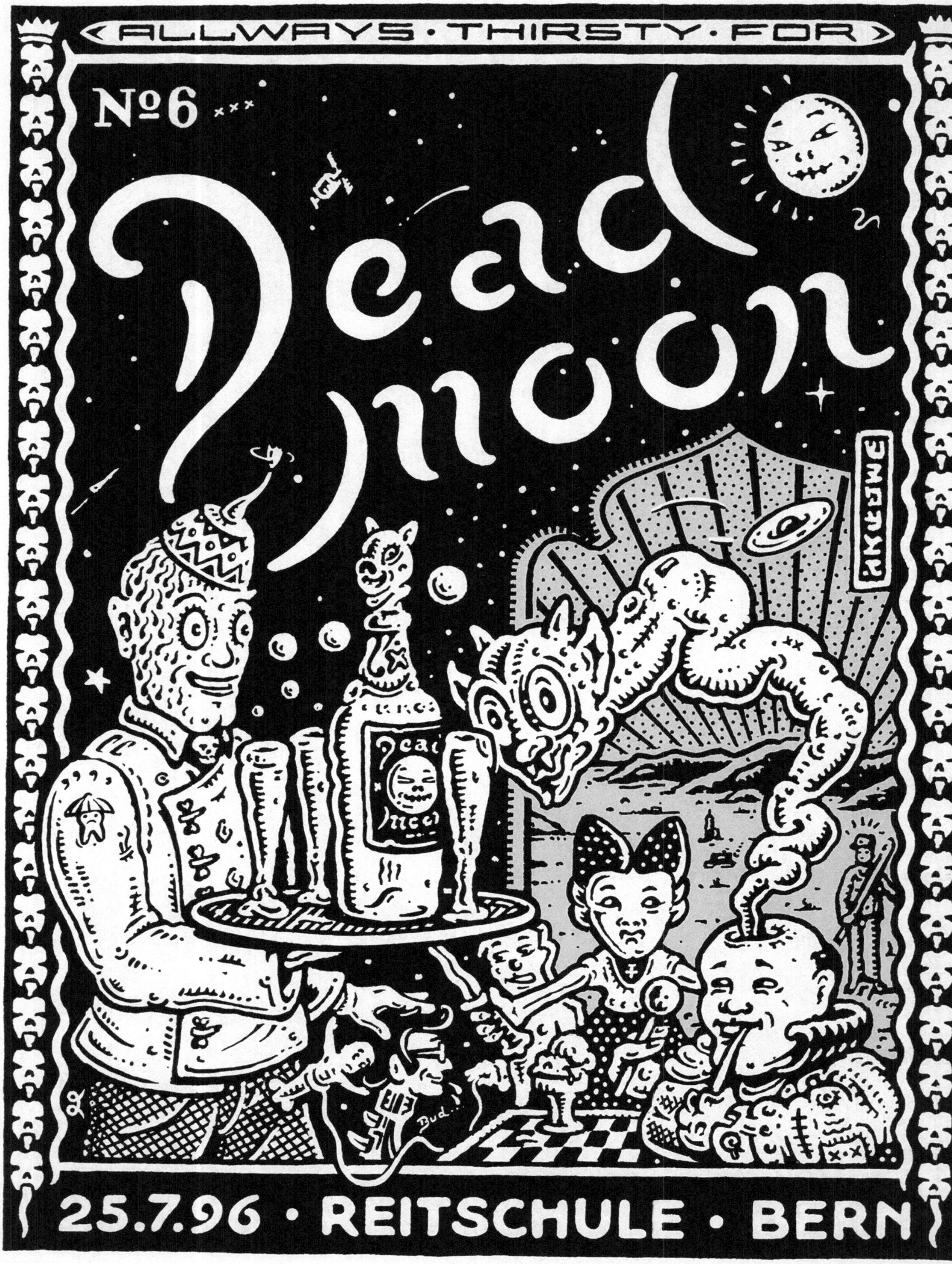
ALLWAYS · THIRSTY · FOR
№6
Dead
moon
25.7.96 · REITSCHULE · BERN

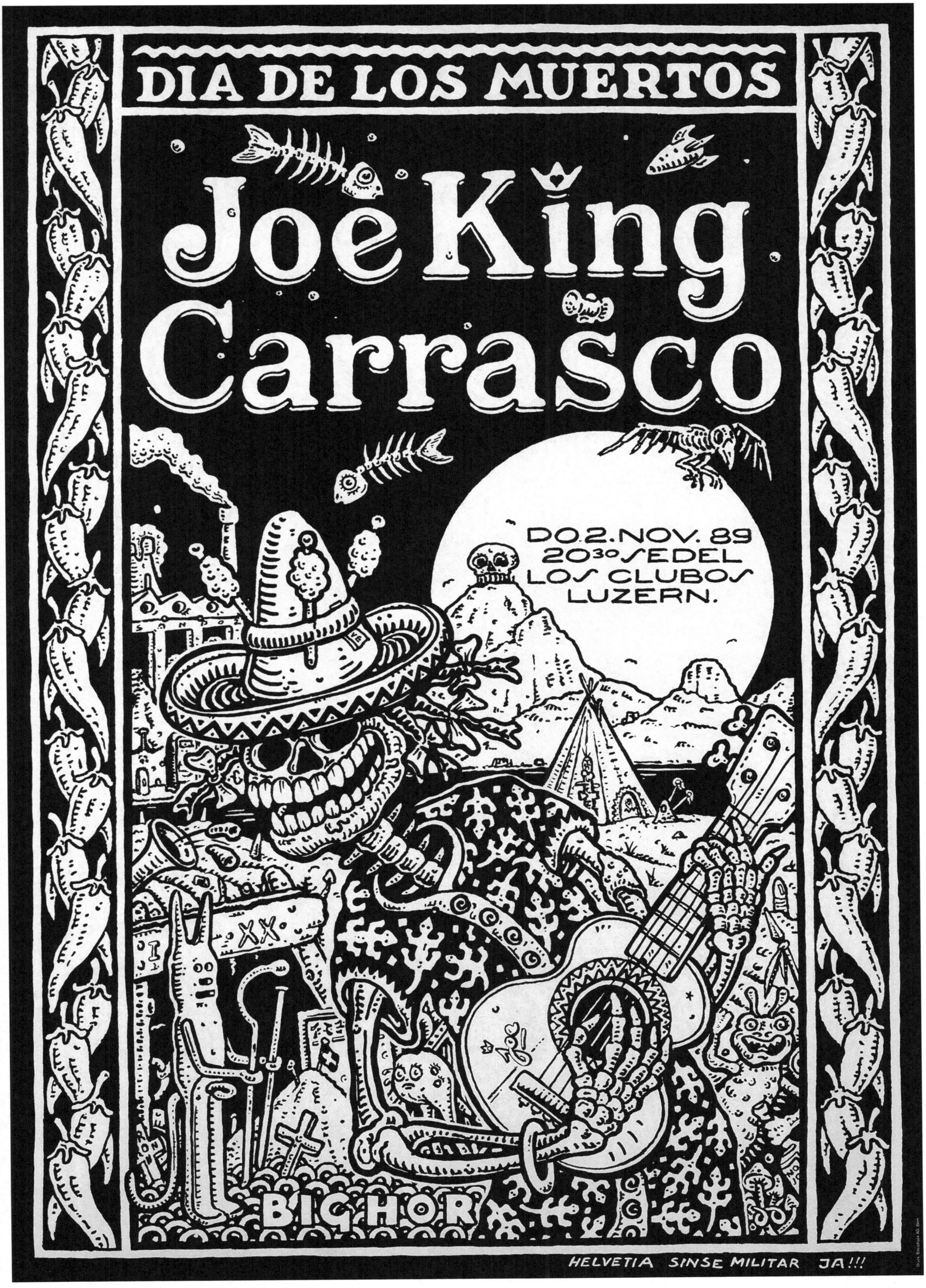
DIA DE LOS MUERTOS
Joe King Carrasco
DO.2.NOV. 89
20³⁰ SEDEL
LOS CLUBOS
LUZERN.
BIGHOR
HELVETIA SINSE MILITAR JA!!!

Project Blue
Dragonslayer
Sky Sunlight Saxon
· Friends: Bishops Daughter · Donnerstag ·
30. März 2030 · Dampfzentrale · Bern
Serigraphie: Albin Uldry

Sky Saxon – Keep it simple!

Der Tag, an dem Michael Jackson starb, war ein trauriger Tag – für Sky-Saxon-Fans. Denn zeitgleich wie der «King of Pop» trat Sky am 25. Juni 2009 seine letzte Reise an, und die Garage-Punk-Szene war um einen genialen Querkopf ärmer. Als Sänger und Texter der Seeds war er in den Sechzigern ein Experte für rohe, berauschende Psychedelicsounds gewesen, Songs wie «Up in Her Room» und «Pushin' Too Hard» begleiteten mich auf allerlei ... naja, whatever. (LP-Tipp: *A Web of Sound*) Und eben dieser Sky Saxon wurde unserer Veranstaltergruppe Project Blue im Januar 1988 angeboten. Niemand wartete zu dieser Zeit auf einen alten Hippiefreak, der mit einer Band namens Dragonslayer sein Comeback versuchte. Umso weniger, da ihm ein Ruf als verschrobener Zeuge Jehovas vorauseilte. Wir haben jedenfalls zugesagt, und etwa sechs Wochen später trudelte die Band in Bern ein ... ohne Sky. Der steckte in Griechenland fest, bad news! Zwei Paniktage später rief seine Agentur an, jemand solle ihn am Flughafen in Zürich abholen. Okay, ich fuhr hin und wartete am entsprechenden Terminal. Braun gebrannte Touris strömten mir entgegen und mittendrin, in wallendem, togaartigem Gewand, Sky mit einer Bouzouki unterm Arm.

Herzliche Begrüssung: «My name is Dirk and I'm from Project Blue.» – «Hi, I'm Sky.» Ein paar Joints, Whiskys und eine Zugfahrt später landeten wir in Bern. Ich wohnte damals mit Freunden in einem grossen alten Rieghaus zwischen den Bahnhofsgleisen und der Murtenstrasse, Sky zog bei uns ein und fühlte sich von Anfang an heimisch. Die Band war im Hotel untergebracht. Der Keyboarder war übrigens Mars Bonfire, hatte bei Steppenwolf gespielt und deren Übersong «Born to Be Wild» komponiert. Ein guter Mensch. Der Rest der Dragonslayer waren allesamt Studiomusiker aus L.A. Wie bei den meisten Project-Blue-Konzerten sorgte ich für ein angemessenes Plakat. Irgendwo hatte ich aufgeschnappt, dass Sky sich an seinem Wohnort auf Hawaii um herrenlose Strassenköter kümmerte, deshalb zeichnete ich eine Art Anubis, umringt von Schmetterlingen, und das Ganze hinter einem Dragonslayer-Raster ... Keep it simple!

Eigentlich hätte das Konzert in der Dampfzentrale Bern stattfinden sollen. Aus irgendwelchen Gründen mussten wir aber in letzter Sekunde nach Thun ins Kühlhaus ausweichen, die Folge war ein unschöner Kleber auf dem Plakat ... aber was soll's. Die Musiker konnten sich jedenfalls in der Zeichnung wiedererkennen, und das Kühlhaus war am Konzertabend proppenvoll. Erstaunlich, weil doch die wenigsten Zuschauer je von dieser Band gehört hatten. Zwei äusserst charmante Jodlerinnen eröffneten die Show: Christine Lauterburg und Josefina Lehmann gaben ihr Bestes, und ein begeisterter Sky jodelte mit oder versuchte es zumindest. Danach heizten die Lokalmatadoren Bishop's Daughter das Kühlhaus auf die richtige Temperatur vor. Die Stimmung war ausgezeichnet und «Sky I swear he was on LSD»-Sunlight-Saxon und die Dragonslayer wussten das zu schätzen. Die Show bleibt unvergesslich. Tage später mussten wir Sky auf Bitten der Band und seiner Agentur überreden, die Tour nicht abzubrechen. Er fühlte sich offensichtlich hier zuhause.

Dirk Bonsma

Sky Saxon — Keep it simple!

The day Michael Jackson died was a sad day — for Sky Saxon fans. Sky left on his final journey on June 25, 2009, at the same time as the "King of Pop" and the garage punk scene was one brilliant, creative mind poorer. As singer and songwriter for the Seeds, he had been an expert on raw and intoxicating psychedelic sounds in the sixties — and songs like "Up in Her Room" and "Pushin' Too Hard" accompanied me while doing all sorts of things ... yeah, whatever. (LP tip: *A Web of Sound*) And it was this Sky Saxon that was offered to Project Blue, our group of event organizers, in January 1988. At that time, no one was waiting for an old hippie freak trying to make his comeback with a band called Dragonslayer. Even less so since a reputation as an eccentric Jehovah's Witness preceded him. Nevertheless we agreed to try and some six weeks later the band rolled into Bern — without Sky. He was stuck in Greece — bad news! Two panicky days later, his agent called and asked for someone to pick him up at the airport in Zurich. OK, I went there and waited at the corresponding terminal. Tanned tourists streamed toward me and, in their midst, in a flowing, toga-like robe, was Sky, with a bouzouki under his arm.

The welcome was warm: "My name is Dirk and I'm from Project Blue," — "Hi, I'm Sky." A couple of joints, whiskeys, and a train trip later, we hit Bern. At the time, I was living with friends in a big, old, half-timbered house between the railroad station tracks and Murtenstrasse, and Sky moved in with us; he felt at home from the start. The band was staying at a hotel. Incidentally, the keyboarder was Mars Bonfire, who had played with Steppenwolf and composed their massive song "Born to Be Wild." A good guy. The rest of Dragonslayer were studio musicians from L.A. As in the case of most Project Blue concerts, I was responsible for making a suitable poster. Somewhere I had picked up the information that Sky took care of stray dogs at his home in Hawaii, which is why I drew a type of Anubis surrounded by butterflies, and super-imposed the whole image with a Dragonslayer raster ... Keep it simple!

The concert should actually have taken place in the Dampfzentrale in Bern. But for some reason, we had to switch to the Kühlhaus in Thun at the last second, and this led to an unsightly sticker on the poster — but what else could we do? At least the musicians were able to recognize themselves in the drawing, and the Kühlhaus was jam-packed on the evening of the concert. This was remarkable as only very few people in the audience had even heard of the band. Two extremely charming yodellers, Christine Lauterburg and Josefina Lehmann, opened the show giving their best and an enthusiastic Sky joined them yodelling — or at least he tried. Afterward, Bishop's Daughter, the local heroes, warmed the Kühlhaus (a former cold store) up to temperature. The mood was excellent and "Sky, I swear he was on LSD"-Sunlight Saxon and Dragonslayer appreciated it. The show remains unforgettable. A few days later, at the band's and his agent's request, we had to persuade Sky not to cancel the tour. Apparently, he felt at home here.

Dirk Bonsma

DIRK BONSMA, LOMBEGO SURFERS, DOUBLE LP, 1990

LOMBEGO SURFERS, LP, 2000

LOMBEGO SURFERS, LP, 2003

LOMBEGO SURFERS, LP, 2010

DIRK BONSMA, LOMBEGO SURFERS, 10", 2012

MANIACS, LP, 1990

LOMBEGO SURFERS, THE FEEBLES, 7", 1996

BODY LOTION, 7", 1984

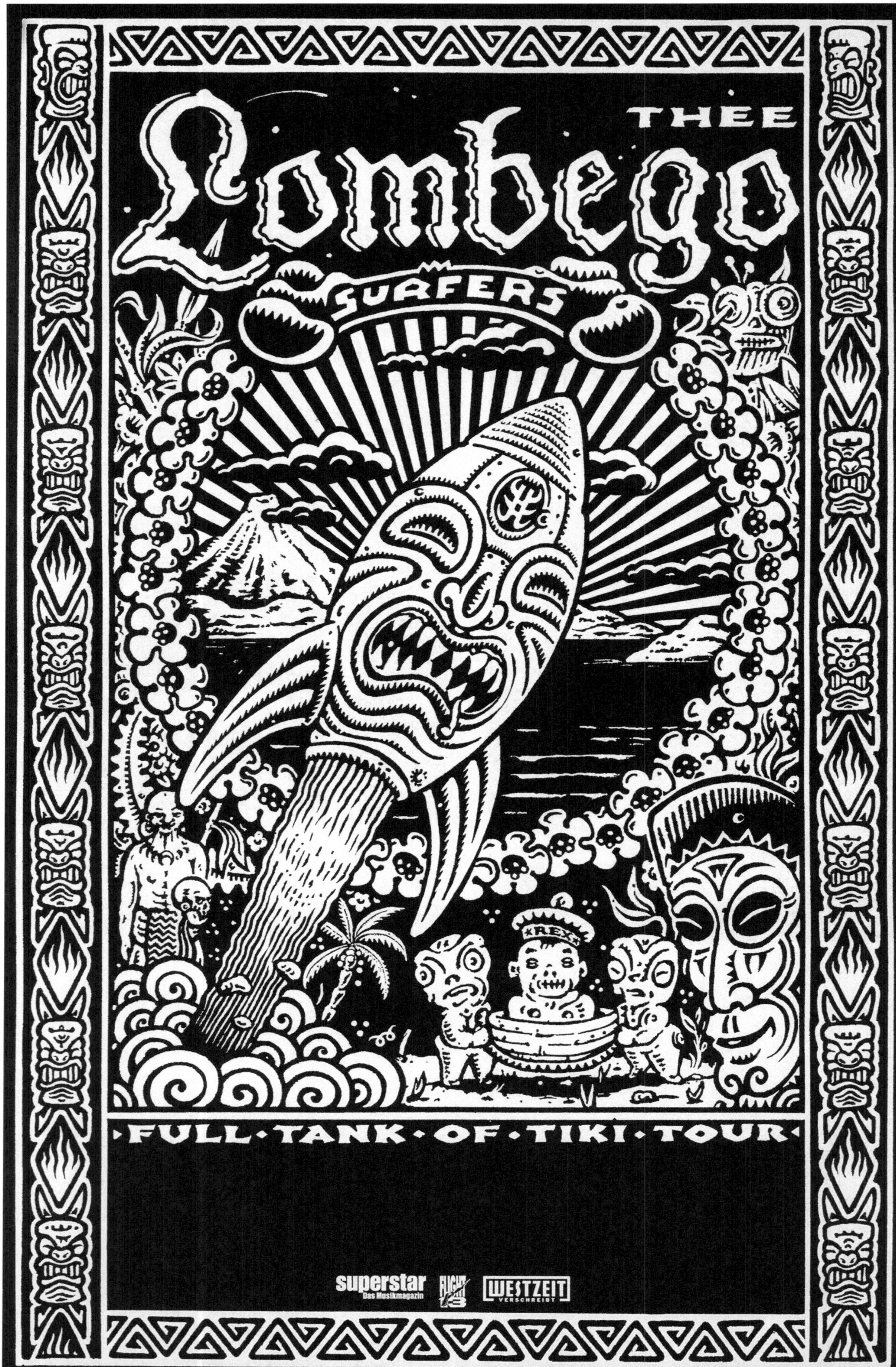
THEE
Lombego
SURFERS
REX
FULL·TANK·OF·TIKI·TOUR
superstar
Das Musikmagazin
WESTZEIT

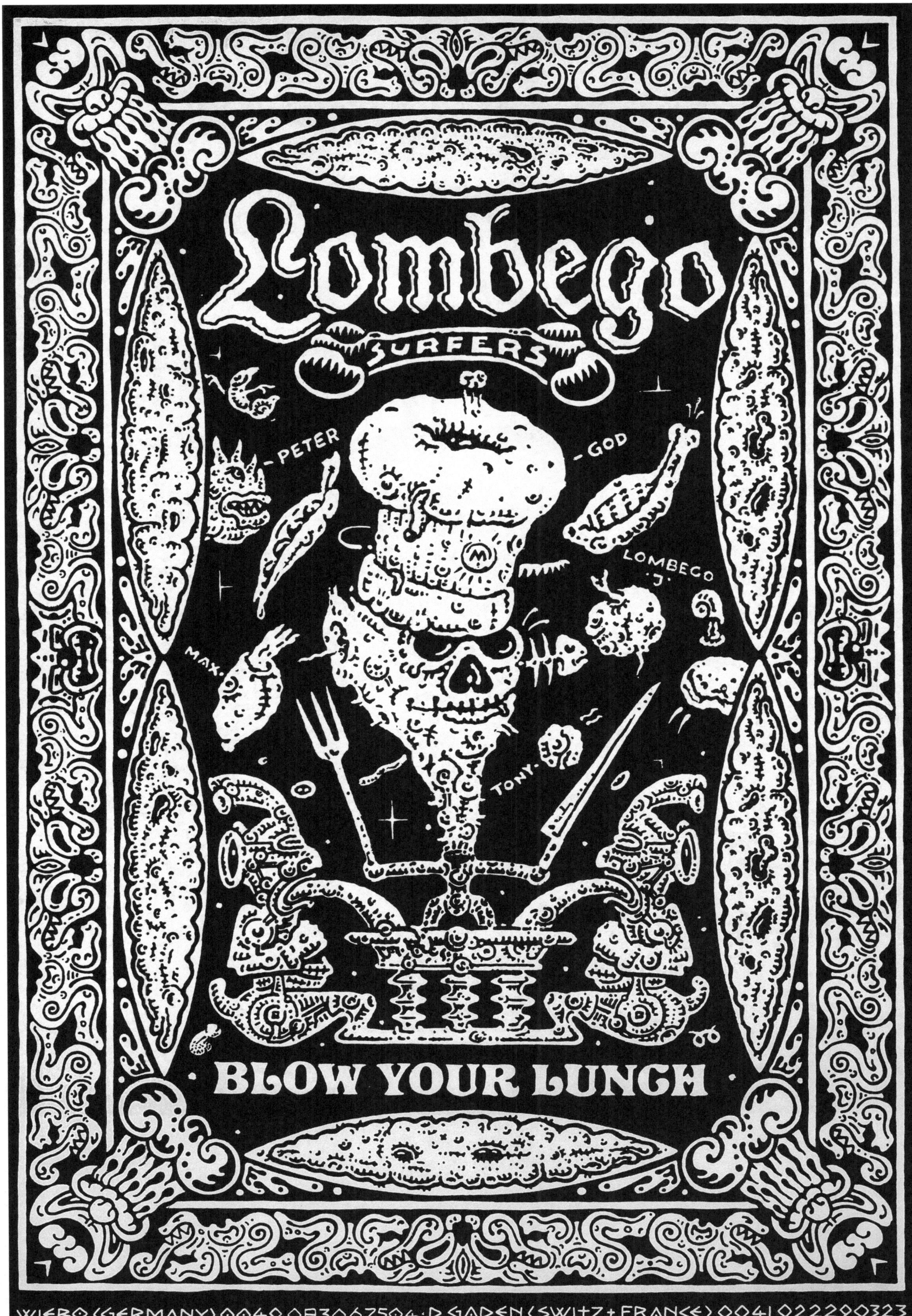
Lombego
SURFERS
PETER
GOD
LOMBEGO
J
MAX
TONY
BLOW YOUR LUNCH
WIEBO (GERMANY) 0049 083067504 · D. GADEN (SWITZ+FRANCE) 0041 022290323

DIRK BONSMA, NICKERS & MONSTERS, 600×750

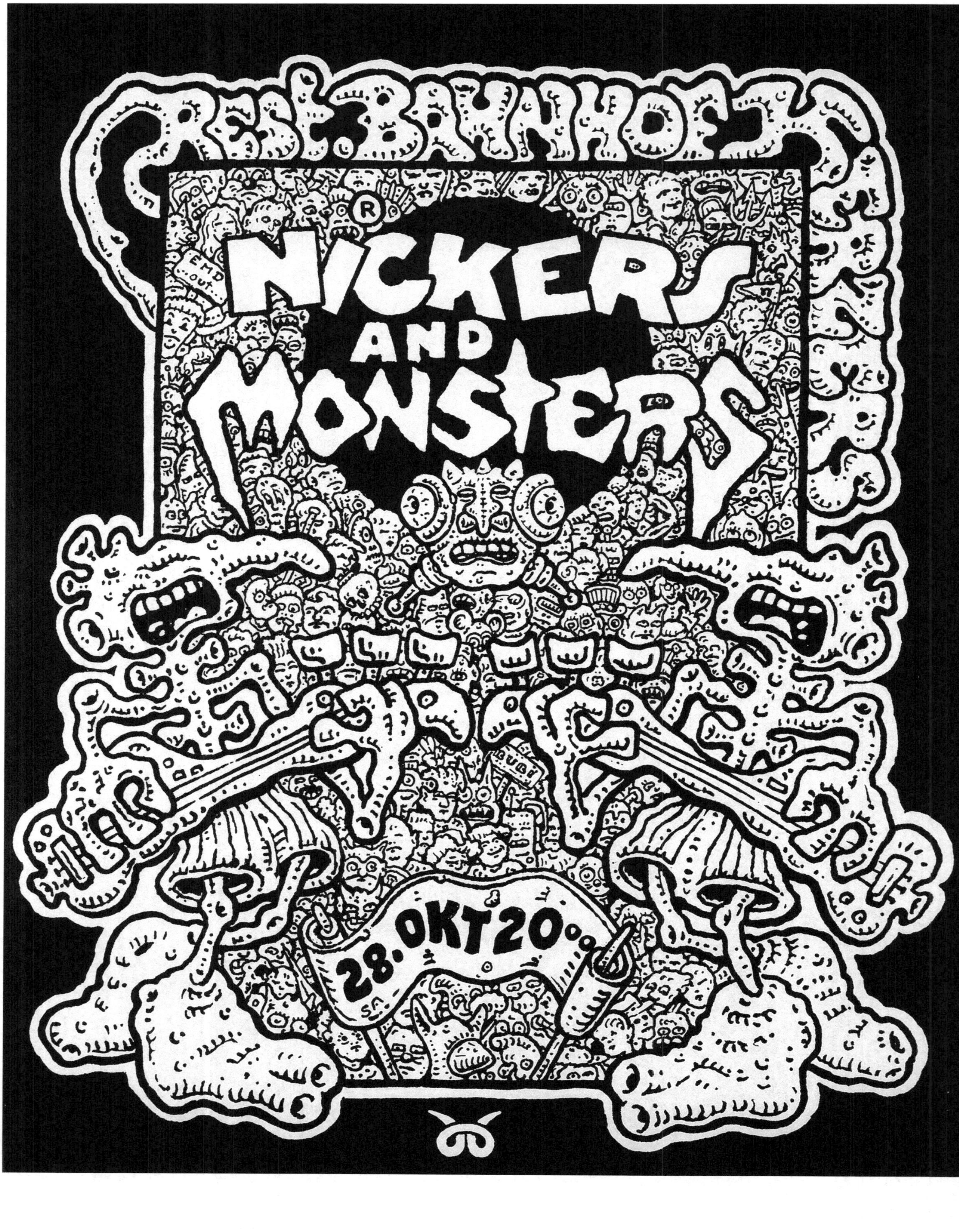

DIRK BONSMA, DEAD MOON, MONSTERS, 1995, 460×600

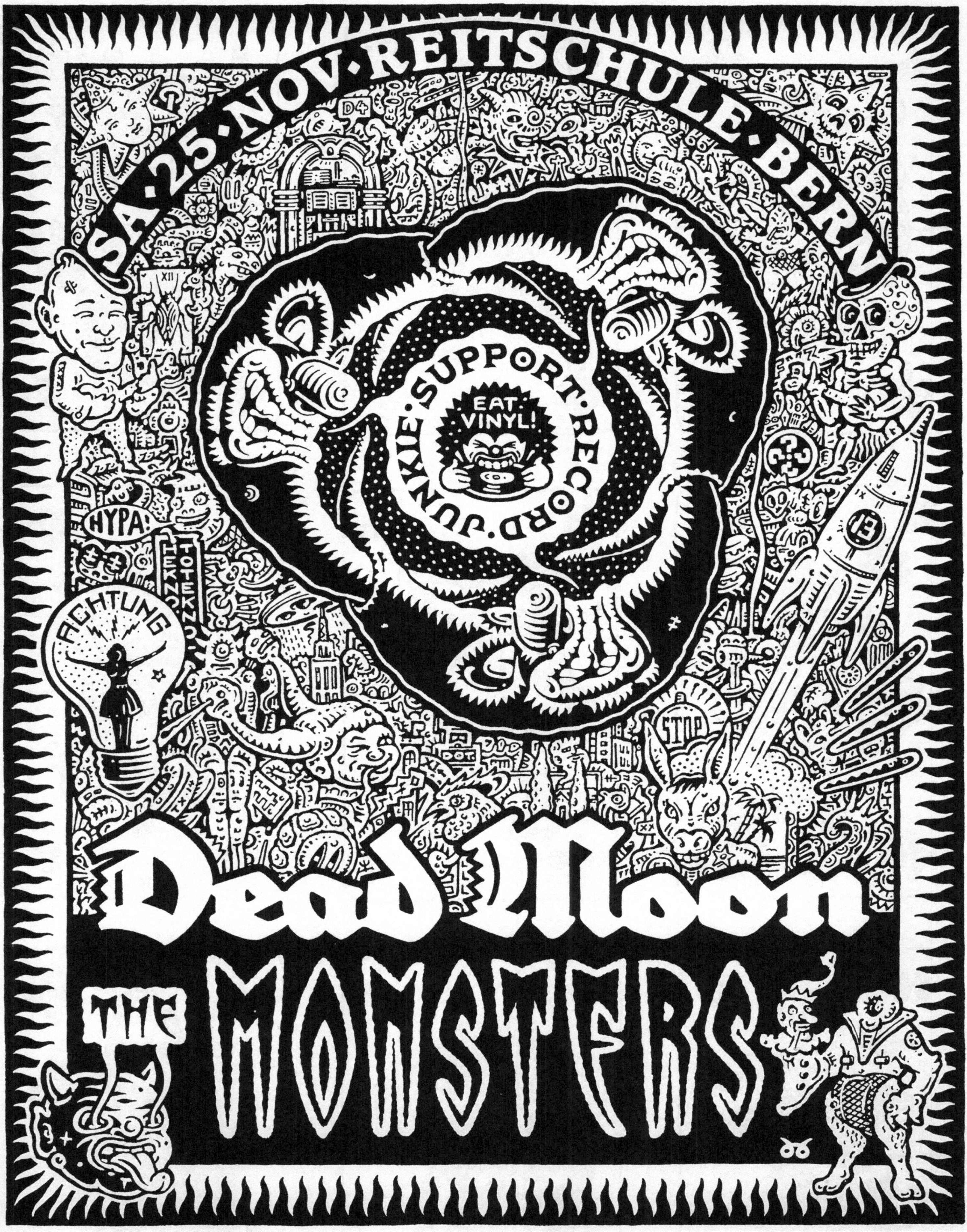

DIRK BONSMA, PLAYING CARD FLYER, FRONT SIDES, 63×95

DIRK BONSMA, PLAYING CARD FLYER, BACK SIDES, 63×95

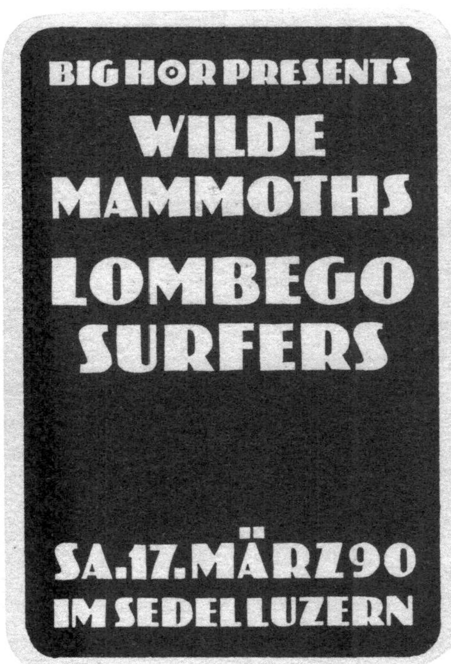

DIRK BONSMA, MIRACLE WORKERS – EUROPE TOUR 87, 1987, 600×840

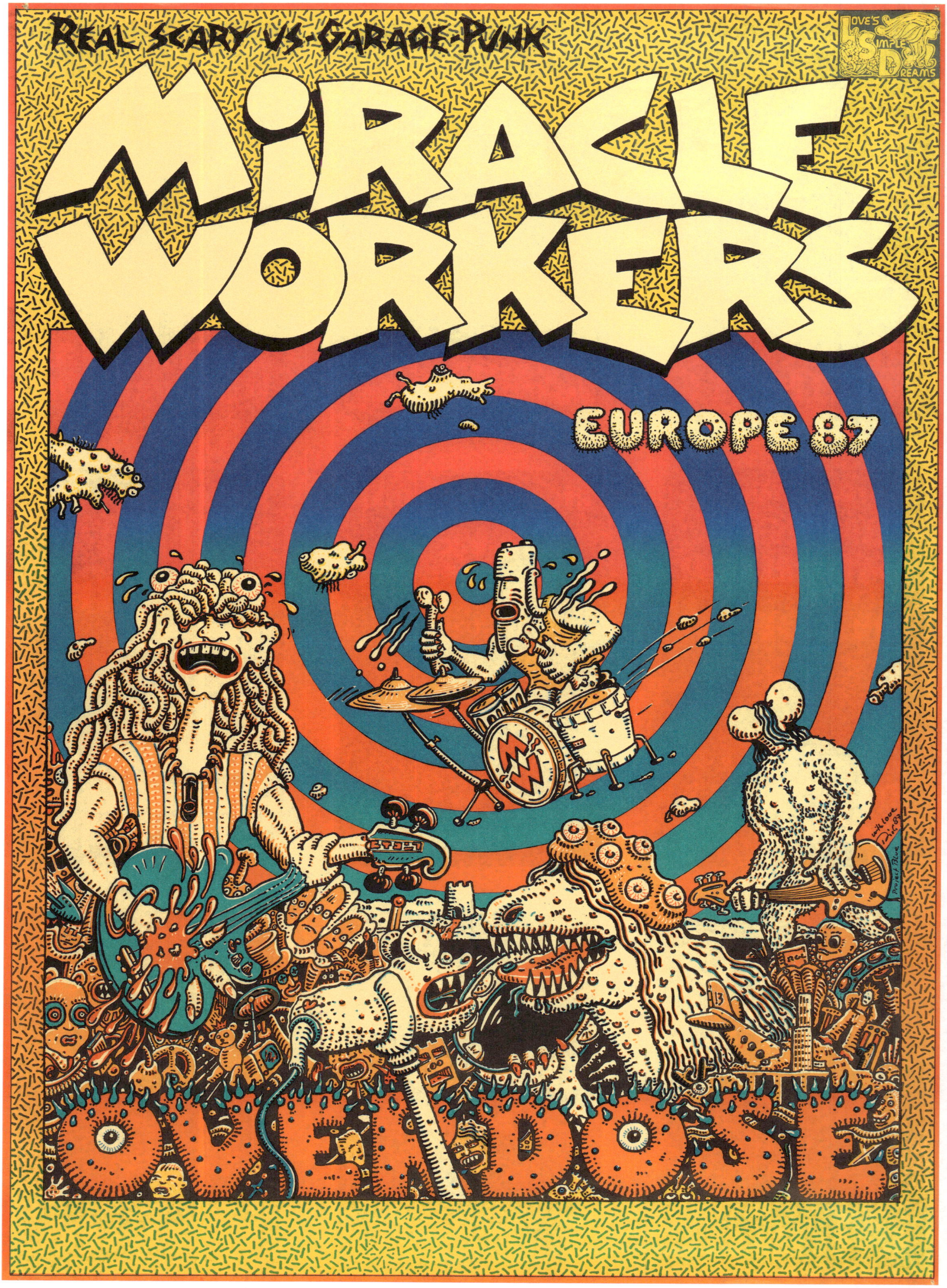

DIRK BONSMA, CHESTERFIELD KINGS – EUROPE TOUR 87, 1987, 600×840

DIRK BONSMA, SCREAMIN J. HAWKINS, 1993, 570×475

DEPT.

ung gods
85 21h
FRI-SON:
rue de l'Industrie 25
FRIBOURG

Jacques Schouwey

Gelernter Hochbauzeichner, der zwischenzeitlich als Schlagzeuger bei der Band Jof and the Ram (mit Franz Treichler von den späteren The Young Gods) agierte und den Plattenladen Cosmos in Fribourg führte. Zusammen mit Pascal Hunkeler war er ab Mitte der Achtzigerjahre für die Konzerte im Fri-Son zuständig. Die beiden führten das alternative Kulturlokal und bestimmten die Auswahl der Konzerte. Schouwey war zudem für die Gestaltung der Plakate und Inserate bis hin zum Layout des eigenen Fanzines *Bleu Royal* zuständig. Er lebte zu dieser Zeit rund um die Uhr wie Peter Bäder und Dirk Bonsma den kompletten Rockkosmos. Seit 1993 führt Jacques Schouwey zusammen mit Pascal Hunkeler die Konzertveranstaltungs- und Promotionsagentur Sofa.

Jacques Schouwey

A trained construction draughtsman, acted as the interim drummer for the band Jof and the Ram (with Franz Treichler of the later The Young Gods) and ran the record shop Cosmos in Fribourg. As of the mid-eighties he was responsible for concerts at the Fri-Son, together with Pascal Hunkeler. The two of them ran the alternative culture centre and also decided the concert selection. Schouwey was also responsible for the design of the posters and advertisements, right up to the layout of the own *Bleu Royal* fanzine. At the time, he lived the complete Rock cosmos 24/7 lifestyle. Since 1993, Jacques Schouwey runs the concert booking and promotion agency Sofa, together with Pascal Hunkeler.

JACQUES SCHOUWEY, I SUONATORI, CYAN REVUE, CLICK CLICK, 1986, 440×605

BISCA
& COPVLATION
sam. 3.5.86 21h
FRI-SON FRIBOURG FRI-SON

FRAUEN IM ROCK
ROCK AU FEMININ
TYPHOON
THE SAN FRANCISCO ALL WOMEN POWER BAND
&
Chin-Chin
20h30
SAM. 11.OCT.86
FRI-SON
rue de l'Industrie 25
FRIBOURG

JACQUES SCHOUWEY, FILM DE GUERRE, EX-BABIES, 1983, 300×420

JACQUES SCHOUWEY, CONCERT ROCK & SOIRÉE FILMS, 1984, 435×605

JACQUES SCHOUWEY, SWANS, EIGERNORDWAND, 1984, 400×575

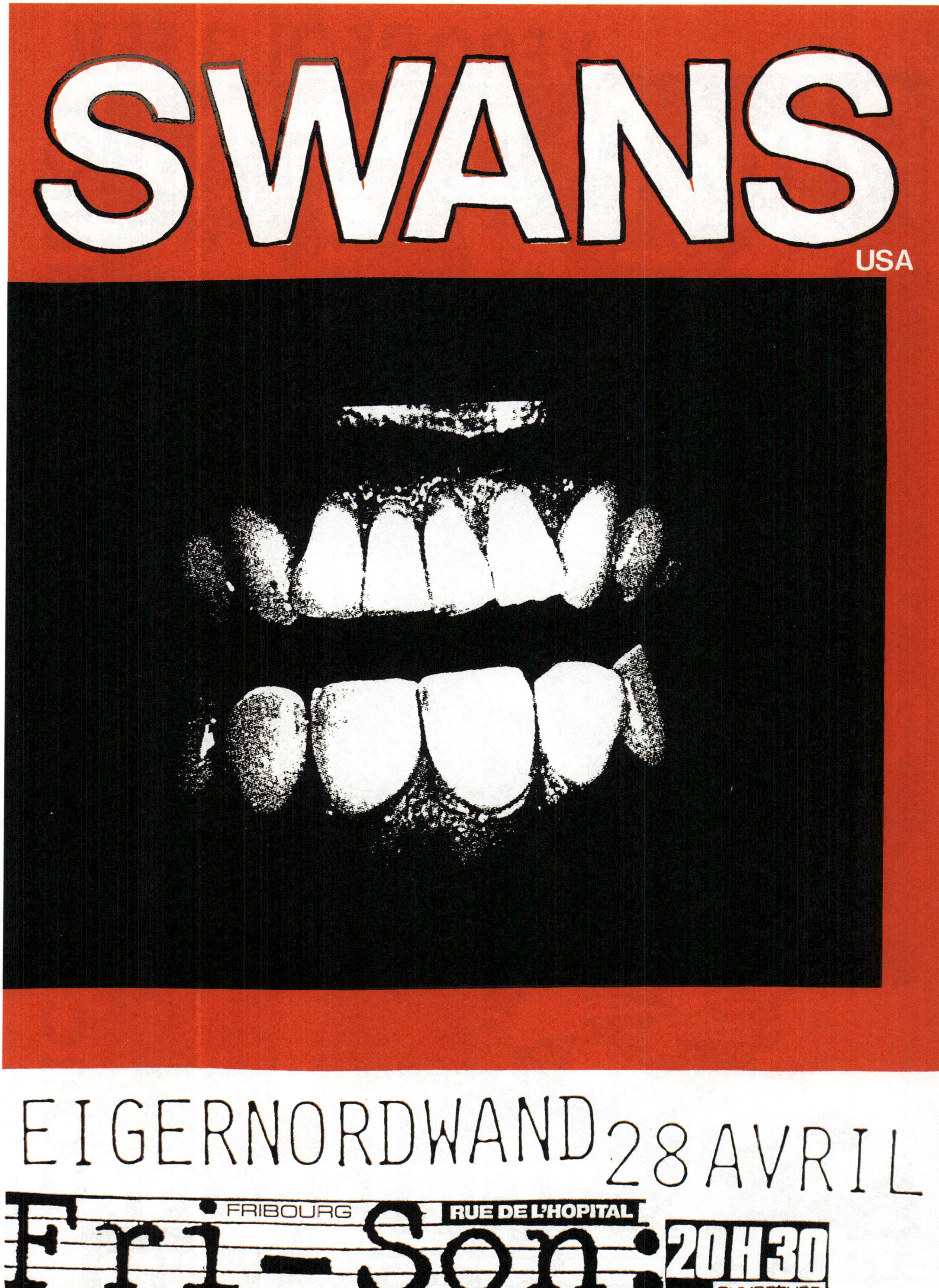

JACQUES SCHOUWEY, LA FURA DELS BAUS, 1985, 415×580

JACQUES SCHOUWEY, TEST DEPT. & THE YOUNG GODS, 1985, 300×420

THE MARCH VIOLETS
IN CONCERT 20H30 FRI-SON
JEUDI 10 MAI 84

GUN CLUB
&
inca babies
FRI-SON
22.11.86
TICKETS
Fr. 18.-
PRELOCATION SEULEMENT
NUR VORVERKAUF
HULLABALOO
OLMO
ROXY
DISCABRAC
VINYL
SOUNDS

Jeffrey Lee Pierce – Eine Flasche Whisky

Jeffrey Lee Pierce und seine Band The Gun Club hatten wir schon seit einiger Zeit auf dem Radar für ein Konzert im Fri-Son in Fribourg. Schliesslich ist es uns für Samstag, den 22. November 1986, auch gelungen, eine Show zu organisieren. Das war die Zeit, als Patricia Morrison noch Mitglied der Band war: eine sehr freundliche, sehr feminine Wahnsinnsfrau. Die Band kam reichlich spät an und begann sofort, Fête zu machen. Als Jeffrey das Fri-Son betrat, war sein Zustand schon so, dass wir uns besorgt fragten: «Oh mein Gott, was wird das bloss für ein Konzert?» Wir behielten die Fassung und dachten uns Sachen wie: Mit etwas Milch kommt der vielleicht auch wieder runter. Nichts von dem! Die Gun-Club-Fête ging weiter. Irgendwann verschwand Jeffrey irgendwo im Lokal. Mittlerweile hatten wir die Anlage aufgestellt und wären eigentlich bereit gewesen, die Türen zu öffnen – aber Jeffrey war nirgends zu sehen. Auf meine Frage an Patricia, wo der Sänger denn geblieben sei, antwortete sie nur: «Ich dachte, er sei bei dir!» Wir fanden ihn dann schnell, weggetreten auf einem Sofa in der Loge, festgeklammert an eine leere Whiskyflasche, die auf ihm lag. Wir: «Scheisse, wie können wir den so wecken, dass er gut drauf ist, er soll ja noch spielen?» Patricia: «Holt eine Flasche Whisky.» Wir: «Kommt nicht infrage, er muss ja noch singen.» Sie: «Eine Flasche Whisky, habe ich gesagt!» Also holte ich eine an der Bar und hielt sie Jeffrey unter die Nase. Das wirkte. Instinktmässig griff er nach der Flasche. Wir mussten ihn anschliessend zu zweit auf die Bühne wuchten, die Flasche sollte niemand sehen. Auf der Bühne war Jeffrey Lee Pierce dann wie ein umgedrehter Handschuh. Die Leute im Publikum hingen an seinen Lippen und realisierten nichts von seinem desolaten Zustand. Dieser erste Gun-Club-Gig im Fri-Son hatte etwas Magisches. Vielleicht gerade darum, weil wir schon gefürchtet hatten, das Konzert absagen zu müssen.

Beim zweiten Gig erschien Jeffrey mit einer komplett neuen Band, mit einer asiatischen Schönheit, die offenbar Patricia Morrisons Rolle übernommen hatte. Pierce selber sagte zwar, er wolle fortan gesund leben, er trank dazu aber ungerührt weiter. Das Konzert ist mir kaum in Erinnerung geblieben. Später gab es noch einen dritten Gig. Pierce war bleich und ausgezehrt, sprach kaum mehr ein Wort und starrte ins Leere. Er verlangte nach Milch, denn er sei auf Entziehungskur. Ansonsten musste man ihn einfach in Ruhe lassen. Das Konzert war grauenhaft. Da spielte der Amy-Winehouse-Effekt. Er konnte nicht ohne Alkohol, doch gleichzeitig konnte er diese hohen Dosen nicht handeln. Zwei Jahre nach seinem dritten Fri-Son-Gig erhielten wir dann die Nachricht, Jeffrey Lee Pierce sei gestorben. Es hatte sich abgezeichnet.

Jacques Schouwey im Gespräch mit Sam Mumenthaler

Jeffrey Lee Pierce — A bottle of whiskey

Jeffrey Lee Pierce and his band, The Gun Club, had already been on our radar for playing a concert at the Fri-Son in Fribourg for some time. Eventually, we managed to organize a show for Saturday, November 22, 1986. At the time, Patricia Morrison — an amazing, very friendly, very feminine woman — was still a member. The band arrived rather late and immediately began partying. When Jeffrey entered the Fri-Son, he was already in such a state that we became concerned: What kind of concert would this be? We kept our composure and thought things like: perhaps some milk would sober him up again. None of that! The Gun Club party continued. At some point, Jeffrey disappeared somewhere in the club. In the meantime, we had set up the sound system and were actually ready to open the doors — but Jeffrey had disappeared. When I asked Patricia where the singer was, she replied: "I thought he was with you!" We soon found him passed out on a sofa in the lodge, clasping an empty whiskey bottle that lay on top of him. We went: "Shit! How can we wake him up so that he's still in a good enough mood to perform?" Patricia said: "Get a bottle of whiskey. We: "That's out of the question. He still has to sing." She: "I told you, a bottle of whiskey!" So I fetched one at the bar and held it under Jeffrey's nose. It worked. He instinctively grabbed the bottle. The two of us then had to drag him onto the stage, yet no one was supposed to see the bottle. On stage, Jeffrey Lee Pierce completely turned. The people in the audience hung on his every word; they didn't have a clue about his desolate condition. This first Gun Club gig at the Fri-Son had something magical about it. Perhaps precisely because of the fact that we had already feared we would have to call off the concert.

Jeffrey turned up for a second gig with a completely new band, with a beautiful Asian woman who had apparently taken over Patricia Morrison's role. Although Pierce himself said that he wanted to live a healthy life from then on, he continued to drink without blinking. I can hardly remember the concert. Later there followed a third gig. Pierce was pale and haggard, hardly said a single word, staring into empty space. He asked for milk since he was in rehab. Beyond that he simply wanted be left in peace. The concert was dreadful. The Amy Winehouse effect. He couldn't do anything without alcohol, but at the same time he couldn't handle such high doses. Two years after his third gig at the Fri-Son, we received the news that Jeffrey Lee Pierce had died. The writing was already on the wall.

Jacques Schouwey in a conversation with Sam Mumenthaler

JACQUES SCHOUWEY, STICKERS PRINTED ON NEONFOIL, DIFFERENT SIZES

THE BEAUTY CONTEST
& NIKKI SUDDEN
JACOBITES
21.2.86
FRI-SON FRIBOURG FRI-SON

Fri-Son (ancien Hôpital)
Sa 1.10.83 20.15
Pink Balloons
Swimming Mannequins
Mask
& Dia Film Video
Entrée Fr.

Fri-Son
new wave
experimental
electronic
improvisation
new music
RUE DE L'HOPITAL

CHRISTIAN DEATH
USA
IN CONCERT
Jeudi 7 JUIN
Fri-Son

The Rose of Avalanche
&
BAROQUE BORDELLO
VEN. 3.10.86
FRI-SON FRIBOURG FRI-SON

Fri-Son
NE TE LAISSE PAS FAIRE ÇA! FREQUENTE PLUTOT

HERTZ
&
SAM FRANK
IN CONCERT
FRI-SON
rue de l'hôpital
vendredi
7 octobre, 20h30
Entrée: Fr. 8.—

Fri-Son
NEW MUSIC

THE MARCH VIOLETS
IN CONCERT FRI-SON
JEUDI 10 MAI 84

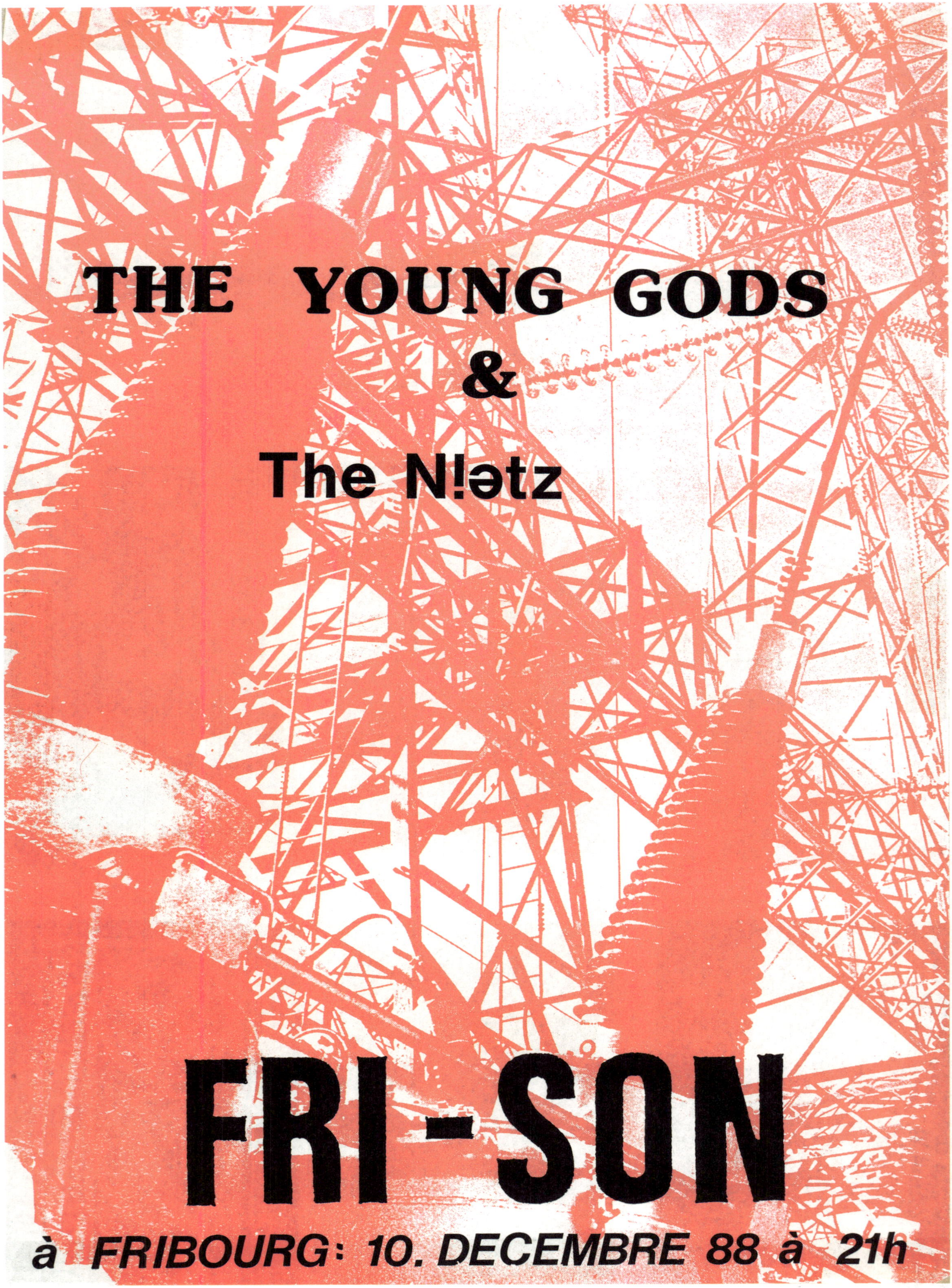
THE YOUNG GODS
&
The N!ətz
FRI-SON
à FRIBOURG: 10. DECEMBRE 88 à 21h

JACQUES SCHOUWEY, T.C.MATIC, 1983, 300×420

JACQUES SCHOUWEY, GIRLS FROM TAHITI & AXEL PRINTEMPS, 1983, 300×420

CARNAVAL ROCK
SAMEDI 8.2.86
DISCO
THE POMOLOGS
THE BABYJAIL
+ SUPPORT
FRI-SON FRIBOURG FRI-SON FRIBO

CONCERT ROCK
CORNET PLASTIC
COEUR
RUE DE L'HOPITAL
20H30
Fri-Son:
5 NOVE

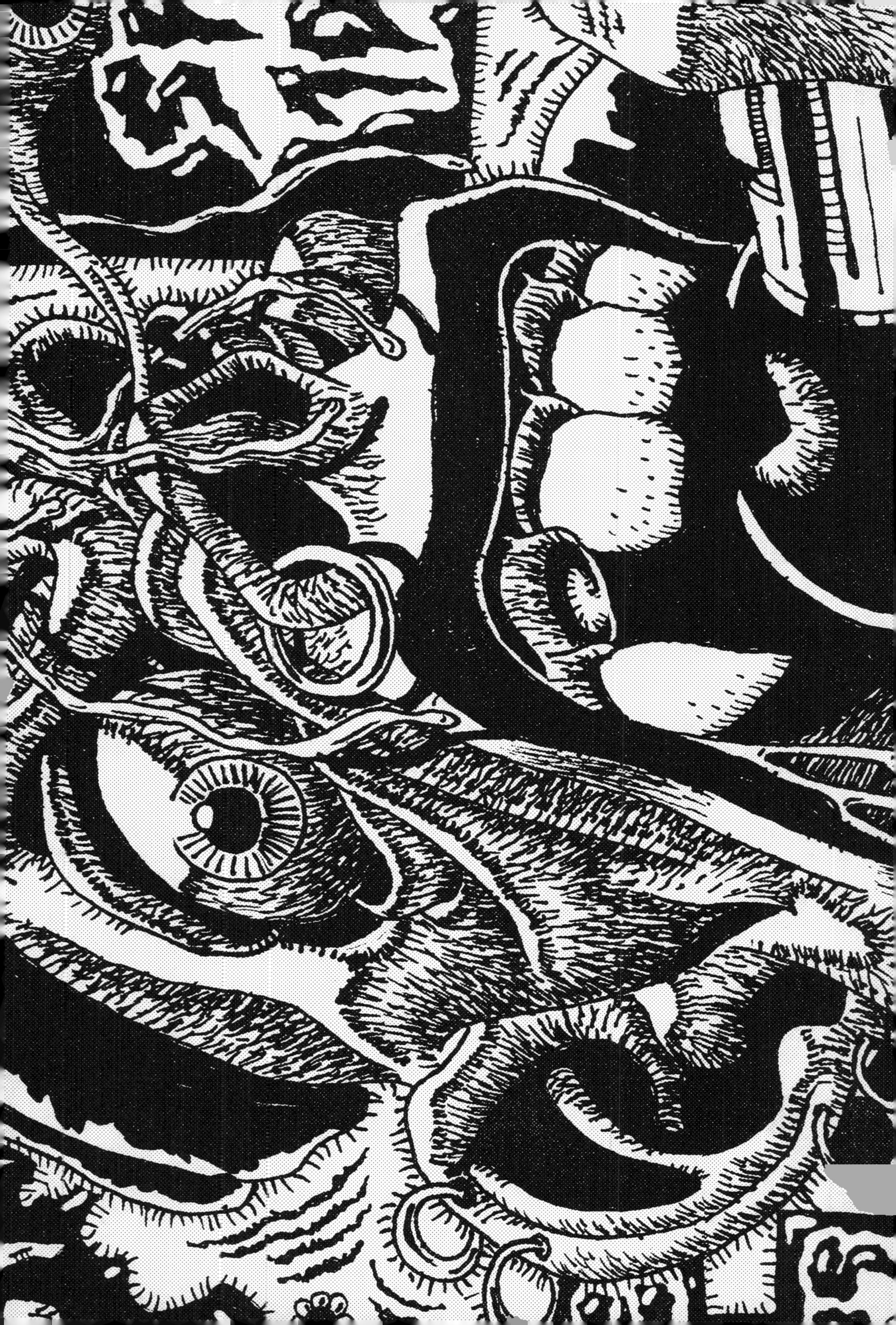

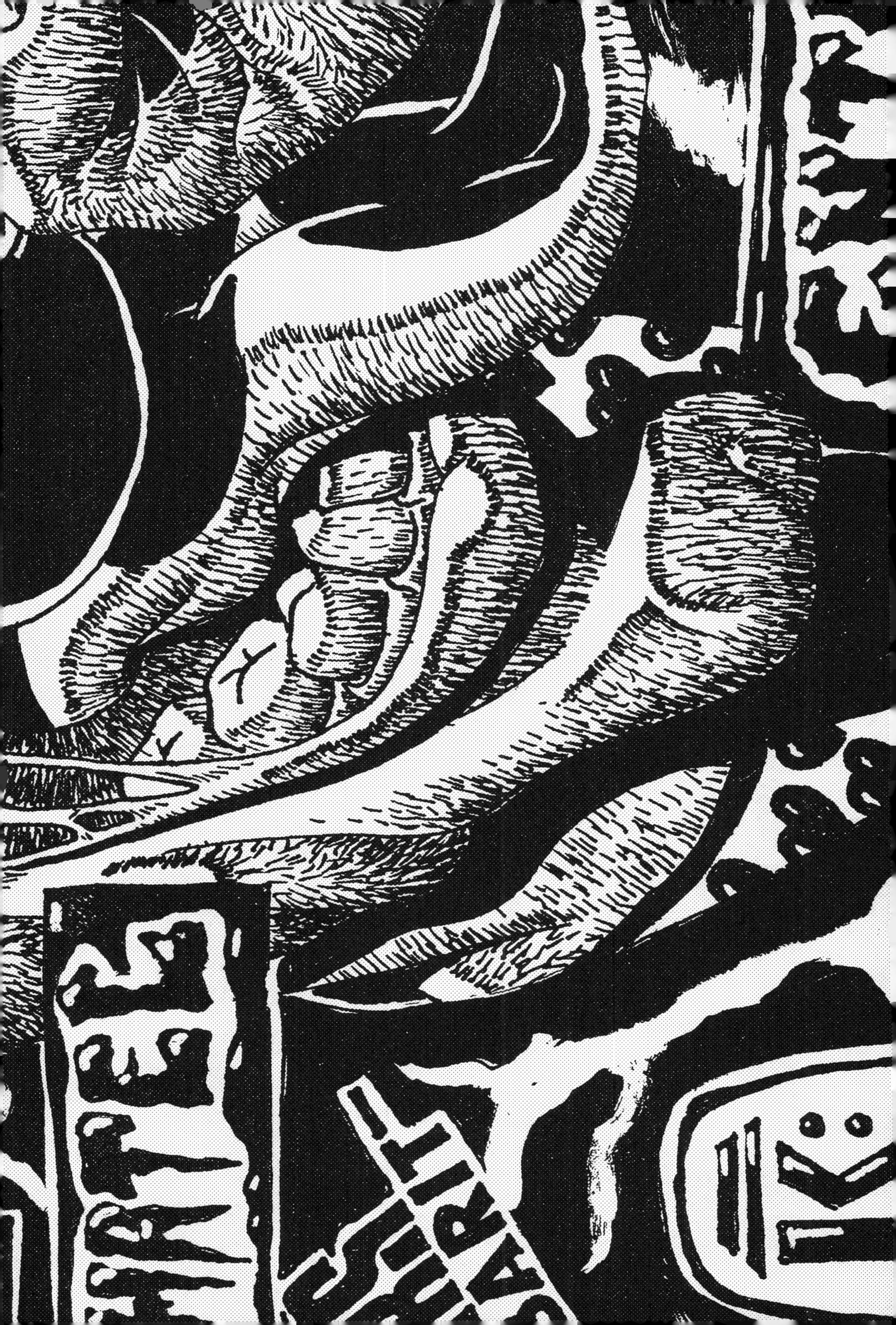

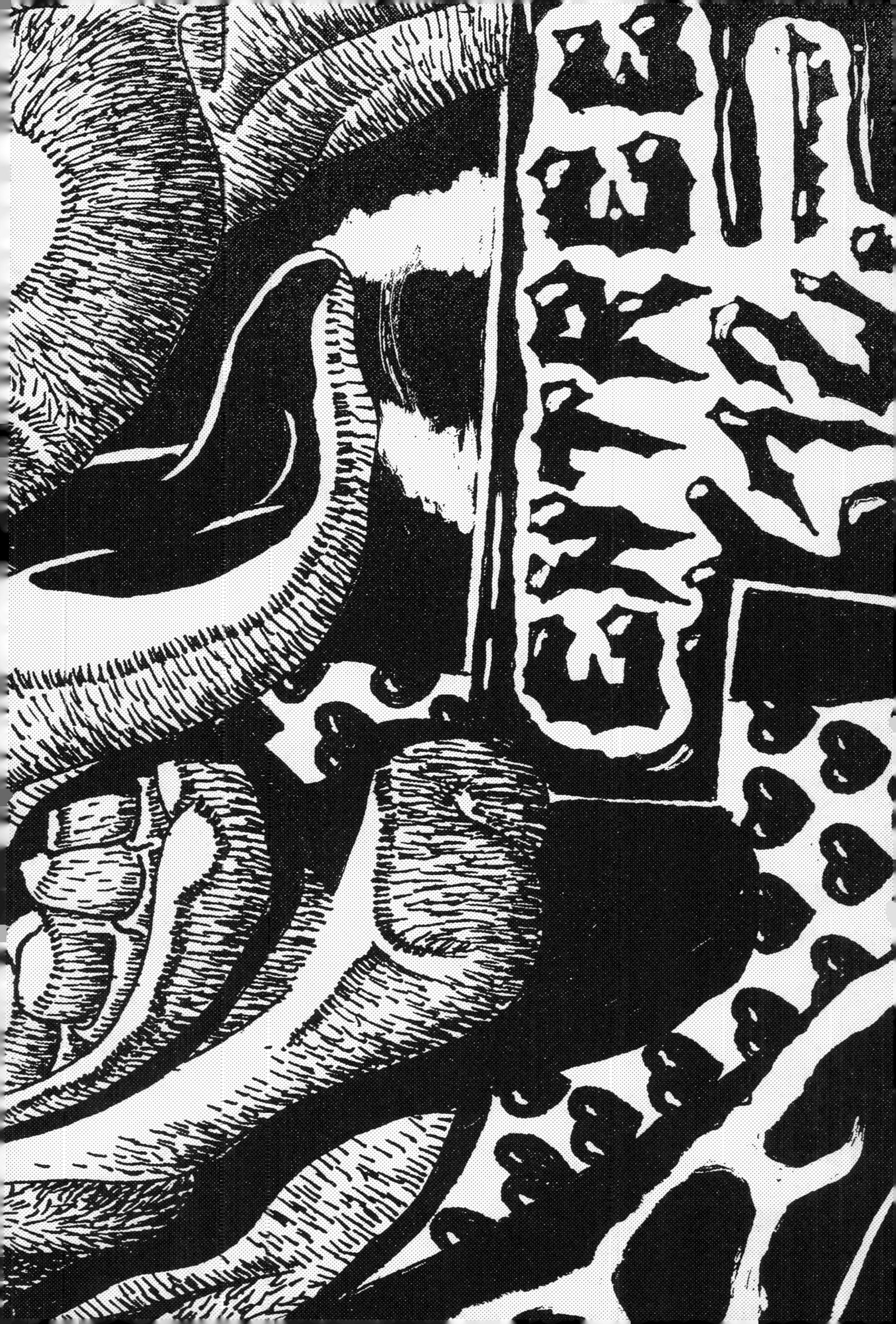

Cédric Magnin, Alain Straubhaar, Luc Torregrossa

Ab Mitte der Achtzigerjahre waren Cédric Magnin, Alain Straubhaar und Luc Torregrossa als Künstlergruppe zuständig für die Visualisierung von Anlässen im Club Bikini Test in La Chaux-de-Fonds. Cédric Magnin hatte zuvor das Zeichenlehrer-Seminar in Bern absolviert, Alain Straubhaar besuchte ein Jahr die École des Beaux-Arts in Paris und danach drei Jahre die École Superieure d'Art Visuel in Genf und Luc Torregrossa die École des Arts Décoratifs in Genf. Das Gestalter-Trio spielte gemeinsam in der Band Redoudables und organisierte im Bikini Test schon früh erste Ausstellungen, in denen es um die Visualisierung von Musik ging. Alle drei blieben bei der Kunst. Cédric ist heute noch Maler, Alain ein Sonntagsmaler, und Luc verstarb 2002. Éditions du Cormoran Blanc publizierte 2009 eine Monografie unter dem Titel *Luc Torregrossa – peintre et dessinateur*.

Cédric Magnin, Alain Straubhaar, Luc Torregrossa

As of the mid-eighties Cédric Magnin, Alain Straubhaar and Luc Torregrossa were responsible as an art group for the visualization of events at the Bikini Test club in La Chaux-de-Fonds. Cédric Magnin had previously passed the art teacher seminary in Bern, Alain Straubhaar attended École des Baux-Arts in Paris for a year and then three years at the École Superieure d'Art Visuel in Genf and Luc Torregrossa the École des Arts Décoratifs in Genf. The designer trio played together in the band Redoudables and, early on, organized exhibitions at the Bikini Test where the focus was on the visualization of music. All three stayed with art. Cédric is still a painter to-date, Alain a Sunday painter and Luc died in 2002. Éditions du Cormoran Blanc published in 2009 a monograph with the title *Luc Torregrossa — peintre et dessinateur*.

LUC TORREGROSSA, DISCO ROCK, 1989, 297×420

LUC TORREGROSSA, I WANT YOU, 1990, 297×420

LUC TORREGROSSA, LE CANCER SAUVAGE, 1990, 297×420

CONCERT
QUARTERED SHADOWS
(BERLIN)
+
GIRL WITH A
GUN
(GENÈVE)
SAMEDI
7 DÉC.
21H.
ENTRÉE
10.–
CAR
LA CHAUX-DE-FONDS

CÉDRIC MAGNIN, PULL MY DAISY, 1989, 297×420

CÉDRIC MAGNIN, LE FASTER, 1989, 297×420

CÉDRIC MAGNIN, IT'S ONLY ROCK AND ROLL, 1989, 297×420

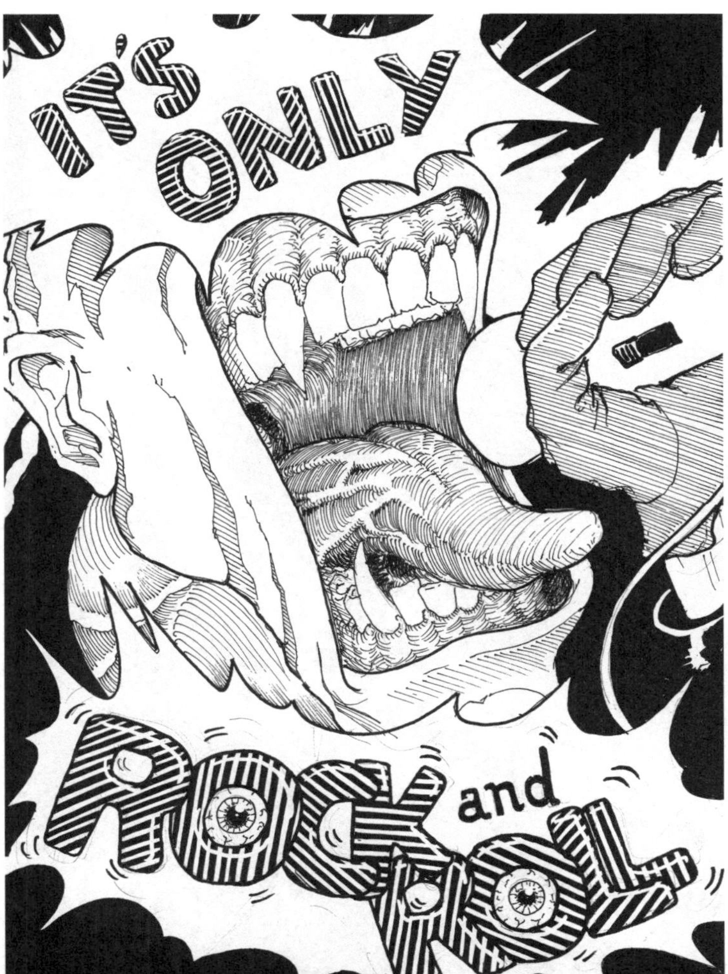

ALAIN STRAUBHAAR, QUARTERED SHADOWS, 1991, 297×420

LE PRÉSENTE
SPANKS
(B)
EN CONCERT
LA CHAUX-DE-FONDS
HALLE AUX ENCHÈRES
- 9 SEPT. - 21 h - 10.-

BUECHSENBEERS
+
SAMEDI
10 JUIN
CENTRE
DES
LOISIRS
NEUCHATEL
HORS GABARIT
ENTREE
12.-

ALAIN STRAUBHAAR, ZÜRI WEST, 1989, 297×420

ALAIN STRAUBHAAR, THE YOUNG GODS, 1989, 297×420

ALAIN STRAUBHAAR, THE SHANGHAI LADIES & CAPHARNRÜM, 1989, 297×420

ALAIN STRAUBHAAR, ACIIID FREAKS, 1989, 297×420

CÉDRIC MAGNIN, FRIGO 6 – EXPOSE, 1989, 297×420

Von Les Frigos zu Bikini Test

Im Sommer '88 hatten wir, sprich Alain Straubhaar, Luc Torregrossa & ich, Cédric Magnin, das grosse Privileg, einen Monat in Paris verbringen zu können. Dies mitten im Quartier Marais in einem grosszügigen Atelier (150 Quadratmeter, rundherum Fenster mit Blick auf den Innenhof, ziemlich abgefahren) des Malers und Kunstkritikers Laurent Wolf. Wir waren jung, wir waren voller Idealismus, wir hatten gerade alle diverse Kunsthochschulen abgeschlossen und waren der Überzeugung, dass die Kunst und der Rock die Welt verändern könnten – eine Welt, die dringend ein Lifting brauchte und, nebenbei gesagt, immer noch braucht. Wir arbeiteten wild und entschlossen und wie besessen mit an der kleinen alternativen Welt des damaligen Paris. Manchmal kam es sogar vor, dass wir nüchtern und ohne Ziel durch die grosse Stadt spazierten. Auf einem dieser Streifzüge entdeckten wir nahe des Pont de Tolbiac, den der Kriminalschriftsteller und Dichter Léo Malet und der berühmte Comic-Autor Jacques Tardi so mochten, in Les Frigos, den ehemaligen Kühlkammern der Stadt, eine Ansammlung von Künstlern unterschiedlichster Sparten; vom Theater über Tanz bis zur Malerei. Sie alle wohnten dort in einem fröhlichen Chaos zusammen, und es roch überall angenehm nach Untergrund und viel Kreativität. Im 3. Stock dieses Kunstlabyrinths lag verborgen ein Atelier, dass sich sechs Maler und Bildhauer teilten. Sie alle waren Anhänger von Figuration Libre (archaische Kunstform, die Anfang der Achtziger in Frankreich entstand), für die wir uns zu diesem Zeitpunkt besonders interessierten, da in der damaligen offiziellen Kunstwelt vor allem abstrakt und konzeptuell gearbeitet wurde und, nebenbei gesagt, heute immer noch.

Wir machten also Bekanntschaft mit frigo6 (so hiess das Kollektiv) und schlugen ihnen vor, bei uns in La Chaux-de-Fonds auszustellen, und zu unserer grossen Freude sagten sie zu. Wir waren Teil des Association-KA-Abenteuers (der Gruppe, die später das Bikini Test gegründet hat), viele von uns wollten, dass sich Kunst und Rock unbedingt parallel, sprich gemeinsam entwickelten. Heute steht aber fest, dass der Rock als grosser Sieger aus diesem Treffen hervorging und die Kunst grösstenteils wie schon damals in Galerien und Museum zu finden ist, schade, wir haben es immerhin versucht ...

Gross war meine Überraschung, als ich beim Durchforsten meiner Vergangenheit für die vorliegende Publikation entdeckte, dass es die Frigos immer noch gibt, dass sie immer noch eine künstlerische Nische im Pariser Untergrund besetzen und dass frigo6 (heute sind sie nur noch zu viert) weiterhin Ausstellungen machen. Ich kann euch nur sagen, wenn ihr das nächste Mal in Paris seid, geht selbst hin und schaut es euch an.

Cédric Magnin

From Les Frigos to Bikini Test

In the summer of 1988, we, Alain Straubhaar, Luc Torregrossa, and I, Cédric Magnin, enjoyed the privilege of spending a month in Paris, in a large studio (150 m², windows all the way around with a view of the inner courtyard, pretty wicked) at the centre of the historic district of Le Marais, belonging to painter and art critic Laurent Wolf. We were young, full of idealism, and had all just graduated from different art colleges. We were convinced that art and rock had the stuff to change the world — a world that urgently needed a facelift and, incidentally, still does. We worked ferociously, with determination, with an obsession for the small alternative world of Paris during that era. Occasionally we even found the time to soberly and aimlessly stroll through the great city. On one of these rambles we discovered a gathering of artists from different genres — theater, dance and painting — in the former city cooling chambers near the Pont de Tolbiac; an area cherished by crime novelist and poet Léo Malet as well as renowned comics author Jacques Tardi. The artists all lived there together in cheerful chaos, and there was an air of underground and total creativity. In a hideout on the third floor of this artistic maze there was a studio shared by six painters and sculptors. They all were followers of Figuration Libre (an archaic art form that arose in France at the beginning of the eighties), which we were particularly interested in at the time. For, in the official art world back then and, incidentally, still to this day, people work in the abstract and conceptual domain.

So we got to know frigo6 (as the collective called itself) and we suggested that they should exhibit at our place in La Chaux-de-Fonds. To our great delight, they agreed. We were part of the KA-Abenteuer group (that later established the Bikini Test club), and many of us essentially wanted to experience a parallel development of art and rock. Today, however, it is clear that rock music emerged from the encounter as the big winner and that art, as was the case back then, is predominantly found in galleries and museums — a pity, but at least we tried ...

As I was combing through my past for this publication, it came as a great surprise to discover that the Frigos still exist, that they still occupy an artistic niche in the Paris underground, and that frigo6 (today only four remain) continues to have exhibitions. All I can say is that you should go there and look for yourselves the next time you visit Paris.

Cédric Magnin

CÉDRIC MAGNIN & ALAIN STRAUBHAAR & LUC TORREGROSSA, 1991, 1500×1500

CÉDRIC MAGNIN & ALAIN STRAUBHAAR & LUC TORREGROSSA, 1991, 1500×1500

CÉDRIC MAGNIN & ALAIN STRAUBHAAR & LUC TORREGROSSA, 1991, 1500×1500

Marlboro

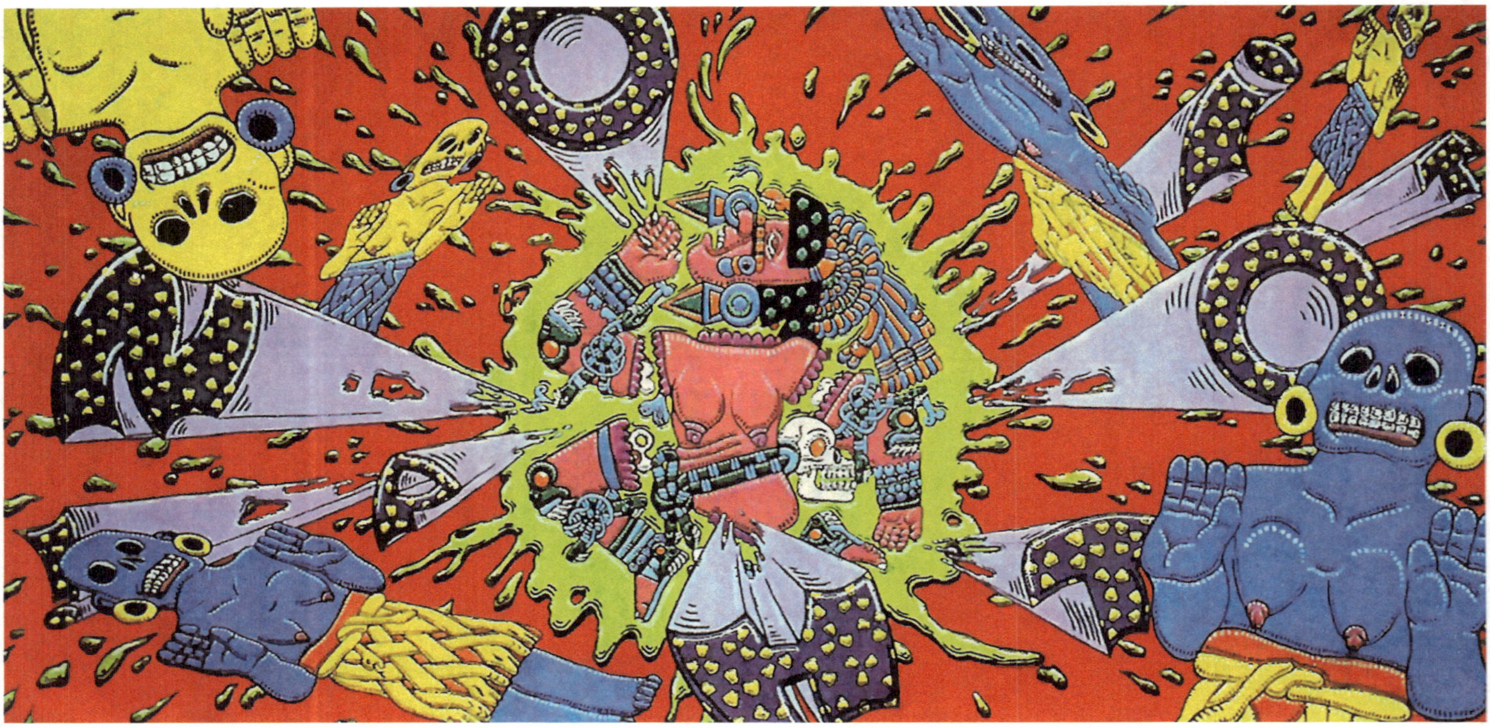

30.10.98
FREITAG 21:30
Luv ZÜRICH
KREUZSTR. 24

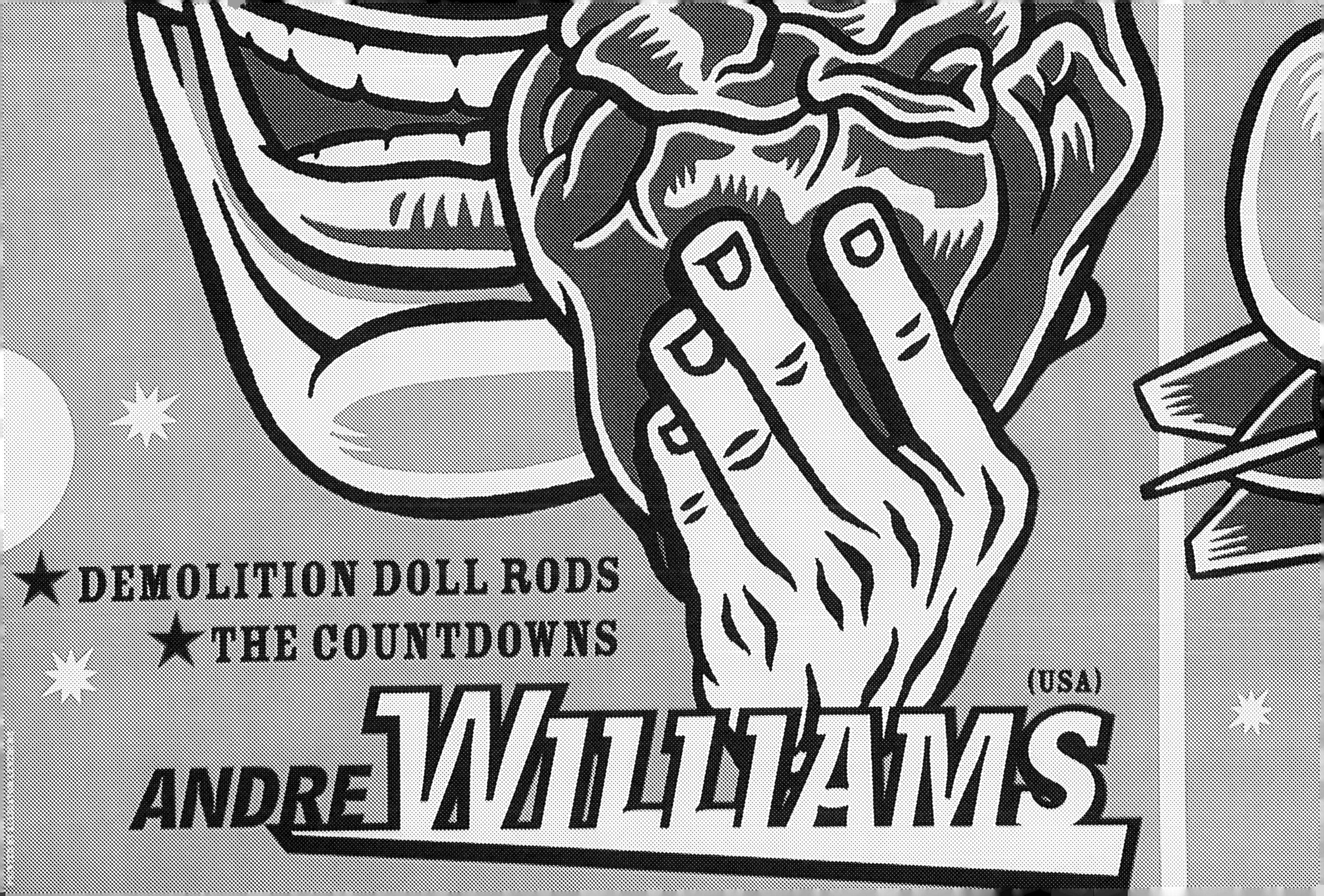
DEMOLITION DOLL RODS
THE COUNTDOWNS
(USA)
ANDRE WILLIAMS

30.10.98
FREITAG 21:30
Luv ZÜRICH
KREUZSTR. 24

Michel Casarramona

Gelernter Grafiker aus Aarau, machte Anfang der Neunzigerjahre mit seinen Konzertveranstaltungen in Zürich und den dafür gestalteten Flyern (Plakate und Plattencover kamen später dazu) auf sich aufmerksam. Zuerst in illegalen Bars, danach im Wohlgroth-Areal und später in der ganzen Stadt Zürich waren seine wunderschön gestalteten Siebdruckplakate und Flyer zu sehen – auch heute noch trifft man in Zürich auf Casarramonas Veranstaltungsplakate. Er war der Initiator und Kurator für den *Garage Sale* im Jahr 2011 und die *Limited Edition* im Jahr 2013, zwei Ausstellungen, die sich dem Grafik-Design, der Illustration, den Comics und der Fotografie widmete.

Michel Casarramona

A trained graphic artist from Aarau, who brought attention to himself at the beginning of the nineties with his concert events in Zurich and the flyers (posters and record covers came later) he designed for them. At first his beautifully designed silkscreen posters could be seen in illegal bars, then at the Wohlgroth grounds and later throughout the entire city of Zurich — to this day one still comes upon Cassaramona's event posters. He was the initiator and curator for the *Garage Sale* in 2011 and the *Limited Edition* in 2013, two exhibitions that dedicate themselves to graphic design, illustration, comics and photography.

MICHEL CASARRAMONA, VENDETTA, KINO, LES ENFANTS DE ST.GALL, NON CONFORM, 105×148, 1992

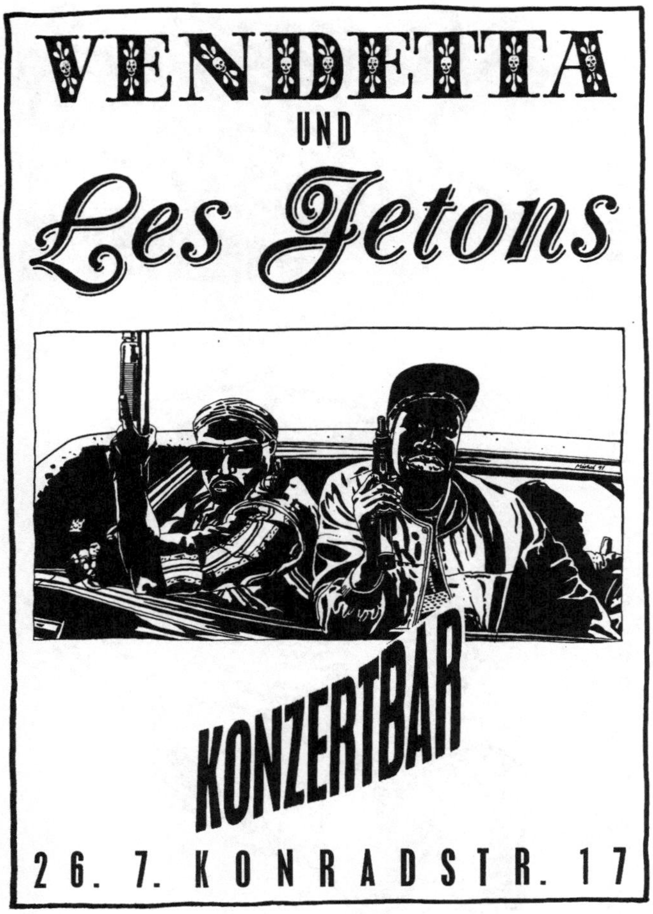

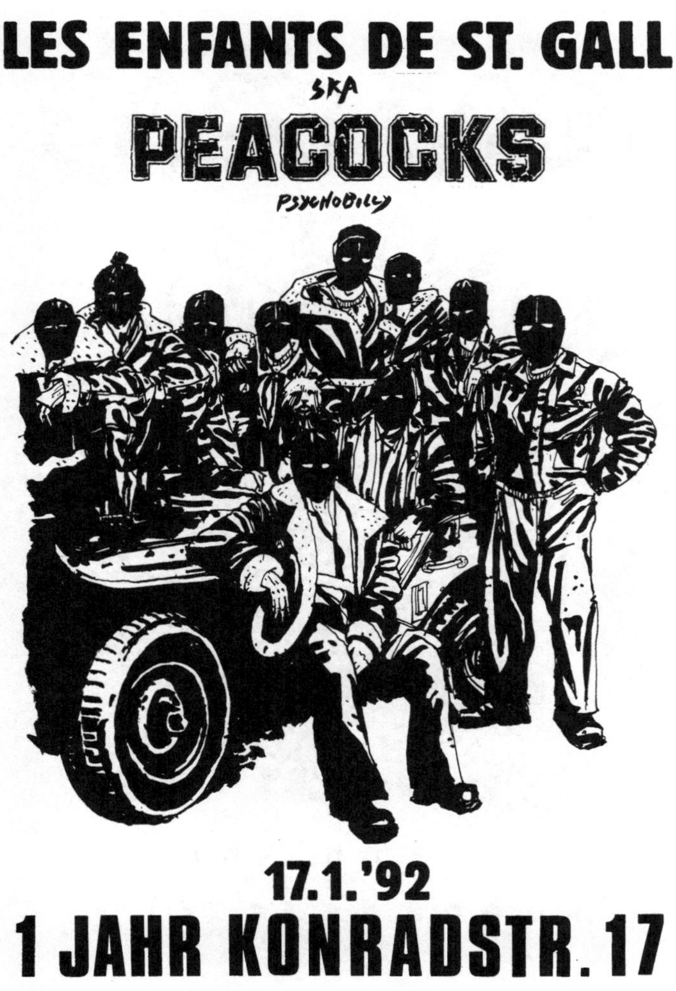

MICHEL CASARRAMONA, CAMP VAMPS, MURPHY'S LAW, TV TV'S, BABY JAIL, 105×148, 1994

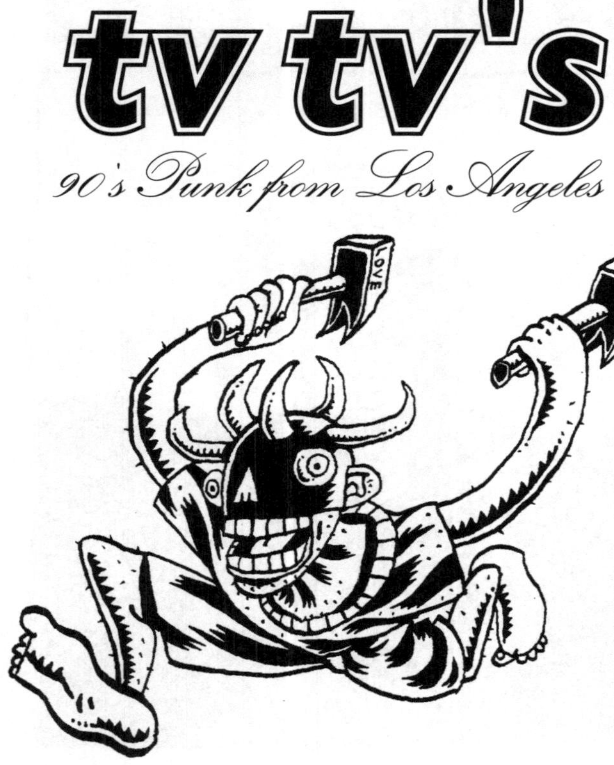

MICHEL CASARRAMONA, KUD IDIJOTI, FRIENDS OF HARRY, WICKED, VENDETTA, 105×148, 1994

MY DEVICE & HELLMUTE
ti/ita-aarau
freitag 17. maerz '95, 22.00 uhr
ambiance, konradstrasse 71

STUMBLE
from newcastle
samstag 18. feb. '95 22.00 uhr
ambiance, konradstrasse 71

PALE SAFIRE
freitag 23. dezember, 22.00 uhr
ambiance, konradstrasse 71

les enfants de st. gall
libanon connection
sonntag 30. april '95, 22.00 uhr
ambiance, konradstrasse 71

bad trip ny/usa
mind over matter
dienstag 30. mai '95 pünktlich 22 uhr
ambiance konradstrasse 71

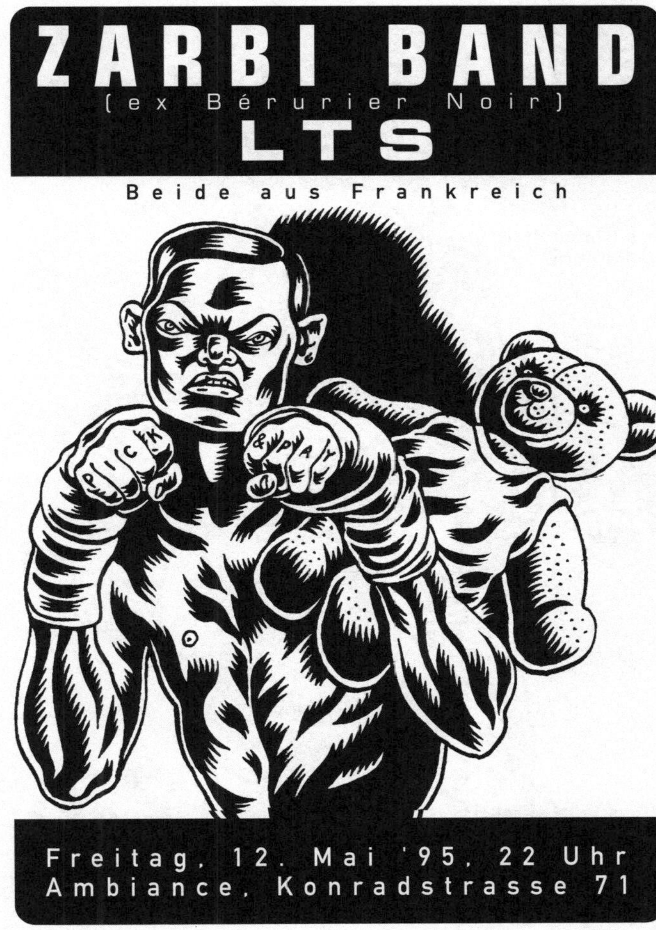
ZARBI BAND
(ex Bérurier Noir)
LTS
Beide aus Frankreich
Freitag, 12. Mai '95, 22 Uhr
Ambiance, Konradstrasse 71

crossover aus deutschland
BHANG DEXTRO
freitag 23. februar '96, 22 uhr
AMBIANCE konradstrasse 71

WALK ALONE
aus frankreich: ex bérurier noir
ZARBI BAND & LTS
freitag 29. märz 1996 22 uhr
ambiance, konradstrasse 71

musikhaus ambiance und g5 präsentieren:
Guttermouth
A.F.I.
surfpunk from california
すきです
samstag 23. November 1996
geroldstrasse 5
pünktlich 22:00 uhr

Ambiance Clubraum präsentiert:
24K
Die Goldenen Zitronen
feat. Hans Platzgumer
and special guests Brüllen Hamburg
Sonntag 15. Dezember 1996
Ernastrasse 20, pünktlich 21:30 Uhr

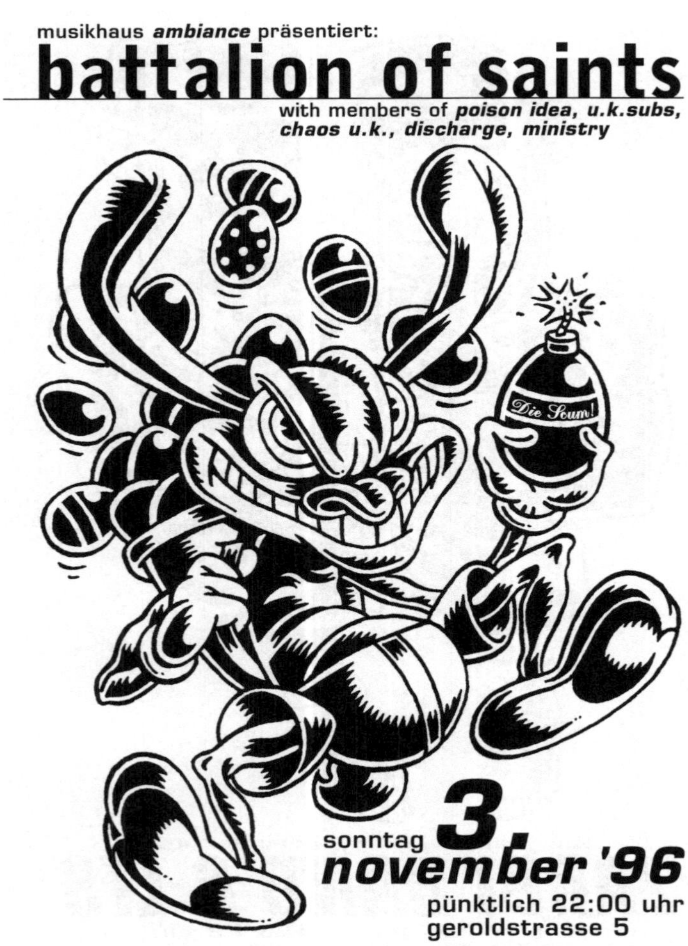
musikhaus ambiance präsentiert:
battalion of saints
with members of poison idea, u.k.subs, chaos u.k., discharge, ministry
Die Scum!
sonntag 3. november '96
pünktlich 22:00 uhr
geroldstrasse 5

Ambiance Clubraum präsentiert:
SISSI DISCO
mit Francoise Cactus & Brezel Göring von
Stereo Total
& Les SuperBonbons
plus DJ Clemens & DJ Buzzawhile
monokini
Do 23. Januar 1997
Ernastrasse 20 pünktlich 21:30 uhr

MICHEL CASARRAMONA, ROCKET FROM THE CRYPT, THE SLACKERS, GUITAR WOLF, FOX FORCE FIVE, 105×148, 1998

MICHEL CASARRAMONA, MAN OR ASTROMAN, COSMIC PSYCHOS, ANDRE WILLIAMS, NEW BOMB TURKS, 195×275, 1998, SILKSCREEN

LUV – Let's get Lock'n'Loll!

Die zweite Hälfte der Neunzigerjahre des 20. Jahrhunderts waren eine beschissene Zeit für den Rock'n'Roll in Zürich. Die Limmatstadt war fest in der Hand der Raver, und die Streetparade war der «place to be».

Aber ein kleiner Club trotzte vehement dem Ansturm der ekstatischen Technokraten. Oder wie es Boris Müller, ehemaliger Türsteher dieses Clubs, 2013 in einem im *Tages-Anzeiger* erschienenen Nachruf zu Zürichs verschwundenen Partytempeln so schön beschrieb: «Mit einer Ladung Schrot und Heroin beförderte sich Kurt Cobain 1994 ins Jenseits. Rock war tot und Gott ein DJ. Wem zu Bumm-Bumm das Herz nicht hüpfen wollte, erlebte Mitte der Neunzigerjahre musikalisch eine schwierige Zeit. Doch eine junge Crew aus der illegalen Barszene eröffnete trotz hartem Gegenwind das Luv. Ein Rockclub im Seefeld – gewagt!»

Mit diesem Wagnis war es 1999, fünf kurze Jahre nach der Eröffnung, schon wieder vorbei. Und wenn es zu dieser Zeit nicht den Michel Casarramona gegeben hätte, so würden sich vielleicht nur noch die wenigen Auserwählten daran erinnern, die damals die Konzerte in diesem verrauchten und verschwitzten 200-Seelen-Club erlebt hatten. Denn es waren neben den Flyern und Monatsprogrammen des Grafikers und Luv-Mitbetreibers Reto Gehrig vor allem die Konzertplakate und Flyer des Zürcher Illustrators und Rock'n'Roll-Aficionados Michel Casarramona, die dem Luv-Club auch nach seinem Ende zu einem über die Grenzen der Stadt hinausreichenden Kultstatus verhalfen. Besonders die von Casarramona liebevoll in Handarbeit gestalteten Konzertplakate waren in diesen Jahren und sind wohl auch heute noch in Dutzenden von Zürcher Haushalten als Wandschmuck zu finden.

So hängt 15 Jahre danach ein 1998 von Michel als Vier-in-einem-Siebdruck gestaltetes Konzertplakat in meinem Atelier. Eigentlich war dieses im Überformat gedruckte und in variabler Serie aufhängbare Polyptychon in seiner Produktion zu aufwändig und zu teuer für einen finanziell unterdotierten Mini-Club wie das Luv. Aber ich durfte mich Michels ansteckendem Enthusiasmus nicht verweigern, denn letztendlich war mir bewusst, dass der Rock'n'Roll neben dem coolen Understatement auch immer des imaginären Grössenwahns bedarf. Oder wie fragte Beat-Man, der Daddy Cool und Doyen des Swiss-Garage-Rock'n'Roll in Referenz an die legendären Cramps so schön: «How Far Can You Go?» So ging Michel keinen Strich zu weit und verewigte dennoch sieben Wahnsinnsbands und vier fantastische Konzerte auf einen Streich: Skeleton Surfers (mit besagtem Beat-Man), Man or Astroman, The Onyas, Cosmic Psychos, Demolition Doll Rods, Andre Williams & The Countdowns und New Bomb Turks. Mein favorisiertes Memento mori an fünf zu kurze Jahre voller Sex, Drugs & Rock'n'Roll.

Apropos Memento mori des Rock'n'Roll: An meinem Kühlschrank hängt mit dem ebenfalls 1998 von Michel geschaffenen Konzertflyer der japanischen Trash-Rocker Guitar Wolf ein weiteres Andenken an die schnelllebige Vergänglichkeit des Rock'n'Roll-Zeitgeists. Der leider viel zu früh verstorbene, in bester Ramones-Manier Bass Wolf genannte Bassist von Guitar Wolf trank an besag-

LUV — Let's get lock'n'loll!

The second half of the nineteen-nineties was a lousy time for rock'n'roll in Zurich. The city on the Limmat river was firmly in the hands of ravers, and the Street Parade was "the place to be." Nevertheless, one small club vigorously defied the onslaught of ecstatic technocrats.

Or, as Boris Müller (a former doorman at this club) so eloquently described it in an obituary for Zurich's vanished party temples published in the *Tages-Anzeiger* in 2013: "Kurt Cobain ferried himself into the afterlife in 1994 with some shotgun ammo and heroin. Rock was dead and God was a DJ. People whose hearts wouldn't beat to the boom-boom sounds had a harsh musical time in the nineteen-nineties. Nevertheless, one young crew from the illegal bar scene opened up the Luv in spite of the strong headwinds. A rock club in the Seefeld district — daring!"

This risky business venture already ended in 1999, five years after its opening. Had it not been for Michel Casarramona, maybe only the chosen few who actually experienced the gigs in this smoky and sweaty club with a capacity for an audience of 200 would still remember it nowadays. For next to the flyers and monthly programs created by Reto Gehrig, acting as the graphic designer and co-operator of the Luv, it was the concert posters and flyers by Michel Casarramona — a Zurich illustrator and rock'n'roll aficionado — that were instrumental in the club achieving cult status; famous far beyond the city limits, even after the club's demise. Especially the concert posters, lovingly handcrafted by Casarramona, were in those days — and probably still today — used as wall decorations in dozens of Zurich households.

Thus, fifteen years later, a concert poster designed by Michel as a four-in-one silkscreen print in 1998 still enhances my studio. To say the least, the production of such a polyptych, printed in an oversized format and available as a series, was far too elaborate and expensive for the financially underfunded mini-club that was the Luv. But I couldn't resist Michel's contagious enthusiasm, for in the end I knew that rock'n'roll always calls not only for cool understatement but also for imaginary delusions of grandeur. Or, as Beat-Man, daddy cool and doyen of Swiss garage rock'n'roll, asked so beguiling with reference to the legendary Cramps: "How Far Can You Go?" Michel, therefore, didn't go one inch too far and still managed to immortalize seven amazing bands and four fantastic concerts in one sweep: Skeleton Surfers (featuring abovementioned Beat-Man), Man Or Astroman, The Onyas, Cosmic Psychos, Demolition Doll Rods, Andre Williams & The Countdowns, and New Bomb Turks. My favorite *memento mori* of the five far too short years filled to the brim with sex, drugs, and rock'n'roll.

Talking about rock'n'roll *memento mori*: Stuck to my refrigerator is the concert flyer Michel created in 1998 for Japanese trash rocker Guitar Wolf, yet another souvenir from the fast-paced transience of the rock'n' roll zeitgeist. On said evening, the bassist of Guitar Wolf — unfortunately, he died far too early — who in line with the Ramones was called Bass Wolf, downed a

tem Abend nach praktisch jedem Song eine Flasche Bier, Kamikaze-Style, auf Ex. Worauf der ebenfalls passend Guitar Wolf genannte Gitarrist und Sänger mit den Worten «Let's Get Lock'n'Loll! One, Two, Thlee, Fole!» jeweils den nächsten Song anzählte. Vor der Zugabe durfte sich Bass Wolf dann auch prompt im Backstage übergeben. Wahrscheinlich hatte ihm niemand erklärt, dass die Biere in der Schweiz hochprozentiger sind als in Japan.

Jedes Mal, wenn ich nun den Kühlschrank öffne, um mir ein Bier zu holen, sehe ich mir den Flyer von Michel an und sage «Let's Get Lock'n'Loll!». Ans Luv denke ich dabei immer, das Exxen lasse ich aber schön bleiben.

R.I.P. Hideaki Sekiguchi, aka Billy, aka Bass Wolf
1967–2005

Martin Ain

bottle of beer after every song in total kamikaze style. At which time, the equally suitably named guitarist and singer, Guitar Wolf, would give the count for the next song with the words: "Let's get lock'n'loll! One, two, thlee, fole!" Before playing the encore, Bass Wolf then promptly threw up backstage. Probably no one had told him that Swiss beer is much stronger than the Japanese equivalent.

Every time I now open the fridge to grab a beer, I look at Michel's flyer and say: "Let's get lock'n'loll!" And, when I do so, I always have to think of the Luv — but I refrain from chugging the beer!

R.I.P. Hideaki Sekiguchi, a.k.a Billy, a.k.a Bass Wolf
1967–2005

Martin Ain

oblivians
THE REVELATORS
Rock & Roll Salvation From
Memphis Tennessee/Columbia Missouri
10. 4. '97
22:00 Uhr, Geroldstr. 5, Zürich

MICHEL CASARRAMONA, HOMETRAINER CONTEST, 2001, 500×700

MICHEL CASARRAMONA, DOCTOR EXPLOSION, 1999, 440×750, SILKSCREEN

MICHEL CASARRAMONA, BOXEN UND TANZ, 2001, 700×500

KEN
UND
TANZ
ÄMPFE
Unter Aufsicht des Schweizerischen Boxverbandes
TS:
CAN
HALL
FEATURING
Buzz
face
BSTAR
BOSS HI-FI
JUNI 2001
ABRIK
AKTIONSHALLE
RESPECT THE CHAMP

MICHEL CASARRAMONA, KING KORA, 1997, 500×750

MICHEL CASARRAMONA, LOS CONEJOS, 1998, 500×700

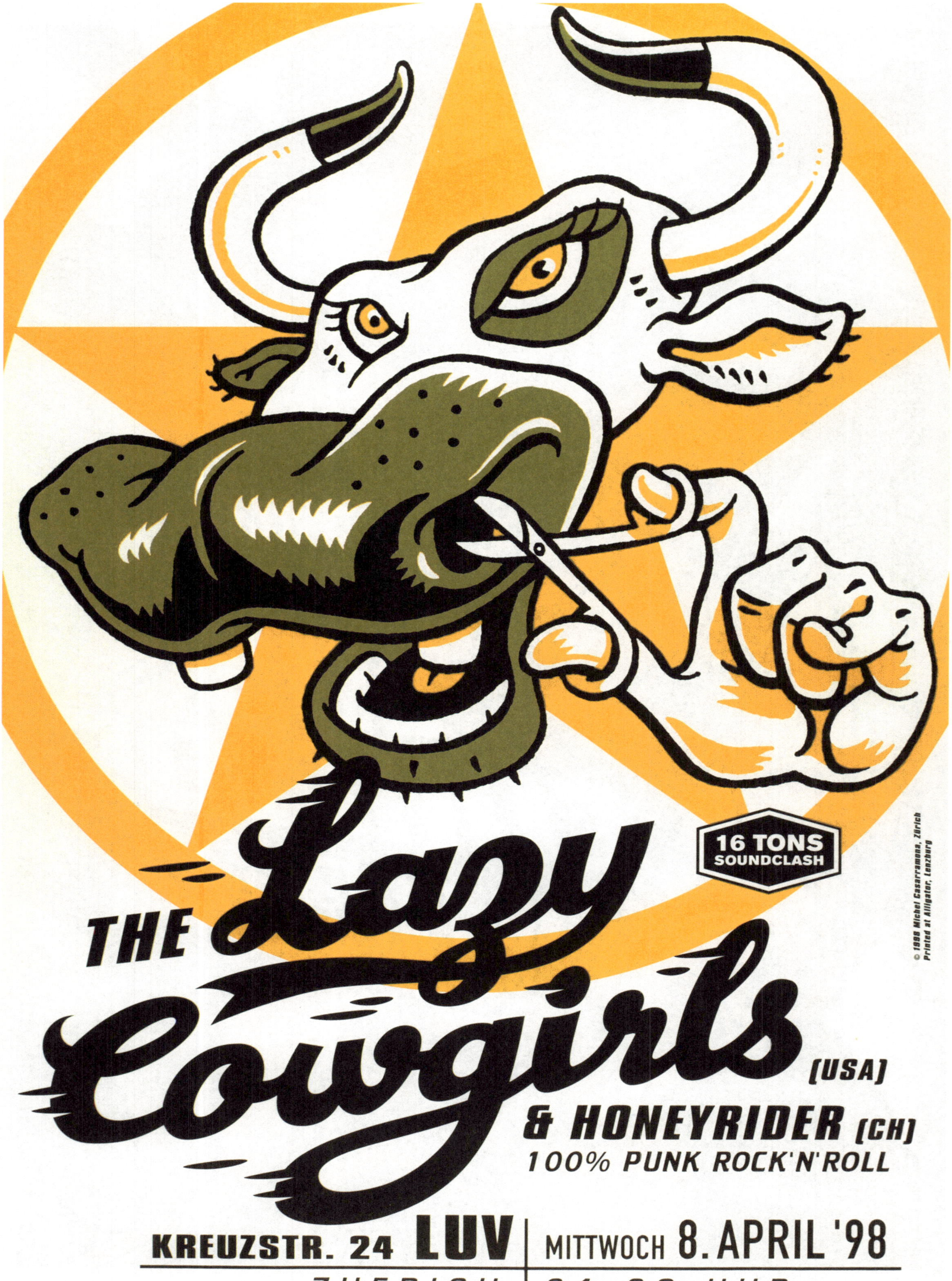
16 TONS
SOUNDCLASH
THE Lazy Cowgirls (USA)
& HONEYRIDER (CH)
100% PUNK ROCK'N'ROLL
KREUZSTR. 24 LUV
ZUERICH
MITTWOCH 8. APRIL '98
21:30 UHR
© 1998 Michel Casarramona, Zürich
Printed at Alligator, Lenzburg

BEYOND ANY HORROR
JOLLY and the FL
spielen au

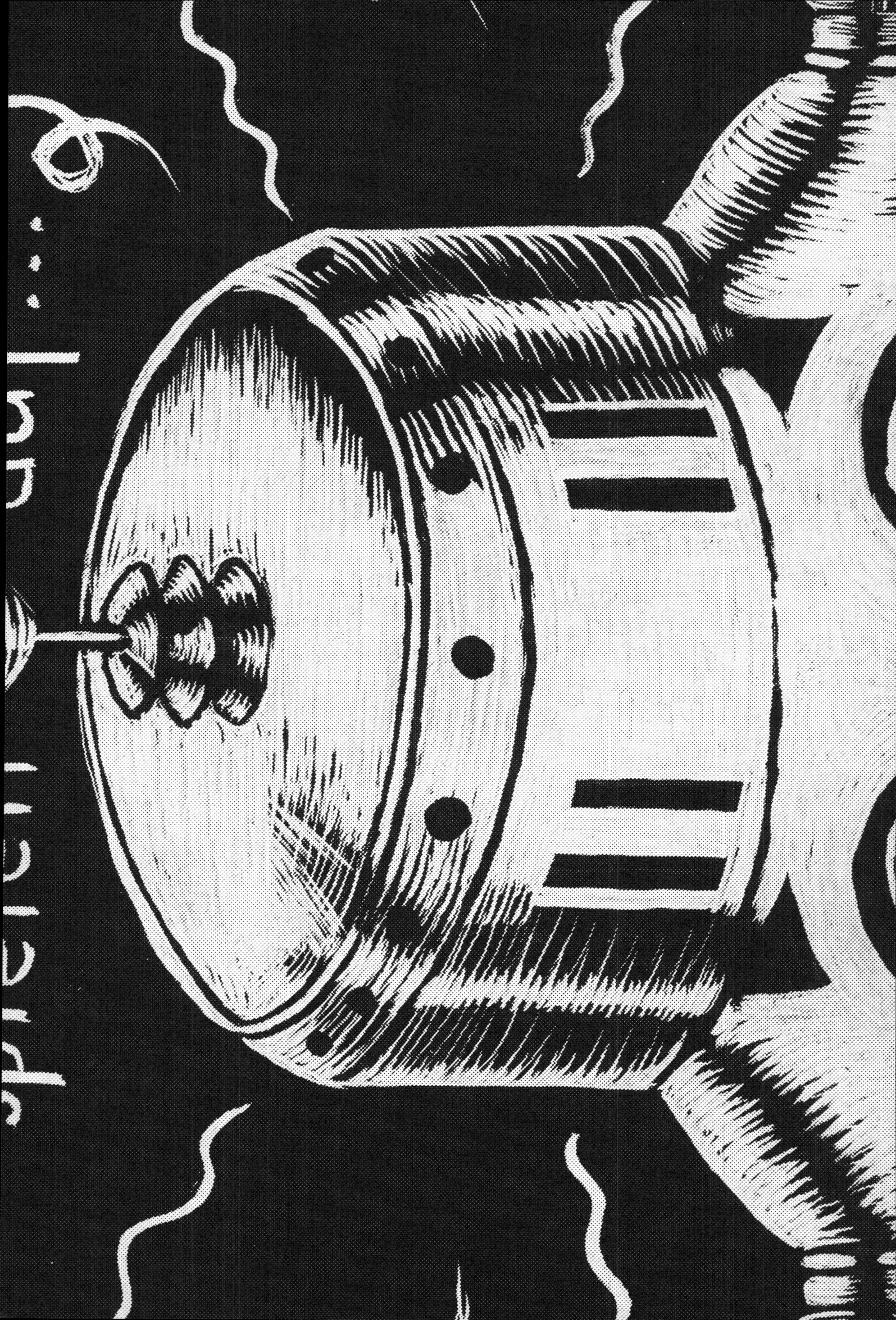
spielen auf…

Märt Infanger

Gelernter Grafiker aus Engelberg und seit Mitte der Achtzigerjahre Akkordeonspieler bei der Band Jolly and the Flytrap. Als Hausgrafiker der Band und Teilhaber des Musiklabels Nomen Records ist er für die Gestaltung der Tonträger, Konzertplakate und Bühnenbilder zuständig. Seit zwei Jahrzehnten erarbeitet er in seinem Atelier «Ultrabazar» Grafiken für Musiklabels und verschiedenste Bands. Seit 2004 unterrichtet er an der Fachklasse Grafik in Luzern.

Märt Infanger

Trained graphic artist from Engelberg and since the mid-eighties accordion player for the band Jolly and the Flytrap. As the domestic graphic artist of the band and part owner of the music label Nomen Records, he is responsible for the design of the recorded media, concert posters and stage scenery. Since two decades he develops graphic art for music labels and various bands at his studio "Ultrabazar." As of 2004 he teaches a class in graphic art in Luzern.

MÄRT INFANGER, JOLLY AND THE FLYTRAP & ALICE IN THUNDERLAND, 1992, 297×420

MÄRT INFANGER, JOLLY AND THE FLYTRAP, 1991, 297×420

JOLLY
and THE
FLYTRAP
BETELGEUZE
26.Sept. 92
Vinylzyklotronisierung
Casino-Kursaal
Planet Engelberg
einbeamung: 19.30 h
mit:
– SIEGFRIED
– PAPA CORAILLE
– JOLLY AND THE FLYTRAP
AND HORNY HÖRNS
MÄRT
LSE-Raumtransporter nach Stans 00.30 h

MÄRT INFANGER, JOLLY AND THE FLYTRAP, 1993, 297×420

MÄRT INFANGER, JOLLY AND THE FLYTRAP, 1993, 297×420

MÄRT INFANGER, JOLLY AND THE FLYTRAP, SWINDLE, PROFAX, 1993, 297×420

MÄRT INFANGER, JOLLY AND THE FLYTRAP, 1992, 297×420

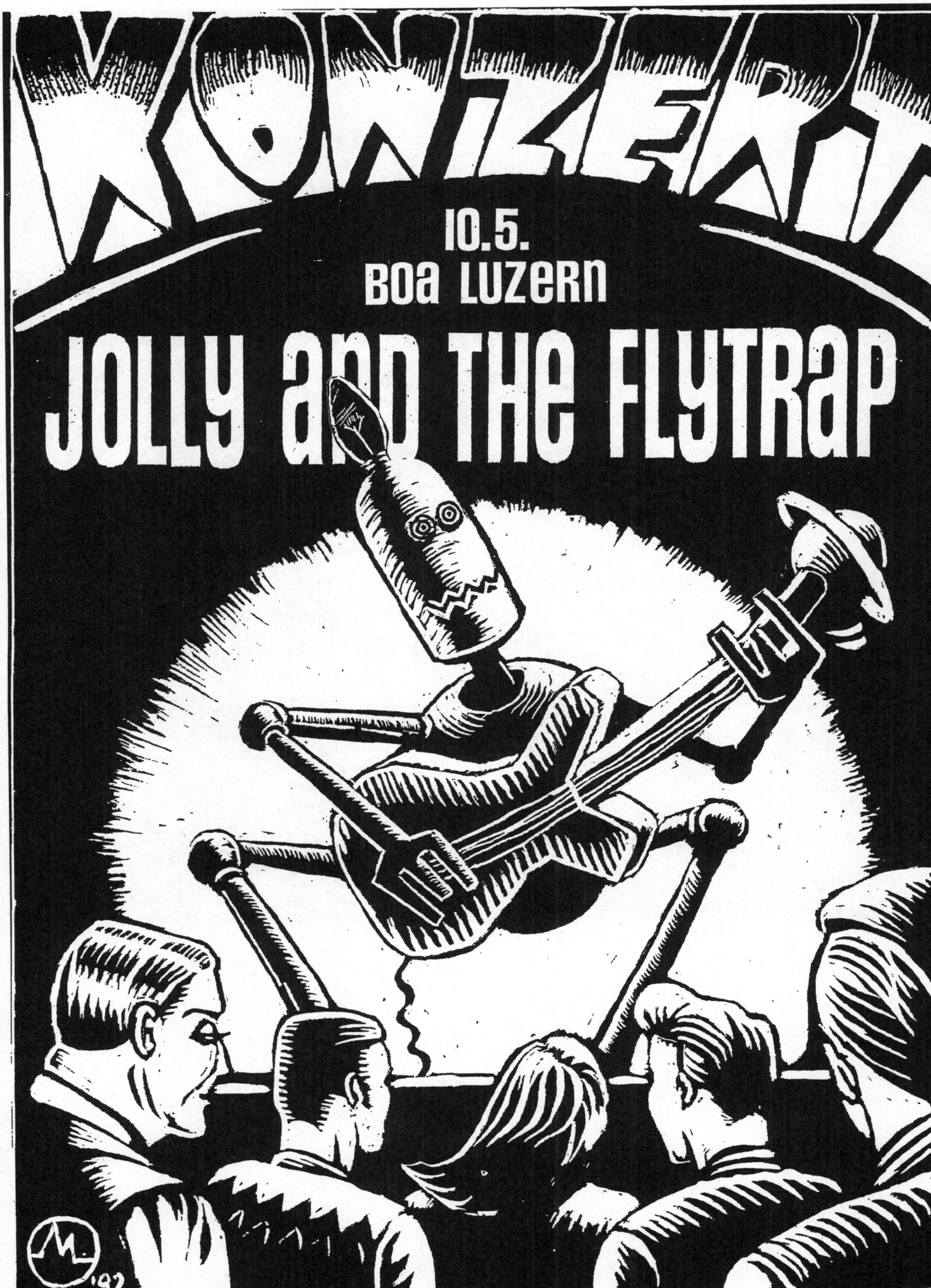

MÄRT INFANGER, JOLLY AND THE FLYTRAP - BETELGEUZE, 7" FRONT COVER, 1992, SILKSCREEN

MÄRT INFANGER, JOLLY AND THE FLYTRAP - BETELGEUZE, 7" BACK COVER, 1992, SILKSCREEN

MÄRT INFANGER, THE DELILAHS, 2006, 500×700, SILKSCREEN

The Delilahs – Wo shoppt Steven Tyler?

Manchmal nimmt Information in der globalisierten Welt seltsame und verschlungene Wege. Anlass war ein Ereignis, das im Gasthaus Grünenwald bei Engelberg seinen Anfang nahm. Dieses ehemalige Gasthaus dient meiner Band Jolly and the Flytrap als Heimatquartier und anderen Bands als Probehotel. Es finden dort auch regelmässig Konzerte und Anlässe statt. Im November 2006 traten im Rahmen des alljährlichen «Seelenwärmers» die Delilahs aus Zug und die Kronzeugen aus Luzern auf. Meine Aufgabe als Mitveranstalter ist es jeweils, das Plakat dafür zu gestalten. Per Zufall stolperte ich über eine Werbung für Damenunterwäsche aus den Fünfzigern und veränderte das Sujet mit einigen Rock'n'Roll-Elementen wie Totenschädel und Tattoos und fügte die Typo hinzu. Die Auflage für den Aushang war zwar eher bescheiden, aber lockte immerhin etwa hundert Besucher an das Konzert. Es wurde ein feiner, astreiner Rockabend, dessen Gitarrenklänge alsbald verblassten und Teil der Geschichte wurden ...

Sechs Jahre vergingen, und plötzlich klingelte bei mir das Telefon, und ein Radiojournalist wollte wissen, warum Steven Tyler von Aerosmith ein «Grünenwald»-Shirt trägt. Ich war total verblüfft, hatte keine blasse Ahnung und wurde zu alledem noch unerwarteterweise auf Sendung geschaltet. Offenbar hatte ein Fan der Delilahs ein Youtube-Video eines Konzerts von Aerosmith in Quebec entdeckt, das Steven Tyler mit einem gelben XS-T-Shirt zeigt, auf dem prominent das Grünenwald-Plakatsujet prangt: «The Delilahs & Kronzeugen – 20.30 Uhr im Gasthaus Grünenwald in Engelberg». Via Facebook machte die Geschichte bald die Runde und wurde im journalistischen Sommerloch zu einer willkommenen Story für Presse und Radio, und ich wurde mit Anfragen überschwemmt:

«Wo shoppt Steven Tyler? Ist Tyler Fan der Innerschweiz? Hat er das Bühnenoutfit aus der Altkleidersammlung? Werden Aerosmith am ‹Halt auf Verlangen›-Festival im Grünenwald auftreten?»

Wir hatten ja weder T-Shirts gedruckt, noch war Herr Tyler nach einer Bergtour auf den Titlis bei uns eingekehrt oder gar versumpft. Auch die Nachforschungen der Journalisten beim Management von Aerosmith endeten erfolglos, und die Geschichte blieb kurios.

Meine Interpretation geht in eine andere Richtung. Ich hoffe nicht, dass es sich um eine serielle Produktion handelt, sondern ich gehe davon aus, dass Tylers Shirt ein Unikat ist und bleibt. So ist es zum Beispiel denkbar, dass Steven Tyler seiner Stylistin den Auftrag erteilte, ein exklusives Bühnenoutfit zu kreieren. Diese stiess wiederum zufällig im Internet auf mein Plakat – nicht wissend, dass die leicht bekleidete Dame auf dem Plakat auf gleiche Weise zu mir gefunden hat.

Märt Infanger

The Delilahs — Where does Steven Tyler do his shopping?

In the globalized world, information sometimes takes strange and intricate routes. One such occasion was an incident that had its beginning at the Gasthaus Grünenwald near Engelberg. This former hotel served my band Jolly and the Flytrap as our home base and other bands used it as a rehearsal hotel. Regular concert evenings and events were also staged there. In November 2006, the Delilahs from Zug and the Kronzeugen from Lucerne performed on the occasion of the annual "Seelenwärmer" (soul warmer) event. It is my responsibility as a co-organizer to design the poster each year. By chance, I came across an advertisement for women's underwear dating back to the nineteen-fifties. I modified the original subject with some rock'n' roll elements — skulls and tattoos — and then added the typography. In spite of the modest print run of the poster, it attracted about a hundred visitors wanting to see the bands perform. It turned out to be an ace rock evening with guitar sounds soon fading to become part of history ...

Six years had passed when my phone suddenly rang. It was a radio reporter wanting to know why Steven Tyler from Aerosmith was seen wearing a "Grünenwald" T-Shirt. I was absolutely flabbergasted; I didn't have the faintest idea and, in addition, was unexpectedly broadcast live on air. Apparently, a fan of the Delilahs had discovered a YouTube video of an Aerosmith concert in Quebec showing Steven Tyler wearing an extra small, yellow T-Shirt prominently featuring the Grünenwald poster design: "The Delilahs & Kronzeugen — 20.30 Uhr im Gasthaus Grünenwald in Engelberg." The story soon made the rounds on Facebook and became a welcome story for the media during the news-dry summer season — I was flooded with questions:

"Where does Steven Tyler do his shopping? Is he a fan of Central Switzerland? Did he get his stage outfit from a used clothes collection? Will Aerosmith be playing the 'Halt auf Verlangen' festival at the Grünenwald?"

We never printed T-Shirts, nor had Mr. Tyler ever stopped by after a mountain tour to the Titlis to join us for late-night drinking. The reporters' queries to Aerosmith's management were equally unsuccessful, so the story remained a curiosity.

My interpretation points in another direction. I'm positive the T-Shirt never reached serial production and instead assume that Tyler's shirt is a one-off and remains unique. It is conceivable that Steven Tyler asked his stylist to create an exclusive stage outfit. In turn, the stylist may have come across my poster on thew Internet merely by chance — not knowing that the scantily dressed lady on the poster had found me in much the same way.

Märt Infanger

MÄRT INFANGER, JOLLY AND THE FLYTRAP, 2007, 420×594

MÄRT INFANGER, JOLLY AND THE FLYTRAP, 2012, 420×594

MÄRT INFANGER, JOLLY AND THE FLYTRAP, 2004, 420×594

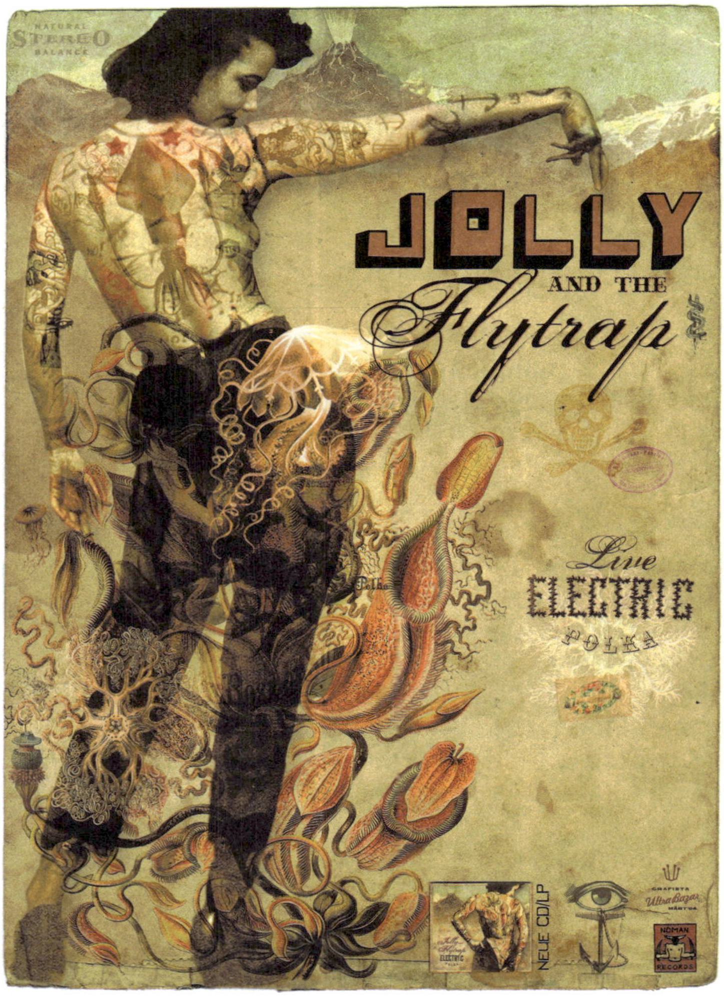

MÄRT INFANGER, JOLLY AND THE FLYTRAP, 2012, 420×594

MÄRT INFANGER, JOLLY AND THE FLYTRAP, TOUR POSTER, 1992, 420×594

MÄRT INFANGER, LOVER, LES CHEVAUX SAUVAGES, 2011, 450×645, SILKSCREEN

MÄRT INFANGER, THE FEELING OF LOVE, 2009, 500×700, SILKSCREEN

MÄRT INFANGER, TEENAGE HATE PUNK NIGHT, 2006, 500×700, SILKSCREEN

MÄRT INFANGER, JE T'AIME & ROLLING ROCK FESTIVAL, 2011, 500×700, SILKSCREEN

Memphisto Produktion presents
Fri. Feb.1.
2002
Doors 9.00 P.M.
10:00 P.M. Show
Boa Bar
Luzern
Voodoo
Gospel
13
R'n'R
Love
Hate
Reverend
BEAT-MAN
& the Unbelievers
Primitive
Preacher
Rock'n'Roll
Sin
Trash
and
DANCING A
GOGO
'till 4.00 A.M.
CPTN. BELOOGA
AND THE KRUSHER
SIEMPRE
187%
GRAFISTA
UltraBazar
MÄRT'02

Rote Fabrik
Sommerbühne
Fr 28.7. 20h
Wu-Tang Cla
& Method Ma
& Raekwon S

ne
coh
Clan
Man Solo
on Solo

Mi 16.8. 20h
Mobb Deep
& Support

Fr 18.8. 20h
Sierra Maestra
(Cuba)

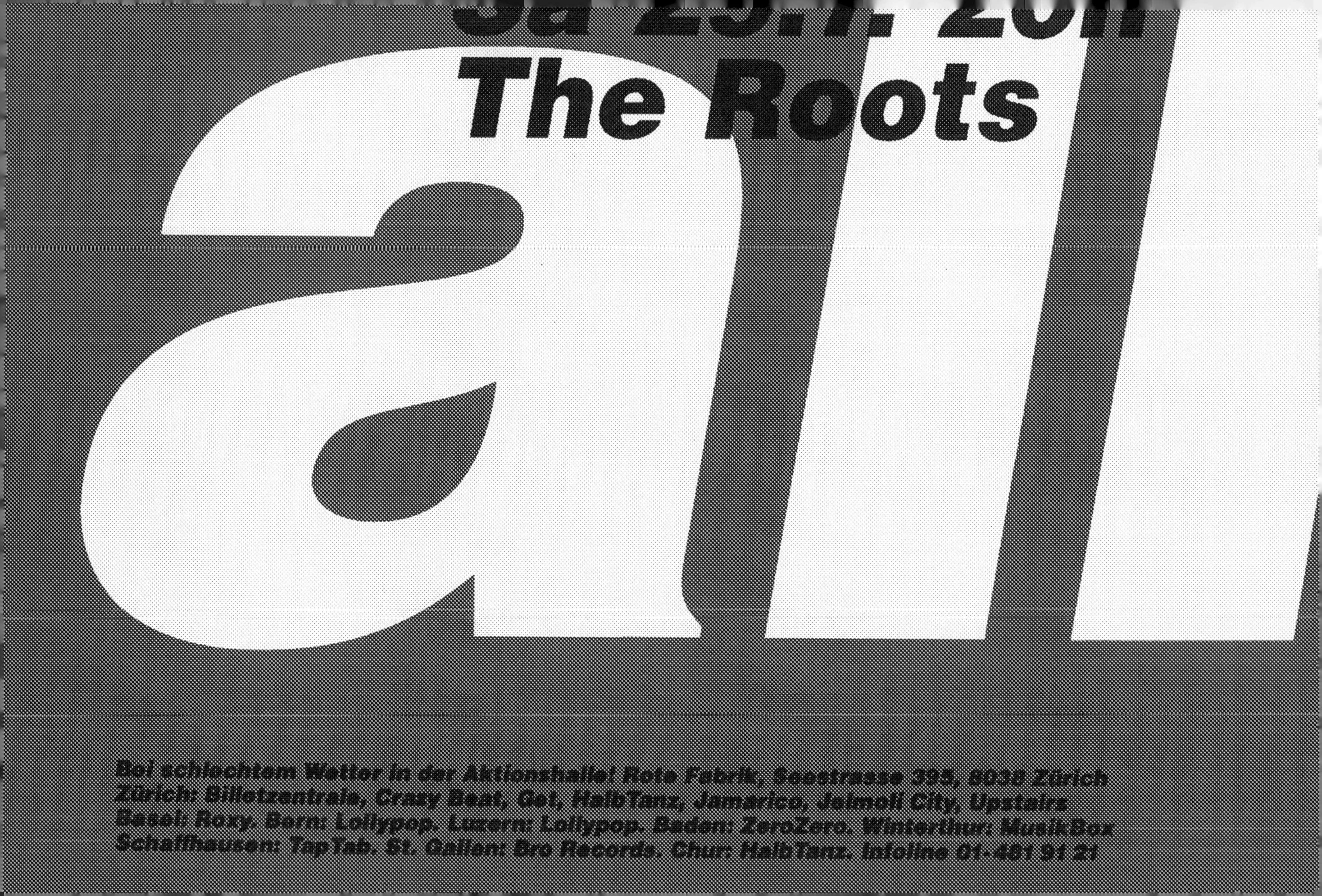
The Roots
Bei schlechtem Wetter in der Aktionshalle! Rote Fabrik, Seestrasse 395, 8038 Zürich
Zürich: Billetzentrale, Crazy Beat, Get, HalbTanz, Jamarico, Jelmoli City, Upstairs
Basel: Roxy. Bern: Lollypop. Luzern: Lollypop. Baden: ZeroZero. Winterthur: MusikBox
Schaffhausen: TapTab. St. Gallen: Bro Records. Chur: HalbTanz. Infoline 01-481 91 21

Cornel Windlin

Machte seinen Abschluss als Grafiker an der Schule für Gestaltung Luzern und arbeitete ab 1988 in London für den Grafikdesigner und Typograf Neville Brody. Ab 1990 war er Art Director des *The Face-Magazins*, machte sich 1991 selbstständig und kehrte 1993 in die Schweiz zurück. Hier gestaltete er unter anderem zwei Jahre lang Konzertplakate für die Rote Fabrik in Zürich, die in diesem Buch gezeigt werden. Von 2007 bis 2010 war Windlin Präsident der Jury der Schönsten Schweizer Bücher. Für die Spielzeit 2009/10 war er verantwortlich für die Konzeption des neuen Gesamterscheinungsbildes des Schauspielhauses Zürich. 2011 erhielt er dafür den Design Preis Schweiz. Heute lebt und arbeitet er in Berlin.

Cornel Windlin

Graduated as graphic artist from the Schule für Gestaltung Luzern and, from 1988, worked in London for the graphic designer and typographer Neville Brody. As of 1990 he was art director of *The Face magazine*, became a freelancer in 1991 and returned to Switzerland in 1993. Here he designed, among other things, concert posters for the Rote Fabrik in Zurich for two years, which are shown in this book. From 2007 to 2010, Windlin was the president of the jury for The Most Beautiful Swiss Books. For the season 2009/10 he was responsible for the concept of the new visual identity of the Schauspielhaus in Zurich. In 2011 he received the Design Prize Switzerland. Today he lives and works in Berlin.

CORNEL WINDLIN, ROTE FABRIK - MAY/JUNE, 1994, 480×680

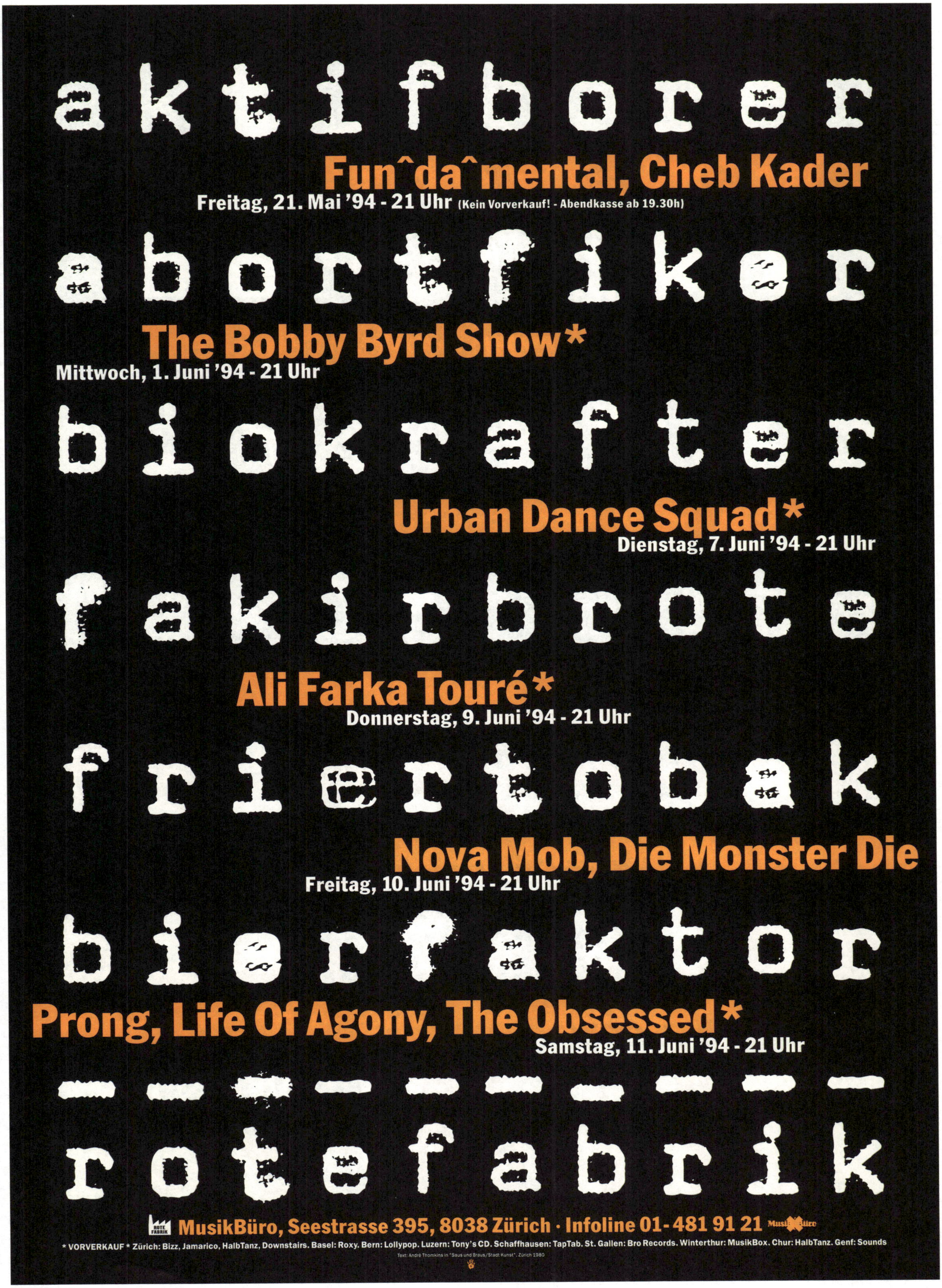

fuck
all ya
Rote Fabrik
Sommerbühne
Fr 28.7. 20h
Wu-Tang Clan
& Method Man Solo
& Raekwon Solo
Sa 29.7. 20h
The Roots
Mi 16.8. 20h
Mobb Deep
& Support
Fr 18.8. 20h
Sierra Maestra
(Cuba)
Bei schlechtem Wetter in der Aktionshalle! Rote Fabrik, Seestrasse 395, 8038 Zürich
Zürich: Billetzentrale, Crazy Beat, Get, HalbTanz, Jamarico, Jelmoli City, Upstairs
Basel: Roxy. Bern: Lollypop. Luzern: Lollypop. Baden: ZeroZero. Winterthur: MusikBox
Schaffhausen: TapTab. St. Gallen: Bro Records. Chur: HalbTanz. Infoline 01-481 91 21

fuck
all ya
Rote Fabrik
Sommerbühne
Fr 28.7. 20h
Wu-Tang Clan
& Method Man Solo
& Raekwon Solo
Sa 29.7. 20h
The Roots
Mi 16.8. 20h
Mobb Deep
& Support
Fr 18.8. 20h
Sierra Maestra
(Cuba)
Bei schlechtem Wetter in der Aktionshalle! Rote Fabrik, Seestrasse 395, 8038 Zürich
Zürich: Billetzentrale, Crazy Beat, Get, HalbTanz, Jamarico, Jelmoli City, Upstairs
Basel: Roxy. Bern: Lollypop. Luzern: Lollypop. Baden: ZeroZero. Winterthur: MusikBox
Schaffhausen: TapTab. St. Gallen: Bro Records. Chur: HalbTanz. Infoline 01-481 91 21

Rote Fabrik – Den Ton in die Stadt tragen

CURIGER Bernd Blankenburg von der Roten Fabrik von 1993 bis 1996, Martin Heller im Museum für Gestaltung von 1994 bis 1999 und Christoph Marthaler vom Schauspielhaus von 1999 bis 2001: Was war an diesen Auftraggebern besonders?

WINDLIN Alle waren sie sehr intelligent und hatten den Mut, mir genügend Spielraum für meine Arbeit anzubieten; aber natürlich taten sie dies auch in ihrem eigenen Interesse und haben genauso davon profitiert wie ich. Zudem hatte jeder von ihnen eine Vision für die Institution, die sie leiten oder geleitet haben. Bei Blankenburg und Marthaler war es sogar so, dass sie damals gerade neu leitende Positionen bei einer Institution antraten und damit auch ein dringendes Bedürfnis hatten, sich mit ihrem Programm zu profilieren. Das war für mich eine interessante Situation und Herausforderung. Da ich von aussen kam und dadurch unabhängig war, konnte ich unbelastet Strategien entwickeln, die diesen Bedürfnissen entsprachen, ohne betriebsblind zu werden oder mich durch interne Konflikte beschneiden zu lassen.

CURIGER Bei der Roten Fabrik hast du Plakate gestaltet, welche für Musikkonzerte im weitesten Sinne stehen sollten. Erstaunlicherweise nahmen deine Plakate kaum Bezug auf die Veranstaltungen an sich.

WINDLIN Das ist etwas zu allgemein formuliert und stimmt so nicht. Natürlich wurde mit etwas anspruchsvolleren Codes operiert als üblich – aber mit Erfolg. Das war auch Teil der Roten Fabrik, in welchem Ton das Programm in die Stadt getragen wurde, und es war ein stark Identität stiftendes Element. Bei allen drei Institutionen ging es darum, Ideen zu kommunizieren oder Inhalte zu vermitteln, die oft nur schwer konkret zu formulieren sind, ohne auf bewährte Muster zurückzugreifen. Auch waren sie bereit, jenseits der bestehenden lokalen Klischees zu kommunizieren, und sind insofern ein Risiko eingegangen – genauso, wie sie in ihrer eigenen Programmation Risiken eingegangen sind. Und sie waren unter Zugzwang: Sie mussten auffallen, um sich von ihrer Konkurrenz abzusetzen. Ich entwickelte Methoden, um adäquate visuelle Entsprechungen zu finden und nicht bloss eine sogenannte «Identity» überzustülpen. Bei diesem Punkt, so scheint mir, haben wir uns dann auch gefunden: Sie versuchten alle, neue Wege zu gehen, waren bereit, andere Darstellungsformen zuzulassen, mit denen sich z.B. Theater, Musik oder Design vermitteln lassen. Man findet denn auch teilweise Ähnlichkeiten im Ansatz: Diversität, Identität durch Mehrstimmigkeit, Überraschung, Widerspruch, Verweigerung, Herausforderung des Publikums usw.

HUG Einerseits geht es hier also um eine gemeinsame Aufbruchstimmung, anderseits scheinst du bei Differenzen auch den Konflikt nicht zu scheuen. Ganz schön anstrengend, stelle ich mir vor…

WINDLIN Ja ja, aber viel weniger anstrengend als zum Beispiel Akkordmaurer zu sein.

WINDLIN Kulturelle Institutionen tendieren dazu, sich von der Kreativität zu entfernen, indem sie den «Dienstleis-

Rote Fabrik — Bringing the sound to the city

CURIGER Bernd Blankenburg at the Rote Fabrik (alternative youth center) from 1993 to 1996, Martin Heller at the Museum für Gestaltung (Museum of Design) from 1994 to 1999, and Christoph Marthaler at the Schauspielhaus (Theater) from 1999 to 2001: What was special about these clients in Zurich?

WINDLIN All of them were very intelligent and had the courage to give me enough latitude for my work; they also did this in their own interest and benefited from it as much as I did, of course. Moreover, each one of them had a vision for the institution they are or were managing. For Blankenburg and Marthaler, this was combined with managerial roles they had assumed in newly established institutions, the reason why they also urgently needed to make a name for themselves with their programs. I found this an interesting situation and a challenge. As I came from outside and was therefore independent, I could develop strategies catering to these needs without politics and unencumbered by internal office conflicts.

CURIGER In the case of the Rote Fabrik, you designed posters that were intended to represent music concerts in the broadest sense. Surprisingly, your posters made hardly any reference to the actual events.

WINDLIN That statement is too general and not strictly true. Of course, the roles implied at the time were more sophisticated than usual — but they were applied successfully. This role intended for the Rote Fabrik, the impression the program should make when it hit the city; this element contributed much to shaping an identity. Communicating ideas or conveying content that may be difficult to express without reverting to conventional patterns was an important requirement for all three institutions. In addition, they were all prepared to communicate beyond existing local clichés, and, in this respect, to take risks — just as they did in their own programming. They also stood under intense pressure: they had to stand out in order to set themselves apart from their competitors. I developed methods for finding suitable visual analogies instead of foisting a so-called "identity" on them. I believe it was at this point that we concurred, inasmuch as they all wanted to leave the beaten path and were prepared to apply new forms for presenting theater, music, or design, for instance. Therefore, one can also find similarities in the approach: diversity, identity through polyphony, surprise, contradiction, non-acceptance, challenging the public, and so on.

HUG So, on the one hand, it's about sharing the feeling of a fresh start, while, on the other hand, you don't seem to shy away from conflicts if differences occur. I imagine that to be quite stressful…

WINDLIN Sure, but much less taxing than being a piece-rate bricklayer.

CURIGER Cultural institutions have a tendency to put a distance between themselves and creativity by emphasizing their "mission to provide services." And graphic designers, in particular, operate in the limbo between being service providers and heralds of art.

tungsauftrag» zu stark betonen. Und gerade ein Grafiker bewegt sich in dieser Grauzone zwischen Dienstleistung und künstlerischer Aussage.

WINDLIN Erstens: «Den» Grafiker gibt es nicht mehr. Dieser Begriff ist missverständlich, und er impliziert vieles, was mit mir und meiner Arbeitsweise nichts zu tun hat. Zweitens: Diese Tendenz ist nicht nur bei kulturellen Institutionen zu sehen, es gelten in den verschiedensten Bereichen sehr ähnliche Spielregeln, die einen auf eine bestimmte Handlungsweise festlegen und gewisse Abläufe und Hierarchien festschreiben wollen. Drittens: Dienstleistung und Aussage schliessen sich nicht aus – sei sie künstlerisch, politisch oder sonstwie motiviert. [...] Es ist mir tatsächlich sehr wichtig, dass meine Arbeit nützlich ist und ihren objektiven Zweck erfüllt, aber – und das ist zentral – wie das geschehen soll, kann ich nicht dem Diktat anderer überlassen. Es gibt die Bedürfnisse des Auftraggebers, die ernst zu nehmen sind, es gibt die unvermeidlichen Interessen des Publikums (eine fiktive Grösse, die oft bloss zur Legitimation der eigenen Interessen bemüht wird: «ist nicht zielgruppenkonform» ist Quatsch und bedeutet bloss, «gefällt der Freundin des CEOs nicht» oder schlicht «passt mir nicht»), und nicht zuletzt gibt es auch meine eigenen Ansprüche. Die Herausforderung für mich ist nun, diese drei Dinge in ein Spannungsverhältnis zu bringen und in Schwingung zu versetzen. Das ist meine Dienstleistung, und das ist meine Kunst.

Cornel Windlin im Gespräch mit Bice Curiger und Catherine Hug

WINDLIN First of all, "the" graphic designer as such no longer exists. The term is unclear and implies many things that have nothing to do with me or with the way I work. Secondly, this tendency is not only apparent with regard to cultural institutions, since similar rules define specific courses of action attempting to codify particular processes and hierarchies in a wide range of fields. Thirdly, service and message — be they motivated artistically, politically, or otherwise — do not exclude each another. [...] That my work is useful and fulfills its objective purpose is, in fact, quite important to me. But — and this is the key — the way this takes place is not something I can leave entirely to others' demands. There are the client's requirements, which must be taken seriously. There are the inevitable interests of the public (a notional variable that often just seeks to lend its own interests' legitimacy). "Doesn't meet the needs of the target group" is nonsense. All this really spells out is "doesn't please the CEO's girlfriend," or simply put, "I don't like it." Last but not least, there are my own requirements. Now what challenges me is how to establish a dynamic relationship between these three elements and attune them to each other. That's the service I provide, and it's my art.

Cornel Windlin in conversation with Bice Curiger and Catherine Hug

CORNEL WINDLIN, DIE SVP HÖRT SOUNDGARDEN, 1995, 700×500

CORNEL WINDLIN, ROTE FABRIK – APRIL, 1994, 690×490

CORNEL WINDLIN, ROTE FABRIK - MAY, 1994, 500×700

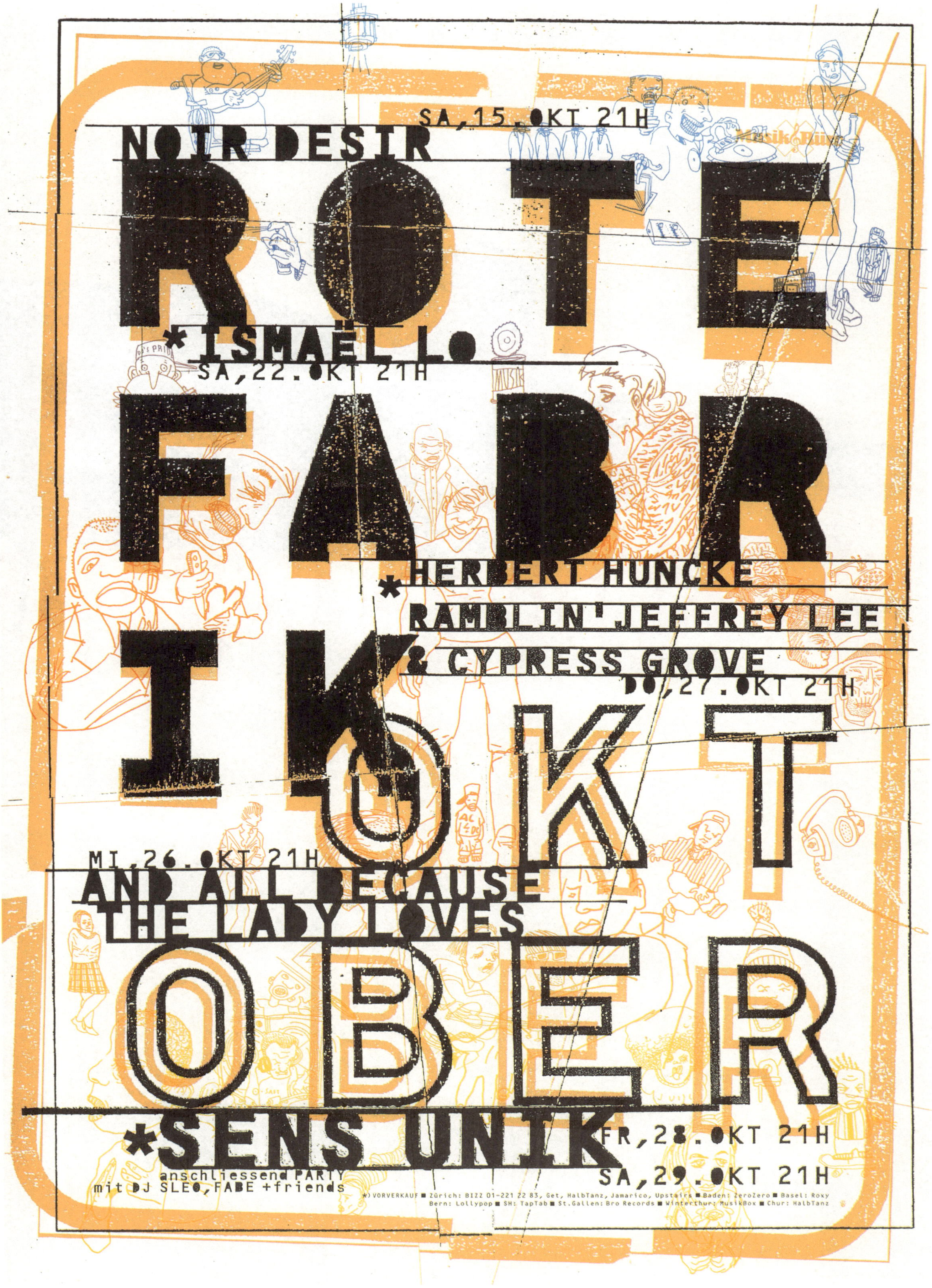
SA,15.OKT 21H
NOIR DESIR
ROTE
*ISMAËL LO
SA,22.OKT 21H
FABR
IK
*HERBERT HUNCKE
RAMBLIN' JEFFREY LEE
& CYPRESS GROVE
DO,27.OKT 21H
OKT
MI,26.OKT 21H
AND ALL BECAUSE
THE LADY LOVES
OBER
*SENS UNIK
FR,28.OKT 21H
SA,29.OKT 21H
anschliessend PARTY
mit DJ SLEO,FABE +friends
*) VORVERKAUF ■ Zürich: BIZZ 01-221 22 83, Get, HalbTanz, Jamarico, Upstairs ■ Baden: ZeroZero ■ Basel: Roxy
Bern: Lollypop ■ SH: TapTab ■ St.Gallen: Bro Records ■ Winterthur: MusikBox ■ Chur: HalbTanz

ZÜRICH: BIZZ 01-221 22 83, CRAZY BEAT, JAMAR
UNIT, UPSTAIRS. WINTERTH
SEASON'S GREETINGS
30 NOV
CYCO MIKO
+INFEC-
TIOUS
GROOVES
METHOD MAN
1 DEZ
+CREW
+VORPREMIERE DES FILMS "THE SHOW"
PJ HAR
+BEN HAR
2 DEZ
ROTE FABRIK FRAKTION
UNTERSTÜTZT DURCH COULEUR 3, NO WAY UND DINGS

NINA'S JAZZ + BLUES,
DEN: ZEROZERO. BASEL: ROXY. BERN: LOLLYPOP. BIEL: LOLLYPOP. LUZERN: LOLLYPOP. SCHAFFHAUSEN: TAPTAB. ST. GALLEN: BRO RECORDS. CHUR: HALBTANZ
LAUSANNE: DISCABRAC. GENÈVE: SOUNDS.
LES MUSICIENS DU NIL
14 DEZ
NTM
+ MELAAZ
15 DEZ
LES REINES PROCHAINES
22 DEZ
ROTE FABRIK
http://www.hugo.ch/hugo/

CORNEL WINDLIN, ROTE FABRIK - MARCH, 1995, 497×698

CORNEL WINDLIN, ROTE FABRIK - NOVEMBER, 1995, 500×700

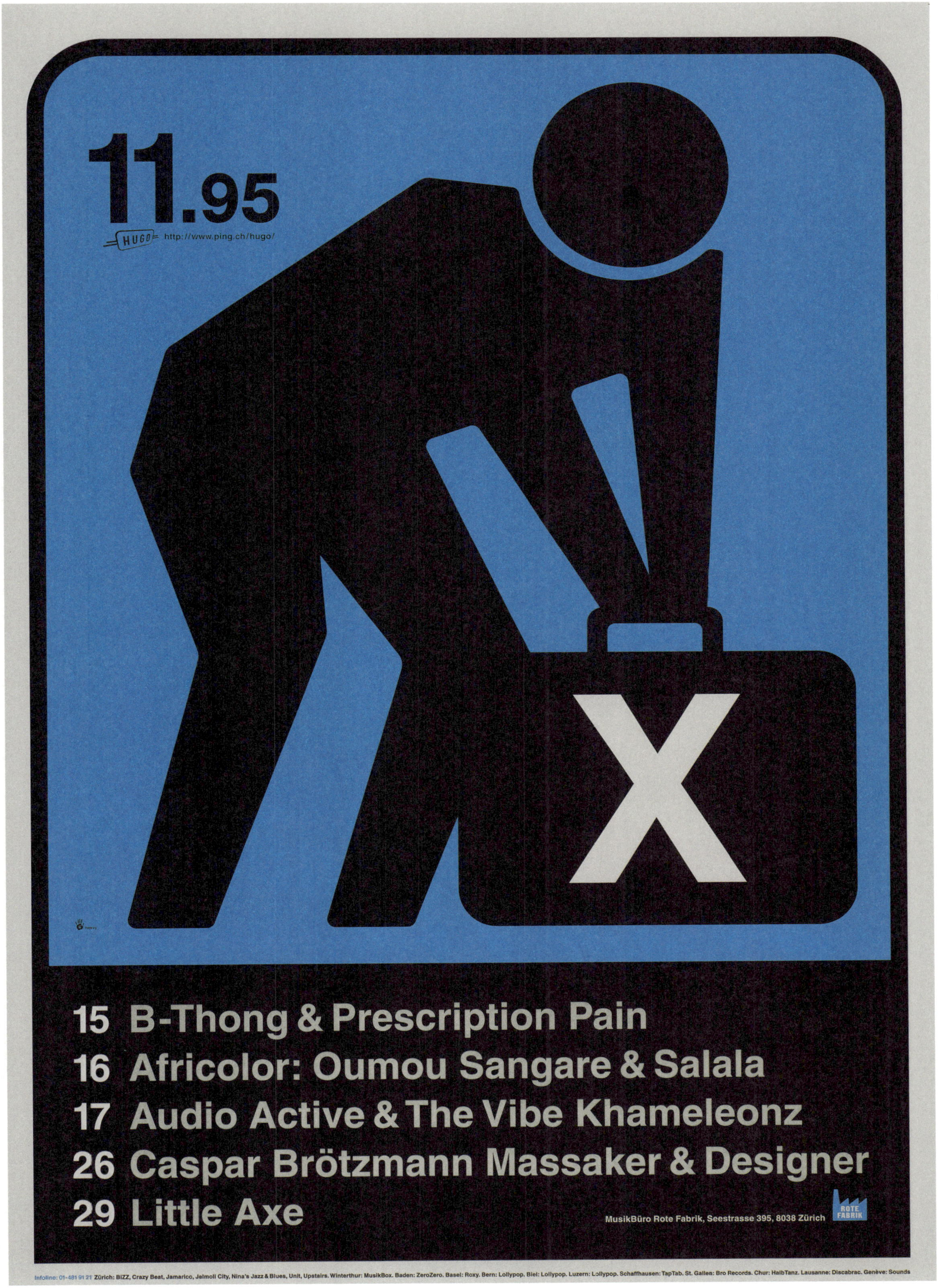

MAI 19 · DJ GOO
Reefer Madness
"ENCHANTÉ"

Reefer Madness – Passt auf, die Schmier' ist da!

Reefer Madness war mein Ding, ja. Ich bin 1993 aus London nach Zürich gekommen und kannte ja noch niemanden. Unter den ersten Leuten, die ich dort durch gemeinsame Freunde kennenlernte, waren Bernd Blankenburg und Connie Hüsser. Ich hab sofort mit Bernd, der damals tagsüber im Musikbüro in der Roten Fabrik tätig war, und Connie, die bei Globus als Dekorateurin arbeitete, Partys organisiert, wo ich selbst hingehen würde. Dabei ging es vor allem um Musik und um eine nette Ambiance.

Anfangs zogen wir von Ort zu Ort. Zum Beispiel in einen Keller an der Seestrasse in Wollishofen, in den Parkring in der Enge, unter Brücken und an den See, wo immer es grad lustig war. Später konnten wir den Keller in einem zwischengenutzten Geschäftshaus an der Zypressenstrasse Sound geprooft ausbauen und als festen Raum einsetzen. Das ging so bis zirka 1997, glaube ich. War ein Riesenspass, das Ganze. Auch, weil es kein Geschäft sein musste bzw. wollte. Und weil wir rechtzeitig damit aufhörten, als es langsam zu gross wurde.

Eines der vielen Highlights war, als David Weiss inkognito mit der Videokamera im Club unterwegs war, um *footage* für die Fischli/Weiss-Video-Installation auf der Biennale 1995 in Venedig zu sammeln (*Ohne Titel* [Venedig-Arbeit], 96 Stunden Videomaterial mit Ausflügen ins Zürcher Umland und Alltagsszenen aus Zürich).

Plötzlich kamen Leute angerannt und zischelten, PASST AUF, DIE SCHMIER' IST DA UND FILMT ALLES. David Weiss, Gott hab ihn selig, sah ja auch wirklich genauso aus wie ein Zivilfahnder. Der coolste Look überhaupt.

Cornel Windlin

Reefer Madness — Watch out, the cops are here!

Reefer madness was indeed my thing. I moved to Zurich from London in 1993 and didn't really know anybody. Among the first people that I got to know through mutual friends were Bernd Blankenburg and Connie Hüsser. I immediately began organizing the kind of parties that I actually wanted to go to myself along with Bernd, who was then working at the music office of the Rote Fabrik during the day, and Connie, who was working as a display artist at Globus department store. At these events, the most important things were the music and a nice ambiance.

At the beginning, we moved itinerantly from place to place. For example, from a cellar on Seestrasse in the suburb of Wollishofen, to Parkring in the Enge area of Zurich, to under bridges and at the lakeside, wherever it was fun at the moment. Later, we were able to soundproof the cellar in a temporarily empty commercial building on Zypressenstrasse and regularly use it as a space. Things went on that way until around 1997, I think. The whole thing was a lot of fun — also because it wasn't supposed to and wasn't trying to be a business. And because we gave it up at the right time, when it was slowly getting too big.

One of the many highlights was when David Weiss came to the club incognito with a video camera to collect *footage* for the Fischli/Weiss video installation for the 1995 Venice Biennale, (*Untitled* [Venice Work], ninety-six hours of video material recording everyday scenes in Zurich and excursions to the countryside around the city).

Suddenly people came running and whispered: "WATCH OUT! THE COPS ARE HERE AND ARE FILMING EVERYTHING." David Weiss, God rest his soul, actually did look exactly like an undercover cop. The coolest look of all.

Cornel Windlin

CORNEL WINDLIN, JUNGLE MADNESS, 1995, 105×105

REEFER MADNESS, 1994, 75×75

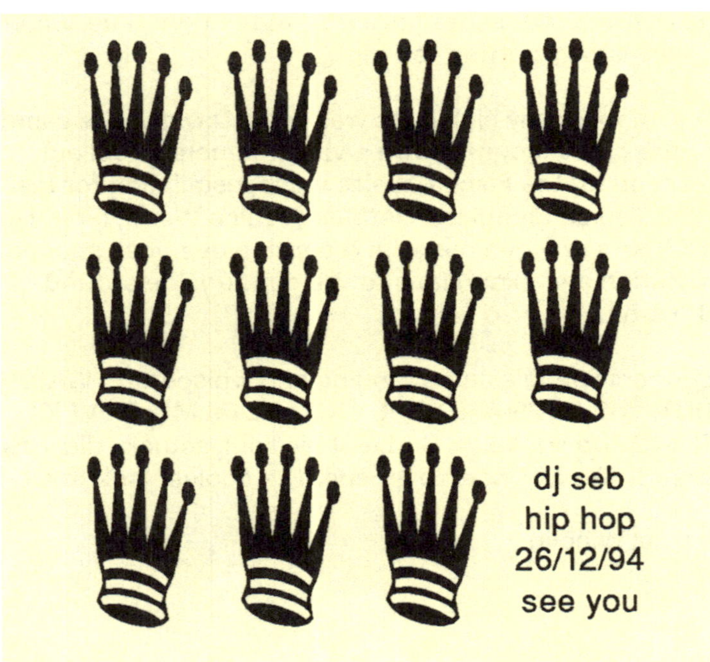

CORNEL WINDLIN, OUR HOUSE IS YOURS, 1994, 148×105

REEFER MADNESS – PASSIER-SCHEIN, 1995, 105×75

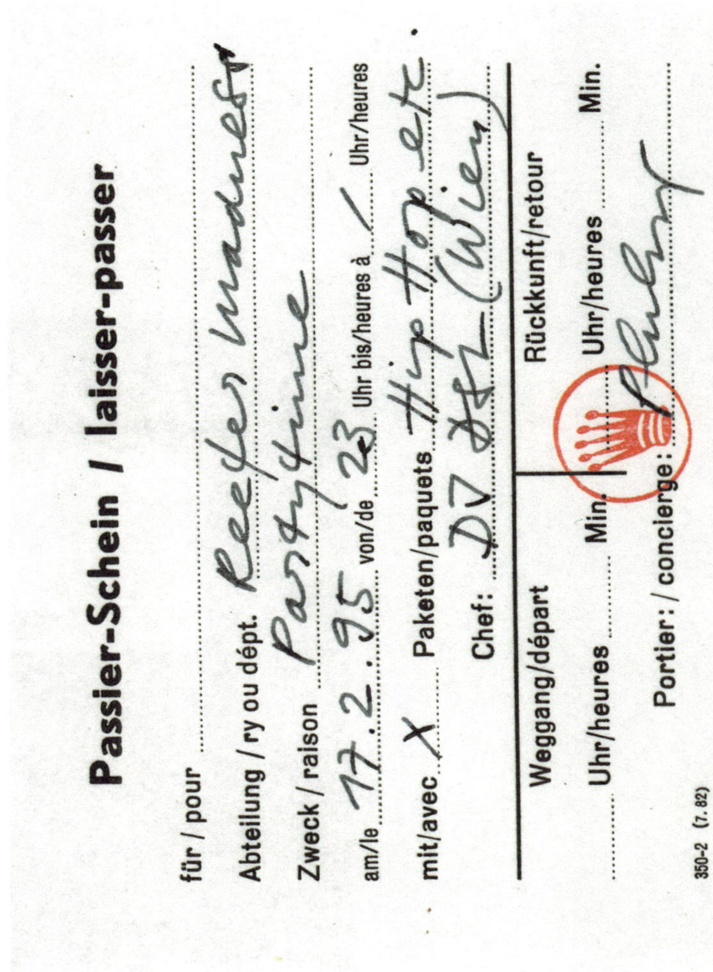

REEFER MADNESS, 1994, 148×105

REEFER MADNESS, 1995, 148×105

CORNEL WINDLIN, ROTE FABRIK – DECEMBER, 1994, 690×490

Super Dolby Stereo Photo: Christoph Eckert

. Dezember, 21 h*
be Called Quest

Do, 8. Dezember, 21 h*
Melvins

Do, 29. Dezember, 21 h
Kadda Chérif Hadria

21 Vorverkauf benützen!*
s. Basel: Roxy. Bern: Lollypop. Baden: ZeroZero. Winterthur: MusikBox. Schaffhausen: TapTab. St. Gallen: Bro Records. Chur: HalbTanz

CORNEL WINDLIN, ROTE FABRIK – MAY/JUNE, 1995, 700×500

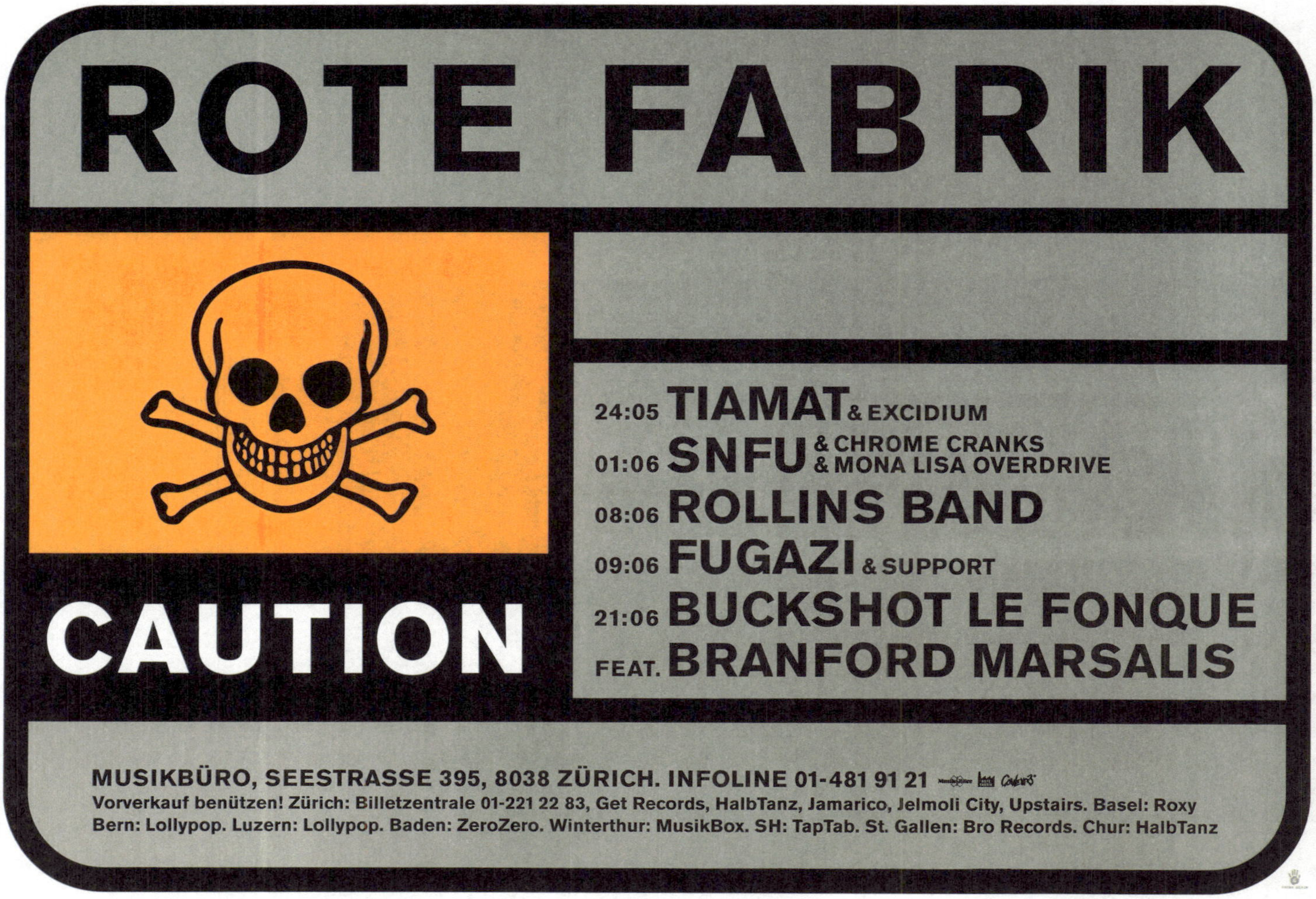

CORNEL WINDLIN, ROTE FABRIK – OCTOBER/NOVEMBER, 1995, 700×500

CORNEL WINDLIN, ROTE FABRIK – NOVEMBER, 1994, 450×630

CORNEL WINDLIN, ROTE FABRIK - APRIL, 1995, 450×630

Bootsy's New
Rubber Band
FEAT.
BERNIE WORRELL 22.FEB
VORVERKAUF BENÜTZEN! INFOLINE 01-481 91 21
ZÜRICH: BIZZ, DINGS, GET, HALBTANZ, JAMARICO, JELMOLI CITY, UPSTAIRS.
BASEL: ROXY. BERN: LOLLYPOP. LUZERN: LOLLYPOP. BADEN: ZEROZERO. WINTERTHUR: MUSIKBOX. SH: TAPTAB
ST. GALLEN: BRO. CHUR: HALBTANZ
ROTE FABRIK
23/FEB
Kyuss
+ MENtal HIPPie BLOOD
Baaba maal
25:Feb.
KOCh/SchUtZ/STUDER (CHOCK SHUT)
1:MÄRZ 20.30h
WEEn +??
SA,17:MÄRZ

s'RoteFabrikli
!!! Slacker's Delight!!!
BOBBY SICHRAN & Band
Mi 1. Feb – Losers and X-Grrrlz only
i'M ©razy for you
1alem
< DON BYRON: >
Music for 6 Musicians; Mi, 8. 2., 20.30h
Do, 9. Feb., SOUL COUGHING-Konzert
Beim letzten Mal standest Du beim Mischpult und hast in mein Bier gekotzt. Du gehst mir nicht mehr aus dem Kopf. Sehen wir uns wieder, same place? Pass auf mein Bier auf. KnowhatImean
Godflesh
(Erleuchtung im Trockeneis)
Lass es uns doch mal versuchen.
Take me higher, baby. Do, 16. Februar
ARNO! Wo bist Du? Treffpunkt Sa, 18.2. in der Fabrik! 21h, oder danach an der Party mit DJ RafNoSleep. Laurence & B.
ROTE FABRIK
ZÜRICH: BILLETZENTRALE, DINGS, GET, HALB TANZ, JAMARICO, JELMOLI CITY, UPSTAIRS. BASEL: ROXY. BERN: LOLLYPOP
LUZERN: LOLLYPOP. BADEN: ZERO ZERO. WINTERTHUR: MUSIKBOX. SH: TAP TAB. ST. GALLEN: BRO. CHUR: HALB TANZ
VORVERKAUF BENÜTZEN! INFOLINE 01-481 91 21

13OGEN13
Sonntag 21 11 ab 21 00
HE MONSTERS
ND THE DEVIL'S MOTORCYCLE
Supporting Act: SHRIMP
ute musik von ROCKMASTER K.
design sucks!

Alain C. Kupper

Auch bekannt unter dem Namen Rockmaster K, zog Alain C. Kupper 1984 von Basel nach Zürich und bildete sich «über das Studium von Plattenumschlägen» zum Grafiker aus. Vier Jahre später veröffentlichte er sein musikalisches Debütalbum *Megasongs* mit der Band Tessin. Seine gestalterischen Projekte im Kontext von Musik- und Szene-Lokalen prägten das Zürich der letzten dreissig Jahre mit. In den Neunzigerjahren gründete er das Musiklabel Suntic Records Zürich sowie den Neue Kunst- und Medienverlag Zürich und 1997 den Raum für aktuelle Kunst, Neuropa – The Modern Institute. Er entwarf die Plakate für das Konzertlokal Bogen 13, erfand den Namen «Zukunft» (für einen Club in Zürich), kochte im «Bananen und Frucht» und gestaltete die Zürcher Restaurants Italia und Lily's sowie die neue Markthalle im Viadukt mit. Als DJ und Musiker tritt er bis heute an zahlreichen Anlässen auf. Er baut Brücken zwischen Sub- und Hochkultur und verwischt vermeintliche Grenzen.

Alain C. Kupper

Today, also known under the name Rockmaster K, Alain C. Kupper moved from Basel to Zurich in 1984 and trained himself as a graphic artist via "the studies of record covers." Four years later he released his debut album *Megasongs*, with his band Tessin. His design projects within the context of music and trendy scene places also shaped Zurich over the last thirty years. In the nineties he founded the music label Suntic Records Zürich as well as the Neuer Kunst- und Medienverlag Zürich and in 1997, the space for contemporary art "Neuropa — The Modern Institute." He designed the posters for the concert hall Bogen 13, invented the name "Zukunft" (for a club in Zurich), cooked in the Bananen und Frucht, and helped fashion Zurich's restaurants Italia and Lily's as well as the new Markthalle im Viadukt. To-date, he performs as a DJ and musician at numerous events. He builds bridges between sub- and established culture and blurs alleged boundaries.

ALAIN C. KUPPER, SPOOKEY RUBEN, 2003, 460×640

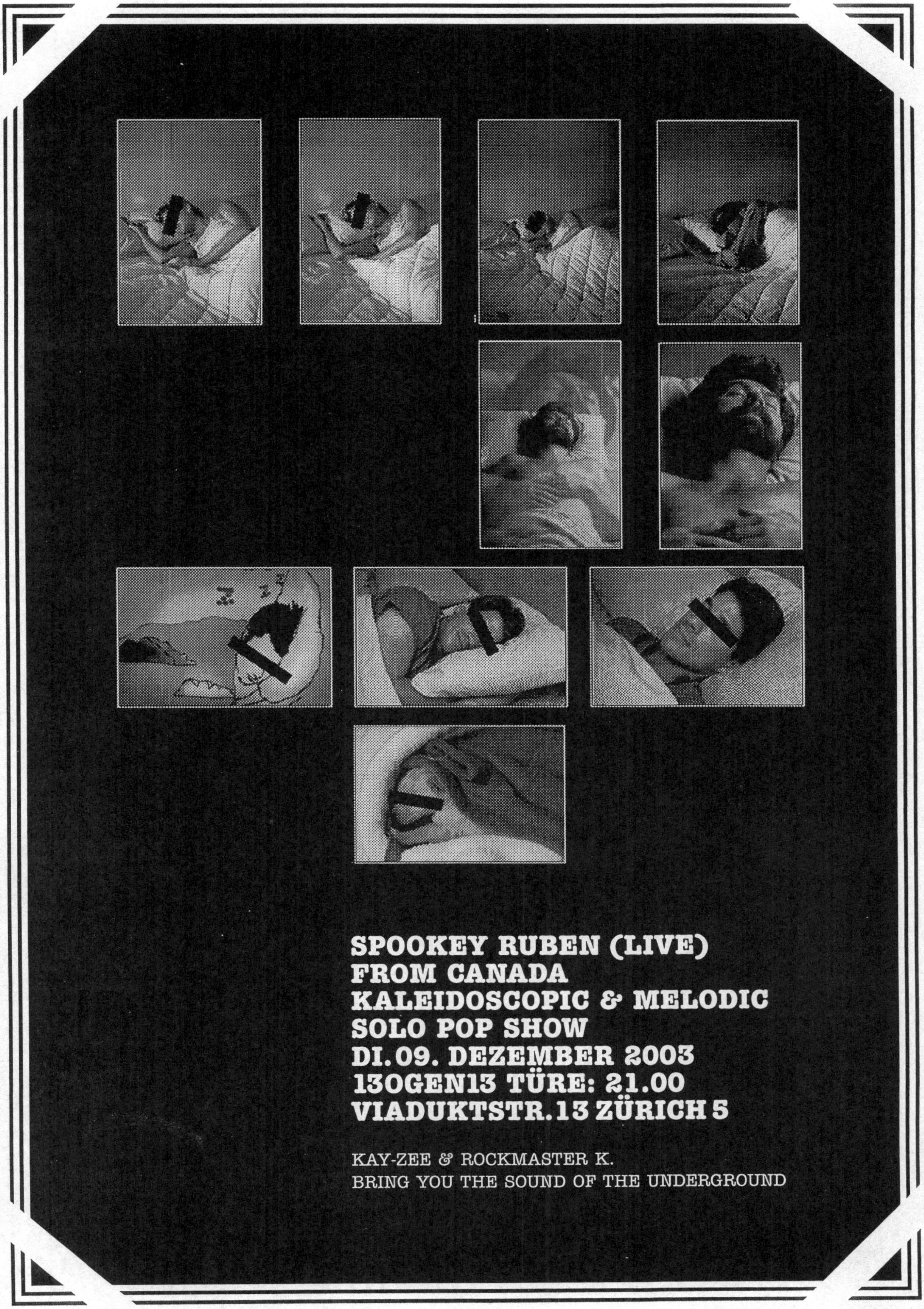

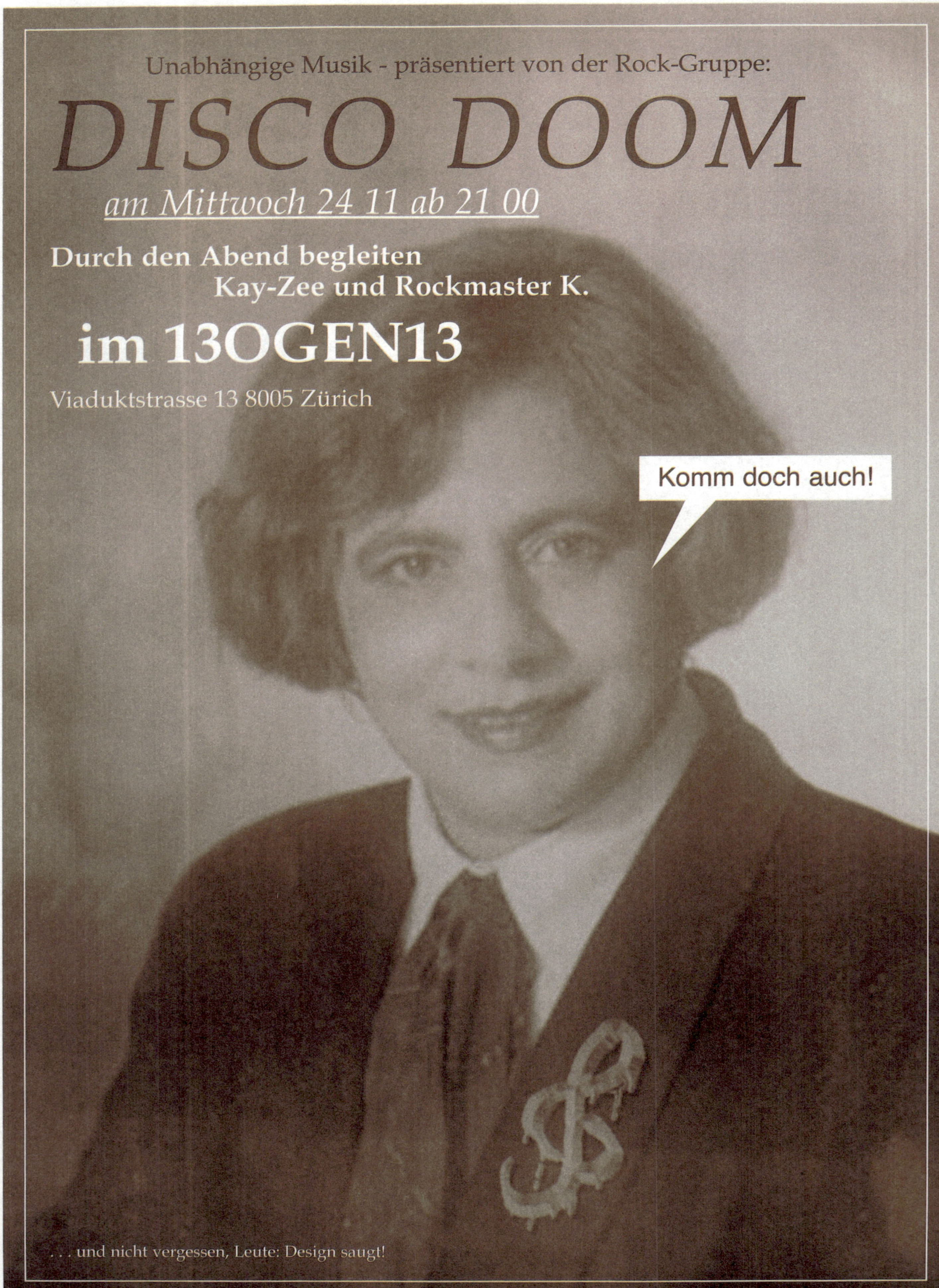
Unabhängige Musik - präsentiert von der Rock-Gruppe:
DISCO DOOM
am Mittwoch 24 11 ab 21 00
Durch den Abend begleiten
Kay-Zee und Rockmaster K.
im 13OGEN13
Viaduktstrasse 13 8005 Zürich
Komm doch auch!
. . . und nicht vergessen, Leute: Design saugt!

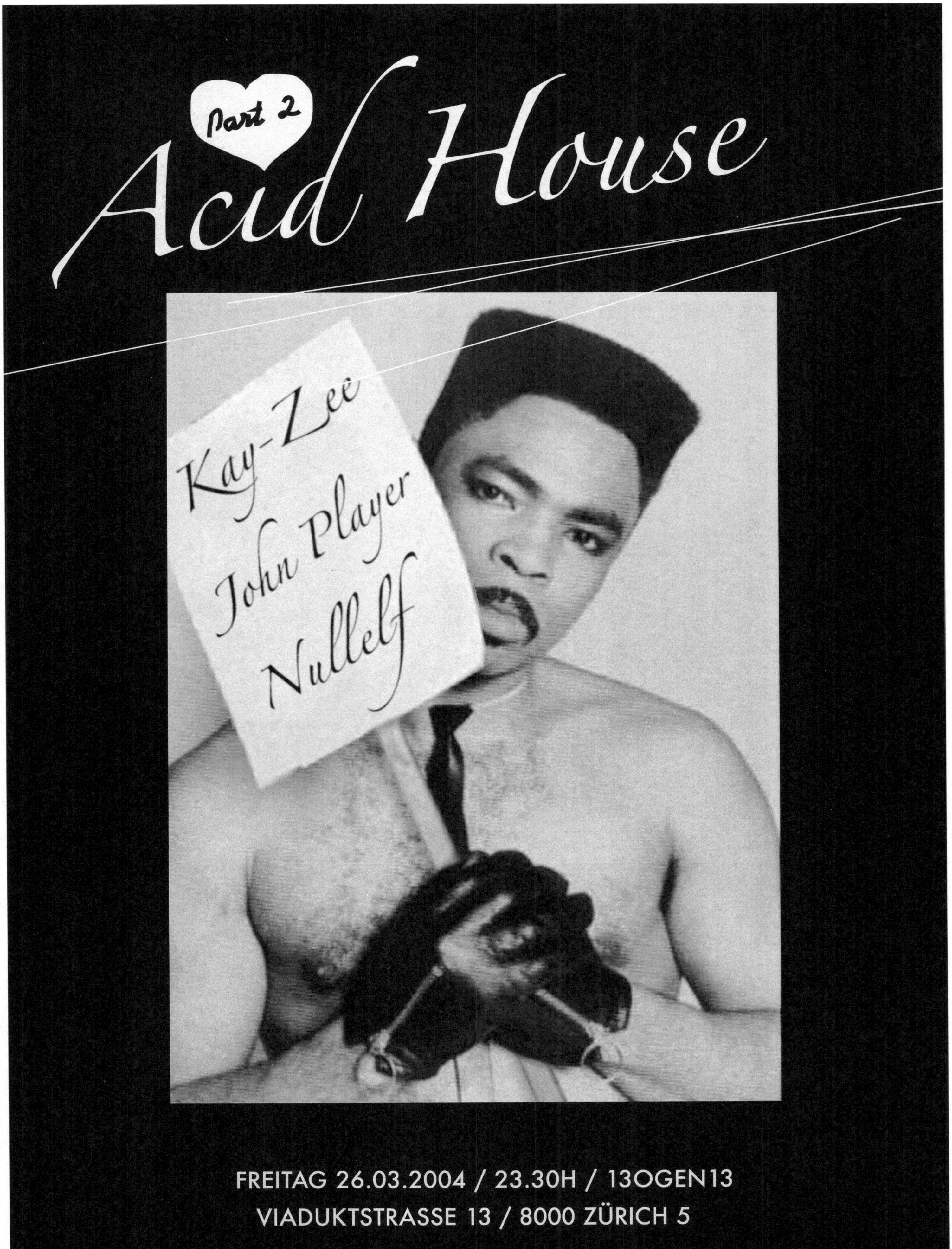
Part 2
Acid House
Kay-Zee
John Player
Nullelf
FREITAG 26.03.2004 / 23.30H / 13OGEN13
VIADUKTSTRASSE 13 / 8000 ZÜRICH 5

13OGEN13
Sonntag 21 11 ab 21 00
THE MONSTERS
ROY AND THE DEVIL'S MOTORCYCLE
Supporting Act: SHRIMP
Gute musik von ROCKMASTER K.
design sucks!
1995

Bogen 13 – Design sucked from 2001 to 2004

Im Wipkinger Eisenbahnviadukt bei der Zürcher Josefswiese ereignete sich in einem umgenutzten Lagerschuppen Anfang dieses Jahrtausends so einiges. Nicht allzu strategisch durchdacht, dafür umso reichhaltiger im Musikangebot und im Fehlen von landläufig bekanntem Komfort. Vieles passierte also durchaus frisch aus einer Musik verliebten Unbekümmertheit, was sich auch direkt in einer Marketingstrategie niederschlug, die vieles erfüllte, am wenigsten jedoch Marketing im Sinne einer Besucher bringenden Wirkung betrieb. Nicht zuletzt weil die Plakate und Flyer oftmals erst wenige Stunden vor Türöffnung des jeweiligen Konzerts erschienen. Das eigentliche Angebot des Konzertlokals Bogen 13 sprach jedoch sowieso für sich.

Als Künstler und Nachtmensch richtete sich Alain C. Kupper aka Rockmaster K. im Gewölbe Nummer 13 der Eisenbahnbrücke als Gast, Freund, Musiker und Mentor vor, auf und hinter der Bühne ein zweites Zuhause ein. Auffassungen der klassischen Werbung wurden unter dem Motto «Design sucks» kopfüber ins ToiToi-Scheisshäuschen vor dem Clubeingang gesteckt.

Es entstanden, teilweise in Zusammenarbeit mit Atelierpartner Cristian Andersen, Werke voll kreativer Wut gepaart mit einem ausgereiften Feingefühl für unangepasste Gestaltung, welche ihre volle Wirkung noch heute in Sammlungen, auf Hauswände gekleistert oder als Kunstinstallation entfalten.

Michi Vollenweider, Murat Erbudak, Dirk Dietz, Dominik Müller

Bogen 13 — Design sucked from 2001 to 2004

A number of extraordinary events happened at the beginning of this millennium inside a converted storage shed under the Wipkingen railroad viaduct, close to the Josefswiese Park in Zurich. These events were not very well devised strategically, yet were all the richer with respect to the music staged and the lack of common comfort. Many rather fresh things therefore came about due to loving music with abandon, something directly reflected in a marketing strategy that achieved many things, but not any success in the sense of attracting visitors. Not least because the posters and flyers often didn't appear more than a few hours before the doors opened for the performance. Nevertheless, what the Bogen 13 venue offered spoke for itself.

As an artist and night owl, Alain C. Kupper a.k.a Rockmaster K., established himself in arch number thirteen under the railroad viaduct as a guest, friend, musician, and mentor; behind the stage he set up a second home for himself. Traditional ideas on advertising were hung upside down in the ToiToi portable toilets outside the club entrance, adhering to the motto "Design sucks."

Partly in cooperation with his studio partner Cristian Andersen, he created works filled with a creative rage paired with a mature sensitivity for unconventional design — works whose impact are still developing to this day, in collections, pasted onto walls, or as art installations.

Michi Vollenweider, Murat Erbudak, Dirk Dietz, Dominik Müller

ALAIN C. KUPPER, PAUL WEIXLER, 2003, 297×420

Paul Weixler "Freiwild" (claudia)Eine merkwürdige Fussnote? Der Paul macht es einem nicht einfach. Da denkt man, endlich mal wieder Schweizer Musik nicht von Patent Ochsner oder von Plüsch, sondern von einem Mann, welcher der heutigen jungen Generation so gar nichts sagt: Paul Weixler. Diejenigen, die noch übrig sind von der Punkszene damals Mitte 70er Jahre werden diesen Text hier gar nicht erst lesen, da sie heute wohl Familie und Kinder zu versorgen haben, falls diese nicht schon ausgezogen sind. "Züri brännt", das waren damals die Schlagwörter und der eine oder andere, der diesen Spruch mit seiner Jugend in Verbindung bringt, wird sich vielleicht noch an die "Zürcher Punk-Rock-Legende" Paul Weixler erinnern. Einer tut es ganz sicher. Sein Name ist Veit F. Stauffer und der war so lieb, seinem langjährigen Freund Paul eine Widmung ins CD-Büchlein zu schreiben und auch noch gleich eine ganze CD-Rezension vorzunehmen. Es fällt einem nach erstmaligem Hören gleich auf: Für Paul sind Frauen vor allem Wix-Grundlagen. Entweder hat er sein Leben lang seine Potenz erheblich einschränken müssen oder aber die Drogen haben sein Bild von der Frau in den Jahren von 20 bis 49 überhaupt nicht verändert (Auflösung im Laufe des Textes). Stellenweise kann der Eindruck aufkommen, ein pubertierender Junge klage über seine Liebesleiden. Aber hey, dieser Mann ist 49, hat erheblich viel durchgemacht, lebt von der IV und hat nach so vielen Jahren endlich seine erste CD draussen. Erwartet man da nicht Texte, die für Gänsehaut sorgen? Erwartet man da nicht biographische Erkenntnisse verpackt in poetischen Worten? Kann man da folgendes erwarten: "Und jetz wett ich, ich wär din Hund" "mir rammled quer durs ganze Programm" "dass es bis zum Himmel sprützt" "de halbi Kosmos fangt a tobe, wenn ich eus eine obenabe hol"... Es ist Paul Weixlers Art sich so auszudrücken, direkt und ohne Umschweife. Es ist nicht sein Ding mit Metaphern zu arbeiten, auch wenn man dies nach all diesen Lebenserfahrungsjahren vielleicht könnte. Es darf jetzt natürlich auch jeder denken, die Autorin sei eine Feministin und hole zum Rundumschlag gegen den in den Köpfen herrschenden Sexismus aus. Paul darf singen, was er will und es ist nun mal so, dass Sex ein vorherrschendes Thema beider Geschlechter ist. Nicht umsonst handeln wohl 70 Prozent (reine Schätzung) aller Lieder dieser Welt von der Liebe. Glücklicherweise hat Paul auch andere Texte geschrieben, die nicht von spritzen und "uf dMatte legge" handeln, sondern Themen wie den Alkoholismus oder Kummer von Kindern oder auch die Hilflosigkeit Pauls der Gesellschaft gegenüber aufgreifen. Das Lied "Chind" ist textlich das Beste, was auf dieser CD zu finden ist. Der Refrain von "Höll" "ich möchte nur no mini Rueh da wiit ewegg vom ganze Gschütz und mit all dem nüt meh ztue ha dune ide Höll und obe am Chrütz" besticht genauso wie folgender Ausschnitt von "Bänkli": "und nöd s'chlinste bitzli Liebi hät er au nie übercho und was eim dänn no übrigbliibi da redt niemer gern devo". Doch wären das bereits die drei Lieder mit etwas anderen Inhalten gewesen. Der Rest spritzt nur so vor sich hin. Doch die Entschuldigung schreibt Paul gleich selbst: "Vor über zehn Jahren wurde ich bei einer Horrorskop-Beratung mit meiner traumatischen Vorvergangenheit konfrontiert. Die urplötzliche Vergegenwärtigung brutaler sexueller Gewalt in meiner Kindheit versetzte mich in Panik und endete in einer geschlossenen psychiatrischen Klinik. Jahrelang lebte ich in Zuständen den heiterhellen Wahnsinn. Um diese Zustände zu bändigen, versuchte ich besonders spannungsgeladene Situationen so weit zu durchschauen, bis ich ein Lied darüber singen konnte." Die ganze, über Jahre hinweg unterdrückte Sexualität liess gar nichts anderes zu als diese Debüt-CD. Seine engsten Freunde werden ihn am besten verstehen, für sich und sie hat er die CD auch gemacht und nicht für die Allgemeinheit, obwohl er sicherlich lieber damit sein Lebensunterhalt verdienen würde als mit der IV. Rocken tut die CD stellenweise allemal, die musikalischen Hintergrundteppiche hören sich gut an. Pauls Stimme jedoch ist gewöhnungsbedürftig und öfters ganz und gar nicht passend. Das Spezielle an dieser CD ist ganz sicher Paul selbst und mit einem wunderschönen Satz : der im CD-Büchlein leider leider keinen Eingang fand -sind all seine textlichen Ausschweifungen entschuldigt: "Diese Lieder sind meine Brücken, die verhindern, dass ich in besonders heiklen Momenten im Strudel meines alten Fahrwassers mitgerissen werde." (Paul Weixler, Frühling 2003) Mehr Informationen: www.recrec.ch "Endlich hat Paul Weixler sein Debutalbum vollendet, nach 25 Jahren Warte- und Leidenszeit, mit 49 Jahren Lebenserfahrung", schreibt Veit F. Stauffer vom RecRec-Laden in den Liner-Notes. Paul Weixler hat den Song "Züri brännt" geschrieben, verlor sich im Hickhack der 80er Unruhen, stürzte ab und hat in den letzten 20 Jahren zwischen Psychiatrie und Gassenszene überlebt. 12 Lieder von wackelndem Mundart-Charme, interpretiert von einer süffig spielenden Band. Mit einer Ausnahme ("Hund"/The Stooges) alles Eigenkompositionen, die mit ihrer Ehrlichkeit und Naivität auch ans Herz rühren. Zwischen Schlager, Kilbirock und Volx-Blues. Paul Weixler: Freiwild (Boy/RecRec) Autor ph. Mail-Adresse des Autors ths.carohuegi@gmx.ch Datum 14.09.2003 11:52 *Chronologie: Basel 1978 - 1993 1978 Erstes AJZ in Basel • Erste Häuserbesetzung in Basel • Projekt Kulturwerkstatt Kaserne. 1980 Gründung des Vereins Kulturwerkstatt Kaserne und Eröffnung des Kulturbetriebs. April 1980 In drei zum Abbruch bestimmten Häusern am Spalenring findet ein Fest mit etwa 150 Personen statt, welche die Häuser als AJZ fordern. Anschliessend Auseinandersetzungen mit der Polizei und Abbruch der Häuser. 25. 4. 1980 Farbschmierereien in der ganzen Stadt: «Stoppt den Frust», «God kill the Queen oder ich mach es». 1. 5. 1980 An der offiziellen 1.-Mai-Feier kommt es zu Gehässigkeiten: Da die Frauenorganisatio-nen keine Rednerin stellen durften, wird das Rednerpult während mehrerer Minuten besetzt. Es kommt zu tumultartigen Szenen. Bei der Anti-Queen-Demo («Mitmarschiere / d'Queen flambiere») kommt es zu Ausschreitungen: 16 Personen werden verhaftet, 10 Personen müssen hospitalisiert werden. 20. 6. 1980 700 Personen nehmen an einem Solidaritätsfest und einer Demo für das AJZ Zürich teil. 23. 6. 1980 2000 Personen versuchen die Gebäude auf dem Gas- und Wasserwerkareal an der Heuwaage zu besetzen. Dort schon bereitstehende Polizisten verhindern das Vorhaben. Auf dem Weg zurück kommt es zu Sachbeschädigungen am Barfi und zu ersten Tränengaseinsätzen der Polizei. Es folgt ein Katz-und- Maus-Spiel zwischen Demonstrierenden und Polizei, bis die Aktionen auf der Mittleren Rheinbrücke mit Einkesselung der übrig gebliebenen DemonstrantInnen und Tränengaseinsätzen gestoppt werden. 25. 6. 1980 Erneute Demo von 500 Personen, die ein Basler AJZ fordern. 27. 6. 1980 Die Häuser an der Ryffstrasse 19–25 werden besetzt. 18. 8. 1980 Nachdem die BesetzerInnen die Häuser an der Ryffstrasse termingerecht geräumt haben, kommt es zu verschiedenen Strassenbarrikaden und Verwüstungen in der Nähe der Häuser. 20. 8. 1980 Ein Trauermarsch von Bewegten setzt sich von der Ryffstrasse in Richtung Gefängnis Lohnhof in Gang, da sich dort eine der Bewegung bekannte Person erhängt hatte. Unterwegs kommt es zu Sachbeschädigungen und dem bisher massivsten Einsatz der Polizei. 65 Personen werden verhaftet. 31. 1. 1981 Lärm, Farbbeutel, Eier und Feuerwerk begleiten die Podiumsdiskussion «Ist der Rechtsstaat gefährdet?» im Bernoullianum, die im Zusammenhang mit der Aktionswoche «Unruhe im Rechtsstaat» des Theaters Basel organisiert wurde. Nach tumultartigen Szenen wird die Veranstaltung vorzeitig abgebrochen. Drei Personen werden festgenommen. Im Anschluss kommt es zu Sachbeschädigungen und Ausschreitungen in der Innenstadt. 14. 2. 1981 Ein ehemaliges Postbetriebsgebäude an der Hochstrasse 16 wird besetzt. Unter Duldung der Eigentümerin bleibt es bis zur Räumung am 5. Mai als AJZ («Europas grösstes autonomes Jugendzentrum») geöffnet. 1. 5. 1981 Krawalle an der 1.-Mai-Feier auf dem Marktplatz: Trotz Redeerlaubnis für die AJZler wird das Mikrofon abgeschaltet. Danach folgen tumultartige Szenen am Rednerpult, und wenig später formiert sich der Demozug, wobei es zu massiven Sachbeschädigungen (1 Mio. Franken) in der Freien Strasse kommt. 10 Demonstrierende werden festgenommen. 3. 5. 1981 Auseinandersetzungen mit 100 «Faschos» und «Babyrockern» auf der Peter Merian-Brücke vor dem AJZ. Der Basler Polizei wird Zusammenarbeit mit den Faschos vorgeworfen. 5. 5. 1981 Räumung des AJZ: Die Polizei trifft am Morgen im AJZ ein und verhaftet 141 Personen, die in die ehemalige Strafanstalt Schällemätteli gebracht werden. Dort kommt es zu Ausbruchversuchen, welche mit Tränengaseinsätzen gestoppt werden. Die abendliche Solidaritätsdemo vor dem Schällemätteli wird mit Tränengas aufgelöst. Beim Rückzug in die Innenstadt kommt es zu Sachbeschädigungen. 9. 5. 1981 AJZ-Grossdemo mit 7000 Personen durch die Stadt. Das alte Gaswerk an der Vogesenstrasse/Gasstrasse wird nicht besetzt, da es sich als «Bruchbude» nicht eignet. Gleichzeitig stellen die Demonstrierenden ein Ultimatum an die Regierung, dass innerhalb einer Woche ein geeignetes Areal zur Verfügung gestellt werden soll. 16. 5. 1981 3000 Personen treffen sich auf dem Marktplatz zu einer Grossdemo. Die Regierung ist auf das Ultimatum nicht eingetreten. Die Bewegung besetzt die ehemalige Audlauerklinik am Petersgraben (AJZ 2). 18. 5. 1981 Räumung der Audlauerklinik durch die Polizei. Zirka 100 Personen werden zwecks Personalien in den Spiegelhof gebracht. Nach der abendlichen VV auf dem Petersplatz folgt eine Demo mit 1000 Personen und Sachbeschädigungen in der Innenstadt. 25. 5. 1981 Besetzung von neun leeren Häusern. 30. 5. 1981 Es kommt zu den bis dahin schwersten Auseinandersetzungen. Die Polizei ist nach dem Fussballländerspiel Schweiz–England (2:1) doppelt gefordert. Einerseits muss sie die englischen Hooligans im Zaum halten, andererseits versuchen AJZ-SympathisantInnen im Anschluss an ein Fest auf dem Theaterplatz, ins Stadttheater einzudringen. Die Polizei interveniert; es kommt zu Strassenbarrikaden am Bankenplatz und Sachbeschädigungen in der Aeschenvorstadt. Die Scharmützel dauern bis zum frühen Morgen. Insgesamt werden 9 Personen verhaftet. 13. 6. 1981 Strassenschlachten zwischen der Polizei und AJZ-AnhängerInnen prägen das Bild der Basler Innenstadt. Am Nachmittag ziehen 1000 Personen vom Marktplatz via Lohnhof zur Heuwaage, wo sie das leer stehende Gas- und Wasserwerk besetzen wollen. Die Gebäude werden bereits von der Polizei bewacht. Es kommt zu Auseinandersetzungen und zur Vertreibung der Demonstrierenden mit Tränengas und Gummigeschossen. Die Scharmützel dauern bis gegen Mitternacht an. 1. 8. 1981 Sabotage der offiziellen 1.-August-Feier auf dem Bruderholz: Es kommt zu Schlägereien zwischen Mitgliedern eines Jodlerklubs und den Demonstrierenden, nachdem der Gesangsvortrag gestört wurde. 15. 8. 1981 Friedliche Demo mit 1000 Personen Richtung Kleinbasel, wo sich einige Demonstrierende in die dortigen Warenhäuser begeben und für beträchtliche Aufregung sorgen. Anschliessend folgt ein Badehappening im Rhein. 6.–9. 10. 1981 Nuclex-Ausstellung in der Musterhalle. 3000 Personen nehmen an der Nix-Nuclex-Demo teil, nachdem zuvor das Rathausdach besetzt worden war und die Nuclex-Zulieferer mit Sitzblockaden gestört wurden. Weihnachten 1981 Erneute AJZ-Besetzung. 14. 2. 1982Demo zum Jubiläum der Besetzung des AJZ an der Hochstrasse. Die weitere Entwicklung in den achtziger Jahren April 1986 Beginn der kulturellen Zwischennutzung der Alten Stadtgärtnerei. Januar 1987Von nun an Nutzung des Areals ohne Bewilligung. 1. 9. 1987 Einreichung der Initiative für einen Kultur- und Naturpark im St. Johann. 8. 5. 1988 Abstimmungsresultat: 44 Prozent Ja- zu 56 Prozent Nein-Stimmen. 21. 6. 1988 Polizeiliche Räumung der Alten Stadtgärtnerei. 20. 9. 1988 Das ehemalige Kino Union wird besetzt. 1. 4. 1989 Polizeiliche Räumung des Union nach einer Demonstration für ein «autonomes Kulturzentrum in der Stadt». Juli 1990 bis Juli 1993 Zwischennutzung des Werkraums Schlotterbeck und der Alten Stückfärberei. Recherchen: Dominik Straumann. Quellen: A. Wüthrich / M. Heimy (Hrsg.). «Frei Sicht uff Basel». Zürich 1982. Andreas Honegger. «Kleine Chronologie der Ereignisse». In: Hugo Bütler und Thomas Häberling (Hrsg.): «Die neuen Verweigerer. Unruhe in Zürich und anderen Städten». Verlag Neue Zürcher Zeitung. Zürich 1981.
WoZ-Online 13.04.2000 Zum Dossier Fotos © by Getrud Vogler, © by Klaus Rozsa, © by Olivia Heussler Hinweis für PC-UserInnen: Verwenden Sie zum Ausdrucken unserer Artikel bitte den Internet Explorer, Netscape unter Windows legt sich quer. Basel | Bern | Schweiz Chronologie: Zürich 1979 - 1991 Herbst 1979 Die Arbeitsgemeinschaft Rock als Revolte (RAR) formiert sich. Ihr Anliegen ist es, die Musikszene in Zürich zu verbessern, das heisst, eine Alternative zu hochkommerzialisierten Konzerten zu schaffen sowie Räumlichkeiten fürs Musikmachen, Festen und Diskutieren zu erwirken. Februar 1980 Die Aktionsgruppe Rote Fabrik (ARF) wird gegründet, um den Forderungen nach Freiräumen Nachdruck zu verschaffen. Sie besteht aus verschiedenen Einzelpersonen, aus den Gruppen Rock und Revolte, Kommunistischer Jugendverband, Jungsozialisten, Freaks am Fritig usw. Der Stadtrat geht auf keine Verhandlungen ein. 17./18. 5. 1980 An einem Protestfest in der Roten Fabrik diskutieren Jugendliche, wie sie Forderungen nach Räumen für ihre Kul-tur Nachdruck verschaffen können. Auf Freitag, den 30. Mai, wird eine Demonstration gegen die Opernhausvorlage angekündigt. 30. 5. 1980 Am Abend des 30. Mai gehen – organisiert durch die ARF – rund 200 Personen auf die Strasse, um vor dem Opernhaus für die Förderung einer alternativen Kultur in der Stadt Zürich zu demonstrieren. Sie wollen die OpernhausbesucherInnen im Vorfeld der städtischen Abstimmung über den 60-Millionen-Kredit für den geplanten Opernhausumbau auf die Bedürfnisse eines alternativen Zürcher Kulturbetriebs aufmerksam machen. Es kommt zum Opernhauskrawall. 4. 6. 1980 Stadtpräsident Widmer und Stadträtin Lieberherr nehmen – zusammen mit rund 2000 Jugendlichen – an einer VV im Volkshaus teil. Zur Einstimmung wird ein Videofilm einer Gruppe von EthnologiestudentInnen über den Opernhauskrawall gezeigt. In Bezug auf das geforderte Jugendzentrum zeigt sich der Zürcher Stadtrat gesprächsbereit – unter der Bedingung, dass keine weiteren Ausschreitungen stattfinden. Sie fordern die Versammelten auf, eine Delegation zu bilden, welche die anstehenden Verhandlungen führen soll. Die VV ist nicht bereit, auf diesen Vorschlag einzugehen, sie beharrt auf direkten Verhandlungen mit dem Stadtrat. 6. 6. 1980 Der kantonale Erziehungsdirektor, Regierungsrat Gilgen, lässt den Videofilm über den Opernhauskrawall wegen politischer Agitation mit wissenschaftlichem Material konfiszieren. 9. 6. 1980 Vor der Universität Zürich findet eine Manifestation statt. Der sofortige Rücktritt von Regierungsrat Gilgen wird gefordert. Am 12. Juni führen an der Universität 2000 StudentInnen einen Protesttag durch. 21. 6. 1980 Nachdem rund 5000 bis 6000 auf dem Helvetiaplatz versammelte Menschen von Präventivverhaftungen von «Rädelsführern der Bewegung» erfahren haben, beschliesst eine Mehrheit, die Diskussion um die von der SP unterbreiteten Vorschläge bezüglich Trägerschaft für ein AJZ zu vertagen und stattdessen sofort zu demonstrieren. Der Menschenzug setzt sich in Richtung Innenstadt in Bewegung. Auf der Quaibrücke trifft er auf die Polizei, welche sich dann aber zurückzieht, worauf die Demonstration friedlich zu Ende geht. 25. 6. 1980 Im Volkshaus beschliesst die Vollversammlung, den Vermittlungsvorschlag der SP anzunehmen, unter der Bedingung, dass das Haus autonom geführt und am darauf folgenden Samstag, dem 28. Juni, geöffnet werden kann. Von der Eröffnung bis zur ersten Schliessung des Autonomen Jugendzentrums 28. 6. 1980 Das Autonome Jugendzentrum wird eröffnet. 15. 6. 1980 Die «Müller-Show» im Fernsehen DRS: Die Bewegung delegiert Anna und Hans Müller an ein Rundtisch-Gespräch mit Vertretern des Stadtrats, der Polizei und der SP. Die «Müllers» nehmen mit ernster Miene den Standpunkt von rechtschaffenen Bürgern ein, fordern mehr Ruhe und Ordnung und scharfe Massnahmen gegen die Krawallmacher. Der Fernsehskandal ist perfekt. Der Begriff «Müllern» wird zur stehenden Wendung für spassige Dialogverweigerung der Jugendbewegung. 1. 8. 1980 4000 Personen beteiligen sich an einer Grossdemonstration für die Einstellung der Strafverfahren. Die Demonstration endet für manche Bewegte mit einem Bad im See sowie mit der Plünderung einer Hotelbar. 9. 8. 1980 JournalistInnen protestieren gegen Druckversuche, die von Politikern und Wirtschaftskreisen auf die Medien ausgeübt werden. 4. 9. 1980 Nach einer Razzia im AJZ beschliesst der Stadtrat, das AJZ zu schliessen. Am Abend kommt es zu heftigen Auseinandersetzungen in der Gegend des Hauptbahnhofs. Der Kampf um die Wiedereröffnung des AJZ 6. 9. 1980 Die Bewegung ruft zu einer Grossdemonstration auf: «Für die sofortige Wiedereröffnung des AJZ, aber subito, susch tätschts!» Es kommt zu heftigen Auseinandersetzungen zwischen den Demonstrierenden und der Polizei bis in die frühen Morgenstunden. Mehrere hundert Personen werden verhaftet. 10. 9. 1980 Die Bewegung diskutiert das weitere Vorgehen an einer VV im Limmathaus. Rund 2500 Bewegte sowie MedienvertreterInnen aus aller Welt sind anwesend. Für die Bewegten ist klar, dass eine fremde Trägerschaft nur dann akzeptiert wird, wenn diese die Autonomie weiterhin gewährleisten kann. 14. 10. 1980 Unbekannte Täter verüben einen Brandanschlag auf eine Baufirma. Es entsteht ein Sachschaden von 2 Millionen Franken. 15. 10. 1980 An der VV in der Roten Fabrik distanziert sich ein Teil der Bewegten von Gewalttaten, andere sind der Ansicht, dass es keine andere Wahl gibt, als solche Wege zu beschreiten. 24. 10. 1980 Die erste Ausgabe einer zweiten Bewegungszeitung – «Der Eisbrecher» – erscheint in einer Auflage von 10.000 Exemplaren. 25. 10. 1980 Teileröffnung der Roten Fabrik. 1. 11. 1980 Premiere des Videofilms «Züri brännt» in der Roten Fabrik. 15. 11. 1980 In zahlreichen Städten machen Jugendliche am Wochenende an einem gesamtschweizerischen Aktionstag mit Demonstrationen auf ihre Anliegen aufmerksam. 24. 12. 1980 An Weihnachten kommt es zu schweren Zusammenstössen zwischen DemonstrantInnen und der Polizei, nachdem Jugendliche versucht hatten, sich Zugang zum geschlossenen AJZ zu verschaffen. 16. 1. 1981 Bereits wenige Tage nach dem Erscheinen der letzten Nummer vom «Eisbrecher» kommt eine neue Zeitung, «Brächise», heraus. 31. 1. 1981 Die TeilnehmerInnen einer unbewilligten Grossdemonstration gegen die Justiz und die laufenden Prozesse werden beim Landesmuseum von der Polizei eingekesselt. Es kommt zu Gewaltexzessen von Seiten der Polizei. Rund 700 Personen müssen sich einer Personenkontrolle unterziehen. 12./14. 2. 1981 Der Verein Pro AJZ organisiert im Volkshaus ein Tribunal, an dem massive Vorwürfe gegen die Behörden und die Polizei erhoben werden. 21. 3. 1981 An der bewilligten Frühlingsdemonstration nehmen rund 8000 Personen teil. Es kommt zu gewalttätigen Auseinandersetzungen und in der Folge zu schweren Sachbeschädigungen in der Gegend des Hauptbahnhofs. 29. 3. 1981 Der Stadtrat orientiert über den Vertrag, der mit den Landeskirchen und der Pro Juventute, welche die Trägerschaft für ein Jugendzentrum an der Limmatstrasse 18/20 übernehmen, abgeschlossen wurde. Von der zweiten Eröffnung bis zur autonomen Schliessung des AJZ 3. 4. 1981 Das AJZ wird mit einer VV und einem Fest ein zweites Mal eröffnet. 23. 5. 1981 Die Bewegung schliesst vorübergehend das AJZ: Einerseits als Protest gegen die verschärfte Repression, aber auch als Signal für jene AJZ-BenützerInnen, die das AJZ als «Konsumtempel» und «Obdachlosenasyl» benützen. Ende August 1981 Bis Ende August 1981 sind insgesamt fast 4000 Personen im Zusammenhang mit den Jugendunruhen verhaftet und rund 1000 Strafverfahren eingeleitet worden. Das Ende des AJZ 12. 10. 1981 Die überforderten Mitglieder der verschiedenen Arbeitsgruppen des AJZ geben auf: Sie schliessen das AJZ. 24. 12. 1981 Das AJZ geht mit einer VV und einem Fest von neuem für 14 Tage auf. Rund 600 Leute nehmen an der Wiedereröffnung teil.
Anfang Januar 1982 Nach dem 14-tägigen Provisorium diskutieren rund 300 Bewegte an einer VV, ob das AJZ weiterhin geöffnet bleiben soll. 17. 3. 1982 Die Trägerschaft des AJZ gibt resigniert auf. Sie löst den Vertrag mit der Stadt Zürich per sofort auf und gibt die Schlüssel für die Gebäude an der Limmatstrasse 18/20 zurück. 23. 3. 1982 Das AJZ wird abgebrochen. Die weitere Entwicklung 1982 bis 1990 Unter der Administration Wagner wird das Budget für alternative und freie Kulturformen von knapp 1 Million auf gut 11 Millionen erhöht (inklusive Rote Fabrik, Gessnerallee, Kanzleizentrum, Rock- und Popkredit, Koprod usw.) 25. 4. 1982 Die Vorlage für ein Zürcher Jugendhaus im Drahtschmidli wird von den StimmbürgerInnen der Stadt Zürich gutgeheissen.1. 9. 1984 Eröffnung des Quartier- und Kulturzentrums Kanzlei.*
1. 1. 1988 Nach einer siebenjährigen Versuchsphase kann das Kulturzentrum Rote Fabrik – vom Souverän abgesegnet – seinen definitiven Betrieb aufnehmen.
1990 Das Kino Xenix erhält nach zehnjährigem Bestehen den Kulturpreis.
8. 12. 1991 Das Zürcher Stimmvolk spricht sich für die definitive Schliessung des Kanzlei aus.

Recherche: Sabine Fischer
Quellen: Chronologie der Zürcher Unruhen vom 30. Mai bis 31. Dezember 1980. In: Olivia Heussler, Malou Muralt, Dieter Oswald, Daniel Schäublin, Andi Zai: «Zürcher Bewegung». Band 32. Verlag ohne Zukunft. Zürich 1981.
Hanspeter Kriesi: «Die Zürcher Bewegung. Bilder, Interaktionen, Zusammenhänge». Campus Verlag. Frankfurt am Main 1984. Andreas Honegger: «Kleine Chronologie der Ereignisse». In: Hugo Bütler und Thomas Häberling (Hrsg.): «Die neuen Verweigerer. Unruhe in Zürich und anderen Städten». Verlag Neue Zürcher Zeitung. Zürich 1981.
Sozialdemokratische Partei der Stadt Zürich: «Eine Stadt in Bewegung. Materialien zu den Zürcher Unruhen». Verlag der Stadt Zürich. Zürich 1981. Max Schmid: «Die Leidensgeschichte des Zürcher Jugendhauses 1945–1980». In: Sozialdemokratische Partei der Stadt Zürich: «Eine Stadt in Bewegung». Verlag der Stadt Zürich. Zürich 1981.

[home]

[home]
WoZ-Online
13.04.2000

Zum Dossier

Fotos © by Lukas Lehmann

Hinweis für PC-UserInnen:
Verwenden Sie zum Ausdrucken unserer Artikel bitte den Internet Explorer, Netscape unter Windows legt sich quer.

Basel I Zürich I Schweiz

Chronologie: Bern

1978- 1997

20. 6. 1980 Nach den Opernhauskrawallen in Zürich wird auch in Bern ein AJZ gefordert. Rund 250 Personen versammeln sich beim Bärengraben, um das alte Tramdepot zu besetzen.
5. 7. 1980 Die Bewegung der Unzufriedenen
mobilisiert für ein Fest der Unzufriedenen in der leer stehenden städtischen Reithalle (RH), die inzwischen von der Bewegung als AJZ gefordert wird.
16. 8. 1980 DemonstrantInnen übergeben den Stadtbehörden eine von 4064 Personen unterschriebene Petition mit der Forderung, die RH «so schnell wie möglich als freies Kultur- und Begegnungszentrum ohne Auflagen zur Verfügung zu stellen».
September 1980 Der Gemeinderat stimmt der Einrichtung eines AJZ in den Stallungen der RH grundsätzlich zu. Weil eine einjährige Kündigungsfrist mit dem bisherigen Mieter besteht, steht die RH erst ab Oktober 1981 als AJZ zur Verfügung.
5. 2. 1981 Eine Kreditvorlage in der Höhe von 600 000 Franken für die Renovation der RH-Stallungen für das geplante AJZ wird vom Stadtrat angenommen.
21. 2. 1981 Das Haus an der Taubenstrasse 12 wird besetzt und zum provisorischen Autonomen Jugendzentrum erklärt
16. 10. 1981 Grosses Eröffnungsfest des Autonomen Begegnungszentrums (ABZ). Zuvor haben über 100 Bewegte am Umbau mitgearbeitet. Es bilden sich verschiedene Arbeitsgruppen wie eine Werkstattgruppe, eine Presse-, eine Sani- und eine Drogengruppe.
30. 3. 1982 Die Behörden haben sich mit den ABZ-BetreiberInnen nicht über ein Betriebskonzept einigen können und sich bis anhin geweigert, Subventionen für das ABZ zu sprechen. Der Gemeinderat stellt ein Ultimatum: «Innert einer Woche sind dem Gemeinderat diejenigen Personen bekannt zu geben, die bereit sind, sich während der Öffnungszeiten des ABZ für einen geordneten Betrieb einzusetzen.»
14. 4. 1982 Das ABZ wird polizeilich geräumt. In der Nacht kommt es zu Strassenschlachten. Die RH wird ein Jahr lang rund um die Uhr polizeilich bewacht.

Die weitere Entwicklung in den achtziger Jahren
18. 5. 1984 Vier besetzte Häuser an der Freiburgstrasse werden geräumt und unter Polizeischutz abgerissen. Noch am gleichen Tag wird das ZAFF im Berner Mattenhofquartier besetzt.
8. 6. 1985 Der Wohn- und Kulturraum ZAFF wird flachgelegt. Verschiedene Nachfolgebesetzungen werden geräumt. Diverse «Strafbars» und unbewilligte Konzerte, die auf die Zerstörung von billigem Wohnraum und auf mangelnden Kulturraum hinweisen, finden statt.
31. 6. 1985 Ehemalige BewohnerInnen des ZAFF lassen sich auf dem Gaswerkareal mit Zelten und Hütten nieder. Das Freie Land Zaffaraya entsteht.
8. 5. 1987 Mit der Besetzung der Dampfzentrale protestieren IKuR, OHM-8 und Hans-Dampf-in-allen-Gassen dagegen, dass «ein weiteres Mal all jene vor der Tür stehen, die sich nicht in eine solche von oben herab diktierte Welt der Kategorien integrieren können oder wollen». Etwa 1000 Leute nehmen am Fest teil, mehrere Rockbands treten auf. Die Gemeinderäte Albisetti und Neukomm an der Spitze der Polizeigrenadiere stellen ab Mitternacht in regelmässigen Abständen Räumungsultimaten, sind aber machtlos.
31. 10. 1987 Kulturstreik in der RH. Nahezu alle kulturellen Institutionen der Region Bern verlegen ihr Programm für einen Abend und eine Nacht in die RH. Das Fest mit Konzerten, Theater und Filmen wird ein voller Erfolg: Gegen 10 000 Leute verfolgen die Auftritte von dreizehn Bands, darunter Stephan Eicher, Polo Hofer, Züri West, die Goldenen Zitronen usw.
21. 11. 1987 Grossdemonstration mit 10 000 TeilnehmerInnen, die die Freigabe des Gaswerkareals zum sofortigen Wiederaufbau des Zaffarayas und die sofortige Öffnung des gesamten Reitschulkomplexes als autonomes Kulturzentrum verlangen. Die Studios der Berner Lokalradios ExtraBern und Förderband werden besetzt. Am Abend findet ein Fest in der besetzten RH statt.
In Zürich werden vor der Roten Fabrik aus Solidarität mit dem Zaffaraya Barrikaden errichtet.
25. 2. 1989 Mit einer Umzugsdemo zieht das Zaffaraya ins Neufeld. Das Gelände bei der Park-and-Ride-Anlage, das dem Kanton Bern gehört und auch als Standplatz der Fahrenden genutzt wird, ist ihnen als weiteres Provisorium angeboten worden. Das inzwischen zu einem Hüttendorf angewachsene Zaffaraya ist auch 1998 noch im Neufeld.
1. 8. 1990 Die Premiere der Tränengasoper «Berner Beben» sorgt für ein volles Kino in der RH. Der Film von Andreas Berger dokumentiert die bewegten achtziger Jahre in Bern: «Mein Film soll eine Selbstdarstellung der Bewegung sein. Ich habe ihn eigentlich für die Leute der Reithalle gemacht.»
1.–3. 11. 1996 Eröffnungsfest Grosse Halle der RH: Mit Filmen, Konzerten, Theater und einer Podiumsdiskussion läutet der Trägerverein Grosse Halle seine Ära ein.
4. 9. 1997 Der Stadtrat spricht einen 480 000-Franken-Projektierungskredit für die Gesamtsanierung der RH. Für einmal ist sich der Stadtrat bezüglich der RH weitgehend einig: Sogar die SVP stimmt mehrheitlich für den Kredit.

Recherchen: David Böher und Michael Fankhauser
Quelle: Hansdampf (Hrsg.): «Reithalle Bern. Autonomie und Kultur im Zentrum». Bern 1998.
[home]

The Ex Factor

Holland's Punk Collective Improvises Anew

Dutch Masters: The new Dizzy Spells shows off the Ex's evolution from earnest punks to musical adventurers.

By John Sewell
No one ever said it was easy being a paragon of righteousness, especially in the world of rock 'n' roll. Even the most overtly political bands tend to get bogged down in their own righteous rhetoric (see Rage Against the Machine), and fans can be fickle--this week's savior can easily become next week's charlatan. But over the course of more than 20 years, the Netherlands' the Ex has evolved from an earnest if somewhat naive punk band into an ambitious, all-encompassing musical collective, all while gaining fans and maintaining respect as a proponent of musical, political, and cultural agitation. In short, the Ex is a European counterpart to America's DIY standard-bearer, Fugazi.

The Fugazi comparison works because of each band's incendiary live shows and strict adherence to a code of self-reliance. (And apparently, it's not just a kinship imagined by critics; the Ex has toured with Fugazi as its opening act.) But sonically, at least in its current permutation, the Ex has a lot more in common with bands like Can, the Pop Group, early Chumbawamba, or English anarcho-punks Crass and the Poison Girls--groups that likewise never followed the dictates of the rock 'n' roll treadmill.

Unlike many of their contemporaries from punk's past who seem content to rehash the same old formula ad nauseam, the members of the Ex have never been satisfied to stick to the same musical blueprint year after year. Instead, the band has continually honed its musical skills, creating an ambling, rhythm-dominated sound that has incorporated any number of new ideas and influences while remaining distinctively its own.

"In a lot of ways, the band hasn't changed," lead vocalist Jos says by phone on the eve of the band's upcoming U.S. tour. (Just "Jos"--though he uses the moniker G.W. Sok in his recordings and writings, he's vague about his actual name. "It really doesn't matter what you call me," he says.)

"When we started out, it was just for fun," Jos says. "It was not such a serious thing because we had no idea if it would last or not. At a certain point we felt like, hey, it's not a throwaway thing anymore--this is basically the thing we want to do because it's our way of communication and where our hearts are.

"We bump into new opportunities and new challenges, and that has allowed [the band] to survive. You get a lot of education out of playing with other people, and that's how we've chosen to work."

Some of those new challenges have come from musicians outside the band. Over the years, the Ex has worked with some of the brightest lights of indie rock and the avant-garde: Tortoise, Sonic Youth guitarists Thurston Moore and Lee Ranaldo, the late cellist and improviser Tom Cora, madcap Dutch jazz drummer Han Bennick, and recording engineer/Shellac guitarist Steve Albini, who has recorded the two most recent of the band's 17 albums. The Ex's collaborative efforts have definitely widened the scope of the band's work, Jos says, though most of the partnerships have come about through happenstance.

"In general, it's hardly ever planned," he says. "Sometimes we'll play at festivals and hear other musicians or whatever. Or we'll start a conversation with another musician and we'll find out we have something in common. We just bump into people and sometimes ideas grow ou t of that. We never look for musicians because that never works. You just meet people and it clicks."

The Ex's newest album, Dizzy Spells (Touch and Go), features only current members Terrie, Andy, Luc, Katrin, and Jos and does a great job showing the band's ongoing growth. Albini's studio skills are perfectly suited to the band, particularly in the way he emphasizes the drums. Drummer Katrin continually pushes the band forward with ceaseless rolls and flourishes that resemble tribal rhythms. From this foundation, the rest of the band hits an interlocking guitar groove far removed from the usual punk-rock power chords. And on top of it all rides Jos' neo-beatnik poetry, more chanted than sung. The songs are tightly wound and powerful, an end result of improvisation and interaction.

By serving no masters and keeping a sharp eye on business practices, the Ex has retained its creative autonomy and built a growing fan base while maintaining its rabble-rousing political ideology. Early on, the band bludgeoned its audience with crudely played songs and bold proclamations. Now the textures are more subtle, the lyrics more oblique.

"When we started in the early '80s, there was a lot of anger," Jos says. "In Europe, there was a lot of unemployment, boredom, and horrible bands. In the Reagan era, we really reacted to the political climate. But I got to the point where I didn't want to say 'fuck the system' every time. I also wanted to say other things and find other ways of saying them. I learned to do it in a more poetic way, or through telling a story or whatever."

Even so, Dizzy Spells is still rife with anti-corporate, anti-materialistic, anti-government sentiments, from the explicit ("Burnsome" goes after PR firm Burson-Marstellar, which has put a positive media face on, among other things, mad cow disease, Three Mile Island, and the Bhopal disaster) to the more poetic ("Nobodies' Dream," based on a text by Eduardo Galeano, centers on the line, "A flea's dream is to buy a dog"). "Walt's Dizzyland" holds up Disney as the embodiment of Hollywood's corporate cultural imperialism and still manages to make a super-catchy chorus out of "Are we fucked/ are we nice/ are we ducks/ are we mice."

"Because we talk about things that concern us and the people around us, and because we sing about political topics, we're considered to be a political band," Jos says. But the band's stand goes beyond taking stances on particular issues: "The music itself--the way we play and how we want to construct our music--we think that's also a political statement because it protests the status quo of pop music. We want to play what we like and we're not so concerned whether it's considered hip or if it sells well.

"I think I am less cynical about the state of things now than I was a few years ago," Jos continues. "In the last couple of years, with the anti-global movement . . . and things like the protests in Seattle and Prague, these movements are all seeming to come together to stop the global dominance of the big companies, and that gives me a bit of hope for the future. I feel like the new action thing is more practical and I feel good about it."

Though the Ex is allied in spirit with many of the protesting factions on the extreme left, the band is wary of being affiliated with a strict political ideology. Generally anti- authoritarian in nature, the Ex purposely avoids following any dogma to the letter.

"We consider ourselves to be friends of anarchism," Jos says. But "the label 'anarchist' is not totally accurate for us. I mean, the way we organize ourselves and the way we live and the things we do with the band, yeah, that's an anarchist thing. But it's not disorganized and it's certainly not chaos.

"I find these labels always a bit confusing. We get labeled as a punk band, and I can see that. But when I see what is called punk nowadays--I have nothing in common with all that Green Day stuff. But the idea of controlling your own life, for me that is punk or that is anarchist. The labels themselves mean nothing to me. You try to live as free as possible."

21.00:

PAUL WEIXLER

«FREIWILD»

SOLO ACAPELLA PERFORMANCE

21.30:

THE EX (HOLLAND)

MONTAG, 10. NOVEMBER 2003

13OGEN13

VIADUKTSTR. 13, 8000 ZH 5

EINTRITT: 18.- FR

ALAIN C. KUPPER & CRISTIAN ANDERSEN, ACID HOUSE, 2003, 460×640

rockmaster k. / andersen

THEY BRING YOU THE BEST SOUND FROM CHICAGO AND DETROIT:

ACID HOUSE

special guest: DJ Mooner (Erkrankung)

ROCCNESS
(Meteorites)

NULLELF
(Swingerclub)

JOHN PLAYER
(7b)

Proto House 1982 - 1984

Like it or not, house was first and foremost a direct descendant of disco. Disco had already been going for ten years when the first electronic drum tracks began to appear out of Chicago, and in that time it had already suffered the slings and arrows of merciless commercial exploitation, dilution and racial and sexual prejudice which culminated in the 'disco sucks' campaign. In one bizarrely extreme incident, people attending a baseball game in Chicago's Komishi Park were invited to bring all their unwanted disco records and after the game they were tossed onto a massive bonfire. Disco eventually collapsed under a heaving weight of crass disco versions of pop records and an ever-increasing volume of records that were simply no good. But the underground scene had already stepped off and was beginning to develop a new style that was deeper, rawer and more designed to make people dance. Disco had already produced the first records to be aimed specifically at DJs with extended 12" versions that included long percussion breaks for mixing purposes and the early eighties proved a vital turning point. Sinnamon's 'Thanks To You', D-Train's 'You're The One For Me' and The Peech Boys' 'Don't Make Me Wait', a record that's been continually sampled over the last decade, took things in a different direction with their sparse, synthesized sounds that introduced dub effects and drop-outs that had never been heard before.

But it wasn't just American music laying the groundwork for house. European music, spanning English electronic pop like Depeche Mode and Soft Cell and the earlier, more disco based sounds of Giorgio Moroder, Klein & MBO and a thousand Italian productions were immensely popular in urban areas like New York and Chicago. One of the reasons for their popularity was two clubs that had simultaneously broken the barriers of race and sexual preference, two clubs that were to pass on into dance music legend - Chicago's Warehouse and New York's Paradise Garage. Up until then, and after, the norm was for black, hispanic, white, straight and gay to segregate themselves, but with the Warehouse, opened in 1977 and presided over by Frankie Knuckles and the Garage where Larry Levan spun, the emphasis was on the music. (Ironically, Levan was first choice for the Warehouse, but he didn't want to leave New York). And the music was as varied as the clienteles - r'n'b based Black dance music and disco peppered with things as diverse as The Clash's 'Magnificent Seven'. For most people, these were the places that acted as breeding grounds for the music that eventually came to be known after the clubs - house and garage.

Right from the start there was a difference in approach between New York and Chicago. "All of the records coming out of New York had been either mid or down tempo, and the kids in Chicago wouldn't do that all night long, they needed more energy" commented Frankie Knuckles after his move to Chicago. The Windy City was seduced to a far greater extent by the European sound and when the records started to come, it showed. Whereas garage in New York evolved more smoothly from First Choice and the labels Salsoul, West End and Prelude, there was no such evolution in Chicago. Opinions still differ as to what the first house record was, but it was certainly made by Jessie Saunders and it was on the Mitchball label - probably Z Factor's 'Fantasy', but there was also another Z Factor tune which went by the name of 'I Like To Do It In Fast Cars'. 'Fantasy' sounds extremely dated now but ten years ago it was like a sound from another planet, with echoes of Kraftwerk's heavily synthesized string sounds, a Eurobeat bassline and a simple, insistent drum machine pattern. Suffice to say, the record remained obscure outside the close-knit urban Chicago scene.

SAMSTAG, 20. DEZEMBER 2003,
13OGEN13 VIADUKTSTRASSE 13
TÜRE 23 UHR

13ØGEN13

ALAIN C. KUPPER, THE METEORITES, 2004, 460×640

ALAIN C. KUPPER, CNUT, DJ MOONER, 2003, 460×640

ALAIN C. KUPPER, TRANS AM, 2004, 640×460

TRANS AM Live
ds: Rockmaster K.
0 Zürich 5

ALAIN C. KUPPER, SUNTIC RECORDS, 2003, 297×420

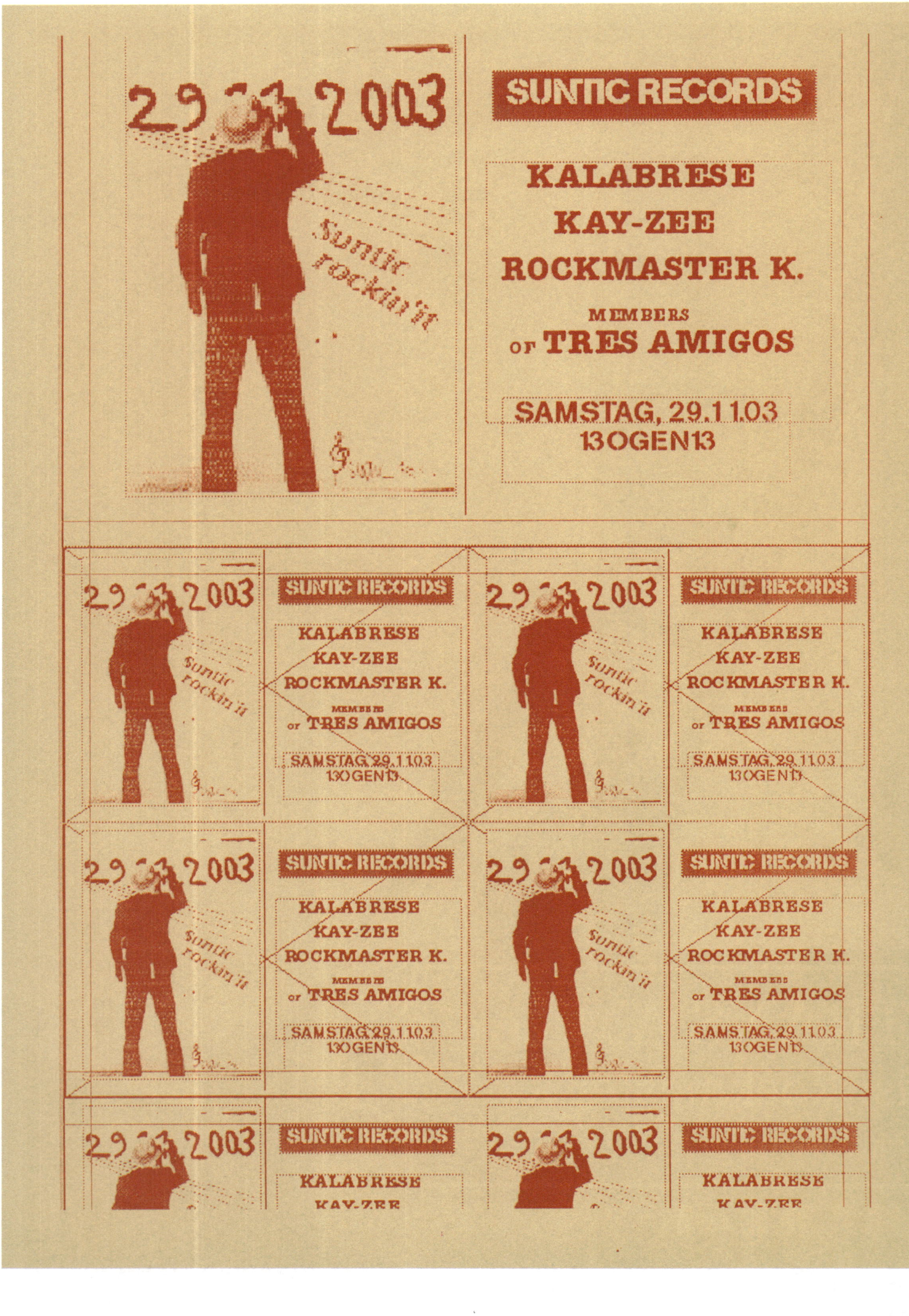

ALAIN C. KUPPER, LOGH, 2003, 297×420

ALAIN C. KUPPER, VOLKSKANTINE ROCKT!, 2004, 640×460

INE ROCKT!

2004 AB 22.00

34 plus 2

y Style)

KMASTER K.+GRAU

OCK+KALABRESE

– Eintritt für gute Musik.

CHKANTINE!!!

design stinks, folks!

ALAIN C. KUPPER, FELIX KUBIN, 2004, 460×640

Best Poster Award
PICCOLO TEATRO MORELLI
MACHT KASPERLITHEATER FÜR UR- UND ANTICHRISTEN & ZEIGT:
«DIE WEIHNACHTSGESCHICHTE»
AM 26./27./28. DEZEMBER 2003,
PÜNKTLICH UM 22H IM 13OGEN13, VIADUKTSTRASSE 13, ZÜRICH 5
AFTER-THEATER-PARTIES:
FR. 26.: DJ VASCOCK UND KING SALAMI
SA. 27.: SURPRISE NIGHT
SO. 28.: HONEY FOR PETZI (LIVE), ROCKMASTER K.

ALAIN C. KUPPER, DÜREFORSÖG, 2003, 460×640

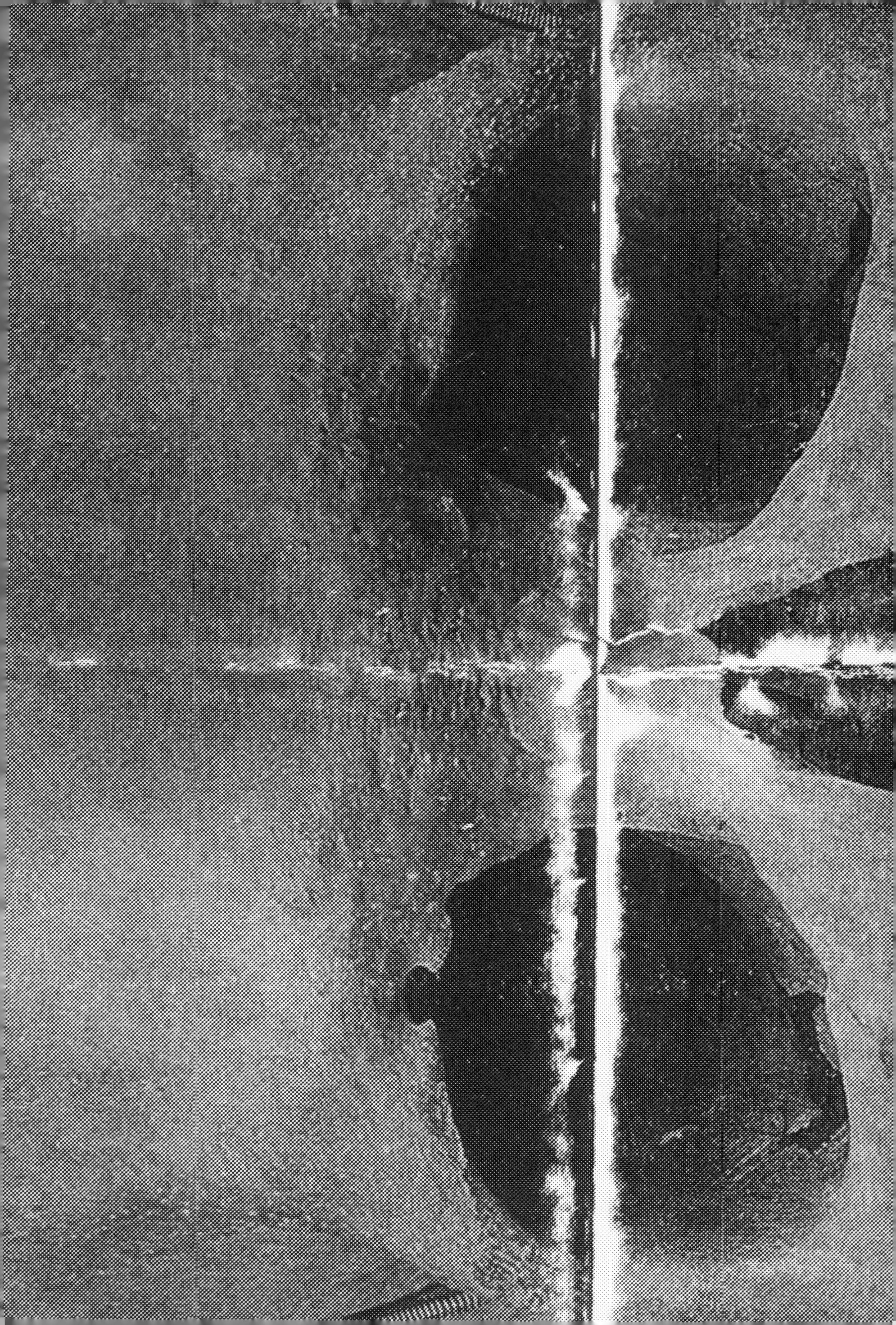

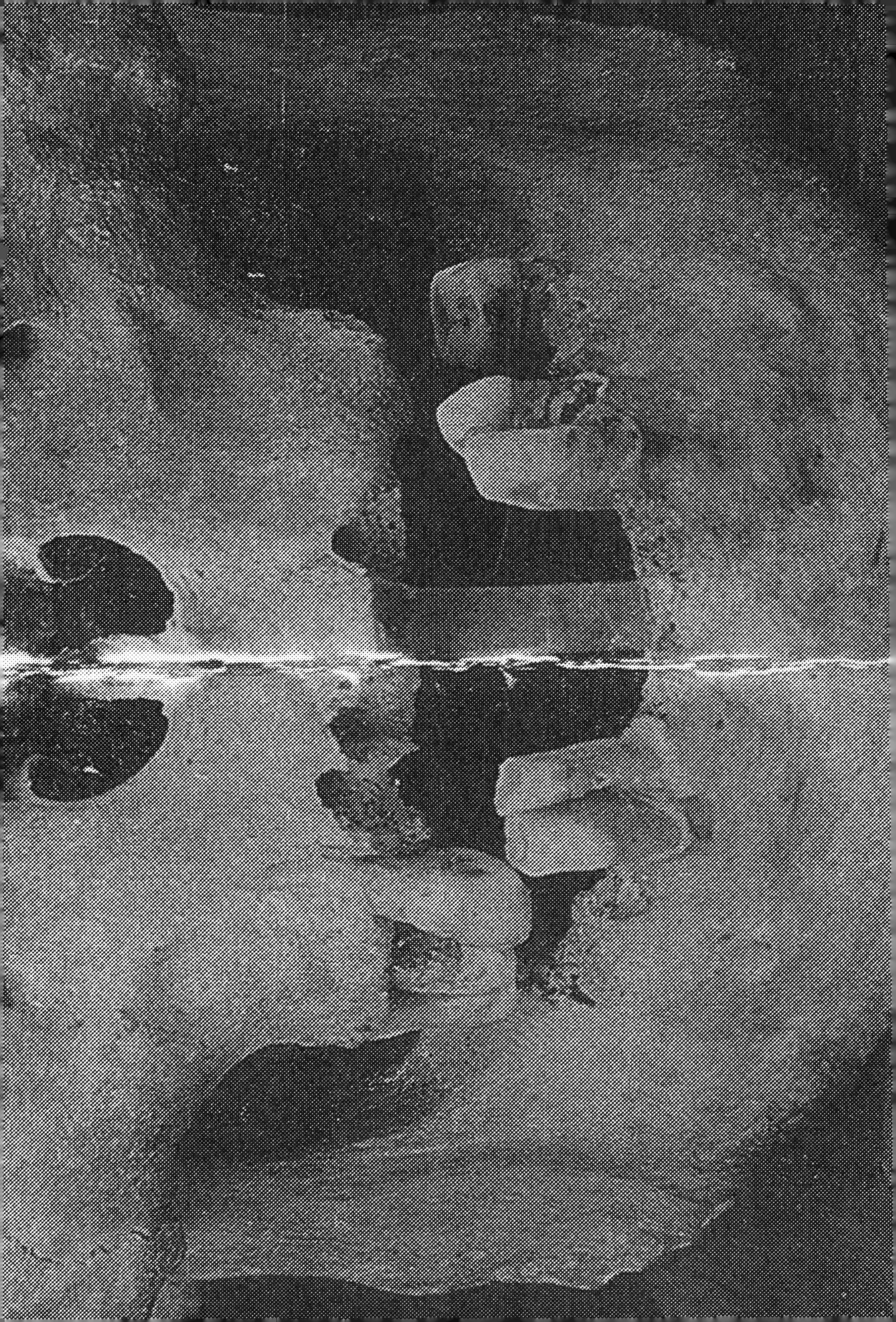

Eric Andersen

Der Zürcher Grafiker und Plakatkünstler macht von der Konzeption bis hin zur Ausführung alles selber. Eric Andersen pflegt einen eigenwilligen Umgang mit traditionellen Druckverfahren wie Holzschnitt, Sieb-, Linol- oder Hochdruck. Er gestaltete bis anhin Programmkarten und Plakate für verschiedene Zürcher Musikclubs und Bands. Politische Plakate stechen in seinem Œuvre besonders hervor – nicht nur wegen ihrer thematischen Brisanz, sondern auch wegen ihrer gestalterischen Eigenständigkeit. 2009 erhielt er dafür den Design Preis Schweiz.

Eric Andersen

The graphic and poster artist from Zurich does everything by himself, from concept to execution. Eric Andersen makes unconventional use of traditional printing processes such as woodcut, silk screen, linoleum or relief printing. Up until now he designed program cards and posters for various music clubs and bands. Political posters stand out prominently from his oeuvre — not just for the thematically explosive nature, but also for the unique designs. In 2009 he received the Design Prize Switzerland for this.

ERIC ANDERSEN, URBAN JUNIOR, 2010, 500×720, SILKSCREEN

BERLIN
Konzert
ALEC EMPIRE
Eat your Heart out
MITTWOCH, 25.11. TÜR: 20.00 UHR, KONZERT: 21.30 UHR / STALL 6 PRODUCTION / ZUERICH
DJ KCOR & DJ MALIK

COLOUR HAZE
JOULES ZH
ZIISCHTIGMUSIG / DI, 17. NOVEMBER 2009 / ZIEGEL OH LAC / 21:30 UHR
SEESTRASSE. 395, 8038 ZUERICH / WWW. ZIISCHTIGMUSIG@ROTEFABRIK.CH

ERIC ANDERSEN, GEISHA, 2009, 500×720, SILKSCREEN

ERIC ANDERSEN, BURN BABY BURN, 2010, 500×720, SILKSCREEN

ERIC ANDERSEN, FUCK FIFA, 2010, 700×1000, SILKSCREEN

Garage 29 – Fuck FIFA

2010 fand die Fussballweltmeisterschaft in Südafrika statt. Der Gestalter Eric Andersen und zwei seiner Kollegen organisierten in den Garagen der Pizzeria Rosso bei der Zürcher Hardbrücke eine Fussball-Bar. Die Idee war, ebenso gemütliche wie gediegene Anlässe für Freunde zu organisieren – so wie es der seit 2006 selbstständig arbeitende Grafiker Andersen auch als Konzertveranstalter tut.

Doch die Bar-Betreiber hatten die Zahl der Spiele unterschätzt – ausserdem fanden viele davon tagsüber, in der Sommerhitze statt. Darum hielt sich auch der Besucherandrang vor den beiden Fernsehgeräten und dem Kühlschrank mit dem Bier oft in sehr überschaubaren Grenzen. So begannen die Betreiber aus Langeweile mit dem Sammeln und Einkleben von Paninibildern von Fussballspielern. Dann hatte jemand die zündende Idee: Die Bilder wurden zerschnipselt und neu montiert, sodass die adretten Fussball-Nationalspieler zu fratzenhaft entstellten Zombies ohne Identität mutierten. Dieses Zerstörungs- und anschliessende Rekonstruktionsspiel begann Wellen zu schlagen. Immer mehr Freunde und auch ganze Familien beteiligten sich und schufen ihre eigenen Fussballmonster – Paninibilder im Wert von weit über 100 Franken mussten dran glauben.

Eric war schon einen Schritt weiter: Er plante, die besten Bilder der «neuen» Fussballer auf einem Protest-Plakat mit dem Titel «Fuck FIFA» zu platzieren. Neben der Musik und anderen Auftragsarbeiten ist das politische Plakat heute eines der zentralen Ausdrucksmittel von Andersen. So gestaltet er seit einiger Zeit Plakate für die 1.-Mai-Demonstrationen, aber auch für einen palästinensischen Grill. Im heissen Sommer 2010 wählte schliesslich eine Jury die Bilder für das Plakat – quasi ein «best of» der hässlichsten Fussballer. Das Plakat «Fuck FIFA», ein Siebdruck, ergänzte Andersen mit einem Text aus der französischen Zeitung *Le Monde*, in der die Machenschaften der FIFA und ihres Schweizer Präsidenten Sepp Blatter mit Fakten und Zahlen kritisch beleuchtet wurden. Die Plakate kleisterten Andersen und seine Kollegen dann in der ganzen Stadt. Das Feedback kam postwendend: Da «Fuck FIFA» in seiner ersten Auflage ein partizipatives Projekt war, freuten sich viele Mitwirkende, dass auch ihr Fussballer es aufs Plakat geschafft hatte.

2014 wiederholt sich das Szenario: Zur Fussball-WM organisiert Andersen in seinen Garagen wieder eine Fussball-Bar. Einerseits, um alte Freunde und Bekannte wieder zu treffen, andererseits, um den voll kommerziellen Public Viewings in der Ausgehmeile von Zürich West etwas entgegenzuhalten. Erneut produziert Andersen auch ein «Fuck FIFA»-Plakat, nach den gleichen Vorgaben wie bei der Erstauflage 2010, diesmal allerdings im Alleingang. Auch die Neuauflage des «Fuck FIFA»-Plakats von 2014 stösst auf grosses Interesse. Andersen hängt 70 Exemplare davon als Installation in die Ausstellungsräume der Kunstmesse Art Basel 2014. Seine Idee, dass die Messebesucher die an die Wand gepinnten Plakate abhängen und mit nach Hause nehmen können und so der Protest noch weitere Kreise zieht, scheitert am Widerstand eines Konservators.

Eric Andersen im Gespräch mit Sam Mumenthaler

Garage 29 — Fuck FIFA

When the Soccer World Cup took place in South Africa in 2010, designer Eric Andersen, together with two colleagues, set up a soccer bar in the garage of Pizzeria Rosso, near the Hardbrücke in Zurich. The idea was to offer relaxed and tasteful events for friends — in the same fashion as Andersen, a freelance graphic designer since 2006, did as a concert organizer.

But the proprietors of the bar had underestimated the sheer number of games. In addition, many took place during the daytime, in the middle of the summer heat. The number of visitors able to watch the two TV sets and the supplies in the beer refrigerator therefore often reached their limits. Out of boredom, the proprietors began collecting the Panini pictures of soccer players and pasting them into the book. Then someone had a brilliant idea: He cut up the pictures and reassembled them in such a manner that the dapper soccer players of the national teams were mutated into grotesquely deformed zombies, without any recognizable identity. The game of destroying and reconstructing caused a stir. More and more friends, even entire families, participated in creating soccer monsters of their own, resulting in the mutilation of Panini pictures worth hundreds of Swiss francs.

But Eric had already gone one step further and was planning to feature the best pictures of these "new" soccer players on a protest poster titled "Fuck Fifa." Besides music and other commissioned works, political posters are today one of Andersen's main means of expression. He's been designing posters for the May 1st demonstrations for a considerable period, and also for a Palestinian snack bar. In the hot summer of 2010, a jury finally selected the pictures to be featured on the "Fuck Fifa" poster: a silkscreen print that was a "best of" the ugliest soccer players. Andersen then added a text with facts and figures from the French newspaper *Le Monde*, criticizing the activities of Fifa and Swiss Fifa president Sepp Blatter. Andersen and his colleagues then pasted it all over town. Feedback came immediately: inasmuch as the first edition of "Fuck Fifa" was a collaborative effort, a number of contributors were pleased to see that their soccer players also made the cut.

This scenario was repeated in 2014: Andersen again organized a soccer bar for the Soccer World Cup in his garage. On the one hand, to meet friends and acquaintances again and on the other, as a response to the completely commercialized "public viewings" staged in the hip area of Zurich West. Again, Andersen produced a "Fuck Fifa" poster following the same rules as the first edition did in 2010, but this time single-handedly. The new 2014 edition once again attracted considerable attention. Andersen posted seventy copies of the poster as an installation in the exhibition rooms of the Art Basel art fair in 2014. His idea of letting visitors to the fair remove the posters from the wall and take them home so that the protest would reach a wider audience, failed due to resistance from one of the curators.

Eric Andersen in a conversation with Sam Mumenthaler

ERIC ANDERSEN, FUCK FIFA, 2014, 700×1000, SILKSCREEN

ERIC ANDERSEN, THE CIRCUS ROCK, 2009, 700×1000, SILKSCREEN

ERIC ANDERSEN, SILENCE, 2011, 700×1000, LEAD TYPE

SILENCE
IS BETTER
THAN
BULLSHIT.

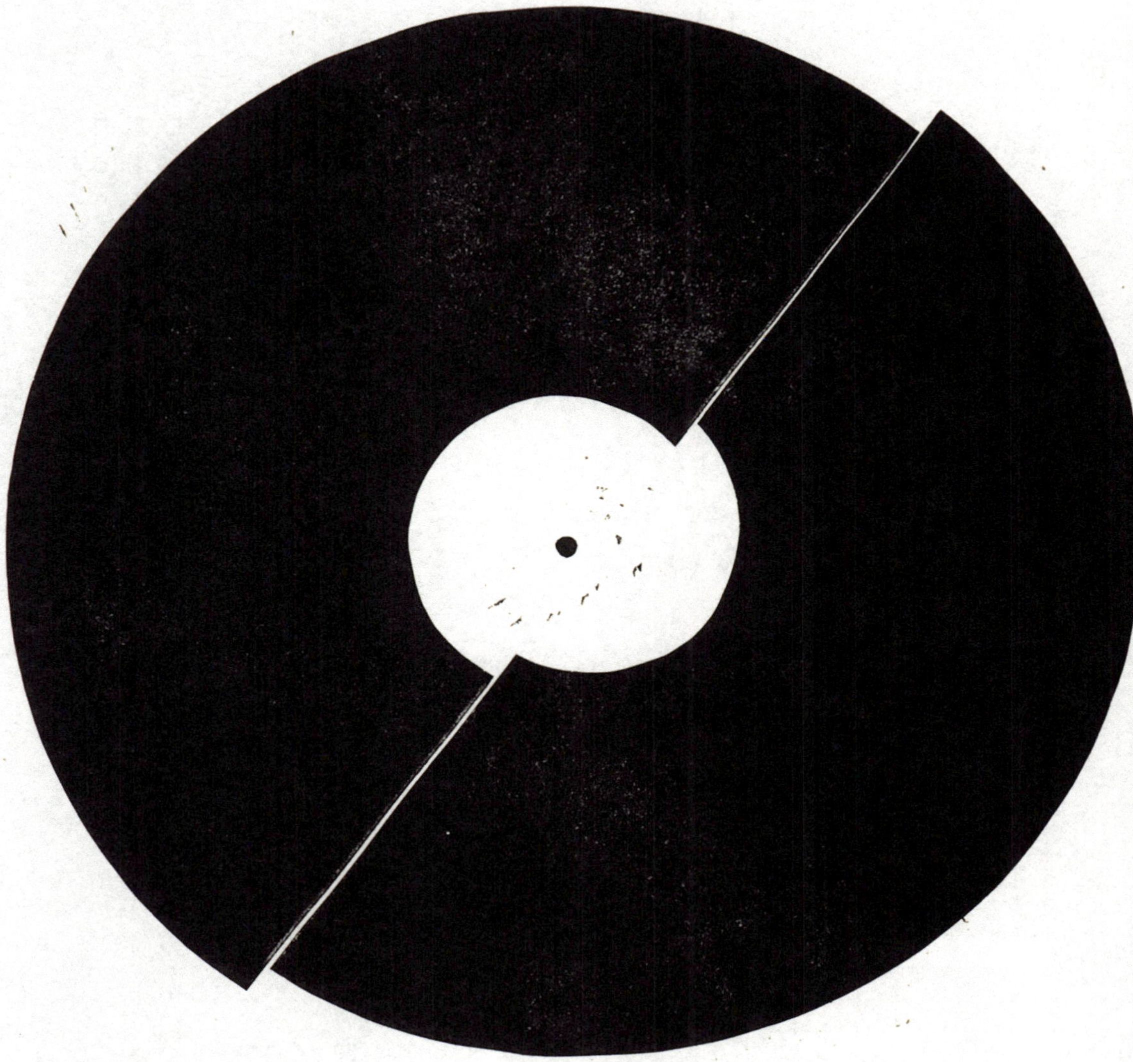

DEMOLITION BLUES

„COULDN'T CARE LESS"
Budget Boozers
RECORD RELEASE
Concert
LOMBEGO SURFERS
(OUTLAW ROCK 'N' ROLL)
BUDGET BOOZERS
(RHYTHM 'N' BOOZE)
CRACKBRAINED SERENADERS
(SPEED-GARAGE ZOMBIE STOMP)
1. 4. 2010/22:00/GÜTERSCHUPPEN/WOLLISHOFEN

ERIC ANDERSEN, VOODOO RHYTHM, 2010, 500×720, SILKSCREEN

ERIC ANDERSEN, STATION 17, 2009, 500×700, WOODCUT

ERIC ANDERSEN, ZUKUNFT – DECEMBER, 2009, 500×700, WOODCUT

ERIC ANDERSEN, BRANT BJORK, MY SLEEPING KARMA, 2010, 500×720, SILKSCREEN

ERIC ANDERSEN, STONEBRIDE, 2009, 500×720, SILKSCREEN

ERIC ANDERSEN, ROCKWOCHE, 2010, 500×720, SILKSCREEN

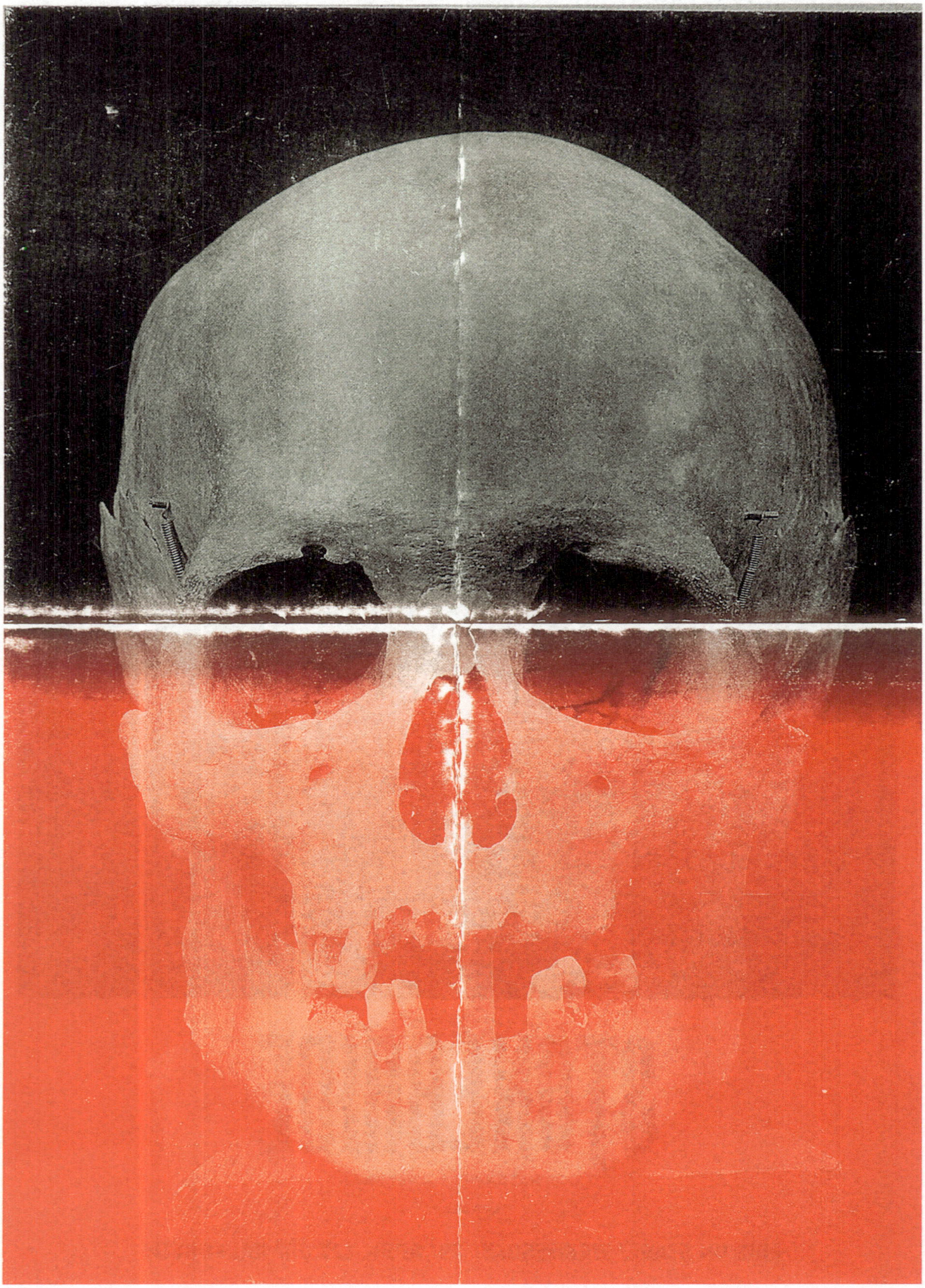

Fan Talk

Ein Diskurs über Schweizer Rockgrafik von Roland Fischbacher und Robert Lzicar

A discourse about Swiss rock graphics from Roland Fischbacher and Robert Lzicar

Was ist Schweizer Rockgrafik? Was haben die Arbeiten der Protagonisten in diesem Buch gemein und was unterscheidet sie? In welchem Zusammenhang sind die Arbeiten entstanden? Und: Wie können diese aus heutiger Perspektive gedeutet werden? Um diese und viele weitere Fragen zu diskutieren, trafen sich Roland Fischbacher, Leiter des Bachelor-Studiengangs «Visuelle Kommunikation» an der Hochschule der Künste Bern, und Robert Lzicar, visueller Gestalter, Dozent und Forscher im Bereich Grafikdesigngeschichte, zu mehreren Gesprächen.

What are Swiss rock graphics? What do the works created by the protagonists of this book have in common and how do they differ? In which context were these works created? And how can they be interpreted from the perspective of today? Roland Fischbacher, director of the “Visual Communication” bachelors program at the Hochschule der Künste (art college) in Bern, and Robert Lzicar, a visual designer, lecturer, and researcher in the field of graphic design history, met for a number of conversations in order to discuss these and many other questions.

Zu den Wurzeln Schweizer Rockgrafik

To the roots of Swiss rock graphics

1: PETER BLUMER, 1969

2: H.R. GIGER, 1998

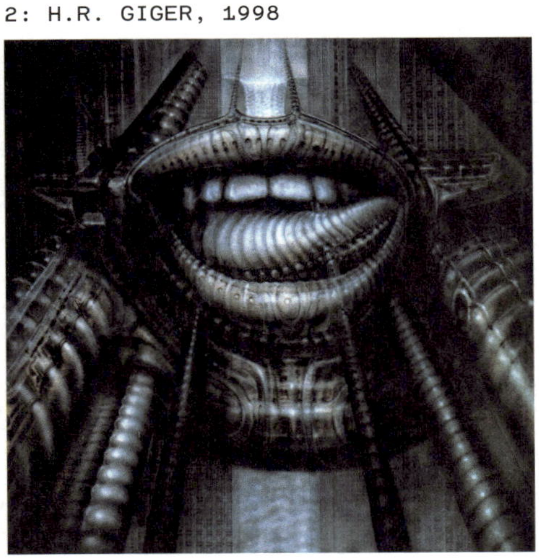

DISKURS

FISCHBACHER Es gibt keine explizit Schweizer Grafik in der Rockkultur. Rock wurde hier nicht erfunden, und mit dem Import des Rock wurde ebenfalls die Ästhetik in die Schweiz importiert. Seit den Sechzigerjahren, aber spätestens seit den Rockplakaten der US-amerikanischen Westküste, verbinden sich Musik und visuelle Sprache, und dies international.

LZICAR Betrachtet man das Buch von vorne bis hinten, lässt sich tatsächlich eine Verbindung zwischen den Arbeiten Düde Dürsts, Peter Blumers, Dirk Bonsmas, Märt Infangers, aber auch Michel Casarramonas herstellen, da sich die Gestalter mehr oder weniger auf die Psychedelic-Poster-Art beziehen.

FISCHBACHER Mit der Umschreibung Psychedelic-Poster-Art bin ich nicht glücklich. Für mich wurzelt dieser Stil im Umfeld der Bewegung der späten Sechzigerjahre in den USA, im speziellen derjenigen der Westküste und der dortigen Sub- und Gegenkultur. Mit der Internationalisierung der Rockmusik internationalisierte sich auch deren Visualisierung. Die Plattencover von Bands wie The Doors, Jefferson Airplaine, Grateful Dead, The Jimi Hendrix Experience und weiteren wurden visuelle Referenzen der Rockmusik. Selbstverständlich auch in der Schweiz. Zum Beispiel in der Form- und Farbgebung der Plakate von Peter Blumer. ABB.1

LZICAR Neben diesem visuellen Stil der Rockmusik haben wir allerdings festgestellt, dass vor allem in der Schweiz viele individuelle Positionen existierten und existieren. Häufig handelt es sich dabei um Grafiker, die in der Tradition von Plakatkünstlern eine individuelle Handschrift entwickeln und pflegen, die sich keinem übergeordneten Stil zuordnen lässt.

FISCHBACHER Und trotzdem hat so ziemlich jede Musikart eine eigene Kultur mit einer ihr eigenen gestalterischen Ästhetik entwickelt. Diese Ästhetiken waren teilweise sehr langlebig. Im Bereich des Prog-Rock waren dies zum Beispiel fantasiereiche Montagen, wie sie auch H.R. Giger produziert hat. ABB.2

LZICAR Mir ist aufgefallen, dass fast alle im Buch behandelten Gestalter als solche ausgebildet wurden.

DISCOURSE

FISCHBACHER There are no specifically Swiss rock graphics in rock culture. Rock wasn't invented here, so the aesthetics were imported to Switzerland along with the music. Music and visual language have been connected since the nineteen-sixties, but at the very latest since the rock posters from the West Coast of the United States were designed — and this applies globally.

LZICAR If you look at the book from front to back, it is actually possible to establish a connection between the works of Düde Dürst, Peter Blumer, Dirk Bonsma, Märt Infanger and Michel Casarramona, since all these designers make reference to the psychedelic poster art to a greater or lesser degree.

FISCHBACHER I'm not happy with the term psychedelic poster art. To me, this style is rooted in the surroundings of the movement thriving in the United States in the late-sixties, particularly on the West Coast and the native sub- and counterculture. As rock music became more international, so did its visualisations. Record covers from bands like The Doors, Jefferson Airplane, Grateful Dead, The Jimi Hendrix Experience and others provided visual reference points for rock music, also in Switzerland, of course. Take, for instance, the form and color of the poster created by Peter Blumer. FIG.1

LZICAR Beside this visual style of rock music, we have, however, also found that there were and are many individual attitudes, most of all in Switzerland. It often occurs that graphic designers develop and cultivate an individual style in the tradition of poster artists, a style that can't be assigned to any over arching style.

FISCHBACHER And nevertheless, pretty much every music genre has developed its own culture and its own design aesthetics. These aesthetics could be quite long-lived. Progressive rock, for example, brought forth fantastical montages produced by H.R. Giger, among others. FIG.2

LZICAR I've noticed that nearly all of the designers dealt with in the book were trained professionals. In the field of graphic design, training is now as important in Switzerland as it was then. Rock graphics therefore appear to have their roots in an

3: VICTOR MOSCOSO, 1974

4: LINDER-STERLING, 1977

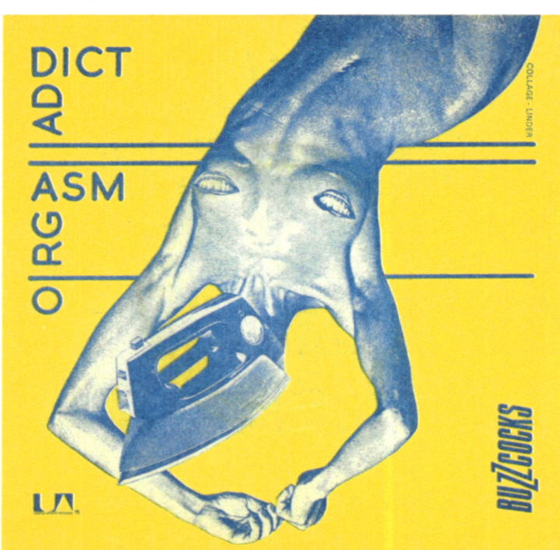

Ausbildung im Bereich der grafischen Gestaltung hat und hatte in der Schweiz einen hohen Stellenwert. Die Rockgrafik scheint also ihre Wurzeln in einem institutionalisierten Umfeld zu haben; anschliessend haben sich die Grafiker dann allerdings wieder herausgelöst, um mit ihren Entwürfen zu einer Subkultur beizutragen.

FISCHBACHER Dies war in den USA und Grossbritannien sicher nicht anders.

LZICAR Du hast recht, Victor Moscoso beispielsweise studierte Kunst an der Cooper Union in New York City und an der Yale University und unterrichtete am San Francisco Art Institute. Interessanterweise handelte es sich hierbei jedoch häufig um künstlerische und nicht um gebrauchsgrafische Karrieren. ABB.3

FISCHBACHER Selbst in der englischen Punk-Bewegung der späten Siebzigerjahre sind Verbindungen zur kreativen Ausbildung nachzuweisen: zum Beispiel bei Linder Sterling, die unter anderem die Collage auf dem Cover der stilprägenden Single *Orgasm Addict* für die Buzzcocks in Zusammenarbeit mit Malcolm Garrett gestaltete. Sie hatte Kunst am früheren Manchester Polytechnic (heute: Manchester Metropolitan University) studiert. Und auch Malcolm Garrett wurde als Grafikdesigner unter anderem am renommierten Departement für Typografie der University of Reading ausgebildet. ABB.4

LZICAR Also ist Professionalität scheinbar auch kein Alleinstellungsmerkmal der Schweizer Rockgrafik. Was ist es denn dann, was alle Beispiele in diesem Buch verbindet? Klar, das Entstehungsland mit dem ihm spezifischen politischen und kulturellen Kontext. Allerdings hatte die Schweiz keine Vorreiterrolle, wie auch im Text von Sam Mumenthaler in diesem Buch klargestellt wird, da es in den Fünfzigerjahren gar keine Schweizer Bands gab, die Rock'n'Roll spielten, und die Beatmusik der Sechziger hierzulande erst relativ spät angekommen ist. Aber trotzdem scheint die Grafik ja so speziell zu sein, dass sie ein eigenes Buch legitimiert.

FISCHBACHER Ich glaube, in den Siebzigerjahren hat sich das Verständnis von Grafik im subkulturellen

institutionalized environment; although the graphic designers later freed themselves, thus, substantially contributing to the subculture with their designs.

FISCHBACHER It was surely no different in the United States or Great Britain.

LZICAR You're right. Victor Moscoso, for example, studied art at both the Cooper Union in New York City and Yale University, then lectured at the San Francisco Art Institute. Interestingly, however, these careers mostly pertained to artistic, not commercial graphics. FIG.3

FISCHBACHER There are also cases that clearly reveal connections to art studies within the English punk movement of the late seventies: for example, Linder Sterling, who, among other things, created the collage on the cover of the Buzzcocks' seminal single, *Orgasm Addict*, in cooperation with Malcolm Garrett. She studied art at the Manchester Polytechnic (today the Manchester Metropolitan University or MMU). And Malcolm Garrett was also a trained graphic designer from the renowned Department of Typography at the University of Reading, among other places. FIG.4

LZICAR Hence, professionalism apparently isn't just a characteristic of Swiss rock graphics. So what connects all the examples in this book? Obviously, their country of origin and a specific political and cultural context. Switzerland certainly didn't play a pioneering role, as Sam Mumenthaler's text in this book demonstrates, since there were not any Swiss bands at all playing rock'n'roll in the fifties, and the beat music of the sixties arrived here relatively late. But the graphic art still appears significant enough to justify a whole book on the subject.

FISCHBACHER In my opinion, the perception of graphic art within the subcultural context of Switzerland changed a lot in the seventies. I believe this also has something to do with the distance to graphics exhibited by the movement of 1968. Many people considered graphics the same as advertising. In spite of exceptions like the works of Peter König or Urban Gwerder, posters of

5: H.R. GIGER, URBAN GWERDER, 1967

6: PETER KÖNIG, 1968

Kontext in der Schweiz stark verändert. Das hat meiner Meinung nach auch mit der Distanz der 68er gegenüber Grafik zu tun. Für viele war Grafik gleichbedeutend mit Werbung. Trotz einiger Beispiele wie den Arbeiten von Peter König oder Urban Gwerder hat das Plakat in der Schweizer Sub- und Politkultur damals nie die Bedeutung gehabt wie zum Beispiel die Arbeiten aus dem Atelier Populaire in Paris. ABB.5+6

LZICAR Trotzdem gab es ja um 1968 auch eine Musikszene in der Schweiz, in der ebenfalls mit Plakaten geworben wurde, oder?

FISCHBACHER Ja, aber die visuellen Künste und auch das Rockplakat haben erst spät eine solch starke Präsenz entwickelt. Die Relevanz des Plakats ist typisch für die späteren Siebziger- und die Achtzigerjahre. Prägnante individuelle Handschriften entwickelten sich in der Schweizer Rockgrafik erst ab den Siebzigern. Dies gilt für mich aber vor allem in der Plakatgestaltung. Eine ganz andere Geschichte erzählen mir die Cover, so die der Schweizer Popgruppe Les Sauterelles, die besonders in den Sechzigerjahren Erfolge feierte. Ich sehe hier einen sehr starken Willen, die formale Sprache internationaler Popkultur zu appropriieren. Bei den Covern der Single *Hongkong / Forget Your Dream* und der LP *View To Heaven* sind die Vorbilder eindeutig erkennbar. Bei der LP *Les Sauterelles* trifft das so nicht zu – zumindest auf der fotografischen Ebene ist die Gestaltung ihrer Zeit sogar voraus. Jedenfalls lässt sich an den Sauterelles beispielhaft darstellen, wie sich Schweizer Bands international zu positionieren versuchten – und dies mit hohen gestalterischen Ansprüchen und Resultaten. Auch die Gestaltung der Cover von The Shiver und Pacific Sound spielen auf internationaler Klaviatur. Dass ich aus meiner heutigen Perspektive die Musik der Bands aufgrund der Gestaltung der Cover falsch eingeordnet habe, widerspricht meinem Anspruch einer gezielten Visualisierung. Aber Totenschädel waren einfach angesagt, ob im Art-Rock oder im Hard-Rock. S.154

Aus den Covern der Rockband Krokodil können die gestalterischen Referenzen und Absichten längst

the Swiss subculture and political culture, at the time, never reached the significance, for instance, of the works produced by the Atelier Populaire in Paris. FIG.5+6

LZICAR At the same time, there also existed a music scene in Switzerland around 1968 advertising with posters, didn't it?

FISCHBACHER Yes, but visual art and rock posters didn't develop such a strong presence until later on. The relevance of posters is typical for the later seventies and the eighties. Clear individual styles at first developed in Swiss rock graphics sometime in the seventies. In my opinion, this applies to poster design, above all. The covers that were to be particularly celebrated in the sixties, like those for Swiss pop group Les Sauterelles, tell a completely different story. Here I recognise a very strong desire to appropriate the formal language of international pop culture. It's easy to recognize the inspiration for the single cover of *Hongkong / Forget Your Dream* and the LP sleeve for *View To Heaven*. This does not apply to the LP *Les Sauterelles* — on a photographic level at least, the design is actually ahead of its time. In any case, Les Sauterelles are a good example of how Swiss bands tried to position themselves on an international level, with high artistic demands and results. The cover design for The Shiver and Pacific Sound pull strings internationally. That I classify the music of the bands incorrectly from my present perspective based on the cover designs, disputes my demand for targeted visualization. But skulls were simply in, whether in art rock or hard rock. P.154

It isn't nearly as easy to read the design references and intentions based on the covers of the rock band Krokodil: On the cover of the self-titled long-player released in 1969, the depiction of the Swiss crest on one hand refers explicitly to the national origins of the band, at the same time as the dominant torch calls to mind the Statue of Liberty, producing a visual link to the United States. The photographs on the cover of *Getting up for the Morning* remind me of living together with flatmates and of a subculture that I grew into over the course of the seventies, but one from which I,

7: ALEC VON TAVEL, 1978

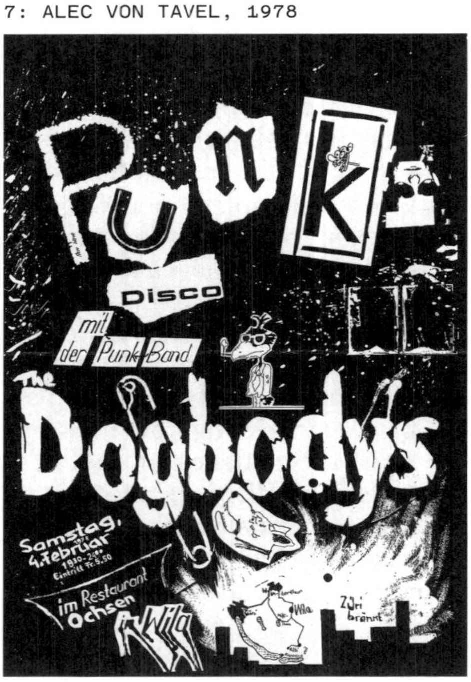

nicht so einfach abgelesen werden: Bei der gleichnamigen Longplayer von 1969 wird durch die Abbildung eines Schweizer Wappens einerseits explizit auf die nationale Herkunft der Band verwiesen und dennoch anhand der dominanten Fackel, die an die Statue of Liberty erinnert, visuell die Verbindung zu den USA hergestellt. Die Fotografien auf dem Cover von *Getting up for the Morning* erinnern mich persönlich an mein WG-Leben und an eine Subkultur, in die ich im Laufe der Siebziger hineingewachsen bin, aber gleichzeitig auch immer einen Schritt daneben stand. S.86+88

Einen ersten Paradigmenwechsel möchte ich für die Siebzigerjahre vorschlagen: Damals wurde der Druck demokratisiert.

LZICAR Demnach war es der Einfluss technologischer Innovationen, der, deiner Meinung nach, die Rockgrafik in der Schweiz grundlegend veränderte?

FISCHBACHER Während meiner Anfangszeiten in der eher politisch geprägten Produktion von Druckerzeugnissen existierte auf einmal der Fotokopiershop. Er war eine Alternative zu den Druckereien, die häufig zu teuer waren. Plötzlich konntest du im Bahnhof zum Copyshop rennen und DIN A3 drucken, einmal falten – und schon hattest du dein Fanzine; oder eben nicht falten und du hattest ein Plakat. Also erstens wurde es billiger und zweitens wurde es «alltäglicher». Die günstigeren Produktionskosten haben sicherlich zur Verbreitung von Rockgrafik beigetragen.

LZICAR Dieser Prozess ist allerdings nicht typisch für die Schweiz. Die Demokratisierung der Produktionsmittel veränderte die Designkultur in den meisten westlichen Ländern.

FISCHBACHER Natürlich, die Technologie hatte immer schon eine starke Auswirkung auf die Gestaltung und die Ästhetik der daraus entstehenden Produkte. So führte der Einsatz des Fotokopierers als Reproduktionsmedium zu einer wiedererkennbaren Ästhetik der fertigen Produkte – der sogenannten Punk- oder Xerox-Ästhetik – und, damit einhergehend, zur extensiven Verbreitung von Kleindrucksachen aus dem subkulturellen Kontext. ABB.7/S.37

at the same time, also always stood apart to a certain degree. PP.86+88

I would like to suggest a first paradigm shift for the seventies: it was the decade when printing was democratised.

LZICAR So, in your opinion, rock graphics in Switzerland were fundamentally changed by the influence of technological innovations?

FISCHBACHER When I just started out producing more political prints, copy shops suddenly cropped up all over the place. They were an alternative to the often far too expensive print shops. All of a sudden you could run to the copy shop in the train station and print DIN A3 sheets. Fold them once, and you had your fanzine; or if you didn't fold them, you had a poster. So first of all it became cheaper and secondly more commonplace. The reduced production costs certainly contributed to the dissemination of rock graphics.

LZICAR But what you've described wasn't typical only for Switzerland. The democratisation of the means of production changed the design culture of most Western countries.

FISCHBACHER As a matter of course, technology has always had a big influence on the design and aesthetics of the respective products. So the use of photocopiers as a means of reproduction led to a clearly recognizable aesthetic in the final products — the so-called punk or Xerox aesthetic — and, consequently, to the widespread dissemination of small printed items from a subcultural context. FIG.7/S.37

LZICAR So, subculture became visible for the first time, developing its own visual codes. But couldn't you say that this development eventually led to the commercialisation of subculture and, ultimately, also to affect alternative rock music?

FISCHBACHER No, at first it was actually the other way around: the new production conditions — including technologies for recording and reproducing music — fuelled a democratisation of rock music. Anyone could participate — "Do it yourself!" was the motto of the hour. Another big step was taken when the first usable computers

8: RUEDI WYSS, 1982

LZICAR Subkultur wurde erstmals sichtbar und entwickelte eigene visuelle Codes. Aber könnte man sagen, dass diese Entwicklung schlussendlich auch zu einer Kommerzialisierung von Subkultur und damit auch von alternativer Rockmusik geführt hat?

FISCHBACHER Nein, zuerst war es eher umgekehrt: Die neuen Produktionsmöglichkeiten – etwa auch Aufnahme- und Reproduktionstechniken von Musik – haben eine Demokratisierung von Rockmusik vorangetrieben. Jeder konnte mitmachen – «Do it yourself!». Ein weiterer Schritt war, als die ersten brauchbaren Computer auf den Markt kamen. So konnten in einfachen Schritten komplexe und farbige Montagen erstellt werden. Dies hatte natürlich grossen Einfluss auf die Ästhetik der in diesem Buch verhandelten Artefakte.

LZICAR An welchen konkreten Beispielen lässt sich der Einfluss des Kopierers und der damit einhergehende ästhetische Umbruch festmachen?

FISCHBACHER Exemplarisch sichtbar wird dies etwa in den Arbeiten von Peter Bäder. Bei ihm war der Fotokopierer ein wichtiges Werkzeug, da man damit erstmals Bilder aus vielfältigen Quellen auf die gleiche Ebene bringen und visuell kombinierbar machen konnte. Aus dem Fotokopierer kamen die Bilder schwarz-weiss und hatten eine ähnliche Struktur. Anschliessend wurden die Bilder von Hand montiert. Die Kombination mehrerer Bilder war der einfachste und effektivste Weg, neue Aussagen zu erzeugen. S.223–242

LZICAR Also wurde die Rockgrafik durch den Fotokopierer um eine neue Dimension bereichert.

FISCHBACHER Das wäre jetzt doch etwas übertrieben. Die Geschichte der Montage in der Grafik ist wahrscheinlich so alt wie die Geschichte der Grafik selber. Nur hat sich bei deren Produktion durch den Umgang mit dem Fotokopierer eine eigene Ästhetik herausgebildet. Dass sich diese Formsprache auch vom Kopierer weg weiterentwickelte, zeigen zum Beispiel die Plakate von Ruedi Wyss für Jazzkonzerte in Bern und Zürich. ABB.8

entered the market. They enabled the creation of complex and colorful montages in simple steps. This, of course, also had a big influence on the aesthetics applied in the artefacts we are dealing with in this book.

LZICAR What concrete examples can be used to identify the influence of photocopiers and the radical change in aesthetics that followed in their wake?

FISCHBACHER As an example, it can be seen in the works of Peter Bäder. He used the photocopier as an important tool, since it enabled placing images from multiple sources on the same plane and to combine them visually. The images left the photocopier in black and white with a similar structure. Afterwards, the images were assembled by hand. The combination of multiple images was the simplest and most effective method for producing new messages. PP.223–242

LZICAR So photocopiers lent rock graphics a completely new dimension.

FISCHBACHER Well, that would be an exaggeration. The history of montage in graphic design is probably as old as the history of graphic design itself. It's only that designs produced by means of a photocopier developed a uniquely individual aesthetic. Ruedi Wyss' posters for jazz concerts in Bern and Zurich, for example, indicate that this formal language continued to develop beyond the photocopier. FIG.8

Internationale Einflüsse

International influences

9: PETER BLUMER, 1972

LZICAR Du hast bereits angedeutet, dass die frühe Rockgrafik internationale Tendenzen zeigte. Dies wird für mich deutlich, wenn man etwa die Arbeiten von Peter Blumer betrachtet. S.123–142

FISCHBACHER Ja, zum Beispiel das Plakat für das Konzert von Pink Floyd im Zürcher Hallenstadion ist eindeutig inspiriert vom sogenannten Westcoast Style. ABB.9

LZICAR Mit dieser grafischen Sprache wurden scheinbar auch ein bestimmtes Lebensgefühl und eine politische Haltung in die Schweiz importiert. Was mich ebenfalls fasziniert, ist, dass zum Beispiel bei der Rockgrafik aus der Schweiz früh auf eine einheitliche Erscheinung geachtet wurde – Rockmusik tritt hierzulande wesentlich institutionalisierter auf, als man es von den US-amerikanischen Vorbildern kennt.

FISCHBACHER Bei Peter Blumers Plakaten für den Konzertveranstalter Good News oder Werner Jekers Reihe für den Electric Circus ist der serielle Gedanke prägend, aber dennoch haben es die Gestalter geschafft, durch Farbe und/oder variierende Sujets den Konzerten eine eigene Identität zu verleihen.

LZICAR Im Gegensatz zu diesen frühen Corporate Design-Ansätzen bezieht H.R. Giger in seinen Entwürfen eine eindeutig künstlerische Position und kreierte einen distinktiven Stil, auf den auch in all seinen anderen Arbeiten zurückgegriffen wird.

FISCHBACHER Die ersten von H.R. Gigers künstlerischen Arbeiten deckten sich mit visuellen Präferenzen eines Teils der Rockmusikszene. Die Tonträger waren mit den von ihm gestalteten Covern über einen langen Zeitraum für viele Künstler eine adäquate Umsetzung ihrer Musik. Dementsprechend gestaltete er seine Cover für international erfolgreiche Bands wie Emerson, Lake and Palmer, Magma, Celtic Frost, Debbie Harry, aber auch für die Politrockband Floh de Cologne. S.147–170

LZICAR H.R. Gigers Arbeiten für Rockmusik nehmen in der Schweizer Rockgrafik eine spezielle Position ein, weil er einer der wenigen Künstler in diesem Buch ist, der

LZICAR You've already mentioned that there were international tendencies in early rock graphics. This becomes clear when I, for instance. look at Peter Blumer's work. PP.123–142

FISCHBACHER Yes, take the Pink Floyd poster for their show at the Hallenstadion in Zurich, which is obviously inspired by the so-called West Coast style. FIG.9

LZICAR A particular attitude toward life and a political set of beliefs were also imported to Switzerland along with this visual language. What also fascinates me about rock graphics from Switzerland is the attention given to a uniform appearance at quite an early stage — rock music developed in a much more institutionalised form than the American role models had.

FISCHBACHER A serial concept characterises both Peter Blumer's posters for the concert organisers at Good News as well as Werner Jeker's series for the Electric Circus. But the designers nevertheless managed to lend concerts their own specific identity by the use of color and/or by varying subjects.

LZICAR In contrast to these early approaches to corporate design, H.R. Giger clearly assumes an artistic attitude, creating a distinctive style and then reiterating it in all of his other works.

FISCHBACHER H.R. Giger's first artistic works catered for the visual preferences of one section within the rock music scene. For a long period of time, the various recorded media sporting covers he had designed were, to many artists, a suitable visual representation of their music. Hence, he designed record covers for internationally successful bands such as Emerson, Lake and Palmer, Magma, Celtic Frost, and Debbie Harry, but also for the political rock band Floh de Cologne. PP.147–170

LZICAR H.R. Giger's work for the rock music industry holds a special position within Swiss rock graphics as he is one of the few artists featured in this book to succeed in establishing himself in the international market. Therefore, his personal style must be recognisable in his artefacts. The works from the

10: MARK PERRY, 1977

sich in einem internationalen Markt etablieren konnte. Seine Handschrift muss deshalb in den Artefakten wiedererkannt werden. Visuell entgegengesetzt funktionieren die Arbeiten aus der Ära des Punk – hier legt das Produkt den Entwurfs- und Produktionsprozess per Kopierer willentlich offen; fast alle Flyer aus der Zeit sind schwarz-weiss, und falls Farbe eingesetzt wird, dann oft nur farbiges Trägerpapier.

FISCHBACHER ... möglichst weg von einer «geschliffenen» Erscheinung. Die Artefakte dienen als Alternative zu den Kommunikationsmitteln der «schönen, heilen» und vor allem ökonomischen Welt. Das Schwarz-Weisse, das Gekritzelte, das Gekratzte, das Gesprayte – all das sind Formen einer gegenkulturellen Haltung.

LZICAR Interessanterweise lässt sich allerdings auch in der Ära des Punk keine lokale Eigenständigkeit feststellen. Die Gestaltung der Beispiele im vorliegenden Buch ähnelt der Erscheinung von Fanzines wie *Sniffin' Glue*, das Mark Perry 1976/77 in England herausgab. Man kann also behaupten, dass es sich bei Punk um eine internationale ästhetische Bewegung handelt, die früh in der Schweiz adaptiert wurde, zum Beispiel im Punk Fanzine *No Fun* von Urs Steiger, erstmals erschienen 1977. ABB.10/S.202+203

punk era work the other way round visually — here the product intentionally reveals the design and production process by means of a photocopier; nearly all of the flyers from this period are black and white, and if color was used, then mostly only in the form of colored paper.

FISCHBACHER ... as far away from a "polished" look as possible. The artefacts serve as an alternative to the means of communication used by the "beautiful, unspoiled," and above all economic world. The monochrome, scribbled, scratched and sprayed — they all signify a countercultural approach.

LZICAR It's interesting to observe that it is indeed impossible to identify any original local style in the punk era. The designs typical of the works in this book resemble the look of fanzines like *Sniffin' Glue*, published by Mark Perry in England in 1976/77. You could therefore argue that punk was an international aesthetic movement that was adapted in Switzerland at an early stage, for instance, by Urs Steiger's punk fanzine *No Fun*, first published in 1977. FIG.10/S.202+203

Individualismus und konzeptionelle Strategien

Individualism and conceptual strategies

LZICAR Parallel zu Punk kam es meiner Meinung nach zu einem eklatanten Bruch – zuerst mit New Wave, danach mit dem sogenannten Post-Punk erhöht sich der Komplexitätsgrad gestalterischer Methoden, und die Relevanz von bildender Kunst und Design für die Rockmusik steigt. Es geht nicht mehr nur darum, ein emotionales Moment visuell zu kommunizieren, sondern es wird versucht, spezifische Ausdrucksformen basierend auf der Musik und dem Image der jeweiligen Band zu kreieren.

FISCHBACHER Typisch erscheint mir der Einsatz präziser Verweise, wie etwa popkultureller Ikonen wie Pacman und Mickey Mouse, oder die Verwendung einer chinesischen Propagandafotografie. Diese werden nicht mehr chaotisch überlagert, sondern genau erkennbar eingesetzt – Strategie statt Chaos. S.175–188

LZICAR Parallel to the development of punk, in my opinion, a substantial breach was taking place — first with new wave, later with so-called post punk; the level of complexity in design methods increases in time with the relevance of visual art and design for rock music. It's no longer about visually communicating an emotional moment. Instead, the attempt is made to create specific forms of expression based on the music and image of a particular band.

FISCHBACHER What seems typical to me is the use of precise references — pop culture icons like Pacman and Mickey Mouse, or a Chinese propaganda photo. Now, these aren't overlapped in a chaotic manner any more, but instead, used in a clearly recognisable way — strategy replaces chaos. PP.175–188

LZICAR Das Referenzsystem wurde dadurch erweitert. Dieses Arbeitsprinzip – also das geplante Beauftragen und Zusammenfügen speziell gefertigter visueller Mittel – würde man heute als Art Direction bezeichnen.

FISCHBACHER Ja, allerdings folgt dieses Prinzip hier einer bewussten Haltung.

LZICAR Würdest du diese als künstlerische oder eher als grafische Attitüde bezeichnen?

FISCHBACHER Ich halte es für schwierig in diesem Zusammenhang, beide Sichtweisen voneinander zu trennen. Die unterschiedlichen Haltungen führen zu einer Parallelität diverser Gestaltungsansätze. Die visuelle Interpretation von Rockmusik ist dadurch vielfältig geworden. Aber auch die Gestaltungsprozesse unterscheiden sich: Peter Fischli inszenierte die Band Kleenex/Liliput visuell und beteiligte sich so an der Konstruktion des Images der Band. Dies wurde möglich, da Künstler und Band sich entweder regelmässig über die Gestaltung austauschten oder sogar zusammen daran arbeiteten. Bei einem Festival kann die Haltung des Grafikers in den Vordergrund treten – oder der Personen, die einen solchen Anlass initiieren.

LZICAR Wir stellen also fest, dass es schwierig ist, ein Plattencover mit einem Festivalplakat zu vergleichen, da Rockgrafik nicht nur vom Kommunikationsmedium, sondern auch von der Auftragssituation und dem Entstehungsprozess abhängig ist. Auch die Langlebigkeit der Artefakte unterscheidet sich grundlegend: Ein Konzert wirbt nur für den kurzen Zeitraum vor der Veranstaltung, während ein Plattencover ab seiner Entstehung bis heute – wenn auch häufig in digitaler Form – mit der Band in Verbindung gebracht wird. Das Plattencover transformiert seine Funktion in diesem Prozess mehrmals: Im Plattenladen soll es zum Kauf anregen, während es später zur Wiedererkennung der Band eingesetzt wird.

FISCHBACHER Doch zurück zu Peter Fischli. Betrachtet man das Coverdesign von *Der Mond / Das Schicksal* der Band Hertz, ist deren Repräsentation auf die typografische Umsetzung des Bandnamens und

11: HERTZ, 1979, ©LIVIO PIATTI

LZICAR That broadened the reference system. Today, this method — I am referring to the planned assignment and arrangement of specifically created visual material — would be called art direction.

FISCHBACHER Yes, but here this principle follows a conscious approach.

LZICAR Would you call this approach an artistic or rather a graphic position?

FISCHBACHER I think it's difficult to separate the two points of view in such a context. The different attitudes led to a parallelism among different approaches to design. They added multiple facets to the visual interpretation of rock music. At the same time, the design processes differ: Peter Fischli staged Kleenex/Liliput on a visual level and, thus, participated in building the band's image. This was possible because artist and band either regularly discussed the design or actually collaborated, in order to create it. With regard to a festival, the graphic designer's position can come to the fore — or the position of the organisers.

LZICAR So we have established that it's hard to compare a record cover with a festival poster since rock graphics not only depend on the communication medium but also on contractual conditions and the creative process. The lifespan of the artefacts is fundamentally different too: a concert is only advertised for a short time prior to the event, while a record cover — albeit in digital form — is connected with the band from the day it is created to the present. The function of the record cover shifts several times during this process: in the record shop, it is supposed to encourage people to buy the album, later it is used to identify the band.

FISCHBACHER Back to Peter Fischli. If you look at his cover design for the Hertz album *Der Mond / Das Schicksal*, the representation is reduced to the typographic design of the band name and the cropped photo picking up the pyramid-like structure of the lettering. The design contains clear references to art. It would be presumptuous to ascribe this to Dadaism. The twenties influence becomes visible on the Liliput

12: LILIPUT, 1980, ©KATJA BECKER

die freigestellte Fotografie, welche die pyramidenartige Struktur des Schriftzugs aufnimmt, reduziert. Die Gestaltung hat klare Bezüge zur Kunst. Diese auf den Dadaismus zurückzuführen wäre verwegen. Sichtbar wird der Zwanzigerjahre-Einfluss auf dem Albumcover der Band Liliput. Die Band wurde darauf in ungewöhnlicher Papp-Verkleidung abgebildet – einerseits erinnert mich das an ein Verkleidungsspiel von Kindern, andererseits kann es als kunsthistorisches Zitat gedeutet werden. Hugo Ball trat 1916 im Zürcher Cabaret Voltaire in einem ähnlichen Kostüm auf, um sein Lautgedicht «Karawane» vorzutragen. ABB.11+12/S.184+188

LZICAR Wird deiner Meinung nach eine vergleichbare Strategie auch von Peter Bäder angewandt?

FISCHBACHER Peter Bäder generiert seine Bildideen hauptsächlich aus sich selbst – man könnte ihn als Bildkonstrukteur bezeichnen –, während Peter Fischli am zeitgenössischen Diskurs über Kunst aktiv teilnimmt und auf diese Weise möglicherweise auch Postmoderne-Theorien rezipiert hat.

LZICAR Gerade bei den Arbeiten von Peter Fischli ist dies schlüssig. Er studierte 1975/76 an der Accademia di Belle Arti in Urbino und 1976/77 an der Accademia di Belle Arti in Bologna. Er führt innovative Strategien in die sogenannte Rockgrafik ein. Die Arbeiten sind eher konzeptuell und weniger bildhaft oder narrativ. Das Visuelle ist dem Intellektuellen untergeordnet. Auch die zunehmende Popularität der Semiotik, also der Lehre der Zeichen, kann anhand der Entwürfe veranschaulicht werden.

FISCHBACHER Der Schritt vom Punk zu allem, was danach kommt, ist, dass es auf einmal ästhetische Strategien gab, welche die Individualität der Bands und Gestalterinnen und Gestalter in den Vordergrund treten liess. Grundsätzlich kann man feststellen, dass mit dem Übergang von Punk zu Post-Punk ein Paradigmenwechsel stattgefunden hat, mit dem das Prinzip der Individualität vor das Prinzip der Kollektivität tritt.

album cover. There the band is portrayed wearing unusual cardboard clothing — on the one hand this reminds me of a children's dressing up game, on the other, it can be interpreted as an art-historical cross-reference. Hugo Ball appeared in a similar costume at the Cabaret Voltaire in Zurich in 1916 to present his sound poem "Karawane". FIG.11+12/S.184+188

LZICAR Does Peter Bäder apply a similar strategy in your opinion?

FISCHBACHER Peter Bäder mainly generates his visual ideas by himself — you could almost call him an engineer of images — while Peter Fischli actively participates in the contemporary art discourse and is, thus, possibly also familiar with postmodernist theories.

LZICAR That makes sense, especially, with regard to the works of Peter Fischli. He studied at the Accademia di Belle Arti in Urbino in 1975/76 and at the Accademia di Belle Arti in Bologna in 1976/77. He implemented innovative strategies in rock graphics. His works are more conceptual and less pictographic or narrative. The visual is subordinate to the intellectual. Based on his designs, it is also possible to perceive the increasing popularity of semiotics (*i.e.* the theory of signs and symbols).

FISCHBACHER The sudden emergence of aesthetic strategies allowing the individuality of the bands and designers to come to the fore is the leap from punk to everything that comes after. Basically, you could say that a simultaneous paradigm shift took place with the transition from punk to post punk, redirecting the focus from the principle of individuality to the principle of collectivity.

Bildkonstruktion und -montage

Image construction and montage

13: PETER BÄDER, 1982

DISKURS

FISCHBACHER Die Arbeiten von Peter Bäder heben sich davon ab, indem sie eine sehr eigene Bildsprache haben – im Sinne einer künstlerischen Handschrift. Einerseits erkennt man in der Unordnung der Bildelemente visuelle Eigenschaften, die dem Punkt zugeschrieben werden, andererseits deutet der hohe Elaborationsgrad seiner Arbeiten auf seine Ausbildung als Grafikdesigner hin. Er hat also eine sehr eigene gestalterische Strategie entwickelt und diese durchgezogen.

LZICAR An dieser Stelle würde ich mir gerne eines der Plakate von Peter Bäder genauer mit dir ansehen.

FISCHBACHER Ich halte das Plakat für das zweite «TonModern»-Festival für repräsentativ.

LZICAR Um den Kontext zu begreifen, in dem das Plakat entstanden ist, wäre es interessant, zu erfahren, um welche Art Veranstaltung es sich bei «TonModern – Laute Nächte in der Roten Fabrik» handelte.

FISCHBACHER Das «TonModern» war ein kleines Festival für «andere Musik» – in diesem Fall alternative und laute Rockmusik – und eine der ersten grösseren Veranstaltungen im neu gegründeten Kulturzentrum Rote Fabrik in Zürich.

LZICAR Was weisst du über die Gestaltung und Produktion des Plakats?

FISCHBACHER Das Besondere an dem Objekt ist, dass es sowohl als Plakat diente als auch als Umschlag für ein Magazin, welches über das Festival informierte. Aus dieser Funktion ergab sich das Querformat. Ich halte es für eine typische Arbeit Peter Bäders in Bezug auf die Technik der Montage. Die Personen im Vordergrund, die Plattenspieler mit den russisch-futuristisch wirkenden trichter förmigen Verstärkern, die vergrösserte Bühne mit Hund – so entsteht aus Bildelementen verschiedener Quellen eine Einheit. Das Plakat produziert eine alternative Realität. ABB.13+14

LZICAR Auch enthält es wenige der Stilismen, die man davor mit Rockgrafik in Verbindung brachte.

FISCHBACHER Die Methode der Montage wurde häufig auch auf Drucksachen aus der Ära des

DISCOURSE

FISCHBACHER The works of Peter Bäder stand out because they have their own pictographic language — an artistic style or handwriting. On the one hand, it is possible to recognize visual characteristics in the disorder of visual elements — something attributed to punk. On the other hand, the high degree of elaboration in his work points to his training as a graphic designer. He has therefore established and followed through a very personal design strategy.

LZICAR At this point, I'd like to take a closer look at one of Peter Bäder's posters.

FISCHBACHER I think the poster for the second "TonModern" festival is representative.

LZICAR In order to understand the context in which the poster was created, it would be interesting to hear what kind of an event "TonModern — Laute Nächte in der Roten Fabrik" (loud nights at the Rote Fabrik) was.

FISCHBACHER "TonModern" was a small festival for "the other music" — in this case alternative and loud rock music — and one of the first large events in the newly established Rote Fabrik cultural centre in Zurich.

LZICAR What do you know about the design and production of the poster?

FISCHBACHER What's special about this item is that it served both as a poster and as a sleeve for an info magazine about the festival. The dual purpose was the reason for the horizontal alignment. I see it as a typical Peter Bäder work because of the montage technique he applies. The people in the foreground, the record player with the funnel-shaped Russian amplifiers in their futuristic look, the enlarged stage accommodating a dog — he creates a unity consisting of different pictographic elements. The poster evokes an alternative reality. FIG.13+14

LZICAR It also contains some of the stylistics previously associated with rock graphics.

FISCHBACHER The montage method was also often used in printed

Punk angewandt, allerdings nicht so raffiniert wie in diesem Entwurf. Hier komponiert Peter Bäder aus den diversen Materialien eine neue visuelle Welt mit einer mehrdeutigen Aussage.

LZICAR Mich interessiert an dem Plakat, dass es Bildelemente und Aussagen kombiniert, die auf den ersten Blick nicht zusammenpassen. Auf diese Weise schafft Peter Bäder eine eigenständige visuelle Interpretation einer Konzertsituation. Nicht die Musik oder Band selbst steht im Mittelpunkt, sondern die Veranstaltung. Für mich stellt das Plakat die Institution des Rockkonzerts infrage und erschafft sie neu als Ort für Experimente. Noch etwas fällt mir auf: Es gibt wenige Elemente, die aus der Montage hervortreten. Alles wirkt demokratisch und gleichwertig.

FISCHBACHER Das Plakat ist auch bewusst nicht auf Lesbarkeit getrimmt.

LZICAR Würdest du sagen, das Plakat wurde willentlich codiert – zum Beispiel, um seine Funktionsweise und Lesbarkeit von herkömmlichen, meist einfach zu rezipierenden Werbeplakaten zu unterscheiden?

material during the punk era, but not in such a refined manner as in this design. Here, Peter Bäder composes a new visual world, with an ambiguous message, using different materials.

LZICAR What I find interesting is the combination of pictographic elements and messages that, at first sight, don't seem to fit together. Hence Peter Bäder creates an independent interpretation of a concert situation. The focus is not on the music or band itself, but on the event. To me, the poster calls the institution of rock concerts into question, recreating them as a field of experimentation. Something else that strikes me, is that there are only few elements that stand out in the montage. Everything appears democratic, set on an equal footing.

FISCHBACHER In addition, the poster is deliberately not designed to be readable.

LZICAR Would you say that the poster was deliberately coded — for example, in order to differentiate its functionality and readability from conventional, generally easy to interpret advertising posters?

14: PETER BÄDER, 1982

FISCHBACHER Dem würde ich zustimmen. Das Plakat verkörpert eine Anti-Haltung gegenüber etablierten Zeichensystemen und Rezeptionsformen.

LZICAR Demnach entwickelt das Plakat eine alternative visuelle Sprache, die bewusst auch mit den tradierten Codes und Stilmitteln der Rockgrafik bricht.

FISCHBACHER Ja, und das war sicherlich neu in Plakaten für Rockmusik in der Schweiz.

FISCHBACHER I would agree with that. The poster embodies an anti-attitude toward established sign systems and forms of reception.

LZICAR So, the poster develops an alternative visual language that also deliberately breaches rock graphics' bequeathed codes and stylistic devices.

FISCHBACHER Yes, and that was surely a novelty in the field of Swiss rock posters.

Lokale Szenen, lokale Stile

Local scenes, local styles

15: DIRK BONSMA, 1988

LZICAR Wie siehst du das bei den Arbeiten von Dirk Bonsma?

FISCHBACHER Für mich ist das etwas ganz anderes: Peter Bäder verfolgt eine grafische Strategie und Dirk Bonsma eine künstlerische. Peter Bäders Entwürfe decken ein wesentlich breiteres mediales Spektrum ab. Dafür setzt er diverse Methoden ein, wie Fotografie, Montage oder Illustration. Dirk Bonsmas Arbeiten hingegen stehen sich methodisch und visuell viel näher und können eindeutig ihm zugeschrieben werden. S.247–266

LZICAR Peter Bäder ist also im Gegensatz zu Dirk Bonsma keinem individuellen Stil verpflichtet, sondern es ist seine individuelle Haltung, welche seine Entwürfe verbindet. Das heisst, du unterscheidest in der Schweizer Rockgrafik grundsätzlich zwischen Grafikern und Künstlern, wobei du davon ausgehst, dass Grafiker mit ihrer Gestaltung auf verschiedene Inhalte anders reagieren als Künstler.

FISCHBACHER Dirk Bonsmas Plakate verweisen auf eine nicht genauer definierte Vergangenheit. Seine Entwürfe wurzeln stark in der US-amerikanischen Gegenkultur mit Protagonisten wie Robert Crumb, Rick Griffin oder R.K. Sloane. Dirk Bonsma erfindet seine Gestaltung nicht für jedes Plakat neu. Er scheint auch musikalisch Freude zu haben an dem, was mal war – und daran ist definitiv nichts Verwerfliches. ABB.16–19

LZICAR Genau, seine visuelle Sprache passt dadurch bestens etwa zur Musik der Fuzztones, die das Garagenrock-Revival zu Beginn der Achtzigerjahre massgeblich

LZICAR How do you assess the works of Dirk Bonsma?

FISCHBACHER I believe his work shows some very distinct traits: Peter Bäder pursues a graphic strategy, Dirk Bonsma pursues an artistic one. Peter Bäder's designs cover a much broader scope of media. Therefore, he applies an array of methods like photography, montage, or illustration. Dirk Bonsma's works, on the other hand, are much closer to each other in a visual sense as well as regarding method and can be clearly attributed to him. S.247–266

LZICAR So, in contrast to Dirk Bonsma, Peter Bäder isn't limited to an individual style, what his designs have in common is his individual attitude. Thus, in Swiss rock graphics, you basically differentiate between graphic designers and artists, starting with the assumption that, through their work, graphic designers react to different content in different manners than do artists.

FISCHBACHER Dirk Bonsma's posters make reference to a past that isn't clearly defined. His designs are strongly rooted in U.S.-American counterculture and contain references to protagonists like Robert Crumb, Rick Griffin, and R.K. Sloane. Dirk Bonsma doesn't reinvent his design for every poster. Moreover, he seems to take pleasure in musical retrospection — and there's definitely nothing wrong with that. FIG.16–19

LZICAR Exactly, that's why his visual language is perfect for the music of the Fuzztones, for example, who played a significant role in the revival of garage rock in the early eighties and for whose Swiss

16: RICK GRIFFIN, 1969

17: R.K. SLOANE, 1984

18: ROBERT CRUMB, 1967

19: DIRK BONSMA, 1987

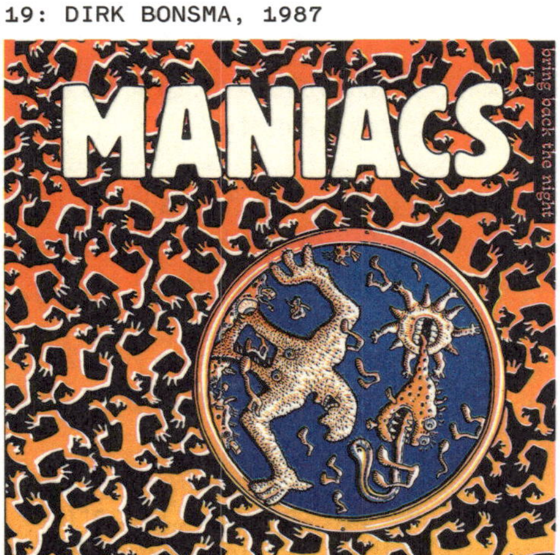

mitgeprägt haben und für deren Auftritte in der Schweiz er ebenfalls die Plakate gestaltet hat. Peter Bäder hingegen repräsentiert in seiner Suche nach einer neuen visuellen Sprache Schweizer Grafik der Achtzigerjahre, als bewusst und explizit mit der grossen Tradition der konstruktiven Gebrauchsgrafik gebrochen wurde, wie dies etwa in der Publikation *Breaking the Rules* der Poster-Sammlung des Museums für Gestaltung Zürich dargestellt wird. ABB.15

Was wir ebenfalls an den beiden Gestaltern Peter Bäder und Dirk Bonsma rekonstruieren können, ist, dass sich aufgrund des Aufkommens verschiedener gestalterischer Positionen lokale Stile entwickelten: Dirk Bonsmas Plakate haben nicht nur die Berner Rockszene stark geprägt, indem er für viele unterschiedliche Institutionen und Anlässe gestaltete. Dies wurde von anderen Veranstaltern und Grafikern übernommen und in ihren Entwürfen verarbeitet.

FISCHBACHER Du meinst, zum Beispiel in den illustrativen Plakaten für den Dachstock der Reitschule?

LZICAR Ja, ich glaube schon … Wie war das in anderen Städten? Ich gehe davon aus, dass etwa in Zürich einfach mehrere «Stimmen» vorhanden waren und sich deshalb kein vorherrschender Stil etablieren konnte, während zum Beispiel in Bern die einzelne «Stimme» Bonsmas lauter geklungen hat, was auch für andere Städte wie Fribourg, Luzern, Biel und viele andere galt.

FISCHBACHER Es gab auch schon eine gewisse Dominanz bestimmter Gestalter oder Institutionen. Eine tatsächliche Demokratisierung hat eigentlich erst mit der Verbreitung des Mediums Flyer eingesetzt.

LZICAR Die Demokratisierung der Organisation der Veranstaltungen brachte also die Demokratisierung der Grafik mit sich – auf einmal wollte und konnte jeder ein Konzert oder eben eine Party organisieren und benötigte dazu eine entsprechende einfach, schnell und billig zu produzierende Ankündigung. Diese Entwicklung wird häufig festgemacht an der Ankunft elektronischer Tanzmusik, gegen Anfang der Neunzigerjahre. S.53

performances he designed the posters. In his search for a new visual language in the Swiss graphic design of the eighties, Peter Bäder, in contrast, represents the deliberate and explicit breach of the long tradition accompanying constructive commercial artwork, as presented, for example, in the publication *Breaking the Rules* from the poster collection of the Museum of Design in Zurich. FIG.15

What we can also reconstruct based on the designers Peter Bäder and Dirk Bonsma, is that local styles developed as a result of different emerging creative positions: Dirk Bonsma's posters had a major influence not only on the Bernese rock scene, whilst he worked for a variety of institutions and events. It was also taken over by other organisers and graphic designers to be reprocessed in their work.

FISCHBACHER Are you for example referring to the illustrative posters for the top floor of the Reitschule (autonomous youth centre in Bern)?

LZICAR Yes, I agree… How was it in other cities? I would imagine that there were, simply more "voices" in Zurich, and that this was the reason why no dominant style developed, while in Bern, for example, Bonsma, as a lone individual could make his "voice" heard more easily; something that also applied to cities like Fribourg, Luzern, Biel and others.

FISCHBACHER There has always existed a certain dominance of particular designers or institutions. True democratisation actually just came about with the frequent use of flyers as a medium.

LZICAR The democratisation of event organisation, thus, entailed a democratisation of graphic design — suddenly everyone who wanted could organise a concert or party and needed an advertisement that could be produced easily, quickly and at a low cost. This development has often been mentioned in connection with the arrival of electronic dance music, at the beginning of the nineties. P.53

FISCHBACHER Nevertheless, there were "professional" or specialized graphic designers who created these flyers and were also known

FISCHBACHER Trotzdem gab es «professionelle» oder spezialisierte Grafikerinnen und Grafiker, die diese Flyer gestaltet haben und als solche bekannt waren. Etwa Cornel Windlin für das Kollektiv Reefer Madness, welches er mitbegründete und mit dem er illegale Partys an diversen Orten veranstaltete, oder Michel Casarramona für Konzerte in den besetzten Häusern in der Konradstrasse in Zürich. Allerdings wurde das Kunstwerk immer kleiner, und die Kommunikation und Gestaltung folgte anderen Strategien. S.319+380

for this. For example, Cornel Windlin, who worked for the Reefer Madness collective, which he had co-founded and with which he organized illegal parties at a wide range of locations, or Michel Casarramona, who advertised the concerts in the squatted houses in the Konradstrasse in Zurich. The artwork became smaller and smaller and communication and design pursued other strategies. PP.320+380

Eigenauftrag und Herzensangelegenheit

Self-assignments and matters of the heart

20: JACQUES SCHOUWEY, 1986

LZICAR Auch in Fribourg gab es eine spezifische Szene, die sich vor allem um das Fri-Son gruppierte. Im Buch sehen wir die Werke von Jacques Schouwey. Kann man dabei von einem regionalen Stil sprechen? S.271–290

FISCHBACHER Nein, ich sehe hier etwa Ähnlichkeiten zu den Bildwelten Peter Bäders, auch wenn die Arbeiten Jacques Schouweys scheinbar stärker im Punk wurzeln. Von 1986 stammt zum Beispiel die Ankündigung für einen Abend mit den Bands Red Lorry Yello Lorry und Domina & The Salves. Das Plakat kann methodisch durch den Einsatz der Fotomontage mit den Plakaten Peter Bäders verglichen werden. Im Vergleich zu Bäders «TonModern»-Plakat ist dieses Plakat Punk. ABB.20

LZICAR Was verstehst du an diesem Beispiel unter Punk?

FISCHBACHER Vielleicht trifft es «unbedarft» besser: Es enthält viele Elemente, die gewollt sind, zum Beispiel die Rahmen und Schatten der Typografie, dies widerspricht der spontanen Gestaltung, die man generell als Punk bezeichnet.

LZICAR Das heisst, du verstehst unter Punk eine amateurhafte Herangehensweise?

FISCHBACHER Ja, aber dies ist eine legitime Haltung, die hier zu einer entsprechend «rotzigen» Form findet.

LZICAR Auch das Konzept erscheint banaler, wenn man es mit dem Plakat für «TonModern» vergleicht.

FISCHBACHER Was mir allerdings am wichtigsten erscheint, ist, dass

LZICAR In Fribourg, there was also a specific scene surrounding the Fri-Son. In this book, we see works by Jacques Schouwey. Can we actually speak of a regional style? PP.271–290

FISCHBACHER No, I see similarities to the pictographic worlds of Peter Bäder, though Jacques Schouwey's work seems more deeply rooted in punk. Take, for example, the advertisement for an evening featuring the Red Lorry Yellow Lorry and Domina & The Slaves in 1986. You can methodologically compare the poster with Peter Bäder's ones he based on photomontage. This poster is punk compared to Bäder's "TonModern" poster. FIG.20

LZICAR What do you mean with "punk" based on this example?

FISCHBACHER Perhaps lowbrow is the more accurate term: it contains many intentional elements, the frame and the shadows of the typography, for instance, but this is counteracted by the spontaneous design, which is generally referred to as punk.

LZICAR So, you refer to punk as an amateurish approach?

FISCHBACHER Yes, but it is a legitimate attitude, which here assumes a "snotty" form, respectively.

LZICAR Compared with the poster for "TonModern", the concept seems to be more banal.

FISCHBACHER But the most important aspects is that, in my opinion, this poster doesn't speak a distinct artistic language — there are simply too many set pieces that are more or less intertwined …

21: JACQUES SCHOUWEY, 1984/85

dieses Plakat für mich keine eindeutige künstlerische Sprache spricht – dafür sind es zu viele Versatzstücke, die mehr oder weniger ineinandergreifen …

LZICAR … und in ihrer Kombination zumindest aus unserer Perspektive auf nichts Übergeordnetes verweisen. In seiner Kleinteiligkeit allerdings ähnelt dieses Plakat dem von Peter Bäder.

FISCHBACHER Ja, aber Peter Bäder konstruiert aus diesen Bestandteilen ein Bild, welches auch zusammenhängend gelesen werden kann. Bei diesem Plakat bleibt die Montage sichtbar, ob bewusst oder unbewusst, ob als Haltung oder einfach, weil der Gestalter es nicht besser konnte – dies kann vom Betrachter nicht beurteilt werden. Diesbezüglich ist das Artefakt ein typisches Produkt seiner Zeit, seine Wirkung geht aber nicht über seine Zeit hinaus. Allerdings erkennt man einen Gestaltungswillen, was die Entwürfe Jacques Schouweys von dem, was man allgemein als Punkgrafik versteht, unterscheidet. Noch stärker kommt dies beim Konzertplakat für die Band Gun Club zum Ausdruck. Hier führt der Gestaltungswille allerdings zu einer eigenständigen und adäquaten Lösung: Die Sujets, welche an B-Movies wie *Godzilla* erinnern, produzieren als Montage eine Atmosphäre, die sich auch mit dem Sound von Gun Club assoziieren lässt. S.282

LZICAR Wir merken also, dass sich das Verhältnis von Grafiker und Rockmusik beziehungsweise -szene entscheidend auf die Gestaltung der Arbeiten auswirkt.

FISCHBACHER Genau, Jacques Schouwey war ja zur gleichen Zeit im Fri-Son als Veranstalter tätig, gestaltete sämtliche Drucksachen für die Location und setzte sich auch inhaltlich mit den einzelnen Bands, die im Fri-Son spielten, auseinander, unter anderem in dem von ihm initiierten Fanzine *Bleu Royal*. Vergleicht man die Positionen von Peter Bäder, Peter Fischli und Jacques Schouwey, würde ich in allen drei Fällen von Gestaltung als Herzensangelegenheit sprechen. Darunter verstehe ich, dass all diese Personen aussergewöhnlich in ihren Umfeldern engagiert waren, und das rund um die Uhr. Das Spezielle an dieser

LZICAR … and, the way they are combined doesn't refer to anything on a higher level, at least from our perspective. In its granularity, however, this poster resembles those of Peter Bäder.

FISCHBACHER Yes, but out of these elements Peter Bäder constructs an image that can still be read cohesively. In this poster, the montage is still visible, whether deliberately or not, whether as an attitude or simply because the designer was unable to do better — the viewer is unable to assess this. In this respect, the artefact is a typical product of its time, but its effect doesn't transcend its time. However, a creative drive is to be recognised, distinguishing Jacques Schouwey's designs from what is, generally, considered punk graphics. This is expressed even more significantly by the concert poster for Gun Club. But here the creative drive leads to an independent and appropriate solution: as a montage, the subjects which are reminiscent of B-movies like *Godzilla*, produce an atmosphere that, at the same time, can be associated with Gun Club's sound.
P.282

LZICAR So we register that the relationship between graphic designer and rock music and/or scene decisively affects the design.

FISCHBACHER Exactly. Jacques Schouwey was at the time actually working as an organiser at the Fri-Son; he designed all printed materials for the venue and also dealt with the content of the different bands playing the Fri-Son in the fanzine *Bleu Royal* that he had founded. Comparing the positions of Peter Bäder, Peter Fischli, and Jacques Schouwey, I would in all three cases speak of design as an affair of the heart. What I mean to say is that all of them were extraordinarily dedicated to their respective scenes, 24/7. The significant element in this period of rock graphics was the symbiosis of what you did, where you did it and with whom you did it. FIG.21

LZICAR Peter Bäder was connected to the RecRec label, Peter Fischli to bands and scene, and Jacques Schouwey arrived at design through his work as a booker and organiser for the Fri-Son. Cédric Magnin, Alain Straubhaar and Luc Torregrossa

22: CHRIS COOPER, 2002

23: FRANK KOZIK, 1994

Phase der Rockgrafik war die Symbiose von, was man macht, mit wem man es macht und wo man es macht. ABB.21

LZICAR Peter Bäder war institutionell an RecRec gebunden, Peter Fischli an Band und Szene, und Jacques Schouwey kam durch seine Aufgabe als Booker und Veranstalter für das Fri-Son zu seiner Tätigkeit als Gestalter. Auch Cédric Magnin, Alain Straubhaar, Luc Torregrossa waren Teil der Gruppe Association KA, der Gruppe, die später das Bikini Test in La Chaux-de-Fonds mitgegründet hat, und gestalteten die Werbemittel für die von ihnen veranstalteten Anlässe. Person und Tätigkeit waren also untrennbar miteinander verbunden – es existierte keine Distanz: Entweder der Grafiker ist selbst Bandmitglied und entwirft Produkte für seine Band – wie Düde Dürst, Märt Infanger oder Alain C. Kupper –, oder er ist Veranstalter einer Reihe oder Mitarbeiter eines Clubs, für die er die visuelle Kommunikation gestaltet – wie nahezu alle anderen Gestalter im Buch –, oder aber er steht ausserhalb von alledem und wird mehr oder weniger klar beauftragt von einer Band oder einem Veranstalter.

FISCHBACHER Wobei in den Beispielen im Buch das dritte Szenario am seltensten vorkommt. Vielleicht am ehesten bei Peter Blumers Plakaten für den Veranstalter Good News. Allerdings wurden die Plakate dermassen stark mit Good News assoziiert, dass Peter Blumer von aussen als Teil der Institution wahrgenommen wird. Die traditionelle Auftragssituation steht hier nicht zentral, weil prägende Grafik in dieser Form wenig präsent ist.

were also part of the group Association KA, later to establish the Bikini Test in La Chaux-de-Fonds and designed the advertising materials for the events they organised. The individual and his activity were, therefore, inseparably linked — there was no distance: either the graphic designer was himself a band member and designed artwork for his band — like Düde Dürst, Märt Infanger or Alain C. Kupper — or he was the organiser of a series or an employee of a club for which he designed the visuals — like nearly all the other designers in the book — or he was on the outside of all this, yet, more or less clearly commissioned by a band or an organiser.

FISCHBACHER From the examples in this book the third scenario is the rarest one. Most likely, it applies to Peter Blumer's posters for the organisers of Good News. Albeit, the posters were so clearly associated with Good News that, from an outside perspective, Peter Blumer himself was perceived to be part of the institution. Traditionally commissioned design isn't at the centre of focus here since there hardly are any relevant points of reference that exist.

Retro-Design und Amerikanismus

Retro design and americanism

LZICAR Betrachten wir die Arbeiten von Michel Casarramona, so lassen sie sich in zwei Phasen unterteilen: die anfänglichen Flyer, meistens in Schwarz-Weiss, und später die farbigen Plakate, mit einer wiederkehrenden Struktur, mit starker Headline und zentraler Bildfigur. S.319-338

FISCHBACHER Auf technisch-formaler Ebene stechen seine Illustrationen heraus: Er hat seinen Stil im Laufe der Zeit gefunden und immer weiter optimiert. Auch seine Plakate

LZICAR Considering the works of Michel Casarramona, they can be divided into two periods: the early flyers, mostly in black and white, and the later color posters, with their recurring structure and astronger headline and central representational figure. PP.319-338

FISCHBACHER His illustrations stand out on a technical, formal level: he found his style over time and continued to optimise it further. His posters also refer to a historical interpretation of American pop

beziehen sich auf eine historische Interpretation von US-amerikanischer Populärkultur, was man zum Beispiel am Einsatz von Sign-Painter-Schriftzügen festmachen kann. Als Vorbilder existierten populäre Plakatgestalter wie Frank Kozik oder der etwas jüngere Coop (Chris Cooper), die an die Tradition der Underground-Comix anschlossen, indem sie Elemente daraus aufgriffen und sie in Form von Siebdruckplakaten für US-Rockbands zu neuen pop-surrealistischen Erzählungen verknüpften. Ihr Einfluss reichte über persönliche Beziehungen bis in die Schweiz, wie dieses Ausstellungsplakat aus dem Jahr 1994 belegt. ABB.22-24

LZICAR Casarramonas Plakate sind eigen, können aber, wie von dir angedeutet, einer bestimmten Strömung im Bereich der Rockgrafik zugeordnet werden. Bis heute veranstaltet er mit Donovan Gregory vom Designer's Club die Zürcher «Garage Sale – Rock'n'Roll, Lowbrow & Underground Culture» – eine Messe, die einerseits den Amerikanismus und andererseits den Lowbrow – zu Deutsch «anspruchslosen» – Stil bereits im Titel trägt. Der gleichen Strömung würde ich auch die Arbeiten von Märt Infanger zuordnen. Beide Gestalter warben sogar für Konzerte derselben Bands, wie etwa von den omnipräsenten The Monsters aus Bern. Man könnte diese Grafik dem Retro-Design zuordnen. S.343-362

FISCHBACHER Dies bedeutet, dass sich diese Gestalter weniger damit beschäftigen, was den zeitgenössischen Diskurs um visuelle Kommunikation und Grafik umtreibt, als vielmehr mit ihrer musikalischen Szene und den damit einhergehenden Stilismen. Es handelt sich um ein in sich geschlossenes Referenzsystem. Demnach könnte man die Geschichte in diesem Buch auch ganz anders erzählen, nämlich entlang der referenzierten Stile, die ja teilweise weit in die Vergangenheit zurückgreifen. Dennoch entwickelte Märt Infanger in seinem System eine distinktive und zeitgemässe visuelle Sprache, zum Beispiel indem er die Merkmale bestimmter Produktionsweisen simuliert und zu etwas Neuem kompiliert.

culture, something thatis hinted at, for example, by the use of sign painter lettering. The role models are popular poster designerslike Frank Kozik or the somewhat younger Coop (Chris Cooper), who followed in the tradition of the Underground Comix, by utilising elements found there and linking them in order to create new pop-surrealistic narratives, realised as silkscreen posters for U.S. rock bands. Via their personal networks, their influence extended all the way to Switzerland, as this exhibition poster from 1994 proves. FIG.22-24

LZICAR Although Casarramona's posters are unique, as you have pointed out, they can also be assigned to a particular current within rock graphics. Casarramona, along with Donovan Gregory of the Designer's Club, continues to organise the "Garage Sale — Rock'n'Roll, Lowbrow & Underground Culture" in Zurich — a fair that already carries both an Americanism and lowbrow style in its name. I would also associate the same current with Märt Infanger's works. Both designers even promoted concerts by the same bands, such as the omnipresent The Monsters from Bern. These graphics could be considered retro design. PP.343-362

FISCHBACHER That means that these designers weren't as worried about what was going on in the current visual communication and graphic design discourse as they were about their music scene and the stylistics associated with it. It's all about a self-contained system of references. Therefore, you could also tell the story in this book in a completely different manner, based on the styles referred to, which indeed reach back far into the past in some cases. At the same time, Märt Infanger developed a distinctive and contemporary visual language in his system by, for example, simulating the characteristics of particular production methods and, rearranging them in order to create something new.

24: FRANK KOZIK, 1994

Sample und Remix

LZICAR Ein weiterer Bruch im dem vom Buch vorgegebenen Kontinuum lässt sich an den Arbeiten von Cornel Windlin festmachen. Vergleichbar mit der künstlerischen Strategie der Assemblage, greift etwa sein Entwurf für die Ankündigung eines Konzerts der Band Codeine – dem Namen und narkotischen Sound der Band entsprechend – typische formale Merkmale pharmazeutischer Produktverpackungen auf. Indem Cornel Windlin diese typische Form mit neuen Texten füllt und als Konzertplakat in einem überraschenden Zusammenhang platziert, manipuliert er dessen Aussage in seinem Sinne. Appropriation dient hier als postmoderne Methode: Der Entwurf irritiert die Sehgewohnheiten des Betrachters. Die Aneignung ist dabei nicht nur ironisches Mittel, wie wir sie aus der heutigen Werbung kennen, sondern verifiziert visuell die gängige Hypothese, dass die Wahrnehmung textueller Information stets von ihrer visuellen Form und dem Rezeptionszusammenhang beeinflusst wird. ABB.25

FISCHBACHER Aus Cornel Windlins Arbeiten lässt sich ein grosses historisches Bewusstsein ablesen. Allerdings gestaltet er nicht im nostalgischen Sinne, sondern bedient sich der Geschichte visueller Konventionen und Stile, immer im Hinblick auf die Kommunikationsabsicht. Ich behaupte allerdings,

Sample and remix

LZICAR It is possible to see another crack in the continuum presented by this book in the works of Cornel Windlin. Comparable with the artistic strategy of assemblage, his design used for advertising a concert by Codeine, for example, — a design that matches the name and narcotic sound of the band — picks up the typical formal characteristics of packaging for pharmaceuticals. By filling this familiar form with new content and placing it in a surprising context such as a concert poster, Cornel Windlin manipulates its message to serve his own needs. Here, appropriation serves as a postmodern technique: the design confounds the viewer's visual expectations. Appropriation is therefore not only an ironic tool as we see it in advertising today, it visually verifies the conventional hypothesis stipulating that how textual information is perceived is always influenced by its visual form and the context in which it is received. FIG.25

FISCHBACHER You can sense a great historical awareness in Cornel Windlin's works. Nevertheless, his design doesn't delve in nostalgia, he helps himself to the history of visual conventions and styles, always with regard to his intended communication. I believe, however, that looking at Cornel Windlin's posters, it is easy to recognise that he designed them. This is because

25: CORNEL WINDLIN, 1994

26: CORNEL WINDLIN, 1994

den Plakaten von Cornel Windlin sieht man sehr wohl an, dass sie von ihm stammen. Und zwar aus dem Grund, dass sie regelmässig zitieren. Es handelt sich also um eine wiederkehrende konzeptionelle Strategie anstelle einer formalen Handschrift. ABB.26

LZICAR Sie appropriieren diverse zeit- und milieuspezifische Ästhetiken und sind dadurch einer bestimmten Ära zuordenbar, wirken aber selten retro. In einem Radiointerview von 2008 distanziert sich Cornel Windlin sogar explizit von der Mode des Retro-Designs. Retro sei für ihn «das Transponieren einer bekannten vergangenen Ästhetik ins Jetzt, ohne sie zu übersetzen und ohne sie inhaltlich weiterzudenken», und er kommt daraufhin zu dem Schluss, dass diese «endlose Perpetuierung von bekannten Evergreens» nirgendwo hinführe (DRS4 Talk 2008). Diese Aussage repräsentiert für mich sein fortschrittliches Geschichtsverständnis: Die gestalterische Interpretation der Vergangenheit muss eine Veränderung des Jetzt oder der Zukunft zum Ziel haben. Meiner Meinung nach ist diese Haltung unter anderem von seinem Arbeitsaufenthalt in England von 1988 bis 1993 geprägt.

FISCHBACHER Auch in diesem Aspekt unterscheidet sich Cornel Windlin von bereits diskutierten Gestaltern, die ihre Inspiration häufiger in der US-amerikanischen Kultur suchten. Die erfolgreiche englische Kreativszene der Neunzigerjahre mit Cool Britannia und Britpop hat sicherlich zu dieser geografischen Verschiebung im kulturellen Refrenzsystem nicht nur der Rockgrafik beigetragen.

LZICAR Betrachtet man etwa das Plakat mit dem Titel «Caution» für die Rote Fabrik, erinnert die Methode – also die Übernahme visueller Eigenschaften von Warnhinweisen – an das Konzertplakat für den Club The Factory von Peter Saville. Allerdings wird bei Cornel Windlins Fassung vor gesundheitsgefährdenden Giftstoffen (im Zusammenhang mit den Konzerten möglicherweise Drogen) und nicht wie bei Peter Saville vor Industrielärm (also lauter Musik) gewarnt. ABB.27+28

FISCHBACHER «Very British» ist ebenso die plakative Verwendung einer Flugzeugkokarde der Royal Air Force, welche später von der

they frequently contain quotations. So it's a recurring conceptual strategy, rather than a formal style. FIG.26

LZICAR Although they appropriate diverse time- and scene-specific aesthetics and can, therefore, be *associated* with a specific era, they seem strangely retro at the same time. In a radio interview from 2008, Cornel Windlin even explicitly dissociated himself from the method of retro design. He believes that retro would be like "transposing a familiar past aesthetic into the present without translating it and without developing it further with regard to content." He then comes to the conclusion that this "endless perpetuation of familiar 'evergreens' can't lead anywhere" (DRS4 Talk 2008). To my mind, this message reveals his progressive concept of history: a creative interpretation of the past must aim at change in the present or the future. The way I see it, this attitude was shaped, among other things, by the time he spent working in England from 1988 to 1993.

FISCHBACHER Also, in this respect, Cornel Windlin differs from the designers we have already discussed, designers who often sought their inspiration in American culture. The successful British creative scene of the nineties, proclaiming Cool Britannia and spawning Britpop, surely contributed to this geographic shift in cultural reference systems, that not only applies to rock graphics.

LZICAR If you look at the poster titled "Caution" for the Rote Fabrik, for example, the method — utilising the visual characteristics of warnings — calls to mind Peter Saville's concert poster for The Factory. However, in Cornel Windlin's version, it warns against substances hazardous to people's health in connection with the concert — drugs, perhaps — and not against industrial noise — loud music, that is — as in Peter Saville's work. FIG.27+28

FISCHBACHER *Very British* is also the eye-catching use of a Royal Air Force cockade, a symbol later appropriated by the Mod subculture movement for example, for their badges, and worn as a sign of belonging to this group. P.387

27: PETER SAVILLE, 1978

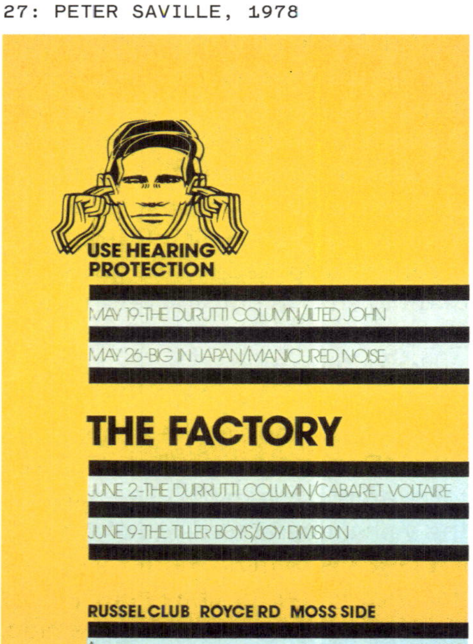

subkulturellen Bewegung der Mods in Besitz genommen wurde und zum Beispiel auf deren typischen Pins die Zugehörigkeit zu dieser Gruppe zum Ausdruck brachte. S.387

LZICAR Um diese Neu-Konnotation so treffend und eingängig umsetzen zu können, ist eine intensive Auseinandersetzung mit den visuellen Codes eines bestimmten Milieus zu einer bestimmten Zeit nötig – ich nenne diese aufwändige und intellektuell herausfordernde Vorarbeit «Visual Research».

FISCHBACHER Cornel Windlin kann die Zeichensysteme und Bildsprachen diverser sozialer Gruppen schnell entschlüsseln und sich aneignen. Dadurch sind seine Arbeiten weniger vergangenheitsorientiert. Obwohl er in all diesen Fällen auf etablierte Wahrnehmungselemente zurückgreift, wirken sie nicht nostalgisch, sondern häufig als das, was sie darstellen: So bleibt eine Fernbedienung eine Fernbedienung und ein Fussballfeld ein Fussballfeld. S.367-390

LZICAR Kunst (*hi-culture*) appropriiert Werbegrafik (*pop-culture*), Werbegrafik (*subculture*) appropriiert Kunst (*hi-culture*) – wo uns diese Doppelhelix hinführen soll, hat uns Cornel Windlin in seinem Radiointerview leider nicht verraten. Der an seinen Arbeiten dargestellte Paradigmenwechsel kann mit dem zeitgleichen Aufkommen des DJs verglichen werden – nicht nur in der elektronischen Musik, sondern auch als Repräsentant für das Öffnen von Genregrenzen, wie es zum Beispiel im Crossover von Bands wie Living Colour, Red Hot Chili Peppers oder den Beastie Boys der Fall ist. In der visuellen Gestaltung ändert sich damit einhergehend die Haltung und Herangehensweise des Grafikers an die Aufgabe.

FISCHBACHER Ich sehe ein Spannungsfeld zwischen Plakaten, die aus der Arbeit am Medium, also aus dem Machen entstanden sind, und solchen, die eher konzeptionell angelegt wurden. Cornel Windlin beherrscht das Mediale, was er auch im Interview auf DRS als sein Hauptinteresse angibt. Damit steht er unter anderem in der Tradition dessen, was man allgemein als «Schweizer Typografie» versteht.

LZICAR In order to transpose this new connotation so aptly and strikingly, you first have to carry out an in-depth examination of the visual codes that apply in a particular environment — I call this time-consuming and intellectually challenging preparatory work "visual research."

FISCHBACHER Cornel Windlin is capable of decoding the sign systems and pictographic language of social groups quickly and appropriate them. This makes his works less retro-oriented. Although he resorts to established elements of cognition in all of these examples, they never appear nostalgic, but instead are often what they depict: a remote control remains a remote control and a soccer field remains a soccer field. PP.367-390

LZICAR Art — highbrow culture — appropriates advertising graphics — pop culture — and advertising graphics — subculture — appropriates art — highbrow culture. Where this double helix will lead us is, unfortunately, not revealed in Cornel Windlins radio interview. The paradigm shift reflected by his works might be compared with the rise of DJ's that occurred around the same time — not only in electronic music, but also as a representative of the dissolving boundaries between genres, as, for example, applies to bands like Living Colour, Red Hot Chili Peppers, or the Beastie Boys. In visual design, graphic designers' positions and approaches to the task at hand changed along the lines of this development.

FISCHBACHER I see an interplay between posters that are created based on working with a medium, *i.e.* based on the production process and more conceptual posters. Cornel Windlin masters the media-related approach and this is also his main field of interest, as he states in the DRS4 interview. He therefore follows the tradition of what is, generally, referred to as "Swiss typography."

LZICAR At the same time, Cornel Windlin goes one step further here, for instance by showing the auxiliary lines used to structure the typographic layout in the poster for the month of November in 1994, thus, demystifying the design. P.387

DISKURS

LZICAR Obwohl Cornel Windlin auch hier einen Schritt weiter geht, zum Beispiel wenn er im Monatsplakat für den November 1994 die Hilfslinien zur Konstruktion des typografischen Layouts offenlegt und so den Entwurf entmystifiziert. S.387

28: CORNEL WINDLIN, 1995

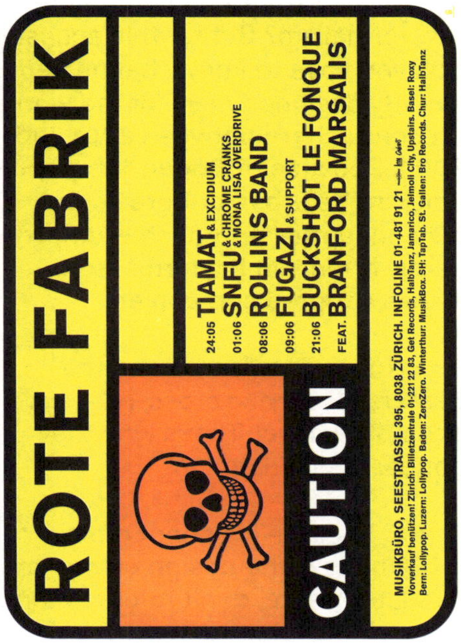

FISCHBACHER Hier stellt sich mir die Frage nach der Zielgruppe und dem daraufhin ausgewählten Referenzsystem. Es sollen ja nicht nur Grafiker durch die Plakate angesprochen werden, und die Plakate wurden hoffentlich nicht nur gestaltet, um damit Grafikdesigngeschichte zu schreiben.

LZICAR Du hast recht, die Grafik vieler von Cornel Windlin für die Rote Fabrik gestalteter Plakate hat Bezüge zu anderer Grafik. Daraus kann aber ein elitäres Spiel werden, nämlich dann, wenn die vermeintlich angesprochene Rezipientengruppe die verwendeten Codes gar nicht entschlüsseln kann – also wenn Grafikdesign auf sich selbst verweist. Im Ausstellungskatalog *Public Affairs* (Curiger & Hug 2002) entgegnet er auf die Behauptung Bice Curigers, dass seine Plakate für die Rote Fabrik «kaum Bezug auf die Veranstaltung an sich» nehmen würden, dass bei der Gestaltung bewusst mit «anspruchsvolleren Codes operiert wurde als üblich». Cornel Windlin hebt allerdings hervor, dass dies «mit Erfolg» geschehen sei, da der «Ton, in welchem das Programm in die Stadt getragen wurde» ein identitätsstiftendes Element für die Rote Fabrik gewesen sei.

FISCHBACHER Dem kann man nicht widersprechen.

DISCOURSE

FISCHBACHER Here, I have to pose the question regarding the target group and the reference system chosen as a result. The posters weren't intended to solely address graphic designers and hopefully not with the idea of making graphic design history.

LZICAR You're right, the graphic design of many posters Cornel Windlin created for the Rote Fabrik contain references to other works of graphic design. But, this can become an elitist game, especially, when the target group can't decipher the codes applied — as when graphic design becomes self-referential. In the exhibition catalogue *Public Affairs* (Curiger & Hug, 2002), he responds to Bice Curiger's allegation that his posters for the Rote Fabrik "hardly refer to the events themselves," that for the design he deliberately "works with codes that are more sophisticated than usual." Cornel Windlin, however, emphasizes how "successful" they were, stressing that the "tone with which the program was brought to the city" contributed to shaping an identity for the Rote Fabrik.

FISCHBACHER You can't disagree with that.

«Design sucks!»

"Design sucks!"

LZICAR Alain C. Kupper bricht mit seinen Plakaten für den Veranstaltungsort Bogen 13, an deren Entwurf teilweise auch sein Atelierkollege Cristian Andersen beteiligt war, radikal mit dem, was wir bisher unter dem Label Schweizer Rockgrafik für dieses Buch betrachtet haben. Auf der Suche nach einem fruchtbaren Vergleich kommt mir am ehesten Peter Fischli in den Sinn. Die Auftraggeber beider Gestalter richten sich an eine urbane Avantgarde und suchen daher bewusst die Nähe zur zeitgenössischen bildenden Kunst. Für mich geht es bei den Plakaten Alain C. Kuppers deshalb weniger um die Ankündi-

LZICAR With his posters for the venue Bogen 13, Alain C. Kupper, who designed them partly in collaboration with his studio mate, Cristian Andersen, radically disbands what we have come to summarise in this book under the label Swiss rock graphics. When I look for a suitable comparison, Peter Fischli is the first person to come to mind. Both designers' clients want to appeal to an urban avantgarde and, thus, deliberately strive for closeness to contemporary visual art. In my opinion, Alain C. Kupper's posters are therefore not so much about announcing a live concert than about actively

gung eines Live-Konzerts, als vielmehr um die aktive Appropriation der Codes dieser Szene durch die Visualisierung intellektueller Konzepte. ABB.29/S.395-416

29: ALAIN C. KUPPER, 2003

FISCHBACHER Ehrlich gesagt fällt es mir schwer, mich zu den Arbeiten zu äussern. Für mich ist es ein bisschen «Heute macht man das halt so».

LZICAR ... also zeitgenössischer Formalismus? Bei diesem Vorwurf muss man allerdings beachten, dass viele der gezeigten Arbeiten bereits zwischen 2001 und 2004 entworfen wurden. Aufgrund der Popularität und Anziehungskraft des Bogen 13 auf die urbane Kulturszene wurde deren konzeptioneller Ansatz – jedoch leider öfter nur deren formaler Stil – aufgegriffen und vervielfacht.

FISCHBACHER Das stimmt, und die Plakate zitieren auf einer anderen Ebene. Daher wirken sie zeitgemäss.

LZICAR Für mich handelt es sich um Meta-Referenzen – die verwendeten Gestaltungselemente verweisen also nicht, um beim Beispiel zu bleiben, auf Formulare, sondern auf die Conceptual Art, welche wiederum auf die Formular-Ästhetik Bezug nahm. Besonders gut sichtbar wird diese Meta-Ebene, wenn man das Plakat für ein Konzert der Band The Monsters im Bogen 13 betrachtet. Alain C. Kupper verzichtet auf sämtliche Retro-Elemente, weil er sich mit dem Plakat an eine andere Szene richtet. Das Plakat visualisiert nicht den Retro-Sound der Band, sondern ausschliesslich den Bandnamen und das Image des Bogen 13. Noch viel wichtiger erscheint mir bei dem Plakat allerdings die unscheinbare Textzeile «design sucks!» – diese lässt einerseits auf eine sehr eingeschränkte Interpretation des Begriffs «Design» durch die Gestalter schliessen und repräsentiert andererseits eine kritische Haltung gegenüber einer US-amerikanischen Konnotation des Wortes «Design», im Sinne von strategischem Marketing. S.400

FISCHBACHER Ich empfinde diese Repräsentationsform der Kritik allerdings als banal, da das Plakat mit vergleichbaren Methoden wie das kritisierte Werbedesign operiert und gestalterisch keine Alternativen dazu anbietet.

appropriating the codes of this scene by visualising intellectual concepts. FIG.29/S.395-416

FISCHBACHER To be honest, I find it hard to comment on the work. To me, it is kind of "that's how it's done nowadays."

LZICAR ... so, it's about contemporary formalism? But for this accusation you have to know that he had already designed many of the works presented here between 2001 and 2004. Because of Bogen 13's popularity in the urban culture scene, his conceptual approach — unfortunately often just his formal style — was adopted and copied.

FISCHBACHER That's true and the posters also make cross-references on another level. That's why they appear up-to-date.

LZICAR I believe it's about meta-references — the design elements used, therefore, don't refer to blank forms, in keeping to the example, but to conceptual art, which in turn refers to the aesthetics of forms and questionnaires. This meta-level becomes particularly visible if you look at the poster for The Monsters' gig at Bogen 13. Alain C. Kupper doesn't apply retro elements because he's targeting a different scene with the poster. So the poster doesn't visualize the retro sound of the band, but only the band name and the image of Bogen 13. I think that a more important element of the poster is the inconspicuous statement: "design sucks!" On the one hand, this suggests that the designer interprets the term "design" in a very limited way, on the other hand, it takes a critical stance towards an American connotation of the word "design," when referring to strategic marketing. P.400

FISCHBACHER But, I find this representational form of criticism banal, as the poster applies similar methods to the commercial design it is criticizing and, in addition, doesn't offer any alternative within the design.

LZICAR This poster designed solely using typography, like a public announcement, appears more radical to me. The demure design steers clear of conventional assumptions and functional analyses for designing posters. FIG.30

LZICAR Radikaler erscheint mir dieses Plakat, welches wie eine öffentliche Bekanntmachung rein typografisch gesetzt wurde. Die spröde Gestaltung entzieht sich jeglicher tradierter Annahmen und Wirkungsanalysen für die Gestaltung von Plakten. ABB.30

30: ALAIN C. KUPPER, 2003

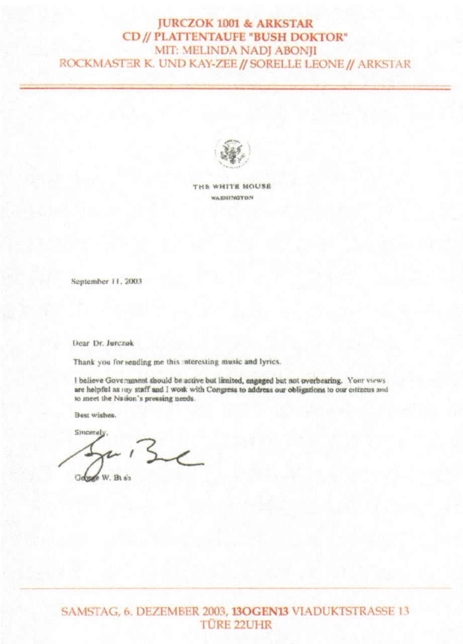

FISCHBACHER Ich nenne das Anti-Grafik!

LZICAR Der Ausdruck trifft es auf den Punkt. Das Plakat entzieht sich all den anerkannten Dimensionen der modernen Konnotation von Grafikdesign, also etwa informieren, stimulieren, instruieren, und repräsentiert auf diese Weise eine zynische Kritik an der Daseinsberechtigung von Grafikdesign als modernes Projekt! Dementgegen verwendet Alain C. Kupper in seinen Arbeiten etwa simple Satzmethoden, wie wir sie aus alltäglicher Office-Software kennen – und suggeriert damit eine amateurhafte Produktionsweise, die wiederum dem Professionalismus der Moderne entgegensteht. Eine ähnliche Strategie wendet der Grafik-Künstler Paul Elliman (hier mit Avigail Moss) in einer Arbeit für die Ausstellung *Forms of Inquiry: The Architecture of Critical Graphic Design* der Architectural Association in London an. ABB.31

31: PAUL ELLIMAN, AVIGAIL MOSS, 2007

FISCHBACHER Es kommt amateurhaft daher, tatsächlich aber handelt es sich um eine geschickt eingesetzte Strategie. Es simuliert eine Anti-Haltung, dabei enthalten die Plakate Alain C. Kuppers durchaus Elemente, die eine klare Haltung erkennen lassen – und Humor.

LZICAR Ja, zum Beispiel wenn mit den Porträts der US-amerikanischen Teenage-Idole Elvis Presley, James Dean und Marlon Brando eine Veranstaltung namens «Acid House», ebenfalls Name einer elektronischen Musikrichtung der späten Achtzigerjahre, beworben wird. Alain C. Kupper lässt hier diverse Kulturen und Zeiten aufeinanderprallen. S.403

FISCHBACHER I'd call that anti-graphic design!

LZICAR Bull's eye! The poster ignores all recognized dimensions of the modern connotation of graphic design — *i.e.* to inform, to stimulate, to instruct — thus, representing a cynical criticism of the right of graphic designers to exist as a modern project! On the other hand, in his works Alain C. Kupper, for example, uses simple typesetting methods like the ones we are familiar with from everyday Office software — and, therefore, suggests an amateurish mode of production which, in turn, precludes contemporary professionalism. Graphic artist Paul Elliman (here with Avigail Moss) uses a similar strategy in a piece for the exhibition *Forms of Inquiry: The Architecture of Critical Graphic Design* at the Architectural Association in London. FIG.31

FISCHBACHER They may seem amateurish, but actually involve a cleverly employed strategy. Alain C. Kupper's posters simulate an anti-attitude but, at the same time, they also contain elements that reveal a clear position — and humor.

LZICAR Certainly, when he, for example, uses portraits of the U.S.-American teenage idols Elvis Presley, James Dean and Marlon Brando, in order to promote an event called "Acid House," referring to an electronic music style of the late eighties. Alain C. Kupper confronts different cultures and eras with each other. P.403

Handwerk und Ideal

Craft and ideal

32: ERIC ANDERSEN, 2007

DISKURS

LZICAR Eric Andersen bewegt sich in einer ähnlichen Zürcher Szene wie Alain C. Kupper und ist freundschaftlich mit ihm verbunden. Beide teilen ähnliche Vorstellungen in Sachen selbstständiges und selbstbestimmtes Leben und Arbeiten.

FISCHBACHER Allerdings sehe ich im Gegensatz zu den konzeptionellen Ansätzen Alain C. Kuppers in den Arbeiten von Eric Andersen eine grössere Affinität zum Grafischen. Die Plakate wehren sich nicht gegen ihre Plakativität. S.421–440

LZICAR Im Gegenteil, Eric Andersen eignet sich historische Produktionsmethoden aus der Technikgeschichte der Grafik an, wie etwa den qualitativ groben Holzdruck, oder aber wesentlich präzisere Drucktechniken, wie beim Poster für «Pauls Boutique». Neu erscheint mir dabei, dass sich der Gestalter keiner bestimmten Drucktechnik verschrieben hat, sondern je nach Anlass und Konzept auf unterschiedliche Vervielfältigungsformen zurückgreift. Er nutzt die Reproduktionstechnik des Plakats als Gestaltungselement. ABB.32

FISCHBACHER Eric Andersen führt weitere gestalterische Traditionen fort, vom handwerklichen Entwurf bis zum formalen Zitat. Die Ideen zu seinen Arbeiten scheinen beim Machen zu entstehen. Damit gehört er etwa mit Michel Casarramona zu den Gestaltern in diesem Buch, die über ihre handwerkliche Entwurfsmethodik zu einer eigenen Sprache gefunden haben – seine Plakate können ihm eindeutig zugeordnet werden.

LZICAR Einen vergleichbaren Ansatz erkenne ich bei weiteren Gestaltern aus Eric Andersens Generation, wie Bert Setzer oder Lukas Zimmermann alias Marsplastik. Beide gestalten und drucken vor allem in und für besetzte Liegenschaften – unter anderem auch Plakate für Konzerte, an deren Organisation sie häufig beteiligt sind. Dabei wenden sie sich ab von standardisierten digitalen Entwurfs- und Produktionsmethoden und entziehen sich so einem rein ökonomisch orientierten Mainstream-Grafikdesign. Jedoch verteufeln sie den Computer nicht. Im Gegeteil. Fast alle genannten Gestalter nutzen das Internet als überregionale Kommunikations- und/oder Vertriebsmöglichkeit

DISCOURSE

LZICAR Eric Andersen is active in a scene in Zurich similar to Alain C. Kupper's. They are also friends. They share similar ideas about being self-determined and about deciding how to live and work independently.

FISCHBACHER At the same time, I see a greater affinity to graphic design in Eric Andersen's works, in contrast to the conceptual approaches of Alain C. Kupper. The posters don't combat their blatant essence. PP.421–440

LZICAR Quite the contrary, Eric Andersen adopts production methods known from the technical history of graphic design, such as the qualitatively coarse woodcut, or much more precise printing techniques as in his poster for "Pauls Boutique". What appears new to me is that the designer doesn't dedicate himself to any specific printing technique, but instead uses different forms of reproduction depending on the event and concept. He uses the technique for reproducing a specific poster like a design element. FIG.32

FISCHBACHER Eric Andersen perpetuates other design traditions, from handcrafted design to formal reference. The ideas for his works seem to arise while he is creating them. Along with Michel Casarramona, he is therefore one of the designers in this book who have found their way to an own language by means of their handcrafted design methods — *i.e.* his posters can clearly be assigned to him.

LZICAR I see a similar approach being used by other designers from Eric Andersen's generation, such as Bert Setzer or Lukas Zimmermann alias Marsplastik. Both of them design and primarily print in and for squatted properties — among other things, posters for concerts they help organize. In their work, they turn their backs on standardised digital design and production methods, thus, avoiding pure commercially-oriented, mainstream graphic design. At the same time, they don't demonise the use of computers. Conversely, nearly all of the designers referred to here, use the Internet for trans-regional communication or to distribute their designs. It's also possible to ascribe a political dimension to their preference for a handcrafted production process. FIG.33+34

33: BERT SETZER, 2005/2008

ihrer Gestaltung. Dem von ihnen bevorzugten handwerklichen Herstellungsprozess kann also eine politische Dimension zugeschrieben werden. ABB.33+34

Eric Andersen wurde etwa angefragt, ob er die analoge Ästhetik seiner Plakate in Photoshop simulieren könne, um eine höhere Auflage eines Plakats zu produzieren. Er hat abgelehnt, da dies seiner Definition von Gestaltung als handwerkliches Prinzip widersprechen würde: Für ihn ist Do-it-yourself kein formaler Stil, der sich beliebig applizieren lässt, sondern eine Ethik, die dem Plakat inhärent ist und über dessen Beschaffenheit in die Öffentlichkeit hinausgetragen wird. Er gestaltet die Plakate auf diese Weise, um deren Betrachter zum Nachdenken über ihren eigenen Lebensentwurf anzuregen. Zu dieser Strategie gehört zum Beispiel auch das gezielte und eigenhändige Anbringen der Plakate an ausgewählten Orten in ausgewählten Stadtteilen. Es hat mich also nicht verwundert, dass ich Eric Andersen als politisch engagierte Person mit einem selbstverständlichen Sendungsbewusstsein kennengelernt habe.

FISCHBACHER Dieses Amateur-Prinzip geht weit über den Diskurs um Grafikdesign hinaus und ist omnipräsent im heutigen Stadtleben. Dessen Protagonisten entscheiden sich etwa dafür, ihr Gemüse im eigenen Garten anzupflanzen, anstatt im Supermarkt zu kaufen. Vergleichbar mit Arts & Crafts, welches sich gegen den Verlust an Qualität und Menschlichkeit durch Massenproduktion infolge uneingeschränkter Industrialisierung auflehnte, scheint sich diese Generation gegen die gleichen Verluste durch Globalisierung als Produkt einer sich selbst überlassenen Ökonomie zu wehren.

LZICAR Damit ist auch die teilweise zynische Abgrenzung sozialer Gruppen anhand visueller Codes zumindest vorübergehend beendet. Die von uns in diesem Kapitel betrachteten Grafiker verstecken sich nicht hinter Zitaten, Meta-Ebenen und Ästhetiken. Sie nutzen ähnliche Methoden, beziehen damit allerdings bewusst Stellung und machen sich angreifbar. Auf diese Weise widersprechen sie dem bisher vorherrschenden urbanen Konzept von Coolness, wonach

Eric Andersen, for example, was asked to simulate the analogue aesthetic of his posters in Photoshop, in order to produce a larger edition of a poster. He refused, since this would have contradicted his definition of design as a craft: in his world do-it-yourself isn't a formal style that can be applied arbitrarily, it is an ethic intrinsic to the poster to be transferred into the public sphere by its quality. He designs posters following this conviction, in order to encourage viewers to reflect on their own life scripts. An element of this strategy is, for instance, to systematically apply the posters in selected locations and city districts by his own hands with a target in mind. It therefore didn't surprise me when I got to know Eric Andersen as a politically dedicated person with a natural sense of mission.

FISCHBACHER This amateur principle extends far beyond a discourse on graphic design and is omnipresent in city life today. Protagonists of this movement, for example, decide to plant their vegetables in their gardens instead of buying them at the supermarket. Likewise, Arts & Crafts rebelled against the loss of quality and humanity, resulting from mass production and unrestrained industrialization; this generation seems to combat the same shortcomings of a globalisation produced by an economy left to its own means.

LZICAR This at least brings a temporary end to the sometimes cynical discrimination of social groups based on visual codes. The graphic designers we are looking at in this chapter don't hide behind cross-references, meta-levels and aesthetics. They use similar methods, but nonetheless deliberately take sides and make themselves vulnerable. Thus, they gain say the urban concept of coolness that has prevailed until now, according to which design is supposed to make an effortless and unintentional impression (see "Marketing und Gestaltung," a lecture held by Diedrich Diederichsen at the Museum für Gestaltung in Zurich as part of the supporting program for the exhibition *Swiss Design 2002 — Netzwerke/Réseaux/Networks*). What Eric Andersen's method really illustrates, are for example, the central aspects outlined by Richard

auch Design möglichst unangestrengt und absichtslos zu wirken habe (vgl. «Marketing und Gestaltung», Vortrag von Diedrich Diederichsen am Museum für Gestaltung Zürich im Rahmenprogramm der Ausstellung *Swiss Design 2002 – Netzwerke/Réseaux/Networks*). Vielmehr lassen sich etwa an der Arbeitsweise von Eric Andersen zentrale Aspekte des soziokulturellen Konzepts des Handwerkers erläutern, welches von Richard Sennett entworfen und mit dem Erfolg seines Buchs *The Craftsman* (2008) verbreitet wurde. Demnach hätten produzierende Menschen das Wissen über ihr Handeln verloren, auch weil Eigeninitiative in komplexen Produktionsprozessen als hinderlich betrachtet und entmutigt wurde.

34: LUKAS ZIMMERMANN, 2011

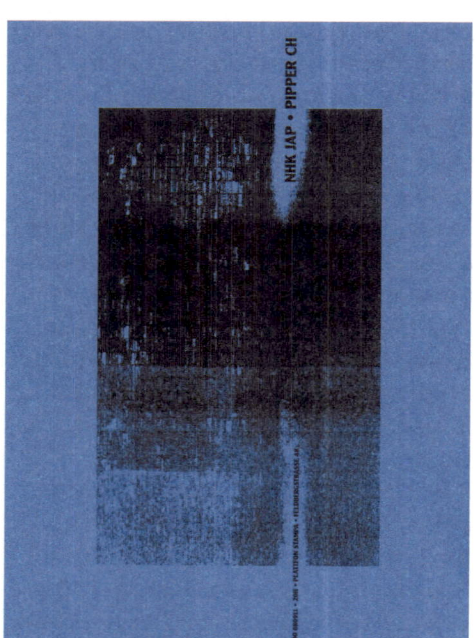

FISCHBACHER Ich bin der Überzeugung, dass sich im Bereich Gestaltung verschiedene Kulturen etabliert haben. Den grösseren Design-Agenturen, wo Eigeninitiative durch Arbeitsteilung, dominante Kundenwünsche, hierarchische Strukturen und enge Corporate Design Manuals eingeschränkt werden, stehen Autoren und Autorinnen, kreative Büros undTrendsurfer gegenüber. Wo der grosse Reibach gemacht wird, ist ja wohl klar.

LZICAR Da habe ich ähnliche Erfahrungen gemacht. Laut Sennett folgen daraus mangelnde Motivation, materielle Gleichgültigkeit und Distanzierung vom Beruf und dessen übergeordneter gesellschaftlicher Funktion. Handwerker hingegen üben eine Tätigkeit aus, die sie um ihrer selbst willen gut machen wollen. Hochwertige und präzise Arbeit zu leisten würde ihnen demnach Selbstachtung und die Achtung anderer bescheren. Eric Andersen ist definitiv Individualist und gestaltet Produkte, die vorrangig ihm selbst gefallen. Aber er ist durchaus bereit, der Gesellschaft etwas von seiner individuellen Leistung zurückzugeben – und dies, ohne dabei einen grösstmöglichen Gewinn erzielen zu wollen. Ich denke, er glaubt und lebt nicht nur nach diesem Prinzip, sondern er repräsentiert es auch nach aussen – durch seine Plakate wie auch durch sein Wesen.

FISCHBACHER Für mich ist das Plakat mit dem Titel «Fuck FIFA!» ein gutes

Sennett pertaining to the sociocultural concept of craftsmanship, disseminated through the success of his novel *The Craftsman* (2008). Hence, producing people had lost the knowledge about their actions, also because personal initiative in complex production processes was considered obstructive and was, therefore, discouraged.

FISCHBACHER I would say that different cultures have established themselves in the field of design. Larger design agencies — where personal initiative is restricted by division of labor, imperative client demands, hierarchical structures and close-mesh corporate design manuals — stand against authors, creative offices and trend surfers. Where the profit is made is obvious.

LZICAR I've had similar experiences. According to Sennett, this promotes a lack of motivation, material indifference and alienation from the profession and its social function in a broader sense. Craftsmen, on the other hand, do things that they want to do well for the sake of it. Delivering high quality and precision, therefore, gives them self-esteem as well as the respect from others. Eric Andersen is definitely an individualist, who designs products that first and foremost please himself, yet he is by all means prepared to give some of his individual achievement back to society, without wanting to make the greatest possible profit. I think he not only believes in and lives according to this principles, but also represents them to the outside world; through his posters as well as through his character.

FISCHBACHER The "Fuck FIFA!" poster is a good example for the principles you just described: it was created as a spontaneous, participatory project connected to the "public viewings" that Eric Andersen organized for his extended group of friends. Although the poster is connected with these occasions, by communicating a political message, it seeks to be more than just a promotional poster. But, at the same time, it is also produced by friends for friends — true to the motto "think global, act local." PP. 428+430

Beispiel für das von dir beschriebene Prinzip: Es entstand als spontanes partizipatives Projekt im Rahmen eines von Eric Andersen organisierten «Public Viewings» für seinen erweiterten Freundeskreis. Obwohl es mit diesem Anlass verbunden ist, möchte es mehr als ein Werbeplakat sein, indem es eine politische Haltung vermittelt. Aber gleichzeitig ist es auch ein Objekt von Freunden für Freunde – getreu dem Motto «Think global, act local». S.428+430

Zur Gegenwart Schweizer Rockgrafik

On Swiss rock graphics today

LZICAR Die jüngsten – und vielleicht lebendigsten – Repräsentanten Schweizer Rockgrafik sind für mich die Plakate von Ronny Hunger alias Comet Substance für den Zürcher Tiefgaragen-Club Elmo Delmo, in dem vor allem unbekannte oder wenig etablierte Bands lauten und unverfälschten Rock spielen. Er folgt der gleichen Do-it-yourself-Ethik wie der Club, wie die Bands, die darin auftreten. Damit stellen seine Plakate und Orte wie das Elmo Delmo Alternativen zum kommerziellen Konzertbusiness dar. Typisch für das auf Freundschaft und freiwilliger Leistung basierende Konzept, die spontane Ästhetik von Einrichtung und Ankündigungen und die dem Jetzt zugewandte Stimmung während der Konzerte ist, dass das Elmo Delmo nur aufgrund von Zwischennutzungsverträgen existiert und seine Zukunft ungewiss ist. ABB.35

LZICAR In my view the most recent — and perhaps also most vibrant — representatives of Swiss rock graphics are the posters by Ronny Hunger, alias Comet Substance, for the underground garage club Elmo Delmo in Zurich, where mostly unknown, hardly established bands play loud and pure rock. He adheres to the same do-it-yourself ethic as the club and the bands that perform there. His posters and venues like the Elmo Delmo represent alternatives to the commercial concert business. Typical for this concept, based on friendship and voluntary contributions, the spontaneous aesthetics of the furnishings and advertisements and the here-and-now atmosphere during the concerts, is the transient nature of the Elmo Delmo, which only exists because of 'interim use contracts' and, therefore faces an uncertain future. FIG.35

35: RONNY HUNGER, 2013

FISCHBACHER Und trotz diesem Bekenntnis zur Rockmusik fällt es mir auch in diesem Zusammenhang schwer, von Rockgrafik zu sprechen. Wie wir festgestellt haben, handelt es sich dabei keinesfalls um einen grafischen Stil, der vor allem Hörer von Rockmusik anspricht. Die Wurzeln einiger der letztgenannten Grafiker liegen bekanntlich in der Hip-Hop-Kultur, und genauso wie sie sich keiner bestimmten Musikart verschrieben haben, lassen sich auch ihre Plakate keiner bestimmten Musikart zuschreiben: Eric Andersen gestaltet politische Plakate mit den gleichen Methoden wie Plakate für Jazz-, Rock- oder Hip-Hop-Konzerte; Lukas Zimmermann überschreitet regelmässig die Grenzen zur Kunst, indem er dem Betrachter zentrale Informationen vorenthält; und Ronny Hungers Plakate erinnern mich an die von Richard Hollis

FISCHBACHER Despite this commitment to rock music, I find it difficult to speak of rock graphics in this connection. As we have already discussed, rock graphic design does by no means designate a graphic style that addresses rock fans. Some representatives discussed here have their roots in hip-hop culture, as is generally known and, just as they have not dedicated themselves to any specific music style, their posters cannot be ascribed to any such genre: Eric Andersen designs political posters, applying the same methods he uses for jazz, rock, or hip-hop concerts; Lukas Zimmermann regularly transcends the boundary to art by withholding central information; and Ronny Hunger's posters remind me of Richard Hollis' so-called "cocktail graphics" from the eighties, which really had very little

sogenannten «cocktail graphics» der Achtzigerjahre, die nun wirklich wenig mit Rock zu tun hatten. Was die grafischen Artefakte in diesem Buch tatsächlich verbindet, ist das ihnen innewohnende Potenzial, alternative Denk-, Seh- und Handlungsweisen anzuregen. ABB.34-36

LZICAR Rockgrafik kann nicht endgültig festgeschrieben werden, da sich das Label mit jedem Blick zurück verändert, genauso wie das, was wir unter Rock verstehen, von Mensch zu Mensch verschieden ist und sich stetig verändert hat und verändern wird. Was wir versucht haben, ist, einen Zusammenhang zwischen vielfältigen Artefakten, Konzepten und Methoden herzustellen, um diese Variante der Visuellen Kommunikation einerseits mit einem eigenständigen Diskurs zu würdigen, und andererseits, um das Potenzial der Interaktion von Grafik- und Rockkultur aufzuzeigen und für die Zukunft nutzbar zu machen.

FISCHBACHER Bei den von uns besprochenen Beispielen zeigt sich, dass sich der eigentliche Bezug zur Musik in den letzten Jahren eher hin zur Gestaltung im Kontext künstlerischer Standpunkte entwickelt hat. Grafik hat eine eigene Kultur entwickelt, die stark mit anderen kulturellen Ausdrucksformen verknüpft ist.

LZICAR Das lässt für die Zukunft der Rockgrafik auf weitere neue Impulse hoffen.

Roland Fischbacher
und Robert Lzicar

to do with rock. What the graphic artefacts in this book actually have in common is their inherent potential to inspire alternative ways of thinking, seeing and acting. FIG.34-36

LZICAR It isn't possible to ultimately codify rock graphics, inasmuch as the label changes with every glance backward, just as what we conceive rock to be differs from person to person and has continually transformed and will continue to do so. We have attempted to establish a connection between an array of products, concepts and methods in order to acknowledge the variations of visual communication with an independent discourse on the one hand, as well as to reveal the potential of the interaction between graphic design and rock culture on the other, making it available for the future.

FISCHBACHER The examples we have discussed, show that the intrinsic reference to music has in recent years developed more toward design within the context of artistic points of view. Graphic design has developed its own culture, a culture strongly linked to other cultural forms of expression.

LZICAR That lets us hope for more new impulses to guide rock graphics into the future.

Roland Fischbacher
and Robert Lzicar

36: ERIC ANDERSEN, 2010

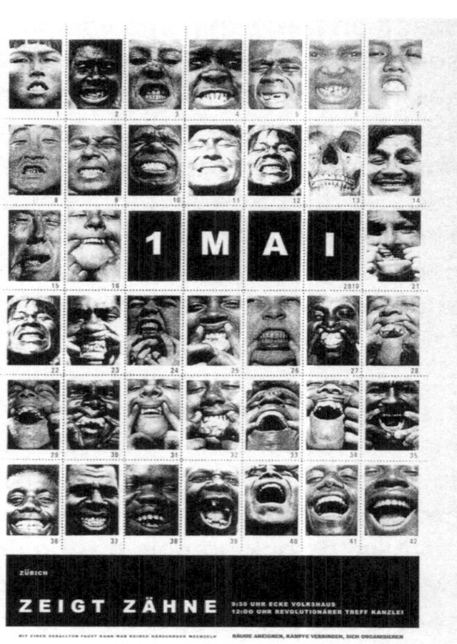

Künstlerindex

Artist index

Bandindex

Band index

BAND INDEX

D

E

BAND INDEX

F

G

BAND INDEX

H

BAND INDEX

I

BAND INDEX

J

K

L

BAND INDEX

BAND INDEX

N

O

P

S

BAND INDEX

X

Y

Z

BAND INDEX

Danke

Thanks

Patrick Frey, Andrea Kempter, Gloria Wismer, Can Asan, André P. Tschan, Colleen Duran, Eric Andersen, Dirk Bonsma, Robert Butler, Düde Dürst, Märt Infanger, Werner Jeker, Cédric Magnin, Urs Steiger, Klaudia Schifferle, Alain Straubhaar, Martin Ain, Leslie Barany, Rock Battaglia, Yvon Baumann, Matthias Belz, Billy Ben, Otto Blumer, Rosmarie Blumer, Sarah Blumer, Noah Bonsma, Bice Curiger, Evelyn Curnis, Bob Fischer, Jessie Fischer, Michel Fishel, Georg Gatsas, Kurt «Guze» Gautschi, Michel van Grondel, Jean-David Gyger, Anna Haas, Markus Hauser, Cornelia Hüsser, Remo Keller, Hans Kunz, Johnny Lopez, Stéphanie Lux, Pietro Mattioli, Marcus May, Ingar Milnes, Daniel Prélaz, Eugen Sorg, Mirco Schiavone, Boris Schlatter, Nik Schlatter, Birgit Schlegel, Martin Schorri, Jean Lou Steinmann, Sandro Sursock, Anthony Thomas, Peter Vitzthum, Michi Vollenweider, Matthias Willi, Marco Witzig, Ruedi Wyss, Peter Zumsteg, and many more …

Impressum

Imprint

Editor:
Lurker Grand, Berlin/Zurich

Text Editor:
Sam Mumenthaler, Bern

Text Authors:
Martin Ain, Leslie Barany, Dirk Bonsma, Bice Curiger, Dirk Dietz, Keith Emerson, Murat Erbudak, Roland Fischbacher, Bob Fischer, H.R. Giger, Lurker Grand, Catherine Hug, Märt Infanger, Robert Lzicar, Cédric Magnin, Marcus May, Dominik Müller, Sam Mumenthaler, Eugen Sorg, André P. Tschan, Michi Vollenweider, Cornel Windlin

English translation and proofreading:
Colleen Duran, Lurker Grand, Amy Klement, Ingar Alan Milnes, André P. Tschan

French translation and proofreading:
Lurker Grand, Stéphanie Lux

German proofreading:
Lurker Grand, Ingar Alan Milnes, Miriam Wiesel

Design:
UFO, Zurich
Ivan Becerro, Sam Linder, Joshua Schenkel
www.ufo.ch

Image Editing:
Can Asan, St. Gallen
www.manipulator.ch

Production:
Offsetdruckerei Karl Grammlich GmbH
Pliezhausen, Germany

Paper:
Munken Lynx Rough 90 g/m2
Munken Lynx Rough 300 g/m2

Typeface:
Bowie & Bowie Mono
by Mirco Schiavone

Captions:
All reproduced artworks in this book originally used offset printing methods unless otherwise noted.
All artwork dimensions are in millimeters.

First edition, 1500 copies
Edition Patrick Frey, 2015
ISBN 978-3-905929-77-5
Printed in Germany

Edition Patrick Frey, Limmatstrasse 268, CH-8005 Zurich
www.editionpatrickfrey.com, mail@editionpatrickfrey.ch

Distribution:

Switzerland:
AVA Verlagsauslieferung, CH – Affoltern am Albis
www.ava.ch

Germany, Austria:
GVA Gemeinsame Verlagsauslieferung, D – Göttingen
www.gva-verlage.de

France, Luxembourg, Belgium:
Les presses du réel, F – Dijon
www.lespressesdureel.com

United Kingdom:
Antenne Books, GB – London
www.antennebooks.com

Japan:
Marginal Press, JP – Tokyo
www.marginal-press.com

Rest of the world:
Edition Patrick Frey, CH – Zurich
www.editionpatrickfrey.com

With the kind support of:

prohelvetia
Stiftung PhonoProduzierende
MIGROS kulturprozent
SWISSLOS Kultur Kanton Bern
Stadt Zürich Kultur
SwissPUNK.ch
Kultur Stadt Bern